AN INTRODUCTION TO
SOCIAL SCIENCE

CONSULTING EDITOR:

Peter I. Rose
Smith College

AN INTRODUCTION TO
SOCIAL SCIENCE

ALFRED APSLER
Clark College

Random House   New York

Copyright © 1971 by Random House, Inc.

All rights reserved under International and Pan-American Copyright Conventions. Published in the United States by Random House, Inc., New York, and simultaneously in Canada by Random House of Canada Limited, Toronto.

ISBN: 0-394-31000-4
Library of Congress Catalog Card Number: 72-133413

Manufactured in the United States of America by H. Wolff Book Mfg. Co., New York, N.Y.

Designed by Two Studio

First Edition
987654321

PREFACE

This book departs from the general pattern of college texts in several ways. It does not deal with one discipline but integrates material from all the social sciences. The discussion of general concepts and methodology is placed not at the beginning of the text, as is usually done, but at the end. In this way the student proceeds from matters that are personally relevant to him to less familiar and more distant problems. This broadened contact can be seen in terms of an ever-widening circle. Finally, the language of this text is quite simple and almost free of technical jargon. Where more sophisticated terms are used, they are defined in the text as well as listed at the end of each chapter for the purpose of review. Anecdotal items are woven freely into the discussion to relieve the student of frustration and boredom. The books and articles selected as suggestions for further reading are likewise nontechnical and have both instructional and entertainment value.

As a community college teacher, the author has taken on the task of imparting an awareness of the social world around us to young and not-so-young adults—that is, to those who are mentally mature but unaccustomed to scholarly presentations. The audience consists of vocational and technical students, students yet unsure of their career plans, and older people anxious to broaden their horizons. The traditional college texts have proved unsuitable for giving this important and growing segment of our student population a brief and easily digestible introduction into the vast areas of man's relations with his fellow-man. This volume is an attempt to fill the gap. Contents and style have been tested in actual classwork and have been met with a favorable reception by the students.

I wish to express my gratitude to a number of colleagues on the Clark College faculty who have sustained me with their most valuable assistance and encouragement, particularly Norman Roberts, Larry Easter, Craig Milnor, Grover Allred, and to our always helpful librarian, Dolores Laners. Professor Peter I. Rose, Consulting Editor for Random House, gave generously of his expertise. I am also indebted to members of the Random House staff, who showed great understanding for this rather new educational project, particularly to Susan Rothstein, who as Manuscript Editor made many valuable suggestions for the improvement of the book. Finally, I must mention the continuous help I received from my wife and fellow teacher Erna, who with understanding and patience participated in the shaping and reshaping of this volume.

It is hoped that the attempt to bring together the vast areas of concern of the social sciences in what must, by the nature of the task, be simplified form will help educators to give the "terminal" student a glimpse into the complexities and urgent needs of our society.

ALFRED APSLER
Vancouver, Washington
Summer 1970

CONTENTS

Preface   v

Introduction   xiii

PART ONE   PEOPLE ALL AROUND YOU   1

1   GET ACQUAINTED WITH YOURSELF   3
your personality

Types of Personalities • Sigmund Freud • Traits and Roles • Self-Concept • Frame of Reference • Learning • Heredity • Motivation

2   IS ANYTHING WRONG WITH YOU?   16
problems of the human mind

Mental Illness • Older Social Attitudes • Misconceptions About Mental Illness • A New Era Begins • Mental Illness and Personality Problems • Stress, Frustration, Conflict • Pressure • The Human Response to Stress • Defensive Behavior • Mental Health • Getting Help

3   WHERE IS THE FIRE?   32
collective behavior

Casual Crowds • Panic • Mobs • Lynching • Riots • Rumor • Social Movements • Leadership • Expressive Crowds • Audiences • Publics • Propaganda

4 CRIME DOES NOT PAY—OR DOES IT?   52
control and deviance

A Monster • Folkways, Mores, Laws • Deviation • Conflict Behavior • Criminal Behavior • Organized Crime • The Criminal Person • How Society Deals with the Violator • Prevention of Crime • Juvenile Delinquency • Retreatist Behavior • Alcoholism • Narcotics • Homosexuality

5 BLACK AND WHITE   74
the question of race

Hatred and Frustration • Race Consciousness • What Is Race? • Race Mixture • Race: A Social Problem • Prejudice • Dominant and Minority Groups • Anti-Semitism • Are There Superior Races? • The Race Issue Today

PART TWO   LOVE, SECURITY, BELONGING   95

6 LOVE IS THE SWEETEST THING ON EARTH   97
love—sex—courtship

Love • Are You in Love? • Sex • Development of Sex and Love • Choosing a Mate • American Courtship • Premarital Sex • Sex Roles • Prospects of Success in Marriage

7 THE FOLKS AT HOME   117
the modern family

Signs of Trouble • Survival • Communication • The Family—A System • The Family—A Social Institution • Monogamy • Nuclear and Extended Families • Whose Name? • Functions • The Unhappy Side • Divorce • The Happy Side

8 HALLOWED BE THY NAME   138
the need for religion

The Need for Comfort • What Is Religion? • Gods • Existence and Death • Important Moments • Ritual and Ceremony • Rules of Conduct • Religious Organization • Many Religions • Drawing Together • American Religion • Secular Religion

PART THREE   THE WORLD OF WORK   161

9 WHAT DO YOU DO FOR A LIVING?   163
work—blessing or curse?

Why Work? • Work—A Curse • The Virtue • Rewards of Work • Work Without Pay • Money and Machine • Busi-

contents ix

ness • Farming • Employment • What Kind of Job? • Finding a Job • Automation • Unemployment • Work Organizations • Leisure

10 MONEY COMES—MONEY GOES   **189**
income and consumption

Money • Inflation • Income • The Consumer • Consumer Habits • How Much Choice Do You Have? • Budgeting • Advertising • Living Standard • Poverty • Fight Against Poverty

11 HOW DO YOU RANK?   **212**
status, caste, and class

Status • Hierarchy • Ascribed and Achieved Status • Stratification • Caste • Classes • Theories of Class • Classes in America • From Upper Upper to Lower Lower • Upper—Middle—Lower

12 TRAINING FOR WORK AND LIFE   **232**
education

What Is Education? • Informal Education • Formal Education • American Schools • Adult Education • How Schools Are Run • Curriculum • Goals of Formal Education • The Teacher • School and the Minority Groups • The Dropout • The Generation Gap

13 GETTING ALONG   **255**
human relations at work

Satisfaction of Needs • Human Relations • Morale • The Group • Leadership

PART FOUR   YOUR COMMUNITY   **271**

14 FROM HAMLET TO MEGALOPOLIS   **273**
the community

The Place Where You Live • The Rural Community • Types of Rural Communities • The City • Origin of Cities • Heterogeneity and Mobility • Ecology of the City • Slums • Suburbia • Megalopolis • Planning

15 CAN YOU FIGHT CITY HALL?   **294**
how the community is run

Local Government • What Local Government Does • Types of Local Government • Types of City Government • Problems of Local Government • The Fifty States • Financing State and Local Government • Voting

x Contents

16 WE, THE PEOPLE 309
the democratic community

What Is Democracy? • Types of Democratic Systems • Rule of Law • Participation • Majority Rule with Respect for Minorities • Democratic Tradition • Democracy and Freedom • Freedom and Order

17 A LARGER COMMUNITY 325
the nation

Nationalism • The Nation • The National Economy • The National Government • The Public and Politics • Problems of the Nation

PART FIVE THE WORLD WE LIVE IN 343

18 IT'S A SMALL WORLD 345
interdependency of states

How Small a World? • Economic Interdependence • The Nation-State in Today's World • Power • Balance of Power • United States Foreign Policy • International Relations

19 A TROUBLED WORLD 359
revolution and war

Rising Expectations • Aid for the "Have-Nots" • Colonial Imperialism • War • Why War? • The Cold War • End of the Cold War? • Foreign Policy and Morality

20 WILL THE WORLD DESTROY ITSELF? 375
the quest for peace

Diplomacy • Collective Security • International Organization • United Nations • The United Nations—Success or Failure? • Disarmament • International Law • World Government

PART SIX SUMMING UP 391

21 ONCE MORE: I AND WE 393
some basic concepts

Personality • Culture • Basic Elements of Culture • Traits and Complexes • Folkways and Mores • Artifacts • Cultural Change • Cultural Diffusion • Groups • Social Problems • Many Cultures

22 GROUPS WITHIN GROUPS **406**
subcultures and contracultures

Regional American Subcultures • Ethnic Subcultures • Religious Subcultures • Contracultures

23 WHAT, WHY, AND FOR WHAT PURPOSE? **420**
the social sciences

Ways of Knowing • What Is Science? • Scientific Attitudes • How Scientific Is Social Science? • How Social Scientists Collect Data • The Various Social Sciences • What Do We Do with Social Science? • Social Science: Good or Bad?

Index **437**

INTRODUCTION

Let us take the year 1969—the year this book was written. You probably knew some people who were fairly satisfied with life and others who felt mistreated by parents, spouses, teachers, by their associates at work, by society in general. Over radio and television you might have heard news about campus riots and snipers in city streets, about drug problems, kidnappings, and the Mafia. You made purchases in stores or regretted that you had no money to do so. The newspapers reported on a rock festival that attracted 300,000 young people. Man reached the moon for the first time. Other stories dealt with housing in the slums, a fight between police and the Black Panthers, a new Supreme Court justice, a young marine from your hometown killed in Vietnam, an Israeli bombing raid on Arab guerrilla camps, stepped-up suppression of the Czechoslovakian people, new trouble on the Russian–Chinese border.

Perhaps you were not too interested in these events and turned quickly to the sports pages, which reported on Lew Alcindor's fabulous contract for his first year in professional basketball, on protests against a player in a South African golf tournament, on the first women jockeys. Advertisements and commercials offered everything from used cars to sprays that fight bad breath.

You lived through the year 1969 involved in a number of personal problems. You thought and talked, you experienced love and hate, friendliness and indifference toward the people around you. In other words, you behaved as a human being living in a society.

This book is about human beings in society. Its aim is to introduce you to the social sciences, which deal with all aspects of man's relations with his fellow-man. We first look at the individual, a person like yourself, and try to see what makes you, your neighbor, and your friend unique and yet, in many ways, similar to other human beings. We give brief attention to those who do not fit the pattern considered normal by the majority and have difficulty getting along. Then we focus on man's behavior in his daily contacts with others. He may follow the throng or cut himself loose; he may be either accepted or rejected. Society invariably affects what he feels, does, and says.

The book then examines men and women as they arrange themselves in groups. The smallest and most intimate group is formed when a couple falls in love, when a family is established. People gather for religious observances, either in small numbers or in large masses. Every society develops some form of religious life.

Next we look at man's efforts to fulfill his physical needs and satisfy his desires for comfort and recognition. This leads us into the world of work, of earning and spending. Each man plays a role according to the place he occupies in society, and he must learn how to properly fill his role.

The circle of man's involvement with his fellow-man widens as he acts as a member of a local community, rural or urban, of a nation, and finally of the whole human society. Whether we like it or not we are involved in the stream of events across the globe.

The affairs of man as he deals with himself and as he makes contact, in ever-widening circles, with other human beings are the subject of the social sciences. This book aims at giving you a view (by no means complete) of the immense variety of topics investigated by social scientists. While everyone has opinions about matters of social concern, the social scientist, like other scientists, observes them carefully and systematically, describes and explains them, and tries, as best he can, to suppress his personal likes and dislikes about them.

As you view the broad picture that social science tries to paint, you will, hopefully, gain added insight into matters close to your own concern. In this book you will encounter problems that are very familiar to you, and perhaps this study will help you to deal with your own problems more rationally. It is also hoped that you will develop a deeper understanding of other people's problems and of the attempts that are being made to deal with them. Above all, you will discover general trends and consistent patterns in the seeming confusion of human acts.

Social science is not just one science but comprises a steadily growing number of specialized fields, each with its own interests and methods. This book does not discuss the various social sciences one by one. Rather, as a general and simple introduction, it cuts across the fields of psychology, anthropology, economics, and others. The last section of the book contains a summary of the concepts with which all social sciences deal and also brief indications as to the concerns of each social science discipline. It is hoped that after becoming acquainted with the broad aspects of human society you will want to examine more closely one or more of the individual fields of social science. If you do, the suggestions for further reading at the end of each chapter should be of some help.

PART ONE **PEOPLE ALL AROUND YOU**

*Let us begin with a person in whom
you are definitely interested: yourself.
Who are you?
What makes you tick?
Do you really know yourself?
"Of course," you answer. "What a
silly question. I've known myself ever
since I was born."*

1 GET ACQUAINTED WITH YOURSELF
your personality

People may claim that they know themselves, but is this really so? What then would explain the hesitation before making a decision or the realization that a wrong one may have been made? How would you account for uncertainty about yourself? If people know themselves so well, why is it so difficult to make others understand them—that is, to "get through" to parents, classmates and co-workers? It would be the unusual person who had never experienced days on which he felt irritated and confused and had perhaps complained, "I am not myself today."

What is this "self"? Or, to put it differently, what is the meaning of "personality"?

Before we continue, let us understand the distinction between the different meanings of the term. We sometimes hear such statements as, "Ethel has lots of personality." What is meant is that Ethel is charming, vivacious, and popular. This is the meaning that the man in the street gives to the term, and from it one could infer that some people have and others don't have personality. However, to the social scientist every individual has a personality. And it is in this more scientific sense that we will use "personality" here. Thus we have an example of a term meaning one thing to the man in

3

the street, but something entirely different to the scientist. We shall encounter other such terms as we go along.

TYPES OF PERSONALITIES

Richard, a young insurance salesman, is active and outspoken. He feels at ease in the company of all kinds of people. He is devoted to his wife and children but flares up quickly when he is annoyed. He grasps new information easily but does not brood over the problems of our time. He likes to watch professional football on television and go hunting with a close friend in the fall. Suspicious of "radicals," he is very anxious to always act correctly and to be appreciated by the "right" people.

On the same block lives Ruth, a college student. Although she is petite and dark-haired, she considers herself unattractive. Since she has had few dates, she is further convinced that she is not attractive to boys. Her constant fear is that she will get fat. She is shy and has a hard time making friends. She agonizes over her schoolwork and lives in fear of poor grades. In her spare time she reads avidly, mostly books that are rather difficult to grasp.

Here we have two people who live in the same neighborhood, have similar social and economic backgrounds, and are close in age, yet who possess very different personalities.
How, then, can we define the human personality? *Personality* is the sum total of an individual's characteristics and ways of behavior. Those characteristics and actions are interdependent elements that form an organized structure, like an airplane or a city.
Psychology is the field of social science that analyzes personality and attempts to explain its functioning. Psychologists form theories of how and why personalities come into existence, and they try to distinguish among the different types. For example, the distinction between *extrovert* and *introvert* personalities is one that is often made. Richard is obviously an extrovert; he gets along well with all kinds of people, engages them easily in conversation, and freely gives his opinions and advice. Ruth would be considered an introvert; she withdraws into herself as if there were an invisible wall separating her from her fellow-men. This is a convenient way to divide people into two classes, but the distinction is too crude to give us an exact description of their personalities or to give any insight into the reasons for their behavior.

SIGMUND FREUD

The thinker whose ideas have made a particularly strong impression, not only on psychologists and social scientists but also on modern man in general, was Sigmund Freud, a Viennese physician who lived from 1856 to 1939. He developed *psychoanalysis*—a revolutionary method for the treatment of mental disorders. Freud's most outstanding contribution was that he went far beyond his medical innovations and developed from them a whole new way of looking at the human personality. Not everybody accepted Freud's ideas; in fact, he became the center of long and bitter controversies. But whether the opinion was one of horror or admiration, the world did take notice of his ideas, which have continued to profoundly influence our literature, art, education, and even philosophy and religion. Freud shares with a few other men the honor of having shaped the thinking of our time.

As a machine runs on some kind of fuel, so man is, according to Freud, propelled by powerful *drives*. He wants to exist as an individual, and he wants to continue his existence as a species. Because of the craving for food, man seeks it and thus assures survival. In the same way, the *libido*, a Latin term commonly translated as the sex drive,[1] makes certain that we keep on reproducing our species.

Sex is, of course, nothing new. Freud certainly did not invent it. It has always been recognized as a device of nature to ensure the continuation of the species. What was new and once extremely startling about Freud's teachings is the idea that the libido is active from birth, not just after sexual maturity. It was this very idea that young children have a sex life that aroused stormy objections at one time. But since the first introduction of his ideas the irate voices have quieted down considerably.

Of course, Freud did not mean that male babies already start to chase female babies. To Freud the libido is a drive for physical pleasure and gratification. Libidinal gratification takes on different forms as the individual grows from infancy into maturity. Infants derive not only nourishment but also pleasure from sucking the mother's breast. Children later show interest in their own genitals and bowel movements and in those of their playmates of either sex.

At one point in his development the boy looks at his father as a rival for the affection of his mother. At this stage feelings of dislike or even of out-and-out hatred on the part of the son are often either secretly harbored or openly shown. Freud calls this the *Oedipus complex*. The relationship between daughter and mother moves through a similar crisis and for the same reasons (*Electra complex*). This theory of sexual jealousy between father and son or mother and daughter has been vehemently criticized by outraged moralists.

When the individual reaches the age of puberty and is now able to reproduce, the libido takes on, in most cases, the form that we usually call sexual desire. Erich Fromm, who was first Freud's student and later his critic, says of Freud that he "sees in the sexual instinct the result of a chemically produced tension in the body which is painful and seeks for relief. The aim of the sexual desire is the removal of this painful tension.

... Sexual desire, in this concept, is an itch, sexual satisfaction the removal of the itch."[2]

Man as an animal seeks to gratify his sex drive, but man is more than an animal. As a member of the human society, he is restricted by its rules and regulations. He has to consider what society presents to him as proper behavior, as worthwhile goals of life. Man must restrain his libido, and he does this in two ways:

1. He *sublimates* part or all of his energies by turning them away from the libidinal to other goals. An explorer who concentrates all his energies on mapping out unknown islands, a sculptor who devotes himself completely to his art, and a monk who lives only for his acts of worship have gone far in sublimating their libidos. An extreme Freudian could interpret any mental or physical activity, as long as it is not connected with sexual fulfillment, as sublimation. Sublimation, then, could be used to explain all human accomplishments from the beginning of time.

2. Man *represses* certain aspects of his libido to the point where he is no longer conscious of them. They have been pushed down into his *subconscious mind*. There rest, seemingly forgotten, not only our lusts, our physical desires, but also our desires to kill, to hurt, to be extremely aggressive—all the feelings that we have repressed because they contrast too much with what society declares to be nice and proper. Pointing out the existence of the subconscious mind has perhaps been Freud's most important achievement. Even those who otherwise oppose him have accepted this thought almost universally.

In Freud's analysis the human personality is broken down into three *interacting* forces, and satisfactory mental health depends on the proper balance between them. Freud labels these forces as the *ego*, the *id*, and the *superego*. These Latin terms, meaning "I," "it," and "over-I," are commonly given the English equivalents of *conscious mind*, *subconscious mind*, and *conscience*.

To use a rather crude picture, let us compare your mind to a room. The space in this room is filled with your conscious mind. Those are your thoughts of which you are aware. You *know* that you love your husband but are annoyed by some of his friends. You know that you dislike science fiction but enjoy bowling once a week. You are aware of your feelings toward your boss or your teacher.

But then there are feelings of which you are unaware. You once wished your father or your mother dead. You disliked a playmate, and when he was badly hurt, you felt responsible for the accident. Seemingly you have forgotten all this, but it is still there buried in your subconscious mind, which can be likened to a container standing inside the room.

The lid on the container that prevents those thoughts from rising into the awareness of the conscious mind is the superego, the conscience. We develop our conscience as we talk, play, and work with parents, teachers, friends, and co-workers, as we watch, read, and listen. Through all these contacts we form ideas of acceptable patterns of action and thought and of the forms of behavior society expects of us. As we mature, we are introduced to the ways of society, which we call its *culture*. (See Chapter 20 for a discussion of culture.)

How then do we know that we have a subconscious mind? According to Freud, there are situations in which the lid is lifted. Our conscience is asleep, and the long hidden becomes known. This happens in dreams or in occasional slips of the tongue. It also occurs during psychoanalysis, the purpose of which is to lift the lid.

This train of thought leads to the conclusion that human personality is not something created at one moment and in one piece. Rather it moves through several phases from infancy to adulthood. Experiences in early childhood have a strong impact on the make-up of the adult personality. Many difficulties that adults encounter have their roots in a lack of maturity, in a failure to progress through the various phases with advancing age. For example, if, as a boy grows older, he fails to overcome the Oedipus complex, he may eventually encounter deep emotional trouble.

We must also conclude that Freudian principles can be applied to the study of any personality, whether that of a living or dead person. Erik H. Erikson's analysis of Martin Luther is a good example of historical and biographical research based on psychoanalytical ideas.[3] Luther, a Catholic monk who broke with his church, led the Protestant Reformation in the sixteenth century. Erikson tries to show that this historic act of defiance was rooted in the personality of the reformer. When Luther was a child, he was dominated by a harsh father, whom he loved and feared at the same time. Throughout his life he retained an intense fear of an avenging God and of eternal punishment. Subconsciously he had transferred his feelings toward his father to his attitude toward God. According to Erikson, when Luther decided to defy the Pope and leave the Catholic church, it was not only a protest against what he felt to be corruption and false beliefs, but it was also a symbolic rebellion against a stern father.

TRAITS AND ROLES

Aside from all other effects, Freud's pronouncements, which first appeared in print in 1895, have generated tremendous interest in psychology and the related social sciences. Since that time the workings of the human mind have been extensively investigated.

Let us go back to the two personalities mentioned in the beginning of the chapter. In describing them we used such terms as "active," "outspoken," "shy," and "fearful." These are *surface traits*. In order to recognize them it is not necessary to dig into the hidden mental recesses. These traits can be easily observed and are rather stable over relatively long periods of time.

Personality contains a number of surface traits. But how do you account for the fact that you, like everybody else, behave one way in one situation and quite differently in another? If you are a student, you exhibit one set of traits in the classroom and quite another at a basketball game. In class you may appear calm, clear thinking, and responsible. But to somebody who watches you in the bleachers of the gymnasium you appear loud, emotional, and rather rough in your expression of applause or disapproval. You as a student in class and you as a fan at the game would seem to be almost two different persons. Actually, you remain the same individual but act out different *roles* in different situations, just as an actor might portray a hero in one performance and a villain in another. The surface traits that you exhibit seem to contradict each other, yet they are fairly consistent within the various roles you play.

Each of us plays a number of roles, depending on whether we are at work, at home, at church, or on a date, whether we are parents or children, students or teachers, leaders or followers. Sometimes situations arise in which there are *role conflicts*. Countless women play the traditional roles of wives and mothers. They cook meals, try to look attractive to their husbands, and take care of their children and household. What if the wife and mother also wants to play the role of the career woman? In that case she also wants to be a successful teacher, businesswoman, or social worker. Role conflicts arise easily in such a situation. It takes a great deal of adjustment and often sacrifice also to bring the roles into harmony, although not all the adjusting would have to come from the wife. The husband too finds that to his well-established role as the sole family provider has now been added the unfamiliar one of equal partner.

SELF-CONCEPT

Whether husband and wife will find a satisfactory solution to their problem of conflicting roles will, to a large extent, depend on their *self-concepts*. The self-concept is a group of traits that you ascribe to yourself. This is how you see yourself regardless of how others may find you. The psychologist Carl Rogers suggests that "most of the ways of behaving are consistent with the concept of self."[4]

Jim is a young man who had been out of school for several years. He had a job but decided to take a few college courses without planning to get a degree. He described himself to one of his teachers as a poor student without the ability to complete the requirements for a bachelor's degree. To his surprise he received all As and Bs at the end of the first quarter. Most students would have been happy but not Jim. He felt confused because the grades were inconsistent with the role he was playing. In the next quarter his grades dropped to the point where they were acceptable to him. Eventually he dropped out of school.

Obviously the roles you choose to play have a lot to do with the place in society in which you find yourself.

your personality 9

FRAME OF REFERENCE

The self-concept is part of a larger concept that we will call the *frame of reference*. We can define the frame of reference as a set of basic assumptions, attitudes, and values that the individual holds about himself and about the world around him. Therefore, your action in any situation that confronts you depends on your frame of reference.

A number of psychologists see our actions as *responses* to *stimuli*. (*Stimulus* [singular] is a Latin term meaning an incentive to action; *stimuli* is the plural.) For example:

A shining toy is dangled before an infant (stimulus); he reaches for it (response).
Somebody stops you in the street with a loud, "Hi Mary" (stimulus); you answer, "Hello Tom" (response).
Driving up to an intersection you see a red stoplight (stimulus); you apply the brakes to your automobile (response).

But people don't always respond to the same stimulus in the same way. Mrs. Johnson shops regularly at a certain grocery store. The same items are always stocked on the shelves, but on some days she notices and buys many more groceries than on others. When asked to explain, Mrs. Johnson declares that she invariably sees more food in the store when she is hungry than when she shops right after having eaten. (See table below.)

Of course, long experience has taught Mrs. Johnson that eating removes hunger. This experience is, in this instance, her frame of reference. The chart below illustrates the relationship between stimulus, frame of reference, and response.

Frame of Reference

Stimulus	Frame of Reference	Response
Food on shelves	Hungry: food removes hunger →	Buys a lot of food
	Not hungry: food not important →	Buys only a few items

We seem to be going through a lot of trouble just to describe how Mrs. Johnson buys her groceries. The purpose is to show the objective of the social scientist: it is to see and to describe a pattern of human behavior. The social scientist operates in the same way as the biologist or physicist, who looks at specific situations in order to discover a general pattern.

When a person is confronted by a situation, he uses one or more of his senses to take notice of it. He interprets what is happening by referring messages from his senses to his existing ideas about himself (self-concept) and to other areas of his frame of reference. He assigns some kind of meaning to these messages. As the messages are interpreted, the person responds to the situation according to the way he perceived it.[5] Since

LEARNING

How does one develop a frame of reference? According to Rogers,[6] we gain ideas about ourselves and others from two main sources: through direct experience and through other people. If you tried to drive an automobile and were successful, you now consider yourself capable of driving. If not, you assume that you cannot drive, at least not without some help or further practice. On the other hand, if you have never tried to fly an airplane, you are probably convinced that you could not do it unless someone else taught you how. Your ideas about driving were formed from direct experience whereas your feelings about your ability to fly came from others. In either case your frame of reference was *learned*. Many psychologists conclude that human behavior in general is mostly a product of learning.

However, what we learn is not always correct. An outdated book or an ill-informed teacher may give the wrong information. Similarly the self-concept may have been formed through the learning of things that are either completely false or quite inaccurate. The girl Ruth, whom we encountered earlier in this chapter, considers herself plain-looking and unattractive to boys. It may very well be—and this happens occasionally—that her parents told her repeatedly that she lacked charm and beauty. They may have compared her unfavorably with a sister or with other girls of their acquaintance. Slowly Ruth accepted the ideas originating with her parents as true, and they became part of her self-concept, affecting her behavior when she was around boys. She tried to avoid boys as much as possible, and when this was not possible, she somehow managed to communicate to them that she did not expect to be asked for a date—and she wasn't.

This girl had convinced herself that she did not measure up to the *norms* of her society, the usual expectations that people hold concerning one another and that they consider normal. Young women are expected to look pretty, and if they are not lucky enough to have an hourglass figure, they must make up for it with stylish clothes, fashionable hairstyles, and cosmetics. Girls must try to appear attractive to boys: this seems to be one of the *values* in our culture. Values give reasons for the norms; they justify them.

If Ruth had been able to improve her appearance and assume a different attitude toward boys she would have benefited enormously, but her self-concept prevented her from changing. Frequently inaccuracies in the self-concept originate with other people. However, whether they have their beginning within ourselves or with other people, they can be very damaging because they keep us from making corrections in ourselves.

Before we go on, let us state once more what psychologists mean by "learning." This term includes, of course, anything you absorb in school or through other forms of instruction. In fact, modern psychology has had much to do with the reform of teaching methods. But you also learn anytime you respond to a stimulus, which may occur in school, at home, on the street, or in the solitude of nature.

Each individual learns different things, but a good portion of everyone's learning experiences are by necessity similar. The society in which we live can be compared to children sitting in the same class, listening to the same teacher, reading the same textbook. By reading the same newspapers and watching the same television programs we respond to the same stimuli as our fellow-men. We obey the same laws and are taught the same rules of proper conduct. Because of standardized industrial production, we must wear the same kind of clothes and pick the same paperbacks from the shelves of drugstores, which all look alike in style and decor. In many ways, a person is *conditioned* to be like all others around him. Many authors point at the danger of *conformity*, a situation in which one personality is just a carbon copy of the next.[7]

If having the same learning experiences tends to make us all alike, those who can manufacture the experiences would have the power to mold our minds into any shape they desire. How justified is this fear of too much conditioning? Alarm has been expressed that massive propaganda, persuasive advertising, and the type of indoctrination that is practiced in some Communist countries are attempts to bring about such widespread molding.

In his novel *Walden Two*, B. F. Skinner describes a fictitious community in which life is scientifically planned to the smallest detail. Members are exposed to only those stimuli that, according to the planners, will make them into faultless personalities. For example, three-year-old children are taught self-control by means of lollipops dusted with sugar. Though they are plainly in sight, the goodies are not supposed to be touched. "We tell [the child] he may eat the lollipop later in the day, provided it hasn't already been licked." At first, the youngsters don't find it easy to resist the temptation, but after the experiment has been repeated several times they are perfectly content to wait for the candy without showing any impatience. The whole process is meticulously prepared and carefully observed.[8]

HEREDITY

It is doubtful that *Walden Two* will be translated into reality though it contains some intriguing ideas. Fortunately complete conformity is not possible. Each one of us still has a unique personality.

Part of this uniqueness is the result of *heredity*. From our parents we inherit the features of our physical appearance, as well as some elements of our temperament and our *intelligence*, which is the capacity to learn. In other words, heredity provides us with the *potentials* for development. The only two people who start life with the same potential are identical twins. They result from a single egg in the female body being fertilized by a single male sperm cell and then dividing in such a way that the two parts develop into two separate individuals. However, this is not the case with fraternal twins. They don't receive the same potential because they are the result of two eggs with different *genetic* components being fertilized at the same time by two different sperm cells. One can see why psychologists have been quite eager to do research on pairs of identical twins.

How important to the formation of the human personality are such hereditary factors as *race*? (We shall have more to say about this in succeeding chapters.) Controversy rages over how much of our behavior can be attributed to heredity and how much to the environment, which furnishes our learning experiences. We can, however, agree that heredity and environment don't function in separate areas that are sealed off from each other. Rather they interact constantly. Nature furnishes you with a strong or weak, a tall or short body, but how this affects your personality depends to a large extent on what you and the people around you make of it. In our society tall boys are expected to turn out for high-school basketball. Coaches indicate that loyalty to the school demands it and that great personal glory will be the reward, and in most cases the boy with the six-foot-plus frame will gladly avail himself of the opportunity.

MOTIVATION

We cannot select either our parents or the society into which we are born, but we must adapt to conditions beyond our control and learn to make the best of them. However, man can change the society into which he is born, and he has done so for as long as he has lived on earth. As we will see in later chapters, there are many aspects of our present society that need changing very urgently.

This brings us to another fundamental argument that has caused heated exchanges for a long time. Both heredity and environment are imposed on man, but is man simply a product of these influences, or does the individual have anything to say, after all, about the kind of person he wants to be? Just like the controversy over Freud, this old battle of ideas between the *determinists* and the proponents of *free will* reaches not only into many aspects of social science but also into religion, philosophy, and the arts. While the theorists will, in all likelihood, keep on struggling for a long time, most of us will probably have to settle for a compromise so that we can get on with our everyday lives.

It is in the nature of science that it leans toward determinism—that is, the idea that whatever we observe is determined by natural causes. The scientist tries to discover trends and regularities and from present or past behavior attempts to predict the future. Astronomers can predict the orbits of stars. Engineers feel sure that they can predict the strength of the bridges they build, and physicians have similar feelings about the predictability of the drugs and diets they prescribe.

In a more limited way the psychologist tries to forecast human behavior. Among the many tools he has fashioned for this purpose are the mental testing procedures. The experts test intelligence, which is man's capacity to understand his environment and to adjust to it. They have also devised means to test interests, aptitudes, and emotional adjustment. It might be a good idea not to overrate the value of all those tests. The experts who put them together are mostly white and move in a middle-class environment. They may not intend to be partial to a particular social group, but the tests still reflect their backgrounds. Blacks, Puerto Ricans, immigrants from other countries, and the poor in general often find that the test questions have little to do with their own experiences and refer to a world that is unknown to them. Therefore, they may score lower than their real capacity. Tests are not meant to relieve you of the responsibility of making decisions concerning yourself, but they can be a distinct help in planning a career, in probing the causes of personality difficulties, and in many other ways.

A person who gets a low rating in tests in verbal expression should think twice before deciding to become a journalist, and one who has difficulty with tests of numerical and spatial relationships might have a hard time as a physicist or mathematician. On the other hand, a test result indicating great ability in communicating with other people might strengthen a young person's ambition to turn toward social work, teaching, or the ministry.

But all that is in us cannot be tested and measured. Man is not only a highly sensitive and extremely complicated machine, he is also a *creative* organism. Creativity, which defies exact study under laboratory conditions, has given mankind its great inventions from the wheel to the spaceship and has produced symphonies and cathedrals, the Song of Solomon, and the plays of Shakespeare. And creativity is not the monopoly of famous persons alone; it can be found in the workshops of craftsmen, in business, in sports. Parents can show creativity in raising their children, and sweethearts in expressing their affection for each other.

What man can accomplish depends not wholly on his physical or mental equipment or his environment but also on the strength of his *motivation*. Motivation is the desire to achieve a certain goal. The will to succeed has at times overcome unbelievable handicaps. The armless artist who has learned to paint with his toes or the one-legged ski enthusiast makes the headlines, but many others have been motivated to overcome equally difficult though less spectacular obstacles.

The Greek philosopher Epicurus said that man's purpose in life is to seek happiness. But what is happiness? For Epicurus it is the same as pleasure. Many have tried to define it in a different way, but it escapes any meaningful description. Rather than running after an elusive happiness, we must settle for more realistic goals. A worthwhile and reachable goal would be to develop into a mature and *integrated* person. Such an individual should retain his uniqueness, yet be reasonably well *socialized*. A mature person neither overrates nor underrates himself to an unreasonable extent. He is motivated to reach goals that are attainable, to face difficulties and challenges rather than to run away from them. Despite unavoidable disappointments and frustrations, a mature person finds life as a whole an interesting and satisfying experience.

How well do you think you fit this description?

Main Ideas
1. Every human being has a personality.
2. We distinguish different types of personalities according to their prominent characteristics. One such distinction is that between extroverts and introverts.
3. Freud spoke of a central driving force in man, the libido. Under its impact the personality functions on three levels: the conscious mind, the subconscious mind, and the conscience.
4. Each individual possesses a number of surface traits and acts out different roles. The roles depend on the social situations in which the individual finds himself.
5. Our behavior is influenced by our self-concept and by the frame of reference, which develop through experience.
6. A major part of our behavior is learned. The learning experience results from responses to stimuli.
7. Those who believe in determinism maintain that heredity and environment in their interaction completely determine the personality.
8. The proponents of free will stress the uniqueness, creativity, and motivation of the individual.
9. A mature individual with an integrated personality is most likely to lead a satisfying life.

Important Terms

Conditioning	Norm
Determinism	Oedipus complex
Drive	Personality
Electra complex	Potential
Extrovert	Psychoanalysis
Frame of reference	Role conflict
Genetic	Self-concept
Heredity	Stimulus
Integrated	Subconscious
Introvert	Sublimation
Libido	Surface trait
Motivation	Value

Conclusion

The human personality is a unified organization of characteristics resulting in the behavior of the individual. Most people in a society behave in a similar way yet also show unique characteristics. An understanding of the general principles involved in the workings of the human personality should make the student more effective in dealing with other people. He should also gain knowledge about himself that will allow him to make reasonable decisions concerning his own future.

Notes

1. Sigmund Freud, *The Psychopathology of Everyday Life* (New York: New American Library, 1952).
2. Erich Fromm, *The Art of Loving* (New York: Harper, 1956), pp. 35–36.
3. Erik H. Erikson, *Young Martin Luther: A Study in Psychoanalysis and History* (New York: W. W. Norton, 1962).
4. Carl R. Rogers, *Client-Centered Therapy* (Boston: Houghton Mifflin, 1951), pp. 481–532.
5. Arthur W. Combs and Donald Snygg, *Individual Behavior* (New York: Harper, 1959), pp. 16–36.
6. Rogers, *op. cit.*, pp. 481–532.
7. B. F. Skinner, *The Technology of Teaching* (New York: Appleton-Century-Crofts, 1968), pp. 169–188.
8. B. F. Skinner, *Walden Two* (New York: Macmillan, 1962), pp. 107–108.

Suggestions for Further Reading

Allport, Gordon (ed.). *Letters from Jenny*. New York: Harcourt, Brace & World, 1965. Study of a woman's personality through a collection of her letters.

Ashley-Montagu, M. F. "Chromosomes and Crime," *Psychology Today*, 2 (October 1968), 42–49. The role of heredity in personality formation.

Eysenck, H. J. *Sense and Nonsense in Psychology*. Baltimore: Penguin Books, 1958 (paperback). Criticism of some psychological notions, especially of psychoanalysis.

Laswell, Harold. "Power and Personality," *Psychology Today*, 2 (October 1968), 64–67. Remarks about the personalities of politicians.

Rosenthal, Robert. "Self-Fulfilling Prophecy," *Psychology Today*, 2 (September 1968), 44–51. People act as one expects them to act.

Salinger, J. D. *The Catcher in the Rye*. New York: New American Library, 1953 (paperback). Novel concerning the development of an adolescent's personality.

Skinner, B. F. *Walden Two*. New York: Macmillan, 1962 (paperback). Novel about a utopian community regulated according to psychological principles.

White, Robert W. *Lives in Progress*, 2nd ed. New York: Holt, Rinehart & Winston, 1966. Collection of descriptive case histories.

Is anything wrong with you? Let's not talk about your body but about your mind.
"Why, not a thing," you answer indignantly. "I am perfectly normal."

2 IS ANYTHING WRONG WITH YOU?
problems of the human mind

First, forget about the term "normal," which is extremely vague. But stop and try to examine yourself for a moment—is there nothing wrong with you? There is probably no one alive who has escaped occasional feelings of anxiety and insecurity, who has never been nervous, never experienced moments of self-doubt. Indeed, if such a person existed, he would be a very dull and uninteresting individual.

There is the story of the two old Quakers walking together. "It seems the whole world is pixilated," remarked one to the other, "except Thee and me, and sometimes I am not so sure about Thee." Now look at the people you know. Don't you find this one a little strange and another somewhat odd or, to use that quaint old-fashioned term, slightly pixilated?

MENTAL ILLNESS

Let us first consider the extreme cases, those of individuals who are more than just "a little strange."

A colleague of the author remembers a scene from his childhood in a small West Coast town. It was a hot summer day, and Annie, about five feet tall and overweight, walked slowly down the street. Her black coat was of heavy wool, the kind of garment suited for a chilly winter day. She seemed completely out of place among the neat rows of homes with their closely cropped lawns and neatly painted fronts.

As she approached a large white house on the corner, a small group of children stopped their game of touch football to watch Annie walk past. Carefully keeping their distance, they shouted, "Hey, crazy Annie, why don't you get a warmer coat?" or "When did they let you out?" The parents of these children, if they heard, made no move to interfere. Annie turned her head, giggled, and made some unintelligible comment.

One day the children saw a dark sedan stop in front of Annie's place. Two men got out and went inside. In a few minutes they brought her out in a white strait jacket, her arms bound securely to her sides. She was never seen again in the neighborhood.

This unfortunate individual needed help and compassion more than most of us. Yet she was treated with cruelty by the young and with cold indifference by the old. The tragedy is that such behavior toward a disturbed person is far from exceptional.

OLDER SOCIAL ATTITUDES

The story of man's behavior toward his mentally afflicted brother covers one of the darkest pages in human history, although there are exceptions to the cruelty. In some pagan societies deranged persons did not fare so badly. They were, in fact, regarded with awe. It was believed that the gods used them as their mouthpieces, and thus their disconnected babbling was respectfully listened to. The priests tried to interpret such incoherent talk as messages from the supernatural world.

But, on the whole, the record is an extremely tragic one, especially with the arrival of Christianity. The insane were thought to be possessed by the devil, and weird rituals were employed to drive him out. When the victims remained unchanged, they were thrown into dungeons, often in heavy chains, and left to die a miserable death from neglect.

When the belief in witchcraft was still widespread, it seemed only natural to pin the label "witch" on an insane person. To punish witches by hanging, drowning, or burning was quite common. In the famous witchcraft trials of 1692 in Salem, Massachusetts, several mentally disturbed women were condemned and executed. When one examines the whole atmosphere of fanaticism and mass hysteria that pervaded Salem and similar places in those days, it is hard to say who was more afflicted, the accusers or the accused.[1]

We don't burn witches anymore, but the habit of treating the mentally ill like criminals has not completely disappeared. Even in these enlightened United States, the mentally ill are still, in some instances, lodged in county jails. Sometimes two or three burly policemen deliver their handcuffed charge into the custody of the sheriff, who then places the arrival into a special padded cell if one is available.

The idea that mental imbalance is a sickness and that the afflicted persons should be treated rather than punished is still not universally accepted, though it is by no means new. In ancient Egypt, 4,000 years ago, cures were attempted by means of *trephining*, which is probably the earliest surgical operation ever performed by men. Part of the skull was chipped away with a crude stone instrument so that the evil spirits could escape through the hole.[2]

Less risky and entirely unbloody was the method employed by the eighteenth-century Austrian healer Franz Anton Mesmer. With a great deal of showmanship he brought the patient into contact with a piece of magnetized metal, proclaiming that this would, in some mysterious way, deliver the patient from his troubles. This hocus-pocus did not cause much harm, and many clients actually believed themselves cured, so strong was their trust in the power of Mesmer's magnetism. What this clever Austrian really possessed was a great *power of suggestion*.[3] We still speak of persons who can "mesmerize" other people. Today the various techniques of *hypnotism* are based on similar strong suggestive devices. Also related to such attempts is what we call *faith healing*, an important ingredient of various religious cults.

The concept of special hospitals for the emotionally disturbed is not new either, but the mental hospital of old (and of not so old) was not exactly a delightful place. It is hard deciding whether or not it constituted an improvement over the traditional jail or dungeon.

An early institution of this kind was the Bethlehem Royal Hospital in London, which dates back to the sixteenth century. It was commonly called by the shortened term "Bedlam," a word still used to indicate utter confusion and senseless turmoil. For a small fee Londoners out for a Sunday stroll could view through a grill the droll antics of the most disturbed patients: it was considered better than a trip to the zoo.

American state hospitals, in which most of our mentally ill were confined, did not raise revenue the way that Bedlam did even though they could have used the additional funds just as well. But until the middle of this century the inmates of these state hospitals did not fare much better than those in Bedlam. The key word describing the attitude of the staff, the state government, and society was neglect, neglect derived from lack of interest. The existence of mental illness was an unpleasant fact, and so people pretended that it just wasn't there.

In the meantime, the mentally ill lingered endlessly in the dim, dreary twilight existence behind the walls and locked doors of overcrowded institutions. Up to the year 1955 practically everyone who was admitted into an institution died there. The patients were kept in custody, but hardly anything was done for them. Psychiatrists were scarce; sometimes not more than two were available for every 1,000 patients. Most of the personnel was untrained and often completely unfit for the job. Filth and boredom prevailed. The motion picture *Snake Pit* offered glimpses into a typical mental hospital of not so long ago, bringing to mind scenes in hell as painted by old masters or as described in the great imagery of the poet Dante.

When treatment was administered at all, it was mostly in some form of shock therapy. Alternating streams of very hot and very cold water were directed at the patient with great force. Or electric currents were passed through his brain by means of electrodes placed on either side of the head. Whether this kind of treatment eventually helped the disturbed person is doubtful. It certainly must have been a frightful experience while it lasted.

Both *hydrotherapy* (cure by water) and *electrotherapy* are still in use today to a limited extent, but the methods have been greatly improved. Very disturbed patients are sometimes put into lukewarm baths for a period of one or more hours. Persons suffering from severe depression may be given slight electric shocks that are not dangerous and cause no damage to the brain. The patients become briefly unconscious, but if the treatment is successful, they wake up calmer and in better spirits.

An extreme measure, now abandoned, was the *lobotomy*, which can be compared to the cutting off of a leg to remove an ingrown toenail. In this procedure particularly violent patients were brought to the operating table where surgeons made an incision into the brain. This quieted them down, to be sure, but in many instances it also turned them into completely unfeeling vegetables.

MISCONCEPTIONS ABOUT MENTAL ILLNESS

In a society that ridicules mentally disturbed persons and bestows on them such telltale colloquial adjectives as "nuts," "crazy," or "cracked" it is not surprising that profound ignorance concerning the mentally ill and their problems is widespread. Progress is being made, but at a very slow pace. We will deal here briefly with some of the more common of the distorted notions.

First, the extent of mental imbalance is widely underestimated. If you are one of those who think, "It can't happen to me," you may be in for a painful surprise. Mental illness may strike your neighbor, a member of your family, and even you. Estimates indicate that one out of every five Americans suffers from an illness caused by a serious emotional problem.[4] Comprehensive studies have shown that in a poor section of midtown Manhattan for every 100 persons who could be considered mentally healthy, 338 were suffering from severe mental disturbances.[5] Thus, there is the very real prospect that almost any person you know may, at some time during his life, be struck by a handicapping emotional disorder.

A widespread misconception is that serious emotional difficulties can be overcome by sheer will power. Such well-meant advice as "Get hold of yourself" or "Face up to your problem" has as little effect in dealing with emotional disorders as it would have in the case of a broken leg or a ruptured appendix. Having observed many mental patients, Watzlawick, Beavin, and Jackson conclude that these patients "usually have tried and failed in all kinds of self-discipline and exercises in will power before they revealed their distress to others."[6] Home remedies just don't work.

We have so long associated mental illness with the strait jacket and the padded cell that we automatically think of the emotionally handicapped person as a raving maniac who will tear to pieces anything that comes within his reach. This is another of those false notions that take a long time to die. Actually violent behavior is the exception rather than the rule. The average disturbed person is more likely to behave like your next-door neighbor than like the murderer who made the front page this morning. Even the deranged man or woman who has actually committed murder is usually quite safe once he or she has been placed in an environment of reduced stress.

Finally, we should be careful not to confuse mental illness with *mental retardation*. Illness, mental or physical, can strike persons of any intelligence level, whereas the mentally retarded have ceased to grow intellectually at a very early age. A mentally deficient adult may be in perfect health, but his *mental age* can be that of a thirteen-year-old or younger. Therefore, he is unable to carry adult responsibilities at work, in the family, and in the general society. Like the mentally ill, the mentally retarded have, in the past, been treated cruelly and have had to carry the full brunt of society's scorn and neglect. But more recently attitudes have slowly begun to change. The retarded are now being trained to perform at the limit of their ability in special classes and schools, and those whose mental age precludes any kind of training are cared for in special institutions where they are made as comfortable as possible.

A NEW ERA BEGINS

Our culture is in a constant process of change. One of the slow changes that has been noticeable in the last two centuries is in man's attitude toward his less fortunate fellow-men. The poor, lawbreakers, cripples, the blind, and the deformed were once handled with callous inhumanity. Gradually we are beginning to see them as victims of circumstances who need our help and who, in many cases, can be helped.

Although this change in attitude has by no means become universal, a new wind is definitely blowing; and one group that has begun to feel the invigorating breeze is the emotionally ill. This new attitude happens to coincide with some very important medical developments that have been made, particularly since 1955. Two new types of drugs were introduced into the armory of the mental therapist, *tranquilizers* and *energizers*. Tranquilizers calm down the overexcited and the violent, and energizers enliven the apathetic and the despondent. Thus, by using these drugs these personality types can be made more amenable to *psychotherapy*, the treatment in which the patient directly confronts his psychiatrist. Psychotherapy (Greek for "healing of the mind") aims at leading the mentally ill patient to a realization of why he feels the way he does and why he acts in a manner harmful to himself and to others. This self-understanding will rid him of his symptoms, and if the therapy is successful, they will not return. The net effect has been that many persons formerly considered hopeless have returned to their homes and jobs or, at least, were so improved that they could continue treatment in outpatient clinics and day-care centers.

In the mid-1950s, Morningside Hospital in Portland, Oregon, was the first institution in the United States to place all patients in "open (unlocked) wards." Many other institutions have since followed suit. The trend is to consider mental illness as another form of illness and a mental hospital as another hospital. Instead of bars or padded cells, teams of competent and sympathetic experts administer all kinds of therapies.

The change of attitude on the part of society will be complete when people can report, "Uncle Hugh is now in a mental hospital recovering from a nervous breakdown," with the same lack of shame that they would tell of his hospitalization because of pneumonia. When this stage is reached, job applicants will no longer have to hide from prospective employers or lovers from prospective in-laws the fact that they have spent time in such an institution.

MENTAL ILLNESS AND PERSONALITY PROBLEMS

Do you feel that we have concentrated too much on this one specific group of people, namely, the mentally ill? "Why not talk about the majority instead," you may ask, "those of us who are of sound mind?" Even though your objection is understandable, it is not completely justified. We *have* been talking about society as a whole though only a small portion of it can be found inside mental institutions. There is no sharp dividing line between those inside and those outside of the hospital. Perhaps this truth is hard to swallow because it hurts our pride. But let's ask ourselves what emotional illness really is.

If we disregard *organic* mental disturbance, which is caused by damage to the brain as a result of accidents or deterioration of the brain tissue, we can define emotional disorders as severe forms of personality disintegration and of failure to adjust to the demands of life and society. The mentally ill separate themselves from reality, play incompatible roles, and face the world with confused and conflicting attitudes. These defects are so strong that the afflicted are unable to function in society. But to lesser degrees all people encounter the same kinds of problems, and so we can discern a gradual progression from the severest cases of personality disintegration to the comparatively mild complications that everyone faces at one time or another.

Types of Mental Disturbances

A. *Psychoses*

Psychotics are unable to deal with their problems. They may become a danger to themselves and to others and must usually be cared for in institutions. Examples of psychotic behavior:
Schizophrenia: This type of psychosis is characterized by emotional indifference and withdrawal from social relations.
Manic-Depressive Psychoses: Patients alternate between extremely depressed and highly excited stages.

B. *Neuroses*

These are milder forms of personality disturbance. Neurotics may be able to act as parents and fulfill their working assignments, but they experience difficulties and need professional help. Examples of neurotic behavior:
Anxiety Neuroses: These are states of unreasonable fear, fear of things that do not exist. Unreasonable fears of special situations, such as being in a small closed room, are also referred to as *phobias*.
Compulsive Neuroses: The neurotic feels compelled to act in a certain way that seems irrational not only to the observer but also to the neurotic himself. For example, a *kleptomaniac* feels compelled to steal though he does not need the stolen objects.

C. *Psychosomatic Illnesses*

These are physical ailments, such as persistent headaches or stomach ulcers, caused by emotional strain. Obviously to treat only the physical symptoms without considering what caused them will have no lasting effect.

D. *Personality Problems*

These are mild and temporary emotional indispositions, such as nervousness, depression, feelings of being persecuted, and so forth.

STRESS, FRUSTRATION, CONFLICT

Mental health, like physical well-being, is not a permanent state that, once achieved, will continue forever. It is something fragile that is constantly being threatened, and it must be protected and repaired through never-ending efforts. Who has never had a nagging cold or a discomforting upset stomach? Although someone with these conditions knows he is probably not dangerously ill, he still has to take some precautions—perhaps a few days of bed rest and a special diet—to restore good health.

Emotional upsets occur at least as frequently as physical ones and require cautious observation and suitable remedies. Some students become highly nervous before important tests. Financial or marital difficulties make people extremely uncomfortable. Rumors of burglaries or muggings in a neighborhood may arouse exaggerated fears and suspicions. Whenever your daily routine is threatened by events like these or by an innumerable variety of others, you experience *stress*. In their dictionary English and English define stress as "a force, applied to a system, sufficient to cause

problems of the human mind   23

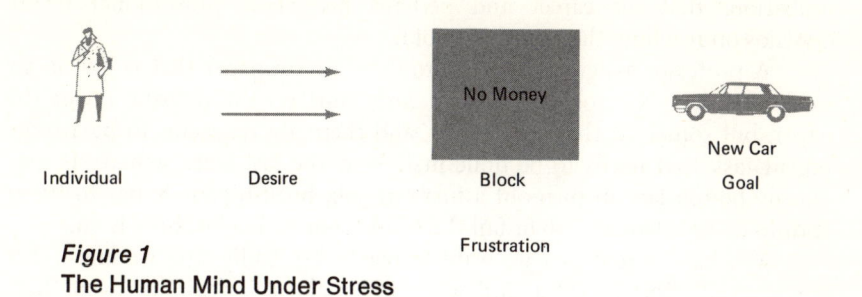

Figure 1
The Human Mind Under Stress

Individual — Desire → Block (No Money) — Frustration — Goal (New Car)

strain or distortion in the system, or, when very great, to alter it into new forms."⁷

The stress you encounter when you are unable to reach a desired goal is called *frustration*. You may want very badly to have a new car, for instance, but this desire is blocked by the simple fact that you don't have the necessary money. Or your favorite girl may tell you one evening that she has decided to go steady with someone else. In either case the result is frustration.

When you are faced with frustration, you may give up any attempt to reach your goal. Perhaps you will just sit back and feel sorry for yourself. But you can also decide to do something about it, to try a course of action. When two or more possibilities of action are open to you and you have to make a choice, then you are faced with a *conflict*.

Some conflicts are trivial, having little or no frustration connected with them. This morning, when you started your day, you probably had to decide what to wear. You may have hesitated for a moment before making your decision, but in the end any choice was acceptable. Perhaps somewhat more important is the choice of dress for a girl about to go out on a date that she has been anticipating with excitement. Yet, in this case too, the conflict between choosing the green or the blue outfit is not very serious. Young persons must sometimes choose between obtaining a college education under severe financial burden and looking for a job that will bring in paychecks immediately. A student would like to try marijuana as his friends have been doing, but he is concerned about the possibilities of being caught and of harmful effects on his health. An unmarried pregnant girl must decide whether to seek an illegal abortion or to bear the child that she would have to give away for adoption. Such conflicts are accompanied by great amounts of stress.

PRESSURE

A new insurance salesman is told by company officials that he is expected to sell $100,000 worth of insurance every month. He knows that he is on probation, that his career and perhaps his whole professional future depends on reaching the monthly quota.

A professor assigns his literature class a term paper that is due in six weeks. Student X resolves to get an early start on the preparation of the paper, but somehow the days slip by, and there always seems to be a more urgent task that needs to be done first. Now the last week is here. It may already be too late to turn out a first-rate job, but Student X has to try at least to do an adequate job or fail the whole course. The pressure is on.

We have a goal that we want to reach very badly, and we know that only special effort or extra-hard work will make this feasible. Even then, success is not assured, for the pressure coming from outside, from parents, teachers, children, bosses, may be too strong.

Let us connect the various concepts illustrated by these two examples: frustration blocks our desire to reach an important goal, and only by means of extraordinary effort can we surmount the difficulties. If there are alternative courses of action open to us, conflict exists, and we must come to a decision whether or not it is worth special and perhaps painful sacrifices to pursue the road to the desired goal. This is a pressure situation. In our own times particularly, when some social situations change rapidly while others lag behind, pressure on individuals and on whole groups exists and perhaps even increases considerably.

THE HUMAN RESPONSE TO STRESS

In striving for success, man is limited by society and by his own frailty. He experiences frustration, conflict, pressure. He feels himself under stress. How does he respond to all this?

As a result of extensive research on humans and on animals, Hans Selye believes that our first reaction to stress is a kind of "generalized call to arms of the defensive forces in the organism."[8] If stress is not excessively heavy, the organism enters a second stage, the stage of resistance, whereby its system develops long-term methods of coping with difficulties. Stress then seems to diminish or even to disappear. If the system cannot solve the problem that produces stress, it enters a third stage. In our efforts to cope with stress-producing situations, we use up energy. The continued loss of energy results in aging and, ultimately, in exhaustion and death. In reality, of course, we don't necessarily die when we get into a tight spot and cannot pull ourselves out of it; we just sort of fold up; we admit defeat. To avoid such a tragic chain of events we must try to remove stress as quickly as possible or, even better, we must avoid situations that bring about excessive stress.

This is not to say that we should avoid stress entirely. Stress is part of life. All great accomplishments of man, whether in peace or war, have come about under stress. For instance, the champion sprinter achieves his record time under stress; the New World was discovered by men laboring under considerable stress; inventors, composers, and performing artists all work under stress. But Selye's advice is to avoid stress-producing situations that produce needless wear and tear. "Whatever happens during the day to threaten my equanimity or throw some doubts upon the value of my action, I just think of this little jingle:

> *Fight always for the highest attainable aim,*
> *But never put up resistance in vain.*[9]

"Never putting up resistance in vain" amounts to *withdrawal*, which is the most sensible course to take in many situations. A girl may have her heart set on becoming a concert singer. But if she is tone-deaf and her voice is of inferior quality, she would be well advised to withdraw from this path and turn her ambitions into different directions. Similarly a young man must give up his aspirations to become a commercial pilot if his eyesight does not measure up to the requirements and if he cannot get the airlines to change their requirements.

However, increased effort can, in certain circumstances, overcome an obstacle. James Coleman classifies this response as *attack*.[10] A student bent on becoming an engineer receives poor grades in mathematics. But instead of giving up, he decides to study harder or to revise his method of study, and he finally succeeds in reaching his goal.

Coleman sees another possibility of successfully responding to stress, *compromise*. A woman has a strong inclination to become a physician. Financial and other circumstances make this impossible, however, and so she settles for the nursing profession. This profession still gives her an opportunity to help the sick, which is part of what she originally wanted.

DEFENSIVE BEHAVIOR

In discussing his broken marriage, a man puts the entire blame on his wife. "She stopped being affectionate," he complains. "She neglected her appearance, she paid no attention to the housework," and so forth. Or a student blames his poor grades on the teacher's dislike for him rather than on his own lack of industry or ability. The teacher, on the other hand, complains about the inferior quality of his class, which never seems to grasp what he is trying to teach. It does not occur to him that at least part of the blame might lie with his poor ways of communicating with the students.

The persons in these situations labor under stress, but they refuse to see its real causes in order to protect their self-images. In this kind of reaction to stress, known as *defensive behavior*, reality is denied or distorted, and the response is inappropriate for the situation. People are usually not conscious of the fact that they are employing defense mechanisms, which are in themselves self-defeating because they hide the real problem and often lead to greater difficulties than those originally encountered.

Blaming someone else for your own faults does not help solve your problem, but it does remove the stress produced by the problem. This unconsciously employed technique is referred to as *projection*, which is a kind of defensive behavior. You project onto others the reasons for conditions that really have their roots in yourself.

The defense mechanism can also exert itself through *repression*. The mind completely refuses to perceive the reasons for an unpleasant situation. Sometimes people who have been involved in a serious accident cannot remember any details even though they remained conscious throughout the incident. A man who complains that other men are constantly trying to seduce him sexually fails to recognize his own hidden homosexual inclinations.

Defensive behavior in some mild form is probably part of every person's life. But in extreme cases it can take on neurotic and even psychotic characteristics. A wildly exaggerated case of projection reveals itself in a letter that was written in all seriousness to a colleague of the author. It reads in part:

> I must tell you, in the name of academic freedom, of the International Jewish Conspiracy. . . . I have suffered beyond belief at the hands of an inhuman Jewish organization. The Jews stunted my growth. They infested me with parasites. They almost emasculated me. They mutilated me. They tried to blind me. They chloroformed and lobotomized me thousands of times in Hoover's demonic attempt to give me brain cancer. . . . They destroyed my marriage. They wrecked my wife. . . .

The letter writer is obviously a deeply troubled individual. Instead of trying to find the causes of his troubles, he blames them all on the Jews. Uncritically he repeats all sorts of slogans that were the stock-in-trade of the German Nazis and that are still proclaimed by various hatemongers in this country. Many people try to shift the blame for their own shortcomings on other individuals or groups though most don't always use such extreme and confused language.

MENTAL HEALTH

It is comparatively easy to describe mental illness; it is quite a bit harder to do the opposite, namely, to delineate clearly the state of mental health. Though body and mind do not always move along parallel tracks, once again it might be useful to compare the mental with the physical situation. Some people afflicted with severe biological diseases require hospitalization or, at least, intensive medical care and medication. Others, suffering from less serious ailments, will get well by following special diets and taking other precautions. The great majority of people, however, are healthy most of the time—but occasionally even these people succumb to short intestinal or respiratory ailments or other minor diseases. Similarly, when we separate the persons suffering from neuroses or psychoses from the rest of the population, there remains the great mass of people who must be considered of basically good mental health despite their occasional inability to deal adequately with frustrating experiences, periods of uncomfortable pressure, or moments of irritating stress.

Mental health could therefore be described as a state of mind in which the individual is able to deal with stresses, frustrations, and pressures that do not go beyond a certain level. You will notice that this description emphasizes negative rather than positive aspects. In fact, we could say: mental health is the absence of mental illness.

But mental health is not merely a holding of the line against mental illness. Resorting again for a moment to the parallel with physical health, we can distinguish between the person who just takes precautions against getting sick and the one who tries to build up his body through rigorous physical exercises. Mentally, too, we can either try to maintain the status quo, that is, the situation as it is now, or we can try to grow; and while there are limits to our physical strength—no matter how much we may exercise—mental and emotional growth does not know any such boundaries.

Abraham H. Maslow speaks of *growth-motivated* persons. Their minds are characterized by superior perception of reality, increased acceptance of self, of others, and of nature. They enjoy periods of privacy and time for reflection and self-examination. They grow in their ability to act independently, in the richness of their emotional reactions. They increase their creativeness and become more democratic in their relationships with others.[11]

Signs of Good Mental Health

1. You feel comfortable about yourself; you have self-respect; you can laugh at yourself; and you can accept your own shortcomings.
2. You feel right about other people; you can give love; you can fit into a group; and you feel a sense of responsibility toward your fellow-men.
3. You are able to meet the demands of life; you set realistic goals for yourself; you welcome new experiences; and you get satisfaction out of what you are doing.

Source: Reprinted with permission of the Macmillan Company from *Social Science: An Introduction to the Study of Society*, 3rd ed. by Elgin P. Hunt. Copyright © The Macmillan Company 1966.

GETTING HELP

As problems of personal adjustment occur, most people try to solve them without outside help, or they talk them over with those closest to them, family members and friends. Often just the fact that somebody will patiently and sympathetically listen to you will give you relief and confidence. A growing literature of personal advice is also available and, judging from the sales figures, is being widely used. These books and feature

28 An Introduction to Social Science

articles cover such topics as how to be successful, how to get along with others, how to make friends.

People in certain occupations—counselors, teachers, ministers, and supervisors in business, industry, and public service—have ample opportunities to help their fellow-men with adjustment problems. More and more it is required that people in such jobs have some training in the area of personal advice or at least show awareness of the problems that come their way.

If problems of personal adjustment take on more serious proportions, expert help can be sought from clinical psychologists, psychiatrists, and psychiatric social workers. Many forms of psychotherapy are provided by these specialists. According to the usual format the therapist meets with his

Through group therapy people work out problems of personal adjustment by interacting with others.
The New York Times

client in a series of personal interviews. Together they probe into the causes of the disturbance and arrive at a way of improving the situation.

In the previous chapter the method of psychoanalysis devised by Freud was mentioned. It is still widely used though it is very time-consuming—lasting sometimes many months or even years—and therefore quite costly for the patient. Since Freud presented his ideas to the world shorter variations of his method have been developed. One kind of crash program is *crisis therapy*, which attacks immediate difficulties without lengthy delving into the distant past. A more recent innovation is *group therapy*, in which several persons experiencing similar difficulties talk out their problems under expert supervision. Various forms of such therapy that have recently found wide use are programs known as sensitivity training, encounter groups, and T-groups. Occupational and recreational therapies are also helpful under certain circumstances.

Whatever the method of therapy used, it is important that the need for outside help is recognized early and that such help is sought without fear or shame.

Main Ideas
1. Historically society's attitude toward the mentally ill has been marked by persecution and neglect.
2. The rate of emotional disturbance in our society is very high.
3. Mental illness is slowly being recognized as a form of illness that is subject to treatment and complete cure.
4. Psychoses, neuroses, and common personality problems differ in the degree of severity, but all are rooted in stress, frustration, and conflict.
5. Our culture creates many pressure situations.
6. People respond to stress situations by withdrawal, attack, or compromise.
7. By employing defense mechanisms, the individual denies or distorts the real causes of stress.
8. Mental health exists when the individual is able to control stress reasonably well. Beyond this point growth-motivated persons constantly attempt to enrich their own emotional reactions and their relations with other people.
9. Society realizes a growing need for various services to assist the population in solving personality problems.

Important Terms
Crisis therapy	Frustration
Defensive behavior	Group therapy
Electrotherapy	Hydrotherapy
Energizer	Hypnotism
Faith healing	Kleptomania

Important Terms (Cont.)

Lobotomy
Manic-depressive psychoses
Mental age
Mental retardation
Neurosis
Organic illness
Phobia
Power of suggestion
Projection

Psychosis
Psychosomatic illness
Psychotherapy
Repression
Schizophrenia
Stress
Tranquilizer
Trephining
Withdrawal

Conclusion

In this chapter we have discussed frustration as a possible contributing cause to personality disorganization. A person in possession of reasonably good mental health is well adjusted to the demands of the world around him. But what if the world itself is topsy-turvy? In later chapters we will deal with such man-made predicaments as overpopulation, the threat of nuclear war, and the pressure of poverty-stricken masses. Some observers have raised the question whether the real madmen are to be found inside or outside our mental institutions, and they are only half joking. The old saying that an ounce of prevention is worth a pound of cure is also true for emotional maladjustment. In this case the most effective prevention ought to be a changed pattern of social life to which it would be easier to adjust.

Notes

1. Marion L. Starkey, *The Devil in Massachusetts* (New York: Time, Inc., 1963).
2. James C. Coleman, *Abnormal Psychology and Modern Life* (Glenview, Ill.: Scott, Foresman, 1964), p. 25.
3. Gardner Murphy, *Historical Introduction to Modern Psychology*, rev. ed. (New York: Harcourt, Brace, 1949), pp. 131–133.
4. Coleman, *op. cit.*, p. 20.
5. Leo Srole, *Mental Health in the Metropolis* (New York: McGraw-Hill, 1962), p. 214.
6. P. Watzlawick, J. Beavin et al., *Pragmatica of Human Communication* (New York: Norton, 1967), p. 237.
7. Horace B. English and Ava C. English, *Psychological and Psychoanalytical Terms* (New York: Longmans, Green, 1958), p. 529.
8. Hans Selye, *The Stress of Life* (New York: McGraw-Hill, 1956), p. 31.
9. Selye, *ibid.*, p. 300.
10. James C. Coleman, *Personality Dynamics and Effective Behavior* (Glenview, Ill.: Scott, Foresman, 1960), pp. 194–205.
11. Abraham H. Maslow, *Toward a Psychology of Being* (New York: Van Nostrand, 1962), pp. 23–24.

Suggestions for Further Reading

Green, Hannah. *I Never Promised You a Rose Garden*. New York: Holt, Rinehart and Winston, 1964. A sensitive book about a mentally disturbed girl.

Hunt, Morton M. *Mental Hospital*. New York: Pyramid Books, 1962 (paperback). Description of a state hospital in which dramatic changes and improvements have taken place.

Kesey, Ken. *One Flew Over the Cuckoo's Nest*. New York: New American Library, 1962 (paperback). Novel set in a mental hospital.

Lindner, Robert. *The Fifty-Minute Hour*. New York: Bantam Books, 1956 (paperback). A practicing psychoanalyst reports on a number of cases involving very disturbed persons.

Maltz, Maxwell. *Psycho-Cybernetics*. New York: Essandess, 1967 (paperback). A book of advice on how to be successful and lead a satisfying life.

Menninger, Karl. *Man Against Himself*. New York: Harcourt, Brace, 1938 (paperback). The well-known psychiatrist argues that at the bottom of man's emotional troubles is self-destructiveness.

Rabkin, Leslie Y. (ed.). *Psychopathology and Literature*. San Francisco: Chandler, 1966. Selections from the works of well-known authors, old and contemporary, involving themes of personality disorganization.

Rokeach, Milton. *The Three Christs of Ypsilanti*. New York: Knopf, 1964. Story of three men who lost their identity and believed themselves to be Christ.

Rubin, Theodore I. *David and Lisa*. New York: Macmillan, 1961. Story of the relationship between two emotionally disturbed adolescents.

Can you walk through this world alone?
Do you want to walk alone?
Are you the master of your actions, your attitudes, your thoughts?
Or do they come about as you interact with the people around you?

3 WHERE IS THE FIRE?
collective behavior

CASUAL CROWDS

There is no lonelier place than a street in a strange city. Though the street is full of people, nobody pays the slightest attention to you as you stroll along, isolated even when passersby brush against your shoulders and elbows. More than ever you yearn for contact with your fellow-men. The desire to *interact*, to receive some sign that others notice your existence, can be overpowering in its urgency.

The wail of a siren rises above the hum of city traffic. A fire truck rumbles by; another one follows. Clumsily they swing out in a wide curve and disappear around a corner. As if charged with electricity, the faceless mass of individuals on the sidewalks finds itself welded together by a common drive: curiosity. People rush after the emergency vehicles. Pushing and huffing they turn to other pedestrians around them—people they have ignored up to this moment—and ask, "Where are they going? Where is the fire?"

You are not alone anymore; you have joined a *crowd*. With hundreds of others you now share a common bond: the excitement and expectation of an unusual experience. Already the intersection is blocked by a rapidly increasing swarm of men and women who don't know each other, who were not even aware of each other's existence a moment ago.

While the fire rages, while the firemen climb ladders and hack their way through flaming debris, you lose your identity and become submerged in the straining, staring mass. You are but a tiny part of a giant organism that has taken on a life of its own independent of your existence. But the life span of this giant organism is short. When the flames are finally extinguished and the fire fighters, tired and besmudged, mount their trucks for the return trip, the giant loses its breath. The mass of people disperses. Once again you are a lonely unnoticed pedestrian on a crowded sidewalk.

Apparently we welcome such events when we feel the breath and hear the voices of other people close by and know that all are moved by the same, though short-lived, stimulus. In *urban* areas, especially, where most contemporary Americans live, many similar occasions to join a crowd present themselves.

People who are closely packed into a narrow space without prearrangement form a *casual crowd.* Obviously something brings them together though the bond they share is neither a strong nor a lasting one: for example, the passing interest in an accident or the necessity of waiting together indoors or outdoors. The interaction, a sharing of feelings in words or gestures or common action of some kind, may be strong or minimal. Hardly any interaction is likely to occur as pedestrians wait at an intersection for the traffic light to change or as strangers sit for hours in a hotel lobby without even looking at each other.

On the other hand, sharing of common concerns is more likely where waiting in line is a regular occurrence. In Russia housewives, workers, or students spend hours waiting in line for groceries, newspapers, and transportation. They chat about trivial matters to while away the time. Commuters who meet morning after morning on the same train can get to know each other quite well. Yet, for the most part, the casual crowd exists only for a limited time and never again assembles with quite the same membership.

Crowds follow rules of behavior that are different from those that their individual members follow when they are alone. This is *collective behavior.* Social scientists have discovered that a person changes his reactions, his expressions, and even his values when he joins the shapeless throng.

PANIC

Let's examine the behavior of a large number of people who are caught in a *panic.* One moment gaiety and a relaxed festive spirit reign in a packed theater, stadium, or night club. Then a shout, "Fire," rings out, or sounds reminding one of shots or of an explosion assault the eardrums. All at once the ability to think rationally disappears. Accustomed habits of chivalry, of concern for the weak are forgotten: senseless pushing blocks the available exits; children are trampled under foot. Whatever avenues of rescue exist are made useless by the very people who want to be rescued. As a result of panic, a disastrous fire in 1942 in the Cocoanut Grove, a Boston night club, claimed the lives of 493 guests. Such tragedies, however, do not occur very often, and a great deal is now known about their prevention. "Excited and irrational behavior can usually be prevented or quickly brought to a stop if effective leadership and realistic information is provided."[1]

Not all societies react to the news of a panic situation with horror like that which accompanied the news of the Cocoanut Grove fire. In India Hindus gather by the hundreds of thousands at religious outdoor festivals along the banks of the Ganges River or at other holy places. From time to time the religious fervor of the masses has exploded in stampedes that cost scores of lives. Yet the survivors of these stampedes were not greatly upset, because Hindus believe in reincarnation. According to their beliefs, when the present body is trampled into the dust, the soul immediately enters another body. And to die on hallowed ground is not at all an abhorrent fate for the pious believer.

MOBS

Sitting in the isolation of his living room, the reader or television viewer is shocked by the behavior of crowds. They seem to violate flagrantly his own loudly professed value system. He may read about how people gathered to stare at the roof of a building where a desperate would-be suicide was getting ready to jump. Even while relatives, clergymen, and police were trying to dissuade him from jumping, the impatient crowd below chanted, "Jump! Jump!" This was something one did not see every day—and the crowd was not to be deprived of its thrill.

Likewise some spectators at boxing matches and car races only seem to be waiting for the sight of bloodied or injured competitors. We are reminded of the sport of the bullring where people crowd together to see blood flow, the blood of the bull, but sometimes even that of the matador or of both. Different only in degree was the taste of the ancient Romans whose sense of excitement was tickled by gladiators tearing each other to pieces or fighting hunger-crazed wild animals. When not content merely to watch violence, a crowd may want to get into the act itself. It then becomes an *acting crowd,* or a *mob.* Crowds are unpredictable: they may be peaceful at one moment and "get out of hand" at the next. Accounts of past and present mob violence are numerous. Many a friendly party on Saturday night has ended in a drunken brawl. Yet mobs hardly ever become violent unless they are conditioned by long-existing social situations or unless they are successfully prodded into violence by mob leaders. Something must compel a crowd to action. An irritant that is strong and immediate can, without delay, cause a crowd to take actions that run counter to generally accepted rules of decent behavior.

In the Middle Ages European peasants, driven by hunger and extreme oppression, stormed the castles of their landlords and pillaged and murdered. During the French Revolution the frustrated masses of Paris broke into the Bastille, a grim prison fortress that had become the symbol of a brutal regime. They slaughtered the guards and carried their severed heads triumphantly through the streets.

Oddly some of the worst mob atrocities have been committed in the name of religion, which proclaims, almost universally, good will toward men. The medieval Crusaders set out to honor the places where the Savior once walked, but along the arduous route to the Holy Land they mercilessly killed armed and unarmed "infidels." In the year 1099 when they conquered Jerusalem, they rode, as one participant triumphantly reported, in the blood of the slain men, women, and children up "to the knees of their horses."[2] More recently Hindus and Moslems, though living as neighbors on the Indian subcontinent, have repeatedly clashed in disastrous civil strife.

LYNCHING

In America mob violence sometimes took the form of *lynching*; that is, when a mob sets out to punish a person whom it, rightly or wrongly, accuses of some unwarranted act. A lynching mob does not wait for judge or jury but takes the law into its own hands. The alleged violator is swiftly executed, often with sickening brutality.

This form of mob violence was used especially in the early American pioneer country, where courts and police forces were not yet functioning effectively. Hard-boiled ranchers strung up horse thieves and cattle rustlers, convinced that only in this way could they protect their exposed settlements.

Until quite recent times lynching was practically synonymous with mob action against blacks in the South. With nauseating frequency crowds of frenzied whites hunted down blacks to flog and otherwise torture them mercilessly. Hanging, shooting, or burning alive usually climaxed those widely approved means of "keeping the nigger in his place." These gruesome actions were the direct outgrowth of the long and loudly preached doctrine of white supremacy, a supremacy often maintained by forcing "inferiors" to remain docile.

After the Civil War the specter of lynching became a substitute for the control that white masters had formerly exercised over black slaves. The height of this trend was reached around the turn of the century. The Tuskegee Institute in Alabama records 161 lynchings of blacks in the year 1892.[3] In 1900 106 cases of lynching were reported. These were only the incidents that came to public attention, however. The actual number of violent mob actions was undoubtedly much higher.[4]

Reports about lynchings do not make very pleasant reading. In 1939 the bank and several stores in the small town of Darien, Georgia, were burglarized. The townspeople were edgy. Then one night two black men were observed walking near the bank. A night watchman challenged them, and shots were exchanged. The blacks ran toward the river and disappeared into the marshland. Even though it was never established that the two fugitives had anything to do with the burglaries, a general alarm brought out a posse of white men. They cornered one black, who then shot and killed a police officer and fled. Next day the posse continued its search with the help of National Guardsmen and bloodhounds. One of the two fugitives was found. He surrendered, protesting all the while that he was not the one who had fired the fatal shot. As he was led to jail, several onlookers urged the crowd to kill him immediately. Some hit him with pistol butts.

He was then placed in a second-floor jail cell. People excitedly surged around the jail and entered its corridors through several unguarded entrances. Women screamed and demanded the death of the prisoner. Suddenly four shots rang out—and a short while later the corpse of the black fugitive was brought out. There were shouts that it should be burned on the spot, but it was eventually taken away in a truck. Exhausted, having relieved its tension, the mob slowly dispersed. The men and women who had been members of it became once again individuals behaving according to ordinary norms and restraints.[5]

A changing social climate in the American South and the pressure of national and world opinion have sharply reduced the number of lynchings. In 1951 one case was reported; several years later there were none. Lynching is an event that is seldom planned in advance. In the South it was swift mob reaction to an occurrence or even to the rumor of an occurrence in which the black man had violated the code by which he was supposed to behave. The black man faced the wrath of white mobs for raising his hand against them, for talking back, for being too prosperous, for insisting on his rights. Brutal acts against him were often excused with the assertion that they were necessary to "protect white womanhood." Suspicion of rape, even innocent bantering with a white girl, could bring swift and bloody retribution to a black man.

White mobs were largely comprised of the poorer and less educated members of the community. These were people whose lives were devoid of healthy, culturally approved outlets for their energy. The periodic atrocities of a lynching mob provided some sort of welcome break in the monotonous daily routine. There was satisfaction in venting one's frustration on somebody else, someone even poorer and lower on the social ladder.

In a mob the individual becomes anonymous, faceless. He is free from individual restraints and control. The mass around him shares in the responsibility for his words and acts. As a fragment of a faceless mob, he can say and do things that he would never dare to say or do when facing society on his own, on a clearly recognizable basis—as John Smith or Jim Brown, for instance.

RIOTS

Mob behavior is not restricted to any one race. Blacks were the traditional victims, but in the 1960s, when the poorer sections of our large cities erupted in dangerous riots, they themselves became the chief participants in mob violence. The street scenes in the Watts district of Los Angeles in 1965 and in Detroit in 1966, to name only two examples, brought about disastrous losses in human lives and massive destruction of property by arson and looting. These riots seemed to be spontaneous outbreaks, but their real causes were the long-standing, deep-seated resentments against a lengthy history of racial discrimination. The black ghettos, left to decay in filth and poverty, were seething with bitterness at the sight of unprecedented national prosperity in which they were not sharing. Inhabitants of the inner city tenements felt that the "Establishment"—that is, the white political and economic leadership—was not interested in remedying their situation. The sight of nearby suburbs where life was pleasant and comfortable infuriated the blacks, who felt trapped in their overcrowded littered streets filled with despair and hopelessness.

It is of little use to argue that riots only hurt the cause of the underprivileged and that the chief victims of the destruction are not the representatives of the Establishment but other poor blacks. Mobs don't reason; they act in a purely emotional manner. If they were capable of logical thinking, they would no longer be mobs. Riots are mob explosions, not carefully worked out campaigns. As in the proverbial powder keg, the explosive material has been long in accumulating. Accidentally a match is lighted, the powder is ignited, and the powder keg is blown to high heaven.

The match that ignites the explosive material is often a quite trivial incident. It may have nothing to do with the main cause of the people's tension. The disastrous Detroit riot was triggered when police mounted a routine raid on an after-hour speak-easy in an abandoned second-floor office. In 1966 in San Francisco a riot followed the shooting of a young suspected car thief by a police officer. The fact that the young man was black may or may not have influenced the policeman's action. Similar events erupted in Newark in 1967 after the police had beaten a black taxi driver.

After the summer of 1967, which was marred by a number of ugly riots, the public demanded to know why these incidents had happened and what could be done to prevent them. President Johnson appointed the National Advisory Commission on Civil Disorder, headed by Otto Kerner,

Governor of Illinois. In its thorough, deep-searching report, the Kerner Commission, as it was generally called, came to the conclusion that no riot that had erupted was triggered by one single incident, though it may have looked that way to the outsider, especially to the news reporter or the television cameraman. But in reality the riots marked the bursting of long festering boils on the social body of the slum communities. Disorder "was generated out of an increasingly disturbed social atmosphere, in which typically a series of tension-heightening incidents over a period of weeks or months became linked in the minds of many in the Negro community with a reservoir of underlying grievances."[6]

One feature stands out among all these tumultuous events: the overt hostility against the police. For the black crowds the uniformed men with their guns and nightsticks are the first and most visible targets of their frustration, their hatred. The cop represents the enemy, the whole thick, impenetrable obstacle that stands in the way of full recognition, full equality. Policemen do frequently show prejudice against those who occupy the lowest position in our social system. Charged with maintaining "law and order," they fail to understand why citizens might question the justice of laws and the fairness of order.

Reform on the part of law enforcement agencies and greater understanding on both sides of the conflict will be required to change the image of the man with the badge. No society can function with any degree of stability unless there is cooperation between the public and those officials whose job it is to enforce the law and keep the peace.

Not all riots occur in city streets. Several times a year our news media report unrest in the nation's prisons. The penitentiary forms a kind of artificial society. In it the lack of privacy is often aggravated by extremely crowded conditions, and days pass slowly under a pall of stark boredom. Normal outlets of physical and mental energy are blocked. These conditions, to which may be added sexual frustration and the general oppressiveness of prison regime, form a highly incendiary fuel—a situation for potential riot—that, once ignited, can burn itself out in a ruinous blaze.

It is comparatively easy to understand how convicts and the desperately poor, people who live under adverse social conditions, may be driven to violence. Yet in the 1960s many college and university campuses in the United States and in other countries were the scenes of arson, large-scale fighting, and general havoc. (See Figure 2.) Young people took time out from their studies in laboratories, libraries, and seminars to express their deep concern over the many wrongs they had been observing inside and outside their schools. University of California students made headlines in 1964 by staging sit-ins at the administration building of the giant Berkeley campus. After much skirmishing 400 policemen broke up the demonstrators by carrying the limp bodies of many protesters to waiting patrol cars. Eight hundred fourteen students were arrested. At one point a crowd of young men and women surrounded a police car carrying an arrested companion and kept it immobilized for more than a day.

collective behavior **39**

"Allen, hurry, our son is on the 11 o'clock news."
Figure 2

Copyright 1968 Saturday Review, Inc. Reprinted with permission of Herbert Goldberg and *Saturday Review*.

In 1968, as if by prearranged signal, a wave of student riots swept Paris, Berlin, Mexico City, New York, and other places. Students ransacked buildings, built barricades in the streets, and fought pitched battles with the police. Neither side gained any laurels for restraint. Much has been said and written about this rash of violent outbreaks. Were the students just "out for a lark," as some observers reprovingly maintained? Youth has always claimed the privilege of being noisier and more radical in its demands than the older generation. Other analysts have hinted darkly at "outside agitators," mysterious political undercover figures who are frequently blamed when trouble arises. Certainly some of these elements were present: youthful exuberance, pranks that got out of hand, political propaganda. Communist, anarchist, and other extremist overtones could be heard unmistakably in the loud clamor. But this does not tell the whole story. For some time students have had serious grievances against the whole system of higher education. They feel ill-at-ease in our mammoth universities, where the individual is reduced to a number in the memory banks of the giant computers.

Undergraduates resent the factory-like system that churns out degrees on the assembly line but does not quench their thirst for purposeful and meaningful experience. They are disappointed by professors who absent themselves from the campus and consider the business of teaching a tedious sideline to more important endeavors, and they quarrel with academic bureaucracies that are unresponsive to their needs. They wish to have a greater voice in what and how they are taught and who teaches it.

In Europe, even more so than in America, universities stick to outdated notions. Their organization and teaching methods, their requirements and testing procedures have not changed much for several centuries. The students of these institutions want their schools to catch up with the twentieth century—no wonder they hardly need any urging to express themselves in tumultuous gestures.

Beyond the preserves of higher education students are voicing their general disgust with an older generation unable to keep society on a course of peace and satisfactory human relations. In their exuberance they are asking: Why isn't this supposedly civilized society doing something drastic to eliminate racial injustice? Why do we still have hunger and malnutrition in the midst of abundance and luxury? Why can't the adults who are in positions of leadership prevent destructive wars, and why do we continue to foul our own earth with deadly pollution?

We hear constantly about street riots and mass cruelty generated by racial and religious antagonism. Add to this the horrors of war, which have grown ever more shocking as history has "progressed," and you wonder just what sort of creature man really is. Is man by nature violent? Is there something in our biological make-up that drives us to destroy our own kind? These questions have baffled philosophers, theologians, and, of course, social scientists for some time. Observation indicates that animals attack members of their own species only when prompted by hunger, sex urge, or the need to defend their territory. Man rarely eats his fellow-men, yet he seems to delight in hurting and killing them.

But there seems to be a glimmer of hope for the human animal. While some anthropologists and zoologists argue that man is by nature violent, others claim that violence has nothing to do with human nature. It is, rather, a product of social conditions. Since it is learned, it can also be unlearned. Peaceful cultures do exist, though we have to go far afield to find them.[7] But American society is not the place to look for a nonviolent way of life, at least not yet. On the contrary, we seem to have a marked preference for the strong-arm solution to our problems; recall, for example, the birth of our nation through revolutionary action or the lusty shoot-outs of pioneer days. The cowboy who is quick on the draw remains the hero of untold motion pictures and television series.[8]

Under what circumstances does man, massed in excitable crowds, tend to become violent? Margaret Mead writes: "Whenever a group that has been required to be docile, segregated, submissive, undemanding and unparticipating, glimpses the possibility of wider participation in the society, we may expect phenomena like these."[9] Thus, it is not the slave who sees no hope, nor the student who is completely cowed by an oppressive educational system who will riot, but the black who begins to see dim outlines of a better life and the student who observes promising cracks in an outdated system: they are ready to speed up the process of change with swinging fists and a few well-aimed Molotov cocktails.

RUMOR

A black youth rapes a white woman.
    A policeman shoots a Puerto Rican.
    Hindus throw a dead pig into the courtyard of a Moslem mosque.
    A bomb planted by an Arab saboteur explodes in a crowded Tel Aviv supermarket. Several Israelis are killed; many more are wounded.
    An epidemic breaks out among the members of a nonliterate tribe. The word passes that it is caused by the magic spells of an old woman who is supposedly well versed in witchcraft.

Such stories spread quickly. Under certain social conditions they are dynamite. The dreadful mechanisms of lynchings and riots have been set in motion many times by such stories. Once the temperature of the mass mind is on the rise, nobody bothers to check on the validity of the rumor. True or false, the rumor has done its job.

    It is in times of extreme tension that rumors circulate easily. Highly prejudiced persons and people with little understanding and deep anxieties usually carry rumors. But anybody can, under the right circumstances, succumb to the whispered sensational word passed excitedly from mouth to mouth. To be the bearer of important news makes the messenger himself important. In the past violence against Jews repeatedly followed the rumor that they had used the blood of Christian children in their religious rites. There was never any truth in such stories, but the long-harbored hostile feeling against Jews made such rumors easily accepted. Many research projects have borne out the thesis that those who spread and those who accept rumors as the truth color the stories according to their long-standing prejudices. Rumors can electrify a crowd whether they are true, or invented, or gross exaggerations of the truth.[10]

SOCIAL MOVEMENTS

When students were battling police in the Latin Quarter of Paris, tourists watched from the balconies of nearby hotels. What they saw were men in blue uniforms charging in wedge formation and students pelting them with broken bottles and chunks of pavement. On the surface it merely looked like another mob scene, but there was more to it than that. The students

42 An Introduction to Social Science

knew what they wanted and had known for some time though their desires were not always clearly articulated. They were following some kind of program, and they had some form of organization. They also had leaders, among them a number of colorful persons, such as Danny "the Red" Cohn-Bendit in Paris, and Rudi Dutschke in Berlin. In other words, the recent student unrest in many American and European cities had many of the characteristics of a *social movement*.

Social movements may be accompanied by mob action, such as that which occurred in Paris in the spring of 1968, or they may be completely free from any mob behavior. They are long lasting and have a clear purpose "aimed at promoting or resisting change in society at large."[11] There are social movements of every conceivable size and importance. Some aim at a complete overhaul of society; others have very modest goals, such as the Anti-Digit Dialing League, which protests the replacement of words (OXford) with digits (69 . . .) in telephone numbers. This particular society feels that words have a warmer and more personalized sound than figures. Nudist movements proclaim that many grave ills of our society would disappear if only we stopped wearing clothes. Vegetarians see the eating of dead animals as the root of all evil.

Broad-based religious and *ideological* movements urge mankind as a whole to take up the banner of radical change. The Quakers and similar groups, for instance, denounce war and any form of violence; socialists want to take business and industry out of the hands of private individuals so that no one person can exploit any other. Other movements restrict their appeal to specific groups, such as the poor, the retired, the highly educated, or lovers of wilderness camping.

Movements need followers, and they also want to see their goals translated into reality. The techniques used to achieve these ends depend on circumstances. Secrecy was the key word of the revolutionary movement in Czarist Russia. That movement depended largely on personal persuasion and the clandestine distribution of pamphlets. In cases where fear of suppression is not a factor, social movements spread their message by means of public meetings, posters, buttons, and through the news media.

Many participants in social movements are satisfied by simply pointing out the benefits to be had in achieving their goals. *Extremists*, on the other hand, prefer tearing down to building up. Attack is their number-one weapon. The extremists' claim that everything vital is at stake, that the world is surely "going to the dogs" unless their recipe for salvation is accepted, is supposed to shock people into joining the ranks. In their opinion the most complex problems facing our society can be solved by applying a simple formula, such as, "Get rid of the Communists in our midst" or, "Liquidate the Wall Street bankers and their lackeys." The spokesmen of the extremist movements, of course, determine who is a Communist or a banker's lackey. Extremists, whether of the right or the left, tend to divide people into either good guys or bad guys with nobody in between. All troubles are blamed on a devil, a *scapegoat*. (See Chapter 5.) Foreigners, Jews, the Pope, United States consulates, the young generation, and the "over-thirty" generation have variously served as scapegoats and targets of abuse for extremists. Eric Hoffer has written:

> Mass movements can rise and spread without belief in a God, but never without belief in a devil. Usually the strength of a mass movement is proportionate to the vividness and tangibility of its devil. . . . People haunted by the purposelessness of their lives try to find a new content not only by dedicating themselves to a holy cause, but also by nursing a fanatical grievance. A mass movement offers unlimited opportunities for both.[12]

LEADERSHIP

Many a harmless crowd has turned into a howling mob bent on blood and terror because a leader suddenly appears who channels the accumulated frustration into a specific direction. Such a leader may mount a soapbox on a street corner or appear shouting and gesturing from an open window. He may scream, "Let's kill that Negro rapist!" or, "Let's free our tortured brethren from the Bastille!" In any case he knows how to establish rapport, how to throw the master switch that sends electric current flowing through the yet docile crowd.

Such a leader may never be known to posterity. He may never again perform the same function, though there are leaders who can repeat such performances because they have sharpened to perfection their talents for whipping up emotions. Leaders like this can forge large numbers of people into rock-hard unity. Radical movements are often manipulated by authoritarian captains who, in the opinion of their dedicated disciples, can do no wrong.

Leaders who can handle the throng as a gifted conductor leads an orchestra, who can elicit obedience and enthusiasm at will, are said to possess *charisma*. Charismatic leaders have inspired profound spiritual renewal, as did Paul of Tarsus or Mahatma Gandhi. Others have fostered hate and played on man's most destructive inner urges. Charisma can work in saint or *demagogue*. Charisma was possessed by Pope Urban II who in 1095 preached to the masses with such religious fervor that they left house and hearth and followed him into the First Crusade shouting, "God wills it." It was a similar talent that enabled Adolf Hitler to set the world ablaze. Civilized Germans completely forgot all moral restraints and committed atrocities of such shocking enormity that words can hardly describe them. Hitler mastered the art of swaying the masses to the point where they gave up all pretense of making up their own minds. He convinced them that in all situations their "Fuehrer" knew best. The rallies and marches of the Nazi movement were in fact carefully staged theatrical performances. Banners and buntings displaying the swastika, the Nazi symbol, framed streets and meeting halls. The ground trembled under the rhythmic stomp of goose-stepping jackboots. Military bands, drums, and fifes intoxicated the listeners with their martial airs. Speaker after speaker shouted belligerent slogans to which the well-rehearsed squads of uniformed storm troopers responded with shouts of *Sieg Heil* (hail to victory).

Finally when the audience had been sufficiently hypnotized, a flare of bugles and a crescendo of drums announced the entry of the Fuehrer himself. The listeners were long past the point where they could critically judge what he had to say. They hung on his words as if every utterance were some kind of divine revelation. In fact, after the Nazi regime came into power, Hitler came to be viewed as God: children were practically taught to worship the demagogue with the little mustache. Still smarting under the humiliating defeat of World War I, Germans under Hitler's leadership felt their breasts swell with an artificially induced vigor, with a feeling of invincibility.

Hitler's techniques are similar to those of successful revival preachers, shocking as this comparison may seem to devout Christians. However worthy the cause may be, the means by which a Billy Graham plays on the emotions of masses of people are not unlike those once employed by a Mussolini or a Hitler. At a Billy Graham rally the stage is also carefully set. The audience is conditioned to give the right response. The music, the prayers, the introductory speeches: all are precisely and professionally geared to enhance the effect of the main message. Then, after his entrance has been prefaced by all of these events, Dr. Graham comes to the pulpit and performs so masterfully that even many who came as doubters go away converted.

EXPRESSIVE CROWDS

The response of a Billy Graham audience is relatively subdued in comparison to other revivals in which the crowd acts out its intense feelings much more dramatically. Shrill shouts of "Amen!" "Hallelujah!" and "Bless the Lord!" underscore the fervent pleas from the pulpit. The faithful cry and gesture in wildly agitated personal prayer. Through progressive *interstimulation* the congregation becomes more overwrought as the revival proceeds.

Such is the behavior pattern of an *expressive crowd.* People like this assembled in one place are certainly not passive, but they are not uncontrolled either. Rather they react in a predictable and acceptable way. Historically, religion has often furnished the spark that ignites expressive crowds. The whirling Dervishes, a Moslem sect, translate their fervor into rhythmic body movements. They dance faster and faster until their agitation reaches such a feverish pitch that their mouths foam and they break down in utter exhaustion. The Shakers, a now extinct American cult, were known to have behaved in a somewhat similar manner. Gatherings of various cults have at times ended in severe self-mutilation. We still hear occasionally of the snake handlers in whose frenzied rites lives have been lost.

Some forms of religious expression would be severely condemned in a different cultural context. In ancient Rome during the Bacchanalia, an annual festival dedicated to Bacchus, the god of wine, rich and poor lost all usual restraint and indulged themselves in orgies of drunkenness and promiscuous sex. In a more mellowed form similar customs still persist during the days before Lent (for example, the Mardi Gras of New Orleans) and also during the famous Oktoberfest in Bavaria, a kind of harvest festival probably dating back to pagan times.

In the United States crowds express themselves in a predictable way whenever they attend a dance. You and your partner go through a well-defined ritual of movements that vary according to the current fashion and the age of the dancers. You applaud the band; you promenade or patronize the refreshment stand during intermission. And it is the exception rather than the rule that dances, under the impact of an enervating rock beat, deteriorate into mob behavior. Participants may smash furniture and get into scuffles on such occasions. A rock festival held in Newport, Rhode Island, in June 1969 ended in a storm of rioting.

Exaggerated hero worship can also cause quite a bit of havoc. During recent years mass hysteria reached its most feverish pitch as fans of the Beatles, a famous quartet of shaggy-haired rock musicians, expressed their adoration of this group. When these idols of countless teen-agers appeared on stage, the audience invariably responded with uproarious shouting, foot stamping, and handclapping. The fact that the performers could not be heard at all above the general din did not cool the ardor of the fans, especially the female fans. One girl told an interviewer: "I can't describe the feeling very well, except to say that the beat and the personalities moved me so that I had to scream my appreciation."[13]

AUDIENCES

Which is your favorite among the currently popular folk-rock groups? What effect does seeing them perform have on you?

Beatle fans regularly turned into an expressive crowd, in fact, an extremely expressive crowd. But when people had paid for their admission tickets, they were expected to be just another *audience*. Audiences assemble not to do something but to watch others do things. An audience is by definition passive rather than active. Some observers of the American scene complain that our society as a whole plays the role of an audience far too much. We are spectators when we should be actors. We watch when we should be creative. The behavior of audiences follows well-established though unwritten rules. For example, concert or theater audiences clap their hands to indicate appreciation. When displeased with the performance they may boo instead or just get up and leave. Even in the concert hall different types of programs exact different audience responses. Audiences feel perfectly free to stomp and sway to an acid-rock band or to sing or hum along to the tunes of a folksinger, but they would hardly do so during a recital of classical music.

On the whole, spectators at a ball game show even less restraint than those at a musical or theatrical performance. In the bleachers you are not out of place when you jump to your feet and shout loudly in language that you would be ashamed to use elsewhere. The fact that everybody around you does the same thing seems to make it acceptable. On occasion stadium audiences have been known to turn into mobs too. That is why in a large South American city the new soccer stadium is equipped with underground passages: the players and umpires can escape in a hurry through these passages should the mood of the spectators turn ugly.

Certain situations of crowd behavior that may look dangerous to the outsider are often kept well under control. Such safely *institutionalized* events as pep rallies at school and the annual conventions of Shriners or the American Legion fall into this category.

PUBLICS

A crowd then consists of many people physically assembled in one place. These people have a common interest, at least for a short time, and some form of interaction is evident. When people are no longer present in one place but are still interacting with one another and sharing common interests, then you have what is called a *public*. The faithful admirers of the television program *Bonanza* form a public. So do the readers of Art Buchwald's newspaper column and the devotees of the comic strip "Peanuts." Their common interest is obvious, and they may even interact through letter writing, wearing buttons, forming fan clubs, and so forth, but they are not likely to ever be assembled all together in one place.

The modern media of mass communications have made a great impact on publics in our society. Whereas the effect of the printed word in books, magazines, and newspapers is limited to those who can and want to read, the impact of modern electronics knows no bounds. Sound motion pictures, radio, and television are creating publics of unheard-of sizes reaching over distant parts of the world. Western cowboys ride on movie screens in Afghanistan, and rock music blares from transistor radios carried on camels in the Sahara desert.

According to Marshall McLuhan these media are not just another way of communicating a message; they themselves determine what is being communicated. "The medium is the message," so he says, and this pronouncement has already become a household expression.[14] McLuhan sees in television, for example, much more than a means of entertainment and information. He suggests that without its vivid blow-by-blow coverage there would have been no civil rights legislation and the war in Vietnam would never have aroused the American public as strongly as it has.

Woodstock 1969.
Ken Regan/Camera 5

The impact of the mass media can also work in reverse. For example, government officials become quite alarmed when criticism of their actions is given wide publicity over the airwaves. In November 1969 Vice-President Spiro Agnew accused the television networks of giving the American people a highly selected and often biased presentation of the news. This accusation aroused considerable alarm among newscasters and news commentators, who saw in it a thinly veiled threat of censorship.

The mass media leave their imprint not only on grave historical developments and government officials but also cater to our lighter whims and fancies. *Fads* of various kinds have always existed, but they were usually restricted to small areas, and it took a long time for them to spread. Now they pop up overnight, whether it is the hula hoop, love beads, psychedelic posters, or male jewelry. But just as quickly as they appear, fads sink back into oblivion—to the relief of many.

If anybody is in need of a sizable public, it is the politician. Contenders for public office recognize the tremendous value of the mass media. A candidate's ability to project a good "image" on the picture tube may have a greater effect on the voters than what he actually stands for. A fairly new corps of professionals—called public opinion analysts—has risen to measure the politician's public image. Through an elaborate system of polls and the expert use of statistics and computer techniques the response of the public to a given issue or to a particular person is recorded. How accurate the polls are is still a matter of much controversy.

PROPAGANDA

Propaganda is a technique or rather a whole arsenal of weapons used to influence the public. More often than not, propaganda tries to create a public where none exists yet. In the ears of many people the word has a nasty ring. "Is it the truth," they will ask, "or is it just propaganda?" People think that propaganda is synonymous with lying. Often it is, but actually we can hardly imagine a complex culture without it. The word itself is derived from the name of a bureau at the papal court in Rome, Congregatio de Propaganda Fide (Department for the Propagation of the Faith). In other words, this is the office of religious propaganda, which is the business of the missionary.

We deplore propaganda efforts in the service of destructive or selfish causes, but few citizens would object to the intensive propaganda campaigns designed to improve our health or to get us to the polls on election day. The list of propaganda devices is endless. Old-fashioned personal persuasion remains as effective as ever. Electronic propaganda—whether by radio, television, films, or records—can at times be subtle, or just barely recognizable, while at others it is poured on heavily. Then there are the testimonials of well-known personalities. For example, a famous film star signs an open letter to the President; the fan is supposed to conclude from this that the cause is righteous. Public relations experts know how to effectively employ fund-raising dinners, leaflets, parades, posters, and many other propaganda devices.

In a free society you may choose to accept propaganda or to ignore it in the same way that water runs off an oily surface—that is, if you have strong enough resistance. The professional propagandist is challenged to employ more intensive devices of persuasion only when met with coolness or resistance. When propaganda is forced upon a defenseless subject, as in the case of a war prisoner or the citizen of a dictatorial regime, we speak of "brainwashing." It is hard, but not impossible, to resist the onslaught of propaganda when it becomes a monopoly, when it is combined with threats and torture, and when it replaces information and education.

Main Ideas
1. People assembled in a sizable number behave differently from the way they do as isolated individuals. This is known as collective behavior.
2. Urban living provides frequent occasions for the formation of casual crowds, which are united by a short-lived common concern.
3. Panic situations can become disastrous if not controlled in time.
4. Acting crowds or mobs behave in a way that society generally disapproves of. Yet mob action arises from long-standing social conditioning. It provides excitement and releases frustration, as in the case of lynchings and riots.
5. Rumors may trigger mob action.
6. Social movements are long-lasting and have a clear purpose of promoting change.
7. The leader establishes rapport with a crowd or a movement by using effective techniques of mass influence.
8. The behavior of expressive crowds and audiences is, for the most part, institutionalized and socially approved.
9. Publics have a common interest that is particularly aroused and maintained by the mass media. The various techniques of persuasion used are often labeled propaganda.

Important Terms
Acting crowd
Audience
Casual crowd
Charisma
Collective behavior
Demagogue
Expressive crowd
Extremist
Fad
Fuehrer
Ideological movement

Interstimulation
Institutionalized
Lynching
Mob
Panic
Propaganda
Public
Scapegoat
Social movement
Urban

Conclusion

Crowds, audiences, publics: rare indeed is the individual who is not part of any of these at some point. Your behavior is partly immersed in collective behavior. Lack of education, maturity, and sound emotional outlets makes us succumb more easily to the lures of collective behavior. On the other hand, the ability to reason, to react critically to potent stimulation makes it possible for us to choose those crowds, movements, and publics with which we wish to identify ourselves.

Notes

1. Duane Schultz, *Panic Behavior* (New York: Random House, 1964), p. 119.
2. H. J. Carroll, *et al.*, eds., *The Development of Civilization: A Documentary and Interpretive Record* (Chicago: Scott, Foresman & Co., 1961), I, 298.
3. *Negro Almanac* (New York: Bellwether, 1967).
4. *The Negro Yearbook* (New York: William H. Wise, 1952), p. 278.
5. Joseph Gittler, *Social Dynamics* (New York: McGraw-Hill, 1952), pp. 88–91.
6. *Report of the National Advisory Commission on Civil Disorders* (New York: Dutton, 1968), p. 6.
7. M. F. Ashley-Montagu (ed.), *Man and Aggression* (New York: Oxford University Press, 1968).
8. Ralph Conant, "Rioting, Insurrection and Civil Disobedience," *American Scholar* (Summer 1968), pp. 420–433.
9. Margaret Mead, "The Wider Significance of the Columbia Upheaval," *Columbia Forum* (October 1968).
10. G. W. Allport and L. Postman, *The Psychology of Rumor* (New York: Henry Holt, 1947).
11. Hans Toch, *The Social Psychology of Social Movements* (Indianapolis, Ind.: Bobbs-Merrill, 1965), p. 5.
12. Eric Hoffer, *The True Believer* (New York: Harper & Row, 1951), pp. 86, 92.
13. J. W. Taylor, "Beatlemania—the Adulation and Exuberance of Some Adolescents," in Marcello Truzzi (ed.), *Sociology and Everyday Life* (Englewood Cliffs, N.J.: Prentice-Hall, 1968), p. 166.
14. Marshall McLuhan, *Understanding Media* (New York: McGraw-Hill, 1964).

Suggestions for Further Reading

"Campus Rebels: Who, Why, What," *Newsweek*, September 30, 1968, pp. 63–68.

Clark, Van Tilbury. *The Oxbow Incident*. New York: American Library, 1940 (paperback). Novel involving mob justice in the Old West.

Heiden, Konrad. *Der Fuehrer: Hitler's Rise to Power.* Boston: Houghton, 1944. A critical biography.

Hoffer, Eric. *The True Believer.* New York: Harper & Row, 1951 (paperback). Analysis of mass movements and their fanatic adherents.

Huxley, Aldous L. *Brave New World Revisited.* New York: Harper, 1958. A sequel to Huxley's novel *Brave New World;* deals with propaganda and brainwashing.

Lewis, Sinclair. *Elmer Gantry.* New York: Harcourt, Brace & World, 1927. Novel about a revival preacher and his way of dealing with the expressive crowd of believers.

"Living Room War," *U.S. News & World Report,* March 4, 1968, pp. 28–29. Effects of the television coverage of the Vietnam war.

"Marshall McLuhan," *Newsweek,* March 6, 1967, pp. 53 ff.

Maschmann, Melita. *Account Rendered.* New York: Abelard-Schuman, 1965. Autobiography of a young woman who was a Nazi youth leader during World War II.

McGinniss, Joe. *The Selling of the President 1968.* New York: Trident, 1969. Deals with the role of television in a political campaign.

Schulberg, Budd. *From the Ashes: Voices of Watts.* New York: New American Library, 1967. Report about developments following the riots in the Watts district of Los Angeles.

Shirer, William L. *The Rise and Fall of the Third Reich.* Greenwich, Connecticut: Fawcett, 1959 (paperback).

Starkey, M. L. *The Devil in Massachusetts.* Garden City, New York: Doubleday, 1961. Mass hysteria and rumors at the time of the witch hunts in Massachusetts.

"The Universities," *The Public Interest,* Special Issue, No. 13 (Fall 1968).

Walker, Daniel. *Rights in Conflict.* New York: Dutton, 1968. Report by the president of the Chicago Crime Commission on the disorders and the police violence that occurred during the Democratic National Convention in Chicago in the summer of 1968.

"When Student Power Gets Out Of Hand," *U.S. News & World Report,* April 1, 1968, pp. 70–72. Reaction to student demonstrations at San Francisco State College.

"Why People Riot," *Science Digest* (October 1967), pp. 56–60.

"Man is born free," we say.
But are you really free?
You are surrounded by rules,
controls, and taboos.
You feel you need them, yet you
sometimes want to rebel against them.
Many others feel as you do.

4 CRIME DOES NOT PAY— OR DOES IT?
control and deviance

A MONSTER

The Boston Strangler was on the loose. An army of detectives and an untold number of amateur fans of Ellery Queen were hunting for him. Tips by the thousands, mostly from cranks, poured into police headquarters. Women were arming themselves with pocket-size tear-gas guns and taking lessons in karate. Hardware stores did a booming business in firearms and strong padlocks for entrance doors. The whole city was on edge. People stayed home evenings and refused to answer their doorbells.

In the meantime the Strangler went about his ghastly business. Before he was securely locked up, he had killed thirteen women. All of these events took place between 1962 and 1964.

A monster? a madman? Certainly, but the Boston Strangler differs only in degree from countless numbers of our society who, without being dangerous criminals, nevertheless flaunt their contempt for society's standards.

What are the standards by which we live? We pride ourselves on residing in a free country. How free are we really to do as we please, to make our own decisions? To what extent do the attitudes of the people around us—family, friends, community—determine what we decide to do and what we find wiser not to do?

FOLKWAYS, MORES, LAWS

Of course it is up to you to decide on the color of the tie you will wear today, whether or not to skip breakfast, or whether to spend Sunday morning in church or out fishing. Wearing ties on certain occasions, eating breakfast, going to church, and fishing are all common activities. They are customary ways of doing things in our society. Social scientists call them *folkways*. Though they are practiced by almost everyone around you, it is still up to you to decide whether or not you will also follow the folkways. If you don't, you will perhaps be considered strange, even uncouth, and not "in," but nothing really painful will happen to you unless you are easily bruised by the disapproving ridicule or astonished looks of the people who surround you.

Just try, on a hot summer day, to go to school or work without wearing any clothes. This would seem to be the most pleasant and most sensible thing to do. In fact, it is being done in other parts of the world. But if you performed this experiment in your hometown, you can imagine what unpleasant consequences there would be.

Or you meet a very attractive member of the opposite sex and marry her despite the fact that you already have a spouse at home. This practice is forbidden in our country, though any good Muslim can have as many as four wives at the same time; King Solomon, of biblical fame, is reported to have had several hundred wives.

What limits our freedom are the *mores*, or rules, that society considers so important for its continued welfare that it is ready to *enforce* them with reward and punishment. Punishment for violating the mores can range all the way from disapproving frowns to the electric chair. On the other hand, *conforming* to the mores is rewarded with recognition, success, and a "good conscience."

Mores are concerned with our *ethical* concepts, the ideas of proper conduct, of right and wrong. We insist that the mores be upheld. A man who neglects his family because of excessive drinking finds himself shunned by co-workers or fellow club members. A woman suspected of stepping out with other women's husbands will be excluded from social gatherings. Nobody invites them or accepts their invitations. In these ways society manifests its disapproval of an individual's behavior. Such rejection by one's close associates can hurt and has driven people to despair, occasionally even to suicide.

Religion can be a powerful agent of *social control* (see Chapter 8). Certain acts are branded as sinful and the sinner is to be punished for them either in this world or in the hereafter or both. Religious statements such as the Ten Commandments make clear to the faithful what is allowed and what is prohibited.

When such rules of conduct become officially enacted and are eventually written down, whether under the auspices of church or government, they become *laws*. One of the oldest and most famous law codes was chiseled into stone 3,700 years ago by order of King Hammurabi of Babylonia. The ancient Romans, about 1,700 years later, made up an elaborate collection of laws that has influenced the administration of justice up to our own day.

Laws are enforced by courts, the police, jailers, and executioners. Most laws are aimed at preventing individuals from committing acts that society believes are unethical. They decree punishment for theft, manslaughter, taking unfair advantage of the weak and the ignorant, and for disregarding the rules of sexual conduct. But we also find laws that have little or nothing to do with ethics. For example, the laws in several northern and central European countries, such as Sweden and Austria, regarding which side of the street vehicles would use were gradually changed, and now everyone in these countries drives on the right side of the street, as we do in the United States. There was no change in moral attitudes; driving on the right side of the street is no more morally justified than hugging the left side. It was merely found to be more convenient to follow the example of most other countries and to avoid confusion, especially in regions where countries are small and border crossings frequent.

Again, how free are you really? Do laws inhibit your freedom? Would you do away with laws? "Certainly not," you might answer the last question. You pride yourself on living under a government by law. It furnishes you with protection; it gives you guidelines for correct behavior. "After all," you say, "we aren't savages," a statement which in itself, by the way, is not very meaningful. So-called savages live by very stringent rules though they may not have written them down.

Now we come to another baffling question: If laws mirror the moral ideas of society, if they serve to protect the individual, why is it necessary to enforce them? Don't the members of a particular society know what is good for them? The truth is that not all laws were made in the interest of society as a whole. Some protect the interests of a powerful ruler, others the privileges of a small ruling class. Besides, we have all kinds of needs, and at times one need conflicts with another. Mores and laws restrain your desire for wealth, for sexual gratification, for power. This can and often does conflict with your need for protection, with your wish to be accepted as a reliable, law-abiding citizen. Our culture places great emphasis on the goal of making a good living but, at the same time, makes it impossible for many to do so. Our laws often deal much more harshly with the poor and the weak than with the wealthy and the strong. Again, all of these situations lead to conflict.

Perhaps in a simpler society the members are always sure of what correct behavior is, and if they are not, there is usually some undisputed authority to guide them. Our more complex social situation, however, breeds doubt and confusion. We live in times of not only rapid transportation and communication but also rapid *cultural change*. The mores and laws are slow in responding to these changes, and so we experience *cultural lags*.

Mothers disagree with daughters on the proper length of a skirt or the best time to return home from a date. Laws penalizing premarital sex relations exist but are rarely enforced because large segments of the public find them outmoded. Even religious spokesmen disagree sharply on the morality of birth control and abortion.

Highly respected businessmen who consider themselves law-abiding citizens see nothing immoral in evading the payment of taxes or in negotiating deals that skirt the line of illegality. Some still work under the outdated assumption that business has no responsibility toward the general society and that the only measure of success is the amount of profit.

Often corruption is uncovered in politics, yet it is very difficult to determine what constitutes a friendly gift to a congressman and what a bribe. When a senator proposes a law that happens to mean good business for a rich campaign contributor, is he paying a debt, or is he convinced that the law is good for all of his constituents?

Thus the question of what is good and what is evil, what is proper and what is improper or shady, often defies an easy answer. It is almost unavoidable to run afoul of mores and laws when the circumstances provoke conflict. The ideas of right and wrong depend on the groups that uphold them. The ways of immigrants conflict with those of native Americans. The poor have standards different from the rich and even the middle class. Homosexuality, which our culture brands as a form of perversion, was openly practiced by males in ancient Greece. The Plains Indians considered *transvestites* (males wearing female clothing) holy persons who acted under orders from gods and spirits.

Even if you are willing to abide by all rules, you may run into trouble if one set of rules conflicts with another. Do you hide a relative who is a criminal from the police, or do you turn him in? Does a Catholic mother whose husband mistreats the children divorce him for their protection or not? Whatever you do in these cases, you violate a cherished principle.

There is no sharp dividing line between the good guys and the bad guys as there is in mediocre comic strips or movies. The study of man in conflict with the accepted standards of his society is complicated. Let us bring its many facets together under the heading of *deviation*.

DEVIATION

In the gripping novel *Lord of the Flies* by William Golding a group of ordinary English children survive a plane crash and are stranded on an uninhabited island. At first these well-behaved boys are thrilled at the prospect of unscheduled adventure. But with every passing day it becomes more evident that the accustomed controls that had previously guided their behavior are now missing. There are no adults to give directions; no daily routines need be observed. From among the bewildered group a new leader arises who encourages violence and disobedience to the old order. In the end factional strife tears the band apart. Theft and murder are committed by the same human beings who had been, only a short while ago, meek, well-behaved schoolboys. A social situation in which accustomed controls were suddenly removed brought about drastic *deviant* action.

Deviance is the failure to obey group rules whether such rules are "formally enacted into law and enforced or informally agreed upon and enforced by informal sanctions."[1] Clearly, what the boys did on that remote island violated all ideas of correct behavior held by the society in which they had formerly lived. But stranded as they were on the island they were beyond the reach of the laws and the enforcement power of that society.

The possibilities of deviant behavior are practically limitless. To give some structure to our discussion, let us distinguish three basic forms, always remembering that we will find much overlapping:

1. Conflict behavior
2. Criminal behavior
3. Retreatist behavior[2]

CONFLICT BEHAVIOR

Many who embark on deviant careers realize quite well that they violate the established norms of their society. They do it anyhow, hoping they will not get caught. The habitual criminals find it profitable to ignore the norms. They break the laws, but they don't challenge them. Quite different is the position of those who oppose the whole set of social rules and decide to confront the society that upholds them.

We encounter the lone rebel who takes out his wrath by assassination and destruction. The 1960s will go down in American history as the decade of political murder. John F. Kennedy, his brother Robert, and Martin Luther King, Jr., were the most prominent victims. A small band of disgruntled men and women tried to blow up the Statue of Liberty as an act of protest. Less spectacular acts of vandalism occur frequently. The hijacking of airplanes while in flight has become another form of protest against United States policy toward Cuba, unless it is done only to obtain transportation to Havana. For the most part, however, the dissatisfied person who wants to destroy or radically alter the present order does not operate alone. This is a field of operation reserved for the broader social movement that has been briefly discussed in the previous chapter and will figure again in later parts of this book.

Let us pause here for a moment to point out that deviance may be something that future generations will find highly praiseworthy. The ancient Hebrew prophets suffered exile and prison when they attacked dishonest priests and cruel kings who suppressed the poor, and the Greek philosopher Socrates was condemned to death because he criticized the religion and government of his time. Though they were persecuted, these critics helped bring about profound changes in human attitudes. Progress often results from the words and the acts of a few who have the courage to deviate from the ways of the many.

CRIMINAL BEHAVIOR

Very obviously the criminal violates what society considers correct behavior. He is by definition a "law breaker," and the law codes provide penalties for him—if he is caught, that is. His violation is a grave one; otherwise we would not call him a criminal.

By sheer volume alone crime is one of the most serious problems of our society. It costs the nation $30 billion or more annually. Here is a sample of the frequency with which certain crimes are being committed in this country:

murder: one every hour
rape: one every thirty-two minutes
robbery: one every five minutes
burglary: one every thirty-two seconds
auto theft: one every minute[3]

Reports also indicate that crime rates are rising about five times faster than the rate of population growth. This sounds quite alarming, but some *criminologists* refuse to be too upset. They point out that at least part of this statistical increase could be the result of better reporting, better police work, and the fact that new offenses have been added to the roster of crimes.

Here are four important questions concerning crime that are often raised by the layman and investigated by the social scientist:

1. What is a crime?
2. Why does a person commit a crime?
3. How does society deal with the violator?
4. Can crime be prevented?

Regarding the first question Sumner shows in his renowned book, *Folkways*,[4] that practically any human act one can think of is allowed in some culture. A husband who kills his wife's lover is not only acting correctly in certain societies, but any other behavior would be considered contemptible. Stealing was taught to boys in ancient Sparta and is still practiced among some wandering Gypsies. In parts of Asia and Africa the mores demand that a man in high government office provide all of his relatives with government jobs or cut them in on lucrative government business. Transplanted to America, such persons, if they continue to do what they have always considered right, may run afoul of various laws.

Cultural standards determine what constitutes crime. Witchcraft was once punished by horrible forms of execution, whereas *incest*—particularly in the case of sexual relations between brother and sister—was deemed commendable when practiced by members of the Egyptian royal family. If we considered everybody a criminal who breaks a law or an ordinance, hardly any noncriminals could be found. Consider traffic violations and the various schemes to avoid paying income taxes. Many business deals are so involved that even lawyers and accountants have a hard time determining whether or not laws have been violated. The car salesman who will sell you a defective automobile for the price of a good one, the real estate broker who will unload low quality property for high prices: Are they criminals or just smart businessmen? Probably the community regards them as respectable members, and only the victims of their sharp practices think differently.

But we shall focus our attention on those acts that are undoubtedly of a criminal nature. We know of persons whom we can, without much disagreement, call criminals. Criminals are people who know very well that they are doing wrong by common moral standards, but who find crime more profitable than pursuing approved ways of behavior.

Now we shall classify the immense variety of illegal acts into three major kinds:

1. Crime against the person, or crimes of violence
2. Crimes against property
3. Crimes without victims

Murder, rape, and assault belong to the first group. The second category applies to criminal acts to obtain material goods without paying the customary price; such acts include larceny, burglary, embezzlement, forgery, and many others. Modern innovations in business and industry give the criminal new ideas, and so he branches out into such enterprises as the large-scale hijacking of trucks or credit card swindles. Our whole economic system is based on the right of private ownership. We rate people by the amount of possessions they have accumulated, and we are therefore very disturbed when we are deprived of what we possess.

Crimes against property far outnumber those against the person. The ratio becomes even more lopsided when we consider that many shootings and other forms of physical violence are actually secondary effects of crimes against property. A burglar who is caught on the premises by the returning owners or a holdup man whose victim refuses to give up his wallet can become violent even though violence was not his original intention.

The term "crimes without victims" comprises a long list of acts that often don't cause physical harm to anybody but are nevertheless definitely classified as illegal. Gambling and prostitution are prominent examples. In certain places and at different times these acts have not only been allowed but also looked upon as quite respectable. The luxurious gambling casinos of the French Riviera once welcomed royalty and still attract the well-heeled social set; but in the United States small-time gamblers and bookies have to retreat to the backrooms of shabby taverns unless they can afford a roundtrip ticket to Las Vegas or to such places where parimutuel betting at race tracks is legal.

Prostitution, the world's "oldest profession," not only violates our laws but is felt to be the most debasing work a female can engage in. Yet at religious shrines of old, priestesses offered themselves to male worshipers in the belief that the sex act symbolizes the life-giving power of the deity. Not so very long ago Japanese and North African girls would engage in prostitution for a limited time so they could earn their dowries. A dowry is the money that a woman brings to her husband at marriage. After marriage these women become respectable matrons, and nobody holds their past against them. In many countries, Austria and Germany, for example (and in some states such as Nevada), the prostitute practices her trade openly. The authorities in these places reason that prostitution will exist anyhow, so they may as well have it properly supervised. The police issue a prostitute a license, and she is required to pass periodic medical examinations. Thereby "honest" women have less to fear from passionate males, and the possibility of contracting venereal disease, especially syphilis, is diminished.

In most parts of the United States "soliciting" is strictly prohibited. But as long as there is a demand for their services, prostitutes will find a way to supply the demand, as police records show. Critics of our traditional mores point at the unfairness of a system that prosecutes a woman who sells her body to alleviate her poverty but not the man who makes the purchase. They also speculate whether women who are the mistresses of wealthy men or who marry only for money have any right to sneer at their sisters who populate the red-light districts.

Prostitution spawns another category of criminals, those who live off the streetwalker's or call girl's earnings: pimps and madams. They may be small operators or part of a powerful and dangerous organization. Here we come face to face with a most sinister threat to our society: organized crime.

ORGANIZED CRIME

Outlaws who operate in bands are nothing new. The legendary Robin Hood and his men who took from the rich to give to the poor have become beloved folk figures. The original *mafiosos* roamed poverty-stricken Sicily in search of illegal spoils with the full support of the peasantry, which feared and detested the corrupt government.

Those earlier bands of outlaws kept to the woods and the villages. But in our time organized crime extends across countries and has taken on the forms of big business. Its leaders live in penthouses and belong to the swankiest clubs. During the era of Prohibition, from 1919 to 1933, their main enterprise was bootlegging. When alcohol was again legalized, they branched out into prostitution, illegal gambling, trafficking in narcotics and pornography, and the masterminding of large-scale thievery. The "protection" rackets extort regular tributes from small businessmen by the threat of violence.

The world of the racketeer has its own code of behavior (see Chapter 22 for a discussion of subcultures) and its own apparatus for enforcing that code. An elaborate rank system separates the big bosses from various levels of underlings down to the toughs who, on orders, rough up or kill disobedient or "unfairly" competing gangsters. Rival gangs, armed with submachine guns and bombs, once engaged in bloody battles, but lately such warfare has largely given way to cooperation. Territories have been staked out, and the various gang leaders even get together occasionally for some sort of underworld summit meeting, such as the now famous meeting of sixty leading racketeers who met to "talk shop" in an elegant home in Appalachia, New York, in 1957. Even though the law enforcement agencies may know all about such gatherings and may have the big-time mobsters under close surveillance, it is often impossible to pin any specific criminal act on them. The bosses are very careful to cover their tracks.

The most notorious racketeers are those of the Cosa Nostra, which grew out of the Sicilian mafias. J. Edgar Hoover, Director of the Federal Bureau of Investigation (F.B.I.), describes it as "the largest organization of the criminal underworld in this country, very closely organized and strictly disciplined. They have committed almost every crime under the sun."[5]

We notice that Italian-sounding names show up prominently in reports about such criminal groups. This does not mean, however, that Italian-Americans as a whole show less respect for our laws than other citizens. In fact, descendants of immigrants from that southern European country have made great contributions in all walks of life. But we have observed that, under certain unfavorable circumstances, especially under the pressure of poverty and discrimination, some immigrants or their sons are susceptible to the temptation of making a career out of crime.

Organized crime helps to corrupt our values because of the vast amounts of money at its disposal. Money buys the assistance of underpaid policemen and even of mayors, union leaders, judges, and legislators. Money pays for elegant offices and helps maintain fronts of legitimate business. Thus, financial power coupled with political influence makes fighting organized crime a most difficult and even dangerous task.

THE CRIMINAL PERSON

What makes a person a habitual criminal? We saw how hard it is to pinpoint what crime really is; therefore we cannot expect an easy answer to this question either. Evil spirits or the devil himself were once blamed as the cause of criminal behavior. Even today the notion persists that some persons are just born criminals.

Cesare Lombroso, an early criminologist who died in 1909, thought he could recognize a criminal type by certain bodily characteristics, especially by the shape of the skull. Theories like his though have largely been discarded in favor of more refined scientific methods. However, other experts investigating the subject from different angles arrive at different answers. "Criminal behavior is learned in interaction with other persons in a process of communication," says Edwin H. Sutherland, whereas Sheldon and Eleanor Glueck trace crime mainly to "primitive impulses of aggression, sexual desire, acquisitiveness and the like." According to the Gluecks we are all potential criminals, but social controls restrain the majority.[6]

There are those who embark on a life of crime because they lack the confidence to succeed in a legitimate occupation. Others learn criminal habits from friends or family members. Crime can also be an act of revolt against rejection. While criminals are found in many walks of life, the highest crime rates occur in the poorest and most neglected sections of our communities. However, studies have shown that in police reports and statistics the lower classes are made to appear more criminal than they really are. This is especially true in the case of young offenders, where it is the policeman who decides whether the juvenile will be referred to the courts or let off with a stern lecture and an admonition not to let himself be caught in the act again. When black youths are arrested, the policemen turn them over to the courts in much greater numbers, even for light offenses, than they would white boys.[7] Many criminals come from broken homes; most of them are too poorly educated though to be successful in the big-time rackets, which require considerable skill and administrative talent. All in all, a person turns to crime through a combination of influences—and the most important of these influences, according to Sheldon and Eleanor Glueck, is family conditions in early childhood. Children who grow up with little or no supervision and affection are most likely to follow the road of deviant behavior.

Some social scientists see the roots of crime not so much in the condition of the individual as in the whole fabric of our society. Children grow up in a world in which the possession of money seems to be the overriding value. Having large quantities of money gives you power and rank, and you can parade before the envious eyes of your neighbors all the things that your money can buy.

Since being wealthy is such a highly desirable goal, we will find a number of people who are determined to reach it, regardless of the means they have to employ. Money acquired by fraud and deception will buy diamonds, Cadillacs, and memberships in exclusive clubs just the same as money gained by honest means. Once a man has struck it rich, it is soon forgotten how he acquired his possessions—at least he hopes so. As Robert K. Merton points out, our society places before its members very desirable "cultural goals," but does not insist very strongly on the "institutionalized means" by which to reach the goals. This gap between the goals and the means invites deviant behavior.[8]

HOW SOCIETY DEALS WITH THE VIOLATOR

The criminal finds himself pitted against an impressive array of police, prosecutors, judges, penal institutions, probation officers, and so forth. How successful are all these organs? According to statistics the record is not too impressive.

Crime is increasing at a rate far exceeding the growth rate of population. Only a fraction of crimes committed are followed up by arrests; an even smaller number lead to conviction and punishment. Of crimes against property only about a third are even reported to the authorities. Victims of swindlers or thieves often remain silent thinking it won't do any good to report incidents, or they feel ashamed of their own negligence. Reluctantly we must admit that there is little evidence to back up the old saying that "crime does not pay."

We hear much criticism of the police, some of which is justified. But the police force is an arm of society and depends on society for direction and recognition, as well as for money and recruits. No doubt, a better relationship between police and the general community, especially in the ghetto areas, is badly needed.

Our Constitution guarantees equality before the law. In practice we sometimes fall short of this ideal. Racial prejudice affects police, judges, and juries as it does other persons. Rich people can pay for top legal talent to defend themselves. Influential citizens can "fix" citations and arrests or at least prevent them from becoming publicized. Contemplating all this, a prisoner in his cell becomes cynical. Justice is not for him. "The difference between me and the guy outside," he reasons bitterly, "is that I got caught."

Our ways of punishing the offender are sadly outdated. Why do we exact penalties? Four basic motives have been found:

1. Revenge
2. Protection of society
3. Punishment as a deterrent
4. Rehabilitation[9]

"Give him what he deserves" is the immediate reaction when we hear of a reprehensible crime, such as the 1966 murder of eight student nurses by Richard Speck in Chicago. The urge to avenge evil is old and persistent; it is charged with emotion. Sex crimes in particular rouse a general outcry of revulsion coupled with the demand for swift retribution.

Society also punishes offenders to protect itself. In this motive we are probably more successful than in any other aspect of punishment, provided, of course, that the criminal is caught. Once he is executed or detained behind bars, he certainly cannot do any further damage.

"See what will happen to you if you misbehave?" Implicit in this rhetorical question is the hope that drastic penalties will serve as a warning to other would-be criminals. How effective this assumption is cannot easily be determined. Fear has probably kept many people law abiding, especially if they have ever watched a public hanging or seen a thief's right hand chopped off. Such scenes were common not too long ago and still occur in some places. But we also know that while pickpockets were publicly hanged in old England, other pickpockets were busy picking the pockets of the spectators.

According to some sociologists offenders are punished not so much to prevent them from repeating their crimes as to keep up the morale of the "good people" who may never see the inside of a jail. Unconsciously most of us want to slip off the strait jacket of proper behavior and give our instincts and secret wishes free run; but we restrain those desires because we also want very much to remain respectable, conforming members of our group. When we self-righteously condemn the violator who takes what is not his or who enjoys forbidden delights, what we are doing is trying to silence the dangerous stirrings within ourselves.[10]

In recent times the motive of reform, or *rehabilitation,* has received growing interest. Social scientists point out that the offender is a maladjusted person and that crime is a kind of sickness. The desirable course to follow is to readjust the person and heal the disease. Besides, we are told that it is far less expensive to return an offender to a constructive existence in society than to keep him in jail at a cost to the taxpayer of $2,000 a year per adult and about $3,500 in the case of a juvenile.[11] Of course, money here is not the only and, hopefully, not the most important consideration.

Our penitentiaries have not yet proved to be very successful instruments of rehabilitation. Over two-thirds of their inmates are repeaters. The psychiatrist Karl Menninger finds prisons completely useless and would replace them with community treatment centers similar to the clinics that tend to our physical ills.[12]

Some model jails make promising efforts to reform the violator. He can learn a useful trade or finish his schooling if he is a dropout. The treatment by the prison personnel is humane; guards are friendly and carry no weapons. Some experiments have been made to allow prisoners to make family visits or to allow them to work on outside jobs during the day. (See Figure 3.) Still, most penitentiaries are dreary and oppressive places.

Whether we go along with such a radical suggestion or not, criminology and psychology have provided much information about the nature of crime. Now society's resistance to change and general apathy need to be overcome so that these findings can actually be applied. Also important is the attitude of "straight" society toward the ex-convict, who needs encouragement and sympathetic guidance, or he may soon be practicing his former occupation again.

"So in view of your enlightened approach to the penal code, we thought you might share our recommendation for a co-ed prison."

Figure 3

Copyright 1969 Saturday Review, Inc. Reprinted by permission of Herbert Goldberg and *Saturday Review*.

PREVENTION OF CRIME

Since we know that certain social conditions foster crime, it stands to reason that changing these conditions will reduce crime. The elimination of poverty and racial discrimination, the improvement of education, and expert counseling for troubled families would slash the ranks of recruits for criminal careers. Furthermore, most serious offenders start out young; they are really progressed juvenile delinquents. Therefore crime prevention must begin with attention to children. Parents, teachers, and guidance personnel can discover problem children early enough for successful treatment. Youth clubs and attractive recreational facilities will also help to keep the growing child from becoming a *juvenile delinquent*.

JUVENILE DELINQUENCY

Newspapers and the other news media frequently point warningly at the alarming extent of juvenile delinquency. What is the distinction between the criminal and the delinquent? When a car is stolen or a murder committed, the act may be considered either a crime or an act of delinquency—depending on the age of the offender. The car is gone and the victim is just as dead in either case, but the delinquent is a junior criminal or the criminal is a graduate delinquent. Various state laws set different cut-off points as to what constitutes a delinquent and what a criminal.

Offenders under the age of sixteen are generally treated as juvenile delinquents. Some states still consider older teen-agers as juveniles, whereas others subject them to the same procedures as adult criminals. In yet another group of states the treatment of the young offender depends on the nature of the offense and also on the decisions of the courts. A person under the age of twenty or, in some cases, twenty-one may be brought before a juvenile court for theft or possession of alcohol, but if he is accused of murder or manslaughter, he will be judged as an adult. A mischief-maker may very well decide whether he wants to be treated as a juvenile or an adult by choosing the state in which he is going to commit the mischief.

The dividing line between the criminal and the delinquent appears to be artificial, especially when we note that most adult criminals are quite young. About three-fourths of those arrested for serious violations are under twenty-five years of age.

But if we continue our observations, we will discover that substantial differences between crime and delinquency do exist and are recognized everywhere in this country. A juvenile becomes a delinquent by committing such acts as truancy, curfew violation, smoking, drinking, and running away. An adult can do such things without penalty. On the other hand, adults are hardly interested in such kid stuff as "joy-riding" (stealing cars for short rides and then abandoning them), which is one of the major headaches of the law enforcement people.

Even the juvenile gang is only remotely related to the adult racket though it may furnish the racket with recruits. Boys gang up to seek companionship and adventure in a drab, frustrating environment. Finding themselves in conflict with the dominant culture around them, they become rebellious and destructive. "To raise his low estimate of himself, the gang boy has carved out his own world and a system of values that entails demands he can easily meet. . . . He makes lying, assault, thievery and unprovoked violence—especially violence—the major activity or dream of his life."[13]

In dealing with the juvenile offender we emphasize rehabilitation even more than when we are confronted with wayward adults. This has not always been the case, however, and one can still find places where children and hardened criminals are locked up together. But it is generally felt that the younger the person the greater the chance of remolding him in the image of the model citizen. This is why juvenile courts have wide leeway in the treatment they can prescribe. The youngsters are put in charge of probation officers or referred to clinics and counselors; they may be placed in foster homes or in special "training schools." Here, as with the adult criminal, the task of rehabilitation is hampered by lack of money, competent personnel, and sympathetic community attitudes.

Concern has also been voiced that the juvenile may, on occasion, be deprived of his civil rights by those procedures that were especially designed for him. Juvenile court is supposed to be an informal session to determine what should be done about the accused, whether he would benefit more from detention in a juvenile hall, in a boys' training school, or in a foster home, and so forth. But the young person himself does not have much to say about the court's decision. He often has no lawyer who can cross-examine witnesses, he cannot appeal the verdict of the court, nor is he entitled to bail. All such privileges are reserved for the adult.

RETREATIST BEHAVIOR

Nonconformists are people whom social conditions have directed into forms of behavior that seem strange to the majority. In the mountains and forests of India one occasionally runs into creatures barely resembling human beings. They have discarded their clothing; their hair is uncut and matted with dirt; they feed on roots and spend their days meditating in a motionless body posture. Hindus regard these mystics as holy and treat them with profound veneration.

Western religion has little tolerance for such extreme behavior. But examples of it do exist. We speak, for instance, of *recluses*, persons who withdraw from a society that they reject or that has rejected them. Often the world only takes notice of recluses after they have died in isolation in rural shacks or city dwellings where they have voluntarily imprisoned themselves for months or years.

People who practice this kind of retreatist behavior usually don't bother anybody, and they seldom break any laws. But some other forms of withdrawal are punishable, and as far as the guardians of the law are concerned, they are classified as crimes. These are habitual drunkenness, the use of narcotics, and certain forms of sex perversion.

ALCOHOLISM

The use of alcoholic beverages can be traced back into man's dim past. In many countries wine is the common drink for old and young. It is also consumed in religious ceremonies of the Jewish and the Catholic faiths. The cocktail is the chief ingredient of many official or private gatherings. Christmas and New Year's Eve celebrations call for alcohol-induced hilarity; so do weddings and diplomatic functions. Many of our cherished folkways involve the use of alcohol.

Yet a sizable number of fellow citizens raise serious objections to the pleasures induced by beer or whiskey. Mormons, Seventh Day Adventists, and other religious denominations consider drinking sinful. More widespread than moral or religious objections is the concern over the dangerous effects of alcohol on the health of body and mind. The need for repeated heavy intoxication is an acute illness. Drinking and driving are a deadly mixture. Moreover, many crimes of violence, untold marital conflicts, absenteeism from work, street brawls, and other undesirable occurrences can be traced to excessive drinking.

Habitual drinking to the point of intoxication is an outward symptom of deep-seated personality problems. It often provides an escape from reality. After the fourth, fifth, or sixth glass, depending on your capacity, your anxieties are forgotten, and your difficulties cease to bother you. Though usually shy, you now become "the life of the party." Tension and guilt feelings are gone, at least until you sober up. The heavy drinker is essentially an immature person, regardless of age. Of him it has been said, "alcohol gives the adult what milk gives the normal infant."[14]

The peculiar attractiveness, coupled with the chemical power, of the fermented drink turns not all but quite a few heavy drinkers into *alcoholics*. Just what causes alcoholism is still a matter of debate among the experts who have researched this illness of body and mind. It is commonly assumed that an alcoholic is a person who falters easily under the stresses and frustrations with which we all must cope. Whatever its cause, chronic alcoholism leads to the gradual destruction of the personality. Drinking becomes a compulsion. The alcoholic must consume ever larger quantities or suffer unbearable agonies. His emotional development is stunted, and he often "has weak sexual drives, his affectional bind being largely with alcohol."[15] He often ends up a social misfit, unable to play his role in family, occupation, and community. Becoming a skidrow derelict is the final stage for some alcoholics.

Alcoholism is not a rare disease. "It has been estimated that about 6 out of 10 adults in the United States use alcoholic beverages, and that one out of every 15 persons who drink becomes an alcoholic."[16]

No sure-fire cure for alcoholism is known. Therapies involving drugs and prolonged hospitalization have met with mixed success. Some compulsive drinkers have been helped by Alcoholics Anonymous and by similar efforts at counseling combined with self-help. The basic question still remains though: What led the alcoholic to excessive drinking in the first place? What made him want to retreat? Both the biological and social sciences will have to combine forces for further research into the nature of this dreadful disease.

NARCOTICS

Needs similar to those that drive some people to excessive drinking lead others to the use of narcotic drugs. Like alcohol, opium, morphine, and heroin bring about a release from tension and create a momentary satisfaction, an *euphoric* feeling. Like alcohol, these drugs are habit forming and can lead to complete physical and mental deterioration.

But there is an important difference between the use of alcohol and drugs, not attributable to chemistry or physiology but to man. While social drinking is acceptable in our culture, the use of drugs is generally outlawed, regardless of the quantity taken. In the United States the mere possession of narcotics, whatever the amount, is labeled as a crime. This has driven drug users underground and forced them to create their own distinct subculture. Isolation and the threat from the outside make them dependent on interaction among their own kind.

Since narcotic drugs cannot be bought openly, racketeers have moved into the very lucrative business of supplying them. Addicts, most of whom reside in large cities, spend $20 and more a day on drugs. To obtain money, the addict frequently "hustles" narcotics to other users. He or she may also engage in other criminal acts, such as theft or prostitution, to support the high cost of the habit.

In the past few years a new sector of society has turned to drugs and received a great deal of public attention. Teen-agers, for whom curiosity, a

Communities protest against drug use.
Charles Gatewood

need for thrills, and a general disgust with the state of our society seem to be the prime motives, have experimented with sniffing airplane glue, which can have very dangerous effects. Many students on college campuses are smoking marijuana. Scientists disagree widely as to the damage this easily obtainable drug can cause. Some consider it far less dangerous than alcohol, while others condemn it strongly. Most agree, however, that not enough is yet known about the effects of "pot" on the human organism. Regardless of the effects of marijuana, there is widespread criticism of the laws concerning it. The heavy penalties for its possession seem out of place, at least until there is more substantial evidence to prove that it presents a definite danger to the user. Furthermore, the smoking of marijuana cigarettes is not, by any means, confined to teen-agers. In many colleges, for professionals as well as students, it has become part of the social ritual, and the users do not consider themselves otherwise at odds with the culture of which they are a part.

Great public excitement has also been aroused by the prophets of the so-called *psychedelic* drugs, particularly LSD. These drugs have become a characteristic ingredient of the hippie movement. Timothy Leary, a former professor of psychology, even promoted LSD as the focal point of what he called a religious cult. His slogan, "Turn on, tune in, drop out," is an invitation to retreat from society into a world of hallucinations conjured up by this easily manufactured drug.

Whereas the dangers of marijuana may perhaps be overrated, the use of LSD is considered extremely risky. "Bad trips" have caused temporary and even permanent mental breakdowns. There is also a possibility that tragic effects may show up long after the drug has been used or even in succeeding generations. Researchers have reported extremely bad trips that occurred many months after the drug had been taken. Some suspect that LSD may alter the body chromosomes, which can, in turn, produce physically or mentally crippled offspring. Fortunately, however, popularity of LSD seems to have passed its crest.

HOMOSEXUALITY

When males turn to other males and women to other women for sexual gratification, "normal" society wonders why. Traditionally homosexuality was condemned in the United States as a repulsive perversion, but we are now beginning to recognize it as another form of retreat from the demands of society. Research into this subject is of quite recent origin since, in the past, scholars, like most other people, shied away from frank discussions of sexual matters and especially of sexual perversion.

Historians find, however, that certain cultures considered sexual relations between male and male or female and female not only permissible but worthy of praise. This was the case in several warrior societies, such as that of ancient Sparta. The term "lesbian," denoting a homosexual female, is derived from the name of the island of Lesbos in Greece, where such relationships were supposedly common during antiquity.

A person may develop strong inferiority feelings in dealing with the opposite sex. After having been rejected by several women whom he wanted to court, a man may convince himself that girls just do not care for him, and so he retreats into male company. Homosexuality is also found where normal sexual outlets are absent, such as in prisons.

The homosexual is subject to very strong contempt from the "straight" majority. In addition he is, like the narcotics user, considered a criminal according to the laws of most states. This situation drives him, as it does the drug addict, into his own subculture, a world of special clubs and bars, homosexual marriages, fierce jealousies, and even prostitutes catering to "gay" customers.

Does society have the right to punish the homosexual as long as he does not harm anybody? And aside from the moral problem, is it wise to do so? The question has been widely discussed. Homosexuals themselves maintain that they are not depraved, not even abnormal, but just different. They claim the right to arrange their lives according to their own designs. Scholars and legislators are beginning to see the problem in the same light. England, for example, has recently taken steps in this direction. Homosexuality as such is no longer considered an offense in the United Kingdom as long as it is practiced "in private among consenting adults."

Main Ideas
1. Society controls the behavior of its members through its folkways and particularly through its mores and laws.
2. Certain conditions, such as cultural change, cultural lag, and various forms of conflict, bring about deviant behavior.
3. The forms of deviant behavior can be grouped under the headings of conflict behavior, criminal behavior, and retreatist behavior.
4. Conflict behavior is exhibited by lone rebels and by social protest movements.
5. Crime, which is punishable by law, is a violation of approved behavior.
6. By its sheer volume crime is a very serious problem in the United States. This is particularly true of organized crime.
7. The criminal person is a product of a combination of influences. Among them poverty, slum conditions, insufficient education, and defective family life are most important.
8. The motives for the punishment of the criminal are revenge, the need to protect society from the criminal, the desire to deter others from committing crimes, and the attempt to rehabilitate the offender.
9. While we profess that rehabilitation is the most desirable treatment of the criminal, we have not been very successful at it.
10. It is being argued that prevention of crime should take precedence over punishment of the criminal. Efforts to prevent and curb juvenile delinquency are considered especially essential.
11. The recluse, the alcoholic, the drug addict, and, in many instances, the homosexual exhibit retreatist behavior.

Important Terms

Alcoholism	Incest
Conformity	Juvenile delinquency
Cosa Nostra	Mafia
Criminology	Mores
Cultural lag	Psychedelic drugs
Deviation	Recluse
Enforcement	Rehabilitation
Ethics	Retreatist behavior
Euphoria	Social control
Folkways	Transvestite

Conclusion
"The socialization process keeps most people law-abiding, not the police," says Jackson Toby.[17] Despite the long list of deviant behavior forms that has just been discussed, most of us exhibit a strong wish

to conform, to be considered reliable and respectable, to be counted among the "ins" rather than the "outs." The norms of society reflect the position of its leading members, who set the tone for the rest. Ultimately the goals of the deviant person are not too different from those of the majority. In his own way he also strives for recognition, economic security, and physical comfort. But the means that he employs to obtain his goals are outlawed or at least strongly disapproved of. A vast variety of deviant behavior patterns can be found in the turbulent whirl of urban life. The task of dealing with deviance is unending, and the methods of dealing with it are undergoing constant change.

Notes

1. Howard Becker, *Outsiders: Studies in the Sociology of Deviance* (New York: The Free Press, 1963), p. 2.
2. Albert Cohen, *Deviance and Control* (Englewood Cliffs, N.J.: Prentice-Hall, 1966), p. 109.
3. Federal Bureau of Investigation, *Uniform Crime Reports* (Washington, D.C.: United States Government Printing Office, 1963), p. 17.
4. William Graham Sumner, *Folkways* (New York: American Library, 1940), pp. 42 ff.
5. *The Challenge of Crime in a Free Society* (Washington, D.C.: United States Government Printing Office, 1967), p. 192.
6. Edwin H. Sutherland, "The Theory of Differential Association" and Sheldon Glueck, "A Critical Look at Differential Association Theory," in David Dressler (ed.), *Readings in Criminology and Penology* (New York: Columbia University Press, 1964), p. 302 and pp. 308–309.
7. Nathan Goldman, *The Differential Selection of Juvenile Offenders for Court Appearance* (National Council on Crime and Delinquency, 1963), p. 42.
8. "Social Structure and Anomie," in Robert K. Merton, *Social Theory and Social Structure*, rev. ed. (Glencoe, Ill.: The Free Press, 1957), pp. 131 ff.
9. Cohen, *op. cit.*, p. 109.
10. Jackson Toby, "Is Punishment Necessary?" in Peter I. Rose (ed.), *The Study of Society: An Integrated Anthology* (New York: Random House, 1967), pp. 779 ff.
11. Robert Rice, *The Challenge of Crime* (Public Affairs Pamphlet, No. 425, 1968), p. 27.
12. Karl Menninger, *The Crime of Punishment* (New York: Viking, 1968).
13. Lewis Yablonsky, *The Violent Gang* (New York: Macmillan, 1963), p. 4.
14. Cohen, *op. cit.*, p. 68.
15. *International Encyclopedia of the Social Sciences* (New York: Macmillan, 1968), IV, 266–267.
16. *Alcoholism* (U.S. Department of Health, Welfare and Education pamphlet, 1963), p. 3.
17. Toby, *op. cit.*, p. 782.

Suggestions for Further Reading

"Abuse of Drugs, a Growing Menace," *UNESCO Courier*, 21 (May 1968), 4-29.

Algren, Nelson. *The Man with the Golden Arm*. New York: Doubleday, 1949. Novel dealing with drug addiction.

Alcoholics Anonymous. Rev. ed. New York: Alcoholics Anonymous World Service, 1955. Personal stories showing the idea and methods of Alcoholics Anonymous.

Burgess, W. C. "Glue Sniffing," *PTA Magazine*, 58 (March 1964), 15-17.

Capote, Truman. *In Cold Blood: A True Account of a Multiple Murder and Its Consequences*. New York: Random House, 1966.

Cavan, Ruth S. (ed.). *Readings in Juvenile Delinquency*. Philadelphia: Lippincott, 1964 (paperback).

Chafetz, M. E. "How Nations Drink: The Puzzle of Alcoholism," *Nation*, 199, November 30, 1964, 401-404.

Conrad, Barnaby. *Dangerfield*. New York: Harper, 1962. Novel based on the life of the writer Sinclair Lewis, who was a heavy drinker.

Cook, Fred. *The F.B.I. Nobody Knows*. New York: Macmillan, 1964.

Davidson, B. "Thrill-Pill Menace," *Saturday Evening Post*, 238, December 4, 1965, 23-27.

Dickens, Charles. *Oliver Twist*. New York: Macmillan, 1932 (paperback). Famous novel about organized crime and delinquent boys in early nineteenth-century London.

Dostoevski, Fyodor. *Crime and Punishment*. New York: Everyman's Library, 1963. Novel by this nineteenth-century Russian writer on the spiritual struggle and redemption of a criminal.

Frank, Stanley. "The Rap Gangsters Fear Most," *Saturday Evening Post*, 231, August 9, 1958, 26, 62-68. Cosa Nostra gangsters and their fear of deportation.

Golding, William. *Lord of the Flies*. New York: Capricorn Books, 1954 (paperback).

Hersey, John. *Too Far to Walk*. New York: Knopf, 1966. Novel dealing with drug use.

Hollister, Hal. "An Ex-Convict Evaluates Prisons," *Harper's Magazine*, 225 (August 1962), 4, 16, 19-20.

Jackson, Charles. *The Lost Weekend*. New York: Noonday Press, 1944. Novel dealing with alcoholism.

Kefauver, Estes. *Crime in America*. Garden City, New York: Doubleday, 1951. The late United States Senator reports on his committee's investigation of crime.

"LSD: Research and Joy Ride," *Nation*, 202, May 16, 1966, 574-576.

Pollack, J. H. "Teenage Drinking and Drug Addiction," *NEA Journal*, 55 (May 1966), 8-12.

Rice, Robert. *The Challenge of Crime*. Public Affairs Pamphlet, No. 425, 1968.

Wade, Rosalind. *Come Fill the Cup*. New York: Pantheon, 1956. Novel dealing with alcoholism.

Whitman, H. "What Is a Problem Drinker?" *Better Homes and Gardens*, 35 (July 1957), 74-75 ff.

Look into a mirror. Do you look different from others? And if so, does it matter?
If your skin color is different, is your mind different too?

5 BLACK AND WHITE
the question of race

HATRED AND FRUSTRATION

It is night. A huge wooden cross burns fiercely on a hill, sending showers of sparks over the men crowding around its base. The men, members of the Ku Klux Klan, hold burning torches in their hands. They are dressed in sheetlike white robes, and pointed hoods—with holes in them for eyes and mouths—cover their faces.

Speaker after speaker mounts the stand that is darkly silhouetted against the fiery cross. Each one in his turn shouts out phrases filled with intense hatred at the white men who have come some distance from several Southern towns. The crowd answers each call for violent action with hoarse shouts of approval. "The way I feel about them niggers who want to integrate our schools," screams a hooded figure from the rostrum, "is this—they don't want an education, they want a funeral."

The crowd seethes with rage. Over and over again the speakers repeat their intention "to maintain forever the God-given supremacy of the white race" with every means at their command. They pledge to rid America of not only black people, but also Jews, socialists, and all other kinds of "undesirables."

Finally the meeting breaks up. The air is thick with smoke and hatred as the Klansmen throw their torches into the embers of the collapsing cross. Before dawn breaks a flimsy wooden Negro church nearby has gone up in flames. A few nights later several sticks of dynamite explode under the house of a black man who has been a leading figure in local voter registration.

Now another scene takes place more than a thousand miles away. We find ourselves on a street corner in a large Northern city. A black youth has climbed onto a small table to address a mass of upturned black faces. Windows in the grimy tenement houses are opened hastily, and more ears strain to catch the youth's message:

"The white man's the devil. You hear me? He's the devil. Did you ever know a white man to do anything right?"

Loud scornful laughter answers the question.

"You know what The Man is preparing for us?"

The listeners know exactly who The Man is.

"He's fixing to exterminate us, to put us all into concentration camps. We need shotguns, machine guns. We must be prepared to kill, or we'll all be killed—!"

Again and again the youth is interrupted by hysterical shouts and shrill whistles. The crowd disperses, muttering curses against the white race and especially against the police.

During the night shots ring out. Blobs of plaster rain from tenement walls, and a window pane shatters under the impact of a brick. A bottle is hurled into a passing car. The sound of shattering glass mingles with the piercing wail of a police siren. Black extremists have incited another explosion of violence in the slums in their attempt to obtain long-denied opportunities.

RACE CONSCIOUSNESS

Many similar scenes and even worse ones have occurred in the last few years, weakening and aggravating the already tense relationship between the black and white races.[1] True, only a comparatively small number of Americans join the ranks of the extremists, black or white. But what the Klan and radical black militants shout and the actions they take are symptoms of a disease that, if untreated, could grow into a deadly epidemic.

We are a *race-conscious* society, which means that the question of skin color divides us sharply and arouses strong, often dangerous, emotions. When nourished by frustration and stirred up by demagogues, such emotions can cause death and destruction. Why does the question of race arouse people so? What is race anyhow?

WHAT IS RACE?

Look into a mirror. Your skin is black, or white, any of an endless variety of shades from dark brown to light tan. Look at your hair. Is it black, brown, red, or blond? Is it kinky, or wavy, or straight? Your nose, your eyelids, your cheekbones may be shaped in any of a number of ways. All these physical characteristics have something to do with race. Yet there is more to race than the shape of eyes and nose. Race is a concept that has long baffled scholars, who strive to bury their emotions and approach the problem reasonably.

Biologists, psychologists, sociologists, anthropologists, and representatives of other sciences are interested in the question of race and study it from different angles. But as scientists they agree on one point: race is not a criterion for determining if a man is good or bad. This is as much out of place as it is to distinguish between good and bad vertebrates or between angelic and devilish garden plants on the basis of their biological makeup.

For the biological scientist racial differences can only mean biological differences. Let us suggest a definition that makes as much sense as any: A race is a group of people with a composite of inherited physical characteristics, such as skin pigmentation, texture of hair, and certain facial features.

It has been assumed for quite some time that mankind can be divided into three main racial groups: Caucasian, Negroid, and Mongoloid. Since we have somehow fallen into the habit of associating race mainly with skin pigmentation, the races are frequently referred to as white, black, and yellow. This is not, of course, the language of the scholar but of the man in the street.

Look again into the mirror. Which of the three labels applies to you? Is your skin black as coal, or white as a sheet, or yellow like a lemon peel? Chances are you will find yourself in a dilemma and soon realize how inaccurate such labels really are. You may be a Caucasian descendant of Turks or Arabs and have an olive complexion; or you may be a very light-skinned "black"; we have yet to find a person who is truly yellow.

Different tribes of native Africans differ from each other in outward appearance more than some whites differ from some blacks. Groups as distant and as different looking as American Indians, Japanese, and inhabitants of the far eastern areas of the Soviet Union are lumped together as members of the Mongoloid race. All these inconsistencies should make us realize that we have, as men are apt to do so often, created an artificial framework into which we try to fit all mankind.

Scholars who want to bring some order into a profusion of different objects try first to arrange them in a few main classes, and if this proves insufficient, they create further subdivisions. Caucasians, for example, can be of the Mediterranean, Alpine, Nordic, or several other subraces. Mediterraneans, such as the inhabitants of Greece, Sicily, and North Africa, are supposed to be of rather short stature and have dark hair and tan complexions. On the other hand, the typical Nordic from Scandinavia or Scotland is thought of as being tall, blond, and blue eyed. But it is hard to find a "typical" Nordic, and when you finally locate one, he may turn out to be an Italian or a Frenchman.

Modern anthropologists distinguish races mainly according to their geographic origins. The chart below follows the text by Beals and Hoijer. In it are listed the racial classifications that most experts agree on and also the names of groups over which there still exists controversy.

Races of Mankind

Name	Location
A. Caucasian Local Races	
1. Larger groups	
Mediterranean	Around Mediterranean Sea, Arabia
Alpine	Central Europe
Northwestern	Scandinavia, Northern Germany, England, Ireland
Northeastern	Russia, Finland, Poland
Iranian	Turkey, Iran, Soviet Union
2. Possibly Archaic (old) races	
Ainu	Japan
Australian	
Dravidian	India
Vedda	Ceylon
B. Negroid Local Races	
Forest Negro	West Africa, Congo
Pygmy	African Ituri Forest
Bushman-Hottentot	Southwest Africa, Kalahari Desert
Nilotic Negro	Sudan, East Africa
Bantu	South and Southeast Africa
C. Mongoloid Local Races	
Asiatic	Siberia, Tibet, China
Southeast Asiatic	Burma, Thailand, Indonesia, Philippines
American Indian (including Eskimos)	North, Central, South America
D. Other Proposed Geographic Races	
Polynesian	South Pacific Islands, Hawaii
Micronesian	West Pacific Islands
Melanesian-Papuan	South and Southwest Pacific Islands, New Guinea

Source: Reprinted with permission of The Macmillan Company from *An Introduction to Anthropology*, 3rd ed., by Ralph L. Beals and Harry Hoijer. © Copyright The Macmillan Company 1953, 1959, 1965.

RACE MIXTURE

Racial groups are not fixed or permanent. Old ones have disappeared or dwindled into insignificance, and new ones seem to emerge. Ideal racial types have little to do with reality. The overwhelming majority of people do not correspond to them and fall somewhere in between.

The fact of migration—as old as mankind itself—would account in part for the impossibility of labeling. Whole populations have moved across the face of the earth. As they settled in new places, their ways of life changed, and after many generations they even began to look different. Interbreeding and intermarrying have mixed up whatever races may have originally existed. A modern Mexican, for example, may have Indian, black, and Spanish ancestors. The Indians were in Mexico first; then came the Spanish conquerors, and finally the blacks, who were brought as slaves. The Spaniards are, in turn, a conglomerate of Celtic aborigines, Roman and Germanic invaders, plus a sizable ingredient of Jews and North African Muslims, who were themselves products of repeated racial mixture. Quite a variety of races and subraces are represented in the modern Mexican. What neat little racial pigeonhole could he possibly fit into?

The fact is that we are all racially "mixed" except for some primitive populations living on remote islands or in inaccessible mountain valleys. Yet people loudly pride themselves on their "racial purity" and vow to uphold it at all cost. Few issues can rouse whites to such a feverish pitch of emotion as the question of intermarriage with blacks. The elaborate system of segregation in the South has often been excused as a means of preventing this interbreeding. This point is a difficult one to discuss calmly and reasonably. Feelings are apt to run high, as is demonstrated in the oft-quoted fictitious argument between a segregationist and a liberal. The argument is this:

The liberal pleads for better treatment of the black man. He wants whites to establish bridges of personal understanding between the races. The segregationist, on the other hand, finds such prospects repulsive. They are against his whole upbringing. And in response to his liberal opponent, the segregationist may ask, "But would you want your sister to marry one?" This is, of course, no argument at all; it is an appeal to a deep-seated prejudice.

If we examine the issue in a calm, rational way, we find there is nothing to support the contention that the mixing of different racial types is in any way harmful to the offspring. The only "harm" done is that to the preconceived ideas of the prejudiced observer.

As for the mixing of black and white, most American blacks have some white ancestors. They are in reality mulattoes, since many black slave women were used by their white masters. A so-called black will not often try to deny that he or she had a white grandfather or great-grandfather. It may be quite a different matter when black ancestors are found in the family tree of a family that thinks of itself as "lily-white," as sometimes happens. This discovery is usually kept secret.

In view of so much confusion some modern anthropologists assert that there is no such thing as race at all. It is a man-made abstraction, no more real than the myths of giants and dwarfs. If we insist on labeling men according to different physical characteristics, then the only scientifically acceptable way would be to label them according to blood types. While it may be questionable whether a person is a Nordic type or even a Caucasian, there can be no doubt that his blood is of the A, B, AB, or O type. A classification according to blood type cuts clearly across races, though people often say "blood" when they mean "race."

RACE: A SOCIAL PROBLEM

Though scientists may find that races don't exist, our attitude toward race continues to haunt us nonetheless. So race becomes one of the major problems in our society causing bitterness and strife, even destruction and bloodshed. We may ask ourselves why we become so aroused about a distinction that isn't even real. But perhaps race does exist after all—even if only as an invention of man.

We often express our feelings through colors. We call a promising young man a "white hope"; a cruel person has a "black heart." In speech and thought people associate the lightness with goodness and darkness with evil. The colors become symbols of our values.

Automatically we fear and distrust that which looks strange and different. In Asia and Africa white Europeans ruled over millions of dark-skinned colonial subjects. In the Western hemisphere white masters swung the whip over dark-skinned slaves. It was the white man who appeared in the superior role.

Even religious authority has been known to justify white supremacy on the one hand and slavery on the other. According to the Bible Noah's three sons, Sem, Ham, and Japhet, were the ancestors of three races, some designated by God to be servants to the others. American slave owners used such statements to soothe their consciences. "To justify the continuation of chattel slavery, Southerners developed an elaborate doctrine of racial superiority. Some even proclaimed that they were, in fact, protecting childlike Negroes from a cruel world in which they could never hope to manage alone."[2] Using such justification, they hoped to show that slavery was divinely ordained and the best thing that could happen to a black man.

Is the white man really superior to other racial groups? First, what do we mean by superiority? Do we speak of physical ability? Here any sports fan can easily refute the white supremacist claim. Blacks have done very well in collecting Olympic medals, not because of their race but because a number of them are simply good athletes. Excellent runners, jumpers, and wrestlers are found among whites and Asiatics, as well as among blacks.

Or do we speak of technical skills and the accomplishments of the human intellect? True, in the last few centuries white Europeans and Americans pioneered in many fields of science, art, politics, and economics.

But this was not always so, nor is anybody assured that it will be so in the future. During much of history the Chinese civilization outshone that of Europe immeasurably. In the tenth century an Arab philosopher commented about Western Europeans, "Ignorance and indolence are dominant among them, as well as crudeness and lack of judgement." And if the white man claims moral superiority, let him consider this statement by a well-known anthropologist:

> Eskimos and Australian aborigines, to take two of the most "primitive" cultures known to anthropologists, are very much more generous, loving and cooperative than are most of the members of civilized societies. By the standards of our own values in these matters, Eskimos and Australian aborigines are better than we are.[3]

PREJUDICE

Clearly then, ideas of racial superiority and inferiority are not the result of proved facts. They are based on *prejudice*. This is the tendency to "prejudge" a person before we get to know him, because we carry with us some notion about the group to which he belongs. Prejudice is widespread; hardly anybody is completely free from it. It is such an easy shortcut, such a lazy substitute for more strenuous thought. You meet somebody on the street, at school, or at work. Immediately you make up your mind about him because you have judged him according to the *stereotype* of his group. Scotchmen are supposedly stubborn, Germans industrious, Chinese sly, and blacks happy-go-lucky. Should you meet a person who does not fit the stereotype, you simply say he is an exception. Only too many people refuse to admit that such *generalizations* are no more accurate than those in the jokes about women drivers or mothers-in-law.

What are the effects of prejudice? You can hate anybody you want, but as long as your hate does not show, no damage results—except to yourself. Or you may translate your prejudices into action. In this case you openly *discriminate*. Discrimination by individuals or in an *institutionalized* pattern occurs in degrees:

1. The prejudiced person speaks out. He voices his hostility, for example, toward blacks, Jews, or Orientals during coffee breaks, meetings, and social gatherings. He condemns all of these groups for what one or several of them may or may not have done.

2. From hostile talk it is not far to the second step: the exclusion of the victimized group by force or by the pressure of public opinion. The targets of discrimination are barred from jobs, schools, places of recreation, various clubs and organizations, and from living in certain parts of the community.

3. In its most drastic form discrimination takes the form of acts of physical violence, ranging from the roughing up of individuals during street brawls to the lynching of blacks by white mobs. The ultimate act is the

planned extermination of the persecuted group, such as practiced by Hitler on the Jews of Europe in the 1930s and 1940s.

DOMINANT AND MINORITY GROUPS

Many societies show signs of racial prejudice, but the practice of discrimination varies a considerable degree from place to place. The United States has a long history of racial discrimination. It appears in even more cruel forms in the Union of South Africa and in Southern Rhodesia.

These countries are ruled by white men whose ancestry is rooted in Europe. They form the *dominant group*—that is, they are the real source of power in politics, in business, and in the making and enforcement of laws. The dominant group has the means to practice discrimination; the minority groups are its victims. In America the dominant group ranks in prestige and influence above the Indians, Mexicans, Puerto Ricans, and blacks, who comprise the *minority groups*. The white man's prestige makes him a model that others try to imitate. It opens for him the doors to the most desirable clubs and social organizations and eases his climb to positions of power. The white man feels superior to other races and expects them to treat him with deference.

Caucasians do not occupy the center of power everywhere, however. In some of the recently independent African countries black people enjoy the role of dominant group while Europeans and Asiatics are forced into the painful minority position. Many of these Europeans and Asiatics have decided to leave their homes and become refugees rather than lose their old privileged status.

Those whose racial prejudices are strong and deep seated are often referred to as *racists*, or *bigots*. They are firmly convinced that other races don't deserve their respect and that it is all right to humiliate them. Since the term "race" is so vague, the racist may even invent races that don't exist, at least not according to the usual definitions. The most prominent example is the myth of the "Aryan race" created by Hitler and the German Nazi movement.

Hitler declared that the Aryan race is destined to be the master race. "Today we rule Germany," he thundered at his brown-shirted followers: "Tomorrow we will rule the world." Scholars use the word "Aryan" to designate an ancient language once spoken in Persia and India, but in the utterances of Nazi propagandists it stood for a people mentally and morally superior to all others. An Aryan was anybody whom Hitler chose to include in this mythical race. Aryans supposedly claimed superiority over such "races" as Poles, Russians, and Jews. In reality Poles and Russians, as well as Frenchmen, Italians, and also Germans, are *nationalities*. We shall discuss nationality problems in later chapters. The Jewish "race," which is mainly a religious group, was branded by Hitler as a group of useless and dangerous parasites and was condemned to extermination.

ANTI-SEMITISM

The misery that the Hitler regime brought upon the Jews defies description. Six million human beings were murdered with machinelike precision in gas chambers or were tortured to death in concentration camps. Millions of Jews who were luckier escaped with their lives to distant lands. And all this occurred because the Jews were considered a race, a race that does not even really exist.

Or does it? "But I know people who look Jewish," you'll perhaps argue. You may have a colleague or a neighbor with a "Jewish nose." "Aren't these inherited physical characteristics?" you contend. "This is exactly how we defined race." You're right about the definition, but there are no particularly Jewish physical characteristics; such features are frequently found in the Mediterranean subrace that was mentioned earlier. Many Arabs, Greeks, and Turks have similar features. And for every Jew who "looks Jewish" there are a number who don't. When you consider the long, arduous history of Jewish migration, this should not be surprising.

Why then does the myth of the Jewish race persist? It is the stock-in-trade of *anti-Semites*, persons who are hostile to Jews. For them the stereotype of the Jew is a clannish individual who is always out to "make a fast buck" and who, at the same time, is secretly plotting to take over the whole world. He has been blamed for capitalism and for communism, for causing wars and for promoting world government.

As with all prejudice, this is, of course, completely irrational. You may ask, "But why the Jews? Why has resentment against this particular group persisted for so long?" Anti-Semitism existed long before Hitler, nor did it end with the Nazi defeat. In earlier times it was nurtured by religious fanaticism. With the shout of "Christ killers" Christian mobs often fell upon their Jewish neighbors. Being a helpless minority in many countries, Jews were singled out as the favorite *scapegoat*. The origin of this term is the Bible (Lev. 16:20–22); it is stated there that Aaron called down upon a goat all the sins of Israel and sent the animal off into the wilderness. The high priest in Jerusalem continued this ceremony once a year on the highest holiday for as long as the Temple was still standing. Thus, instead of blaming ourselves for poor grades, loss of a job, or any other misfortunes, we like to look around for others to blame—for scapegoats. When nations were suffering and began to grumble against their leaders, it was convenient for the men in charge to divert the anger of the masses by turning it toward the Jews.

What then are the Jews if they are not a race? Some people would answer: a Jew is a person who identifies himself with or is identified by others as being of the Jewish religion. But this is not the whole story. Many people who don't practice the Jewish religion still consider themselves Jews. They hum Jewish songs and laugh at the humor of Jewish jokes. They enjoy certain Jewish foods, especially when meals are taken in the company of other Jews. A Jew, then, whether he attends a synagogue often, rarely, or not at all, is a person who has "a sense of community with a particular cultural and historical tradition."[4]

Most American Jews trace their ancestry back to Eastern Europe where they were once forced to live in *ghettos* as a punishment for their refusal to become Christians. In fact, the word "ghetto" originally designated the Jewish quarters of a medieval city. Sometimes streets leading out of the ghetto were closed off with heavy chains at night and on Sundays. Jewish segregation from the Christian community was made complete.

In this forced isolation the ghetto dwellers built up their own culture. Not only a different religion was practiced inside those chained-off quarters but different customs and institutions also prevailed. Dress and food, music and sanitary habits: the way of life led by the Jew in the ghetto was strange to the majority outside. The ghetto even had a language of its own—Yiddish, an old German dialect mixed with Hebrew words—that Jews spoke among themselves, while Hebrew was reserved for worship and religious study.

The stranger the ways of the Jews seemed to the dominant group, the stronger became mistrust and prejudice, punctuated by periodic cruel persecutions. As they fled to America, Eastern European Jews carried their customs with them. Scared and confused, they crowded together into certain city streets, where they continued for a time the life of the ghetto that they had left behind. But gradually American Jews have been abandoning the old way of life. For example, at one time a number of Yiddish newspapers were published in the larger cities, but today only very few are left, and these are read mostly by older people.

ARE THERE SUPERIOR RACES?

Thus we have races that fit some sort of scientific definition, and we have groups that are still called races even though they don't fit the definition at all. This is very confusing. Therefore some scholars suggest forgetting about the misleading term "race" altogether and using the designation *ethnic group* instead. Under this heading, derived from a Greek word meaning nation, could then be listed racial groups in the biological sense, such as Caucasians, Negroids, and Mongoloids, as well as groups based on a common place of origin, a common religion, common language, customs, and moral standards—in short, on anything passed down through the generations. We had therefore best speak of Chicanos (Mexican-Americans), Polish-Americans, American Jews, and others as ethnic groups.

The racist does not bother about such distinctions. His prejudices exist whether his victims are members of real or imagined races. No matter what the experts say, he divides mankind into those who are "superior" and those who are "inferior." Some races he calls talented, noble, and virtuous, especially the one to which he himself claims to belong, and others he calls unchangeably stupid, unambitious, and immoral.

What has the serious researcher to say about this? All the data have not yet been compiled, but so far nothing has been found to indicate that race determines anybody's IQ, ability, or character. The intelligence and the attitudes that children acquire as they grow up depend largely on their environment. Without exposure to love, books, art, and beauty, any child will turn into an adult deprived of life's fullness.

During World War II various intelligence tests were given to groups of white and black soldiers. Five Northern and eight Southern states were represented. Blacks scored lower than whites as a whole, but Northerners, black or white, had higher marks than Southerners, black or white. Anthropologist Ruth Benedict commented on this:

> Everybody knows that Southerners are inborn equals of Northerners, but in 1917 many Southern States' per capita expenditures for schools were only fractions of those in Northern states, and housing and diet and income were far below average too. . . . The differences did not arise because people were from the North or the South, or because they were white or black, but because of differences in income, education, cultural advantages and other opportunities.[5]

Prejudice divides society into "we" and "they" groups, and such division helps bring about the very faults of which the "we" group accuses the "they" group. "Blacks are ignorant" say many whites, but the whole story is that for a long time "they" have been prevented from obtaining a good education and therefore seem "ignorant." "*We* told you so" then proclaim the very people who are responsible for the defects.

Why is there prejudice? How did it come about? Is it inherent in human nature? No, we are certainly not born prejudiced. Group together black and white, Caucasian and Mongoloid, or any other combination of small children, and they will get along marvelously. They may have their little arguments but not any more so than a group of children all of the same shade of skin. Prejudice is, therefore, learned. It is acquired by growing up in a prejudiced society.

The dominant group in society enjoys its position and wants to preserve it. It will use, at times, harsh means to keep any challenger in his place. If the challenger persists, the social climate may become stormy and thunderous.

In the South violence has often been the response of enraged whites to blacks who attempt to improve their lot. In the spring of 1970, when the courts ordered that the schools of Lamar, South Carolina, be integrated, a white mob attacked a bus carrying black children to a formerly all-white school. The bus was overturned, and the children barely escaped serious physical harm.

Psychologists find that prejudice grows most abundantly in the soil of personal frustration, and this is true of both dominant and minority groups. When Northern blacks demonstrated for better housing, hordes of angry young whites showered them with obscenities and, what was considerably more dangerous, with broken bottles and pieces of metal. Many of the attackers were the sons of immigrant workers who had themselves belonged to minority groups and had suffered from prejudices a few decades earlier. Those who have experienced disappointments often take it out on those who rank below them in social status.

Minority groups may not have the power to punish others for their lack of success, but, at least in their own minds, they can blame misfortune on discrimination, something that is beyond their control. A Jewish applicant is denied admission to a high-ranking school. Is it because of his personal shortcomings or because of his being Jewish? A black is refused a job. Can he believe that the employer gave the job to a better qualified candidate, or did the employer disqualify him because of race? Discrimination, real or imagined, builds walls between men.

THE RACE ISSUE TODAY

A number of racial minorities living in the United States have very real complaints against their treatment by the dominant group. Mexican-Americans, particularly in the southwestern states, have known what it means to be treated as second-class citizens; so have Puerto Ricans who migrated to New York City in quest of a nebulous promised land full of "milk and honey."

The fate of a half million American Indians continues to be a shameful blot on the American record. The white man subdued the Indians by disregarding all the loudly professed principles of justice and mercy. Excusing his cruel discriminatory acts by declaring that the Indian is not quite human, the white American drove the Indian from his land, deprived him of his livelihood, and destroyed his tribal way of life. Indians were forced into reservations, usually located in the most barren sections of the country, where most of them are still kept in conditions of chronic need and ill health. "Indian reservations exist as poverty-stricken islands surrounded by an ocean of American bounty."[6]

But the problem of the black American overshadows that of all other racial issues, by sheer numbers alone, if not for other reasons. According to estimates made by the United States Bureau of the Census our total population numbered approximately 203,000,000 by mid-1968. A little over 22,350,000 people, or over 10 percent, were black.[7]

Blacks and whites have lived in this country for a long time, but not until the former—the largest minority group in the country—began to strain against the bounds of the role assigned to them as an inferior group did the argument about race mushroom into a crisis. Many have even called it a revolution.

For almost a century after the Emancipation Proclamation *segre-*

gation was the code of the South, where most Negroes lived. By state laws and by custom the races were kept apart everywhere from streetcars to cemeteries and from churches to taverns. This practice, the "Jim Crow" arrangement, as blacks dubbed it, always underscored their inferior position. In certain areas a black man could enter a white man's home only by the back door, the servants' entrance. He could enjoy a motion picture if he had the money for the ticket but only from the balcony. Segregation has contributed to the poverty and backwardness of the South. A community that could have supported one good high school had to maintain two inferior ones instead. Two sets of lavatories, drinking fountains, or waiting rooms had to be provided where one would have been sufficient. Often the white society did not even bother to duplicate facilities. Blacks were simply denied access to those that existed. In many towns, for example, black children did not have the public parks or swimming pools that white children enjoyed.

Although segregation by law (*de jure*) is absent in the North, segregation in fact (*de facto*) is not. Minority groups are kept out of white residential areas. Many avenues to employment and business remain blocked. Lodges and fraternities proudly assert their "lily-whiteness," and so do many churches. "Sunday from eleven to twelve is the most segregated hour of the week," blacks bitterly complain.

All of these segregationist practices have nurtured the growth of black ghettos in our large cities. Neglect and overcrowding have turned these districts into slums where crime and delinquency are rampant. Employment for people living in the ghetto is scarce, especially for the male. Where a man is deprived of his role as the family provider, desertion and broken homes frequently result. The future of race relations is further clouded by the fact that young ghetto dwellers and white youths are complete strangers to each other. Though they may live only a few city blocks apart, so little contact exists between them that they could just as well be the inhabitants of different planets.

In the past several years racial problems have become the all-encompassing topic. In the newspapers the subject is found on the front page, on the editorial page, in the sports section, and even in advertisements. It is also the major topic in religious news.

For a long time blacks played their "inferior" roles in sullen but passive silence. Then a change began to take place. Some had gone to college; some had worked themselves up to middle-class status. Having tasted the educational and economic opportunities that whites enjoyed, blacks began to resent the neglect and contempt that they had previously put up with. "We too have studied the Constitution and the Bill of Rights," they declared. "We know the meaning of the Pledge of Allegiance: 'liberty and justice for all'—that includes us. It is time that white society lived up to its solemn pledges."

Through television and other mass media the whole black community became aware of the prosperity and the comfort that the majority of Americans enjoyed. Blacks saw only white children playing on the well-tended suburban lawns pictured in commercials. White couples were shown strolling in luxurious resorts; behind the desks of well-appointed offices sat white executives dictating to white secretaries, white pharmacists, white road surveyors, white housewives chatted in front of their split-level bungalows: it was a world that the black had constantly before his eyes, yet a world from which he was excluded.

As a result, black resistance to various forms of discrimination stiffened. Methods long used by political groups and labor unions were adopted for the struggle. The pressure of voluntary organization was brought into play. The National Association for the Advancement of Colored People (NAACP), founded in 1909, jolted white consciences by taking the most glaring cases of racial injustice to court. Another organization, the Urban League, only two years younger, is still trying to assure the black his fair share of jobs and decent housing.

In 1954 racial segregation of schoolchildren became the most dramatic point of contention. In one of its most significant decisions the Supreme Court of the United States declared school segregation to be contrary to the spirit of the Constitution. Obviously the decision did not change overnight long ingrained racist attitudes and practices, but it gave support and encouragement to the forces struggling to end discrimination.

In this struggle a voice was raised loudly and clearly, the voice of a black Baptist preacher from Georgia. Dr. Martin Luther King, Jr., became the spokesman of the oppressed and the poor. When Mrs. Rosa Parks was arrested in Montgomery, Alabama, for refusing to move to the "colored" section of a city bus, Dr. King organized a bus strike. This economic boycott engaged the interest of the whole world. Grudgingly the bus company gave up one of the South's time-honored customs. Seating became *integrated*.

Martin Luther King became an international figure, and in 1964 he received the coveted Nobel Prize for Peace. His call for nonviolent protest was heard, and this method caught on. Long discouraged and intimidated, blacks found a new sense of pride. Many sympathetic whites, among them students, teachers, and clergymen, rallied to their support. By means of peaceful demonstrations they protested segregation in Southern parks and bus depots, on beaches and at lunch counters. The defenders of the old order fought back viciously. The nonviolent demonstrators were clubbed by Southern state troopers and sheriffs' deputies. They were set upon by police dogs and drenched by high-pressure water hoses. Several civil rights workers, among them not only blacks but also a white minister and a white housewife, lost their lives.

The new thrust of the black movement expressed itself in new organizational forms, more forceful and more impatient than any that had existed before. Dr. King himself led the Southern Christian Leadership

Conference (SCLC) until his assassination. More radical in their public expressions and in their tactics were the Student Nonviolent Coordinating Committee (SNCC) and the Congress of Racial Equality (CORE).

The climax of this whole attempt to make public some glaring faults in our democratic system came with the civil rights march into Washington, D.C., on August 28, 1963. This mass rally of Americans demanding that the words of our Constitution be finally translated into action also marked the high point in the career of Dr. King as a leader in the nonviolent tradition of India's Mahatma Gandhi.

Impressed and pressured by this newly exhibited vigor among minority groups, Congress passed several laws destined to right old wrongs. The most far reaching of these new federal laws was the Civil Rights Act of 1964. It provided that citizens, especially blacks, may not be kept from voting through the use of phony literacy tests; it also asserted the right of all persons to be equally served in hotels, restaurants, theaters, and other places of public accommodation. Such laws may look good on paper, but their enforcement was, in many instances, sabotaged by Southern state officials—and they hardly touched Northern problems.

Still, significant progress has been made. Blacks now vote in increas-

Blacks in America today are voicing an intense pride in their heritage.
Charles Gatewood

ing numbers, and a few are even being elected to political offices. In 1968 there were 385 elected black officials scattered through the South, among them several state legislators and even law enforcement officers such as Sheriff Lucius D. Amerson of Macon County, Alabama.[8] One must remember that in some parts of the South sheriffs wield almost absolute power, especially over blacks. In 1969 Charles Evers became the mayor of Fayette, Mississippi, the first black man to hold such an office in the Deep South.

Despite these token successes the plight of the poor in our cities still remains, and most of these poor are Puerto Ricans, Mexican-Americans, and Negroes. The black population in the inner city is, in fact, constantly increasing. Despite civil rights laws housing is becoming not less but more segregated as whites move to the suburbs. This is *de facto* segregation.

Tension grew in the slums. New black leaders appeared, young and forceful, who were impatient with the slow results of peaceful protest and complicated court proceedings. They wanted action. Their shrill voices shouted hatred and vengeance. The cry of "black power" echoed through streets and meeting halls, a slogan open to many interpretations, but characteristic of the new defiant attitude among many blacks. In the ghetto riots that erupted lives and property were lost, and the victims were mostly other blacks.

Extremists, such as the Black Muslim leader Muhammad Elijah, were no longer satisfied with only ending segregation.

> The Muslims want a national state of their own. Muhammad states flatly that "there can be no peace in the world until every man is in his own country." The white man's country, he says, is in Europe. Nevertheless, the Muslims are willing to divide the country with the white man at least on a temporary basis.[9]

One of the most eloquent apostles of black power is Stokely Carmichael who declares: "Black people should and must fight back. Nothing more quickly repels someone bent on destroying you than the unequivocal message, 'O.K., fool, make your move, and run the risk I run—of dying.' "[10]

The violent language and gestures that express a sharpening of black resistance are used by only a small number of blacks, however. Far more widespread is a new pride in being black. The old custom of aping the white man, of applying cosmetics to whiten the skin and straighten the hair, has lost much of its appeal. There was a time when light-skinned blacks looked contemptuously upon their darker brethren, even refusing to date them or allow them into their social circles. Now many emphasize their blackness. Pointing to their African heritage, which has lain dormant for so long, blacks display African dress and hair styles. And at high schools and colleges they press for curriculums that study African culture and languages in addition to the long-neglected study of the black man's contribution to American history.

Yet despite the new search for identity by a proud young generation, most blacks, like other minority groups, would probably agree with the distinguished writer Louis E. Lomax who points out that the American black is, after all, still more American than he is African. He has adopted the language, the religion, the ways of thought and action of this country even though his ancestors were unwillingly brought here as slaves. What he wants is to be fully recognized as a member of the cultural community to which he belongs anyhow.[11]

The whole question of racial problems has been vastly complicated by the armed conflict in Vietnam which took on all the features of a bloody war in 1964. Many blacks who were drafted or who volunteered for military duty found in the armed forces their first chance to act as men, to be accepted as equals. Others, however, protested that they were being forced to fight a "white man's war" that they found unjust and in which they felt they had no stake.

Today, the race problem is still an open sore on the body of our society (as is Vietnam). Discrimination against blacks runs high, and so does the resentment of the black man. But even though a satisfactory solution seems far away, it can be reached. Prejudice is acquired, not inborn. It need not be permanent. The Japanese attack on Pearl Harbor in

1941 brought to the surface a long-smoldering hatred for Japanese-Americans, especially on the West Coast. Citizens of Japanese background were indiscriminately rounded up and shipped off to places resembling concentration camps. The human damage in ruined careers and interrupted education, not to speak of emotional pains and economic losses, can hardly be estimated. Yet twenty-five years later, raw hostility has been largely replaced by warm sympathy and a genuine liking of Japanese ways and products.

Again, prejudice is learned, not inborn. What can be learned, can also be unlearned. Even persons who have long practiced discrimination cannot help but have their cherished prejudices profoundly shaken when they come into close day-by-day contact with members of other ethnic groups or when they make a sincere effort to study the history, special problems, and contributions to art, music, sports, or any other field of human endeavor of such groups.

Main Ideas
1. We live in a race-conscious society.
2. A race is a group of people with a composite of inherited physical characteristics.
3. The division of mankind into races remains inexact.
4. Racial prejudice often leads to discrimination by the dominant group against minority groups.
5. The term "race" has been incorrectly applied to various national groups and also to members of the Jewish religion.
6. The Jewish minority has been the favorite scapegoat in various societies.
7. There is no evidence that there are intellectually and morally superior or inferior races or ethnic groups.
8. The race issue, and particularly the relationship between blacks and whites, is now one of the most important—perhaps the most important—domestic problems in the United States.
9. A new militancy and a new racial pride among American blacks have given the problem particular urgency.

Important Terms
Anti-Semitism
Bigot
De facto segregation
De jure segregation
Discrimination
Dominant group
Ethnic group
Extremist
Ghetto
Integration

Minority group
Nationality
Prejudice
Race
Race consciousness
Racist
Scapegoat
Segregation
Stereotype

Conclusion

What can be done about all this? Let's not look to the social scientist for a specific answer, for he is not a fighter or a propagandist. He observes society and then interprets what he sees. He is in a position to describe the effects of prejudice and discriminatory practices on mental health, economic life, and the democratic process. This information is then made available to civic, spiritual, and educational leaders who want to take action against social ills. The social scientist who has studied racial problems can also point out what changes are taking place. He steps back, so to speak, and reviews the turbulent scene from a distance. Thus he can, with some degree of accuracy, predict what actions will help speed reform along.

Notes

1. These two scenes are composites of actual occurrences that were reported by various news media and also mentioned in several books, such as James W. Vander Zanden, "The Klan Revival," in Peter I. Rose (ed.), *The Study of Society: An Integrated Anthology* (New York: Random House, 1967), pp. 860 ff. and Louis E. Lomax, *The Negro Revolution* (New York: Harper & Row, 1962).
2. Peter I. Rose, *The Subject Is Race* (New York: Oxford University Press, 1968), p. 21.
3. M. F. Ashley-Montagu, *Race, Science and Humanity* (Princeton, N.J.: Van Nostrand, 1963), p. 132.
4. Kenneth Stern, "Is Religion Necessary?" in Peter I. Rose (ed.), *The Ghetto and Beyond* (New York: Random House, 1969), p. 190.
5. Ruth Benedict, *The Races of Mankind* (New York: Public Affairs Committee, 1944), pp. 17–18.
6. Peter Farb, "The American Indian: A Portrait in Limbo," *Saturday Review*, October 12, 1968, p. 29.
7. U.S. Department of Commerce, Bureau of the Census, *Population Estimates*, July 1, 1968.
8. Walter Rugaber, "Blacks in Power," *New York Times Student Weekly*, December 16, 1968, p. 4.
9. C. Eric Lincoln, "The Black Muslim Movement," in Rose, *The Study of Society, op. cit.*, p. 874.
10. Stokely Carmichael and Charles V. Hamilton, *Black Power: The Politics of Liberation in America* (New York: Random House, 1967), p. 52.
11. Lomax, *op. cit.*

Suggestions for Further Reading

Baldwin, James. *Nobody Knows My Name.* New York: Dell, 1963 (paperback).
  The well-known novelist writes about discrimination.
Brown, Claude. *Manchild in the Promised Land.* New York: Macmillan, 1965.
  Autobiographical account of a childhood in Harlem.

Dimont, Max I. *Jews, God and History*. New York: New American Library, 1962 (paperback). History of the Jews emphasizing their contributions and the persecutions they suffered.

Griffin, John Howard. *Black Like Me*. New York: New American Library, 1960 (paperback). A white journalist disguised as a Negro experiences discrimination in the South.

Hoover, Dwight W. (ed.). *Understanding Negro History*. Chicago: Quadrangle Books, 1968 (paperback).

King, Martin Luther. *Why We Can't Wait*. New York: Harper & Row, 1964. The since-martyred black leader explains his program of nonviolent resistance.

Kitagawa, Daisuke. *Issei and Nisei: The Internment Years*. New York: Seabury Press, 1967. Discrimination against Japanese-Americans during World War II.

Lee, Harper. *To Kill a Mockingbird*. New York: Popular Library, 1962 (paperback). Novel set against the background of race relations in the South.

Malcolm X. *The Autobiography of Malcolm X*. New York: Grove Press, 1964. Written shortly before the assassination of this black extremist.

Paton, Alan. *Cry, the Beloved Country*. New York: Scribner, 1961. Novel depicting race relations in South Africa.

Styron, William. *The Confessions of Nat Turner*. New York: Random House, 1966. Novel about a slave rebellion that failed.

Wright, Richard. *Black Boy*. New York: Harper & Row, 1966 (paperback). Autobiography of a black writer.

PART TWO: LOVE, SECURITY, BELONGING

What is love?
How do you find a partner
for marriage?
What are the chances of success
in marriage?
Where does sex fit in?

6   LOVE IS THE SWEETEST THING ON EARTH
love—sex—courtship

LOVE

The love between a man and a woman is a topic of never-ending fascination. Songs of all styles, from classic to Western and acid rock, rejoice over happy love and lament unhappy love. Love inspires the pens of poets and the brushes of painters. Its complications supply endless material for story, stage, and film. We never tire of hearing about the trials of Romeo and Juliet and other famous lovers of literature and history. Our language is replete with such phrases as "falling in love" and "love at first sight." *Romantic love* is described as something wonderful. It is associated with flowers and springtime, with moonlight, beauty, and youth.

    But what is love really? If we are to believe what we see on television and at the movies, it must be the most unselfish feeling there is. Romeo is willing to die for his Juliet. He wants to give her everything she fancies, including the moon. Yet psychology tells us that love is selfish, that our true aim in loving is to satisfy our own needs. "Every person, as a separate individual, experiences aloneness. And so we strive actively to overcome our aloneness by some form of love."[1] Man must overcome his loneliness, or he will ruin his life. Without love he lives in an unbearable prison. "The awareness

97

of human separation without reunion by love . . . is the source of shame. It is at the same time the source of guilt and anxiety."[2]

In loving we become increasingly vulnerable. When two people love each other, they become adept at providing needed satisfaction for one another. As their love increases, their dependence on one another must likewise increase. If, for any reason, the relationship should end, the shock of the loss may produce extreme pain. Such loss has frequently been the cause of suicide, murder, and other violent acts.

Love then has two components: first, doing something for the other person in order to satisfy yourself; second, having the other person do something for you, which will further satisfy your desires. Love is mutual dependence. It takes time to learn how to satisfy the other person, and the greater the love, the more vulnerable we become to mishaps in the love relationship. We must be willing to place our trust entirely in the other person. This is the real test of love. It is such a difficult task that many love relationships never progress past the beginning stages of interdependence.

Occasionally a father will claim that his children owe him devotion because of the sacrifices he has made in raising them. He feels that he has done more for them than they have ever done for him and that a time will come when they should repay him. Such a father certainly demonstrates the selfishness of love, for he has not received the gratification he needs. Because he was not truly able to love his children, despite the shelter, clothing, and other necessities he provided for them, he hopes to force love from them instead. The gratification of loving a child should more than compensate for any hardship experienced by the parent while raising it. We hear of mothers whose love looks not like love at all but more like a desire to dominate and control their children even when they are old enough to chart their own course. But many more mothers exhibit a completely unselfish love, the delight of which is to watch the unfolding of the child's personality. The mother may want very badly to keep the growing child close to her, but she does not stand in his way no matter what direction his life may take.

Young children love their parents despite what the parents may do to them, but in adult relationships, especially those between husband and wife, the possibilities of conflict and frustration are much greater. If you lovingly give yourself up to your mate only to discover that your trust is not returned, that your spouse is, for some reason, incapable of loving you, the shock could be shattering, and the wound deep and beyond the chance of healing. The love relationship between adults requires constant work to keep it whole.

ARE YOU IN LOVE?

Certainly a young person knows when he or she is in love. But what some young people experience may be romantic love and not the abiding love that we have discussed. Beautiful and exhilarating as romantic love is, it brings about a fairly superficial relationship. Deep love takes time to develop because one cannot learn overnight how to satisfy another's needs. Some persons are very adept in forming relationships quickly, but what may first look as if it could develop into a highly rewarding experience for two people may sometimes run into a dead end very quickly. This can happen if one of the partners has failed to develop real trust in the other.

Abiding love can also fail to blossom when communication between the lovers is lacking. Suppose a girl is not successful in satisfying her boyfriend's need for companionship. If she notices the difficulty, she may be able to do something about it, but if the boy is unable to communicate his lack of satisfaction, she may be unable to make the necessary corrections, and their love is in danger of foundering.

It is easy to fall in love. One only needs to find a person of the opposite sex who is physically attractive and behaves in a pleasing manner. It is infinitely more difficult to remain in love over a long period. One necessary requirement for abiding love is to become well acquainted with the true personality of the partner. Another is that each person sees himself accurately. If we misjudge ourselves in order to protect our self-concept, we will, in all likelihood, also misjudge the person with whom we deal intimately.

SEX

The word "love" is often used when "sex" would be the more appropriate term. "Making love" is considered a more acceptable synonym for having sexual relations. When we speak of sex, or *erotic passion*, we have in mind the desire of males and females to have intimate physical contact with each other. This physical contact results in offspring. Without the sex drive there would be very few new human beings.

The purely biological sex urge, however, cannot be separated from the emotional attachment that we have called love. Human beings don't mate—as most animals do—with just any available member of the opposite sex. How we express or restrain the sex urge depends largely on the standards set by the society in which we live. In fact, even the male who engages the services of a prostitute is socially conditioned, and he will probably try to select an attractive female though love does not enter the picture. Whereas love has long been a very desirable topic to write, talk, and sing about, the topic of sex has not always been treated with such freedom. We can distinguish a whole range of social attitudes toward sex, from extremely *permissive* to extremely *restrictive*.

Members of Western societies who tolerate no other standards but their own might display shock about the permissiveness of the Lepcha in India. Lepcha girls regularly engage in sexual intercourse by the time they are eleven or twelve years old. It is thought that this aids in their maturation. Such societies usually allow children to observe adult sexual behavior. Talk about sex and much of the sex play is quite open.

The Indian society, as well as other Oriental societies, displays a frankness in sexual matters that often embarrasses American visitors, who are used to a more prudish attitude toward sex. When tourists visit Hindu temples, they can see carved figures of men and women in the most frankly sexual embraces. Sex is not set apart as something unclean and forbidden but is included in art, religion, and in everyday life as something natural. "No one tells children stories about babies brought in little baskets by doctors or storks. When the children ask questions about physiological facts, they are given the answers."[3]

On the other hand, highly restrictive attitudes are found among the Kwoma in New Guinea where boys are warned not to touch their genitals. If a woman sees a boy with an erection, she will beat his penis with a stick. Murngin boys in Australia are moved to a separate house when they are five years old to prevent them from watching the sex act at home.[4]

Our own society shows strangely contradictory attitudes. It is "sex-centric but sex-rejecting." Whether the American watches television or movies, whether he looks at the covers of magazines or paperbacks or at advertisements for perfumes and hair tonics, he finds sex staring in his face. Sexual stimulation is everywhere, "but when teen-agers do what they have obviously been invited to do, society either punishes them or looks embarrassedly the other way."[5]

The attitude of embarrassment and shocked righteousness dates back a long time and has its roots mainly in religious teachings. In the past Christian spokesmen condemned any sexual expression outside the marriage bed as a grave sin. Even marital relations were looked upon as a necessary evil, and religious people who had completely renounced any sex life were considered models of virtue and were praised for their purity. Anything connected with sex, then, was seen as impure, improper, and dirty.

In the United States the strong *Puritan* influence strengthened this negative attitude toward sex. The best way of dealing with sex was not to discuss it or write about it—that is, to pretend that it did not exist. A complicated restrictive code developed with various penalties for *obscene* behavior, foul language, premarital intercourse, prostitution, and homosexuality.

However, laws and penalties did not do away with all these expressions of sexuality; they only drove them underground. Frequently people professed a virtuous attitude publicly but followed more liberal rules privately. This hypocrisy is now under attack by a young generation that recognizes the contradiction between the way adults expect young people to behave and the way that adults themselves behave.

In recent years, especially since World War II, a significant change has come about in what observers call "the public aspect of sex." In print and in lecture halls the topic is being thoroughly discussed. Students seriously question the old standards and demand justification for the rules imposed on them. Best-selling books describe sexual activity in great detail, often with ample use of "four-letter words." Nudity, long banned and restricted to burlesque houses, has made its appearance on stage and screen. Magazines are also letting down barriers to sexual expression in their stories as well as in their illustrations. Significant in this regard is the great popularity of *Playboy* magazine among young men. This well-adorned magazine is not exclusively devoted to sex, but it deals with the subject unashamedly. Its pictures of nude beauties openly cater to the male interest in the female body.

Painters and sculptors have long seen in the human body an object of beauty that gives enjoyment to the beholder. And today we hear it asserted more and more that the physical union of human bodies is not degrading but rather an enriching and ennobling experience. The writer Terry Southern suggests that we should perhaps substitute another word for "sex," which, in the minds of many people, has taken on the meaning of something dirty, something to leer at, and to scribble about on the walls of rest rooms.

> I think we should talk about "eroticism." It's a good word, you know, deriving from Eros [the Greek god of love] and having to do with love. There is such a thing that is esthetically erotic which is very positive and beautiful. I think what is described as "pornography" is usually something erotic that just didn't make it.[6]

Sex is finally being brought into the open. But does this also herald a change in the private relationships between males and females? Scientists are not sure.

> In looking at [the changes], it is important to differentiate between the public and private faces of sex. The changes in the public face of sexuality are easy to discern. The hard part is to find the implications of these public changes for the private face of sexuality.[7]

DEVELOPMENT OF SEX AND LOVE

Human beings are ready to perform the sex act and to reproduce after they have reached *puberty*. But the sex drive has not appeared overnight. It has been developing and maturing throughout childhood (see Chapter 1).

According to psychoanalytical theory the ability to love a mate develops through several stages. These stages follow each other according to a definitely set pattern. But an individual may have difficulty in developing from one stage to the next. Such difficulties are primarily rooted in his environment. A baby's first love object is his mother because she provides nourishment and *oral* stimulation either from her breast or from a bottle. Only when the child receives adequate stimulation from the mother can he

102 An Introduction to Social Science

move successfully into the next stage. If the child does not receive adequate stimulation, *fixation* (partial or complete stopping) may result.

Between the first and the second year of life the child moves on to the second stage of development, the *anal stage*. His source of gratification shifts from the mouth to the *anus*. His mother continues to please him by changing his diapers and cleaning up the messes he creates. Eventually the child tries to please his mother by learning bowel and bladder control. This is his first attempt to show love and affection.

If nothing interferes, the child progresses to the *phallic stage* at about the age of three. His source of gratification now comes from playing with the genitals. He will ask questions about sex and may engage in some sex play with other children. The *Oedipus complex* (a boy's jealousy of his own father) and the *Electra complex* (a girl's jealousy of her own mother) become apparent.

In the next stage of development, the *latent stage*, the Oedipus and Electra complexes are being resolved. Realizing that he cannot replace his father as his mother's love object, a male child instead *identifies* with his father and tries to imitate him. He assumes his father's values and he will later seek a mate in much the same manner as, in his knowledge, his father found his mother. But if the Oedipus complex cannot be resolved, perhaps because the mother encourages the son's attachment to her, he may become a "mama's boy" and never be able to find a mate.

The latent stage continues into puberty. Now the genitals become fully developed, and the *secondary sex characteristics* appear, such as the female breast and *pubic hair* around the genitals. For a while the young person rejects any intimate contact with the opposite sex. Homosexual play and *masturbation* are not infrequent.

Finally, after the individual has successfully passed through the preliminary stages, he enters the *genital stage*. In this stage of development the active and conscious search for a mate begins.[8]

Stages of Sexual Development in the Child
Oral
Anal
Phallic
Latent
Genital

As a child's body develops and grows to maturity, he also learns the art of loving. The first love objects are his own parents; other love objects appear later. People who do not learn to love deeply at an early age may have great difficulty loving deeply as adults. This was borne out by a study undertaken in 1938. Seven hundred ninety-two married couples answered questions about their childhood and sexual adjustment in marriage. Childhood background was found to have a definite relationship to marital happiness. Four items in particular were listed as basic to success in marriage: superior happiness of parents in their marital relationship, childhood happiness, lack of conflict with mother, and home discipline that was firm but not harsh.[9]

CHOOSING A MATE

After a child has grown to maturity, it is time to get married and start a family. This requires that two people of the opposite sex somehow get together. How, among the millions of human beings, do a particular male and a particular female find each other for the purpose of marriage?

The way it happens in countless stories is that boy meets girl at a party, at work, at college. Hearts pound; bells ring. Boy falls in love with girl and vice versa. Boy declares his love for girl and proposes marriage. Girl accepts, and a wedding date is set. We are used to the idea that love is all that matters in the selection of a mate. We tend to look upon any other considerations with contempt or ridicule.

Actually, being in love is not at all a common reason among human societies for getting married. In fact, only a small number of societies recognize it as a valid reason, and this recognition is fairly recent in time. Love rarely figures, for instance, in the marriage arrangements of primitive people, and it has also been downgraded by some higher civilizations. "Love between a man and a woman is not a phenomenon of uncivilized society. . . . The Greeks conceived of it as a madness by which a person was afflicted through the practice or malevolence of some god or goddess."[10]

Most societies set up strict rules to assure that desirable marriages take place and even stricter rules to prevent undesirable ones. The prohibition of *incest*, the mating of close blood relatives, is almost universal, but there are differences concerning the degree of "closeness." The Catholic Church, for example, forbids marriage between first cousins, but such marriage is not considered improper in other religions. Isolated tribes, on the other hand, may rule out marriage between tribal members completely, probably because it is felt that everyone has become related to everyone else through long periods of intermarriage.

Young people of the Kurnai tribe in Australia get around this rule by eloping. Filled with moral indignation, the whole village sets out in hot pursuit of the pair. If the offending couple is caught, they are killed outright. But if they manage to stay hidden until the birth of a child, they are then received back into the community.[11] Another people, the Jie of Uganda, go to extremes in keeping their marriageable young people from choosing their own mates. Not only must both families give their permission, but even close friends of the parents.[12]

Most social groups find it desirable for their members to choose mates from within the group (*endogamy*). If young people are allowed to make their selection solely on the basis of romantic love, they may violate this rule. Therefore it is often thought safest that the parents take care of mate selection. It was and still is common in many parts of the world for two families to arrange a marriage between their children. In India this arrangement was often made while the children involved were barely able to walk. Thus love could not be an obstacle. The aim of each family was to connect itself with another family of equal or higher social standing. In Japan and medieval Europe, where wealth was measured in land, prearranged marriages were mainly real estate transactions. The bride and groom had little or nothing to say in the matter.

Where matches are arranged by parents, it is necessary that two families that consider each other desirable come in contact with one another. This has often been brought about with the help of a matchmaker. He or she knows all about eligible families with children of the proper age. The matchmaker acts as a go-between for the families and expects, of course, some reward for his services. The musical play *Fiddler on the Roof* shows *Yenta*, a matchmaker, in action in a Jewish *shtetl* of old Russia. In America many people like to make amateurish attempts at matchmaking, but it is hardly a profitable occupation.

The higher the social rank of the family, the more limited, it seems, is the freedom of the children to marry for love. Young people of higher social rank are, in many instances, closely watched by chaperons so that there is no opportunity for private meetings between lovers. Love is deemed a threat to the upper ranks, and nowhere can this be better observed than among the royal families of old. The king of France, let us say, wanted an alliance with Spain; so he arranged a marriage between his son and the Spanish royal princess. Nobody considered love, and the young couple was expected to produce children, preferably a male heir. No wonder that kings so often sought real affection in the arms of mistresses.

Of the many strange ways of choosing a mate that we find in different cultures let us mention several more, such as wife buying and wife stealing. During the past several decades males in certain parts of East Africa have been complaining that the price of wives has gone up considerably since the influx of Western ideas of sex equality. According to legend, when ancient Rome had a shortage of young women, her men went out and attacked the Sabines, a neighboring tribe, and carried off a number of girls. When the enraged Sabine men came to reclaim their women, the girls declared they were quite happy to stay with their captors. Peace was arranged, and in time the two tribes became one. The legend indicates that such occurrences were not unknown.

In a "suitor service marriage" a man must work for his future wife's family in order to earn her. The Bible tells how Jacob worked for seven years to earn his beloved Rachel. Sometimes a man inherits a wife. According to old Hebrew law the brother of a deceased husband had to marry the widow in order to give her a home and protection.

Today a man who obviously marries a woman for her money is an object of perpetual sneers. A century or two ago marrying for money was not at all uncommon in the highest social circles of England and Germany. Aristocrats with exalted titles and little cash wooed young ladies whose fathers were rich but of lowlier background, and when they were married, everybody was happy. The groom had his finances straightened out, and the bride obtained a much coveted title.

AMERICAN COURTSHIP

The term *courtship* dates from a time when young men were supposed to "court," or woo, their ladies in a very romantic fashion by serenading them under windows, sending them love poems and presents, and praising their beauty in exaggerated terms. For our purpose we will use the word to indicate all the customary contacts between the sexes before marriage.

At first glance American society seems to offer its young people a wide choice of mates, but a closer look indicates that we, too, are subject to many conditions and restraints. First of all, if young people are to select their own mates, they must have occasions to meet suitable persons of the opposite sex. Where do single males and single females meet one another? Since many American schools and colleges are *coeducational,* they are obvious meeting places. School-sponsored dances and other social activities are particularly aimed at helping young people get better acquainted. Usually it is the boy's task to ask the girl out for the evening, but some dances are strictly "stag," and others leave the initiative to the girls.

Young people living in the same neighborhood have ample chances to get acquainted. Some of the ways they meet are through hobby groups, sports activities, and church activities. Churches are particularly interested in having their members marry within the flock. Their young people's groups or singles' clubs serve this purpose more or less openly.

A technique that is often frowned upon, especially by girls, is the "pickup." Boys will approach previously unknown girls on the street, in a movie theater, or in an eating place patronized by the younger set. The idea is that a very desirable girl should not have to depend on such chance meetings.

Although he may be free from his family's intervention in contacting a possible mate, the young person may find the job a burden. It can be a hardship, especially in the cold, impersonal environment of the modern city or when a strong feeling of insecurity holds a person back.

Modern business practices offer some assistance in such cases. In certain magazines one can advertise his wish to make the acquaintance of someone of the opposite sex. The various underground papers that are published in our large cities and near university campuses specialize in classified ads for people seeking not only companionship but also a great variety of sexual pleasures. Or a prospective candidate for marriage can enroll in a "lonely hearts club." All he has to do is send in a description of himself and the kind of mate he would like to find, together with the required fee. The "club" will then furnish him with the names of likely persons to contact.

A novel twist to the "lonely hearts" approach is the selection of a date or dance partner by computer. For some reason the help of a computer is quite acceptable to many people who hold "lonely hearts clubs" in rather low esteem.

Once a male and a female have met through one means or other, they usually begin *dating*. Dating is a peculiarly American habit, quite incomprehensible to persons raised in some other cultures. Tom may date Mary one weekend and Linda the next. Girls may vary their dates the same way. There need not be any serious commitment to a single person. Rather, young people are encouraged to "play the field" so that they will have a wider sampling from which to make their final choices.

Aside from romance dating is an important part of our recreational life. Many sports and entertainment activities call for attendance by couples. Parents encourage dating by providing money and transportation and by welcoming the companions of their children into their homes.

The real purpose of dating is accomplished when two partners decide that their meetings are more satisfactory than any other dates. They fall in love, and from now on they "go steady." Falling in love is not only "wonderful," as the song proclaims, it is also an experience for which the child is being prepared during his whole upbringing. At home, at school, and in various youth activities the child is, by degrees, encouraged to make his own decisions. Less and less he relies on father and mother in the selection of friends or in the choice of pastimes. The moment when he or she finds an abiding love brings about the final freedom from parental attachment.

As romantic love progresses, the loved person appears to be increasingly desirable in the other person's eyes. Feelings are expressed by kissing and other intimate gestures, commonly called "necking." The sex urge is aroused, and physical intimacy may culminate in sexual intercourse. But the moral standards of our society often restrain sexual behavior. It is primarily the girl who sets the limits to the relationship.

As the two lovers become more certain of their love, they want to make public their intention of staying together permanently. Following the custom of the American middle class, they become engaged. A date is set for the wedding, which climaxes and also brings to an end the period of courtship. Society shows its vital interest in the act of engagement and even more so in the wedding by surrounding these events with rich ceremonies and many customs of a symbolic nature. The participants may be only dimly aware of the original meanings attached to the symbols. For example, the white dress of the bride denotes her virginity, throwing rice at the bridal couple symbolizes a wish for fertility, and so on.

The wedding ceremony signifies, at least in theory, the moment at which the relationship between a man and a woman becomes permanent.

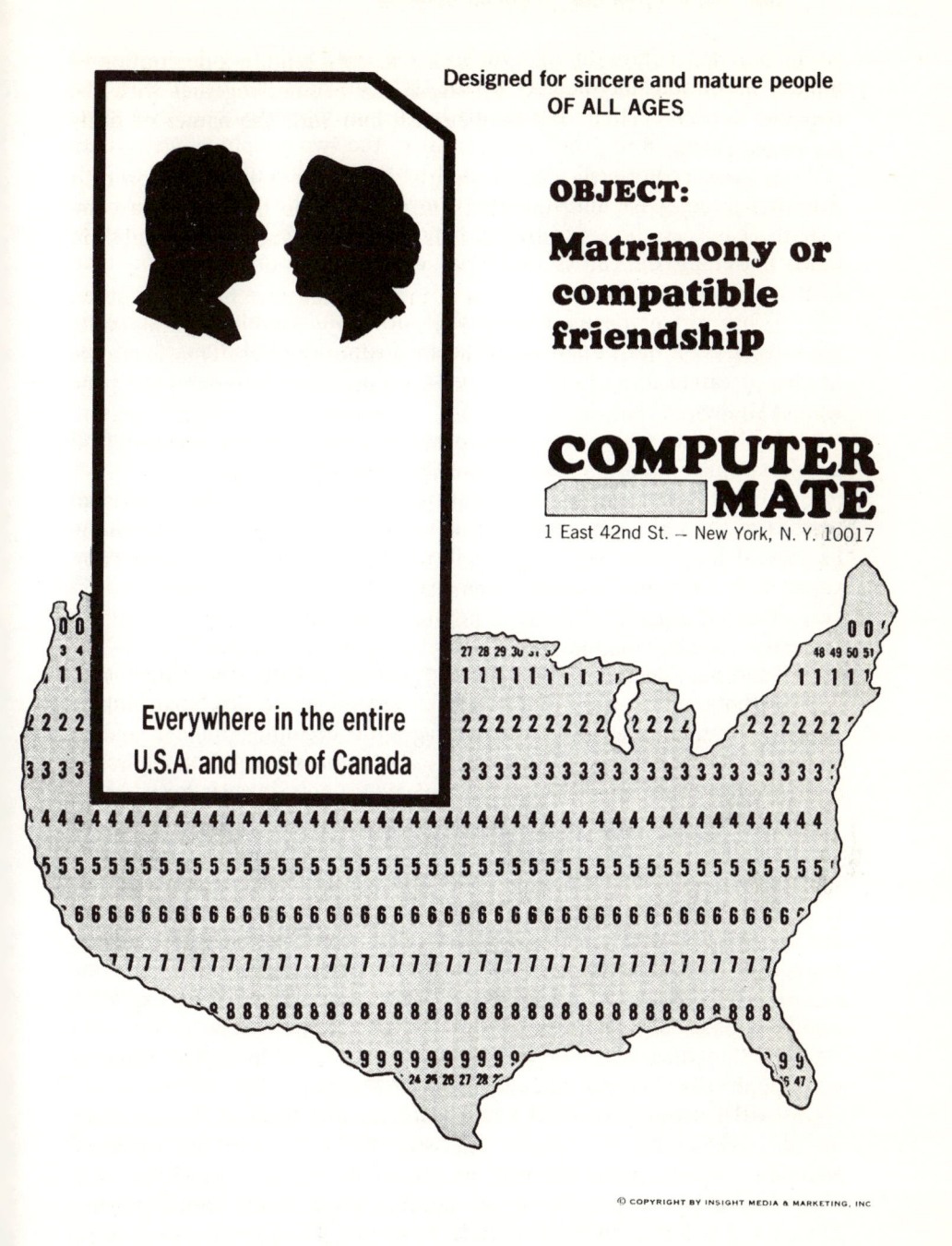

Dating by computer.
Reproduced courtesy of Computer Mate

At all previous points during courtship the relationship could have been broken off without any penalty by society. This does not mean, however, that such a breakup, after the couple has begun to go steady or even after the engagement, cannot be very painful to the two people concerned. In addition to the emotional upset caused by the couple's difficulties, the rift will often cause grave embarrassment, especially to the girl, who may feel that she has been discarded by her fiancé. Yet in the long run it may be much better for difficulties to surface during the courtship period than later during married life.

What sort of people are we likely to choose as marriage partners? This depends on individual tastes and inclinations and also on whom one has had occasion to meet. We can make certain general observations from various studies.

We tend to marry people like ourselves. A boy is most likely to meet a girl of similar social background, and he knows that his family will look favorably on such a meeting. Consequently, dating occurs mainly between persons of the same class, though it is not uncommon for class barriers to be crossed by people who find qualities other than social standing more valuable. For example, a wealthy boy may date a laborer's daughter who is very pretty. A girl whose father is prominent may want to be seen with a successful athlete though his family may be very poor.

Most marriages occur between partners of the same educational level. Not without justification are colleges sometimes called matrimonial bureaus. Furthermore, interfaith marriages are becoming more common, though only about 10 to 15 percent of all Catholics marry non-Catholics, and less than 5 percent of American Jews marry outside their faith. Much more frequent are marriages between the members of various Protestant denominations, as most Protestants pay very little attention to individual differences in creed and ritual.

Interracial marriages are rare; they account for approximately 1 percent of all marriages in the United States. Yet as the bars of segregation are being broken, it is likely that more people of different races will meet, get to know each other, and fall in love. College campuses and places of work should provide such opportunities. There have been some well-publicized interracial marriages in the entertainment world, where talent and box office popularity outweigh traditional race prejudice.

In the majority of black-white marriages the black partner is male, and the white partner is female. Usually the male is of higher social standing than his mate. He may be financially successful or have some claim to fame through professional, artistic, or athletic accomplishments. Since in the American class system, being black has traditionally been looked on as being inferior, marriage to a white woman could mean a growth in status for a black man. However, with the recent rise of black pride and "black power" interracial marriage is becoming far less desirable in the eyes of blacks who stress black identity.

Finally, studies indicate that we show a tendency to marry people whose physical and mental characteristics are similar to our own. Husbands and wives resemble each other to a startling degree in height, eye color, weight, memory, intelligence, drinking habits, the number of children desired, and even in the number of brothers and sisters.[13]

PREMARITAL SEX

How far may couples go in their sexual contacts during the courtship period? Is "heavy petting" all right? Should sexual intercourse take place when the two people are in love? When they are engaged? When marriage has to be postponed for financial reasons? The answers to these questions depend on the moral standards of the particular society. These standards can differ vastly from society to society, and they are, moreover, subject to change, especially during periods of rapid social change when there may be widespread confusion and disagreement.

In alpine villages girls quite commonly received their beaus in their bedchambers. If pregnancy resulted, it was not judged a disgrace. On the contrary, the girl had demonstrated that she was able to conceive children, which was considered a very important asset. Furthermore, children were needed as helpers in the field.

By and large, however, moralists demanded that girls enter marriage as virgins. The wedding night was considered the appropriate time to end this stage. On the following morning, it was customary in some Eastern European rural areas to display publicly the bloody bed sheet as a proof that the bride had indeed kept her virtue up to that moment.

Premarital intercourse and also heavy necking are still frowned upon in our society, especially in the name of religion. But the gap between official attitudes and private views seems to be widening. Official attitudes are expressed in sermons, political speeches, newspaper editorials, and in the laws enacted by our legislators, whereas private views guide the individual in what he actually does. We find four variations of such private views.

> 1. Complete *abstinence* from premarital intercourse is demanded for both men and women.
> 2. Premarital intercourse is all right in case of love, stable relationship, and engagement.
> 3. Premarital intercourse is all right when there is physical attraction.
> 4. *Double standard:* premarital intercourse is acceptable for males but not for females.[14]

In the late 1940s and early 1950s a good deal of attention was given to the massive statistical studies of private sexual behavior undertaken by the late Alfred Kinsey.[15] It was found that 85 percent of the total male population and 50 percent of the female population had engaged in premarital intercourse.

Many of the people interviewed by Kinsey and his team of researchers are now the parents of adolescents and young adults. Have our private sexual habits changed even further since these studies were undertaken? Though it is too early to tell, many observers feel that such recent developments as the increasingly open discussion of sex in general and the use of new contraceptives, particularly the pill, are having some effect. Complete freedom in premarital sexual expression seems unlikely, however, but young people are talking more about "trial marriages" and about the right to gain some sexual experience with a potential marriage partner.

Kinsey also reported on the educational level of the persons who were interviewed. It was found that 87 percent of the males with only a grade school education, 84 percent of those with a high school education, and 67 percent of those with a college education had experienced premarital sex relations. The more education people had, the more reluctant they were to break long-established rules.

But more recently the situation seems to have reversed itself. A poll conducted in 1969 by a national television network brought out the fact that college students are now pleading for greater sexual permissiveness than are noncollege people. It was also found that whereas young people in our colleges and universities renounce the standards officially held by their parents, working young people stick closer to the values esteemed by their elders. The different attitudes seem to be related not so much to schooling or economic standing as to *liberal* and *conservative* positions.[16] Conservatives want to maintain the old official standards of premarital abstinence, whereas liberals recommend greater freedom.

We hear it said with increasing emphasis, especially by quite serious young people, that the sex act can be a very precious symbol of a beautiful relationship between a man and a woman whether they are married or not. Nor does it matter if this relationship lasts a short while or for life. As long as the relationship is warm and deep, the sex act has its place in it.

Such a point of view is also in line with the growing freedom of women to arrange their lives according to their own designs. In the area of sex, as in other areas, the woman tends to be considered man's equal. When such liberal opinions prevail, the decision to engage in physical intimacy is a mutual one, as is the decision to end the relationship.

Social scientists do not pass judgment on whether premarital sex relations are right or wrong; they simply point out the results of their observations. One expert concludes, "Generally speaking, premarital relations cannot be carried out with complete satisfaction in our society."[17] Several reasons are given:

1. It takes several years until a couple learns to perform the sex act with complete satisfaction. Premarital experiences can seldom be shared so long.
2. Because society officially condemns premarital sex relations, strong feelings of guilt may result.

3. The fear of discovery and of pregnancy may lead to very disappointing premarital sex experiences.

SEX ROLES

Are you a male or a female? There are few people who could not answer this question. One's sex can be easily established biologically, yet there have been men who wanted to be women and women who wanted to be men. In some cases a medical operation has fulfilled these wishes. Biological facts alone, however, are not enough to confirm the sex role of many humans. "The human mind, in its perversity, does not completely trust anatomical characteristics and insists upon including psychological factors in the final judgment."[18]

It is more difficult for males to establish an adequate sex role than for females. According to Western standards the male plays the role of the active partner, but in order to do so he must be *potent* (physically able to perform the sex act), whereas the female can more easily fulfill her more passive role. This situation puts extra pressure on a man, who must prove his manhood anew at every occasion. But the very anxiety about his sexual potency may make it more difficult for him to perform adequately.

On a different level, some females still strive to constantly prove their identity. They wear padded bras, and a few resort to the more radical silicone treatment to enlarge their breasts in order to emphasize their femininity.

Traditionally girls lived more sheltered lives than boys. They were strictly supervised by their mothers and had little chance of pursuing their own inclinations, while boys were able to cut loose sooner from parental control.[19] After marriage husband and wife continued to play the roles they had assumed while growing into adolescence. The woman spent her days at home caring for house and children. She made her husband comfortable when he returned from work and was available when he desired sexual satisfaction. Unless she retained strong ties with her own family or made friends easily with other females, she led a rather lonely life.

The husband's role was to go out and work, which required that he be away from home for most of his waking hours. After work he felt entitled to join his male companions for drink, talk, or cardplaying. He might even engage in some casual sexual activities with other women, but he would not stand for his wife to do likewise.

Recent investigations have discovered that men and women still continue to play these established sex roles but not in all social classes. These sex roles remain typical for the blue-collar workers and low-income groups.[20] "For working-class couples there is no issue over who does what around the house."[21] This does not mean that man and woman, especially

112 An Introduction to Social Science

"Some day all this will be yours"

Figure 4

Copyright 1968 Saturday Review, Inc. Reprinted with permission of Robert M. Hageman and *Saturday Review*.

the woman, are always happy in playing those roles, but they play them anyhow. (See Figure 4.)

It is in observing people of the middle class, and particularly those who have received much formal education, that we see women having difficulty combining the conventional role of the "weaker sex" with the newly assumed roles of college students and professional workers. A young coed reported that her mother had admonished her by saying: "That 'A' in Philosophy is very nice, dear. But please don't become so deep that no man will be good enough for you."[22] Girls of superior intelligence have been known to play the role of a "dumb blonde" on dates because this was what they thought their male companions expected.

PROSPECTS OF SUCCESS IN MARRIAGE

In old fairy tales a valiant prince falls in love with a beautiful princess. After overcoming many obstacles the lovers fall into each other's arms, marry, and—we are told—"live happily ever after."

Not every wedding ceremony, however, is followed by permanent happiness, as we will see in the following chapter. Marriage is a difficult undertaking, and many of the difficulties encountered have their root in courtship days. Through tested love, as described earlier in this chapter, a couple will be able to iron out many rough spots, but abiding love is the product of a long relationship between mature people. "Falling in love" and having a short romantic courtship may not provide a strong enough foundation for a successful marriage. In marriage superficial affection must stand the harsh test of a daily routine, without the glamour of evening and weekend dates. Sexual frustration and general disappointment often result when abiding love does not replace the romantic illusion.

The social scientist cannot predict success in marriage with the same accuracy as the astronomer predicts an eclipse of the moon. But he can venture some advice based on careful observations. Studies indicate that hasty marriages have a high rate of breakup; and that in general the prospects for a successful marriage are gloomiest when both partners are seventeen years of age or younger, are school dropouts, have been acquainted less than six months, and have had a limited number of dating partners before marriage.[23]

Main Ideas

1. Modern Western society glorifies romantic love as the most beautiful experience possible.
2. Two human beings who love each other deeply depend on one another for self-satisfaction.
3. The attitudes toward the biological aspects of sex differ with time and culture; they range from extreme permissiveness to extreme restriction.
4. Our society is at the same time "sex-centric" and "sex-rejecting."
5. The development of sexual interest and of the ability to love goes through several stages as the human being grows from infancy to adulthood. Successful passage through the early stages develops in the person the ability to love completely.
6. In many societies the task of mate selection falls to the parents.
7. Families in which the parents choose mates try to select mates of equal or higher social rank.
8. In the United States young people appear to be free to select their own mates, but in reality they are subject to many restraints.
9. Dating is a typical part of American courtship and is also an important factor in recreational life.
10. Persons who select each other as marriage partners frequently show similar physical, mental, and social characteristics.
11. Interracial marriages are still rare, but with decreasing segregation their number can be expected to increase.
12. Premarital sexual intercourse is condemned by our official moral

standards but is privately practiced by a very substantial number of unmarried people.

13. Young people, especially on college campuses, are seriously questioning the accepted adult standards concerning premarital sex relations.

14. Sex roles and sex identity are determined not only by biological factors but also by psychological and social attitudes.

15. Success in marriage depends to a considerable degree on the length and the quality of the courtship period.

Important Terms

Abstinence	Obscenity
Anal stage	Oral stage
Coeducation	Permissive attitude
Courtship	Phallic stage
Double standard	Puberty
Endogamy	Puritan
Erotic passion	Restrictive attitude
Fixation	Romantic love
Incest	Secondary sex characteristics
Masturbation	

Conclusion

No society can continue to exist unless its young members mate and produce offspring. Since the perpetuation of a society is so vital, great stress is put on the rules of sexual conduct and mate selection. Such rules exist in all known cultures and are usually supported by religious teachings and by the laws of the community. In these times of rapid technological and social change there is much disagreement about the standards of courtship and sexual behavior, as well as a contrast between publicly professed morality and private attitudes and behavior.

Notes

1. Rollo May, "The Daemonic: Love and Death," *Psychology Today*, 1, No. 9 (1968), 16–25.
2. Erich Fromm, *The Art of Loving* (New York: Harper, 1956), p. 9.
3. David and Vera Mace, *Marriage: East and West* (Garden City, N.Y.: Doubleday, 1960), p. 85.
4. C. S. Ford and F. A. Beach, *Patterns of Sexual Behavior* (New York: Harper, 1951), pp. 178–192.
5. Richard F. Hettlinger, *Living with Sex: The Student's Dilemma* (New York: Seabury Press, 1966), p. 4.
6. *Time*, July 11, 1969, p. 64.
7. William Simon, "Sex," *Psychology Today*, 3, No. 2 (1969), 23–27.

8. Ruth Monroe, *Schools of Psychoanalytic Thought* (New York: Dryden Press, 1955), pp. 184–227.
9. Lewis M. Terman, *Psychological Factors in Marital Happiness* (New York: McGraw-Hill, 1938).
10. William Graham Sumner, *Folkways* (New York: Mentor Books, 1940), pp. 310–311.
11. Ruth Benedict, *Patterns of Culture* (New York: Mentor Books, 1934), p. 31.
12. P. H. Gulliver, "Jie Marriage," *Journal of the Royal African Society*, 52 (1953), 149–55.
13. Bernard Berelson and Gary Steiner, *Human Behavior*, short ed. (New York: Harcourt, Brace & World, 1964), pp. 39–42.
14. Ira L. Reiss, *Premarital Sexual Standards in America* (Glencoe, Ill.: The Free Press, 1960), pp. 83–84.
15. A. C. Kinsey, W. B. Pomeroy, *et al.*, *Sexual Behavior of the Human Male* (Philadelphia: Saunders, 1948); and A. C. Kinsey, W. B. Pomeroy, *et al.*, *Sexual Behavior of the Human Female* (Philadelphia: Saunders, 1953).
16. Ira L. Reiss, "Social Class and Premarital Sexual Permissiveness," in Marvin B. Sussman (ed.), *Sourcebook in Marriage and the Family*, 3rd ed. (Boston: Houghton Mifflin, 1968), pp. 227–236.
17. L. Q. Crawley, J. L. Malfetti, *et al.*, *Reproduction, Sex, and Preparation for Marriage* (Englewood Cliffs, N.J.: Prentice-Hall, 1964), p. 128.
18. Jerome Kagan, "Check one: ☐ Male ☐ Female," *Psychology Today*, 3, No. 2 (1969), 39.
19. Mirra Komarovsky, "Functional Analysis of Sex Roles," in Marvin B. Sussman (ed.), *Sourcebook in Marriage and the Family*, 2nd ed. (Boston: Houghton Mifflin, 1963), pp. 258 ff.
20. Lee Rainwater, "Social Class and Conjugal Role Relationship," in Sussman, *op. cit.*, pp. 275 ff.
21. Mirra Komarovsky, "Blue-Collar Families," in Philip Ehrensaft and A. Etzioni (eds.), *Anatomies of America* (New York: Macmillan, 1969), p. 483.
22. Mirra Komarovsky, "Cultural Contradictions and Sex Roles," in R. F. Winch, R. McGinnis, *et al.* (eds.), *Selected Studies in Marriage and the Family*, rev. ed. (New York: Holt, Rinehart & Winston, 1962), p. 128.
23. Lee G. Burchinal, "Trends and Prospects for Young Marriages," *Journal for Marriage and the Family*, 27 (1965), 243–254.

Suggestions for Further Reading

Brown, Helen. *Sex and the Single Girl*. New York: Geis, 1962. Candid, humorous, and nonpatronizing advice to unmarried women.

Crawley, L. Q., J. L. Malfetti, *et al.*, *Reproduction, Sex, and Preparation for Marriage*. Englewood Cliffs, N.J.: Prentice-Hall, 1964. Facts and clinical insights for the young adult reader.

Duvall, Evelyn M. *Love and the Facts of Life*. New York: Association Press, 1963. Answers to questions that disturb young people; the questions concern boy-girl relationships.

Duvall, Sylvanus M. *Before You Marry*. Rev. ed. New York: Association Press, 1959. Advice to young people concerning courtship and marriage.

Fromm, Erich. *The Art of Loving*. New York: Bantam Books, 1956. Thoughtful discussion of romantic and other kinds of love.

Lindner, Robert. *The Fifty-Minute Hour*. New York: Rinehart, 1955. Collection of case histories of psychosexual development.

Morris, Desmond. *The Naked Ape*. New York: McGraw-Hill, 1967. A biologist looks at the hereditary and environmental factors of human sexual behavior.

Popenoe, Paul. *Marriage Is What You Make It*. New York: Macmillan, 1950. An expert on family problems discusses marriage.

Sheed, Wilfrid. "We Overrate Love," *Saturday Evening Post*, March 25, 1967, pp. 10 ff.

*What happened to the good old days
when a home was still a home?
Is the American family going
to pieces?
Will it soon be a thing of the past?*

7 THE FOLKS AT HOME
the modern family

SIGNS OF TROUBLE

The picture of a glamorous film star adorns the cover of a movie magazine. The star's eyes are sad. The magazine's feature story asks, "Is she happy with her fifth husband whom she married six months ago?" Lately she has been seen frequently in the company of her new leading man. What will be the fate of the several children whom she has given birth to during her previous marriages?

Marital problems make headlines when film stars or politicians are involved, but on the back pages of your daily newspaper you can find listed the divorces of the little-known people. Looking around you, at relatives, friends, and neighbors, you can also see couples who have broken up and couples whose partners are having trouble living together. What is happening to the stability of family life?

There are other disturbing signs of trouble. The man in the upstairs apartment has disappeared, leaving the mother of four children to wait for a welfare check. Fatherless households like this one can be found in the low-income sections of the city. Divorces are expensive, and so *desertion* becomes the poor man's divorce.

Bewildered children tell their teachers that their parents have been arguing again. Some children return home after school to an empty house, where they have to fend for themselves till their working mother shows up. Older youngsters rebel against their parents. A disconsolate mother reports to the police that her daughter, barely in her early teens, has run away from home. Adolescents speak of the "generation gap": their parents don't understand them, they assert, and parental rules and regulations are outmoded. Homes, from coast to coast, resound with arguments, some quiet and reasonable and many loud and defiant.

SURVIVAL

Where is all this going to end?

No doubt, the modern family has problems. We find them in this country and in others as well. But before we examine problems, let us look at the many signs that assure us that the family will survive, though perhaps not in the form to which we or our parents have grown accustomed.

Actually, conditions in the family today are not necessarily worse than those in the family of a generation or a century ago. Not all homes were peaceful and happy then either. Not all husbands and wives were faithful to each other. Not all children were raised with love and returned love to their parents. Much of what we deplore today was here yesterday as well, but we have a tendency to idealize the past. "We look backward wistfully to the idealized past, and agree with one another in [our] thoughtful moments on how much better the past family system used to be, in the good old days that never were."[1]

We must remember that the family has existed for a long, long time. It was here before the school, the church, or the theater. And today, despite its problems, the family is a going concern. True, the divorce rate is high, yet it is noteworthy that it has not risen in the last twenty-five years but has remained constant at about one divorce granted for every four marriage licenses issued per year.

This means that more families are being started than dissolved. Of every twenty young people nineteen get married, which is a rate at least as high as ever before. Members of families travel together, picnic together, and join in many activities in the family rooms of their homes. Children today receive more attention than children ever have. A housewife may spend much of her time as a den mother, or a helper in a cooperative kindergarten, or chauffeuring her children to and from piano lessons and school parties. From school counselors, newspaper columnists, television lecturers, and Dr. Spock she receives in a year more information on how to bring up children properly than her mother did in a lifetime.

All this would seem to indicate that the family is not about to disappear. Human nature is not changing. At birth human beings are still more helpless than most other creatures, and they remain in a dependent state so much longer than other species in the animal kingdom. A child's first social contact is with his family. The earliest years are spent in the most intimate relations with his parents, especially with his mother. In the first five years of his life a child learns more than at any period thereafter. This is the time when his main personality traits are formed, when he receives his initial *socialization*. For the young child the family is a miniature society with himself as an important, well-recognized member.

The family is not merely the sum of two, three, or more people. Nobody knows this better than merchants and advertisers. Much of their sales appeal is directed at the housewife, who shops not only for herself but for the whole family unit. Perhaps the father, or the mother, or both bring home wages, but they spend only a small part of them for individual needs. Most purchases made by family units are for food, furniture, curtains, rugs, and other items that add to comfort and ease. It is the whole family that usually rents an apartment, buys a house, or goes off on a vacation trip.

In later chapters we will see that your family has much to do with the occupation you choose, the religion you practice, the friends you select, and the formal or informal organizations you join. Who you are and how you rank with your associates depend, to a large extent, on your family.

Now we turn to the very acute problems of the modern family. Numerous studies of these problems have been made. It is unfortunate, though, that they have for the most part been restricted to the examination of the urban middle-class family. Thus, sufficient information about family life in the low-income sections of our large cities and among the poor who live in the rural countryside has not been gathered.

The psychologist gives much attention to the problem of *communication* among the members of the family, while the sociologist regards the family as an *institution* within a changing society. We shall now look at both of those approaches.

COMMUNICATION

A married couple seem to be drifting hopelessly apart. Neither partner is able to do anything about it. Though both partners are intelligent and serious people, they just cannot bring themselves to discuss the situation calmly with each other. In another situation a father complains of his son: "It's impossible to talk with John. I just can't get through to him." In each case a breakdown of communication has occurred.

We communicate most easily about topics that are not too important, that don't affect us too personally. For example, you can always talk about the weather, and it will probably not upset you—that is, unless you have more than ordinary personal interest in the weather, like a weather forecaster. On the other hand, studies have shown that married couples find it very difficult to discuss money matters calmly with each other.

Conflict over finances is the most commonly listed complaint in divorce actions.

Young people of college age hesitate to discuss sex with their parents. The subject is certainly important to them, and they know that the older generation is not unaware of this. Yet an invisible wall prevents a frank discussion that may be urgently needed.

According to psychologist John Wallen "the closer the feelings are to here-and-now, to you-and-me, in this present moment—the more difficult they are to discuss openly."[2] It is in the family that the feelings of the members are closest to "here-and-now" and to "you-and-me." Children often find it hard to open their innermost feelings to their parents, though they see them every day and have known them all their lives. Parents experience similar blocks in talking freely with their children. Husbands and wives hesitate to confide in each other without holding back, without shame, anger, or envy.

Scale Indicating Range of Difficulty in Communicating Various Feelings

Most Distant   *Least Difficult to Communicate*

"Joe was angry with Jim." (Past feelings of persons neither of whom is present)
"I was angry with Susan." (Past feelings about somebody not present)
"I am angry with Susan." (Present feelings about somebody not present)
"I was angry with you last month." (Past feelings about you)
"I am angry with you." (Present feelings about you)

Here and Now   *Most Difficult to Communicate*

Source: Adapted from John Wallen, *Emotions as Problems* (unpublished paper prepared for the Northwest Regional Educational Laboratory, Portland, Oregon, 1967).

THE FAMILY—A SYSTEM

A family does not seem to be much like a television set, yet they have something in common: both are *systems*. Suppose, for example, that you take a screwdriver and completely dismantle your television set. You then carefully stack up all parts on a table or place them in a box. What you then have is lots of bolts, nuts, wires, and tubes but no television set. In order for these pieces to be a complete television set once again, they must be assembled in a certain way, with each part in a particular relationship to all the other parts. The correctly assembled set is something more than the sum of its parts. It is a system, an assemblage of items held together by some force of interaction or interdependence.[3]

The family is likewise more than the sum of its individual members. Father, Mother, son Bill, and daughters Mary and Beth are the parts of a system that functions well when the individual parts *interact* properly with each other.

To interact is to communicate. Husband and wife, parents and chil-

"By George, son, do you realize what we are doing? We are communicating."

Figure 5

Copyright 1969 Saturday Review. Reprinted with permission of Barney Tobey and *Saturday Review*.

dren remain strangers, disconnected parts like the tubes and wires of the disassembled television set, unless there is communication among them. To have a well-functioning family, communication must be frequent and intensive, at least as frequent and intensive and possibly more so than the communication between individual family members and persons outside the family. (See Figure 5.)

What actually takes place when members of a family attempt to communicate with one another? Let us assume you are an adolescent boy. It is Friday, and you would like to use the family car for an evening date. Your wish is formed into a signal that passes from you to your father. This first step is the *encoding process*. (See Figure 6.) The signal is your request, "Dad, may I have the car this evening?"

Your father receives the signal and *decodes* it—that is, he converts it into the idea that you want the car and the rest of the family will have to do without it. He then says: "O.K., son. Here are the keys but be careful and observe the speed laws." His reply to your signal is the *feedback*. You, in turn, respond to your father's feedback by taking the keys and saying, "Thank you, Dad, and don't worry."

122 An Introduction to Social Science

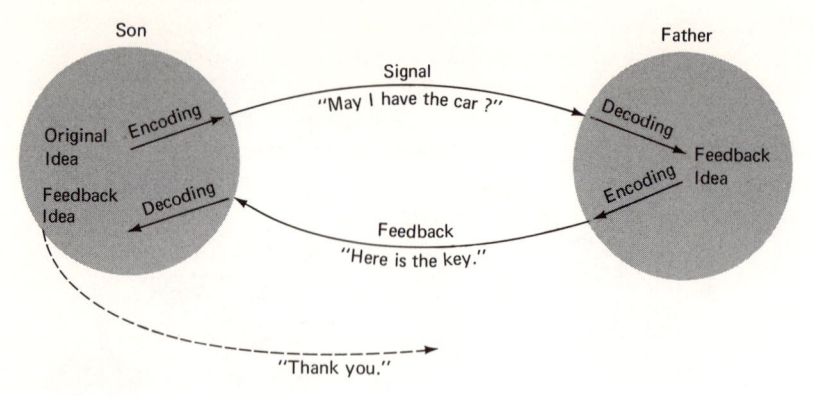

Figure 6
Communication from Person to Person

[Diagram: Son (Original Idea) — Encoding → Signal "May I have the car?" → Decoding → Father (Feedback Idea); Father — Encoding → Feedback "Here is the key." → Decoding → Son (Feedback Idea); dashed arrow "Thank you."]

Communication has a kind of circular nature. It is a daily necessity to communicate with people who are close to you. The process has no beginning and no end. The trouble is that the process of communication can break down at any point in the circle. The receiver may never get the message, or he may get an idea that is so different from what was sent that he completely misunderstands the message.

Your plan for Friday night is to take your girl to a dance. After the dance you intend to stop at a drive-in restaurant for a bite to eat and then to park for a while in a secluded spot and engage in a bit of necking. When you ask for the car, you tell your father about the dance and the food but not about the necking, since you don't feel like discussing sex freely. Here is the first breakdown of communication. You have failed to encode the entire idea, and so your father does not see the situation as you see it.

You take the car and have a very pleasant evening, but because of the time spent necking, you arrive home much later than your parents had anticipated. Since the topic of sex is taboo in your family, they keep their thoughts to themselves. They conclude that you, in turn, are not telling them what really happened, namely that you were necking heavily with your date. This is something they would not approve of.

None of this is brought out into the open by either you or your parents. Next time you ask for the use of the family car, your father may be defensive and embarrassed. He imposes some unreasonable restrictions, and you react with open hostility, which puts your parents even more on the defensive. A more severe breakdown of communications has occurred.

As a tiny faulty plug can keep a whole television set from functioning, so trivial misunderstandings have often disrupted communication within the family. In the morning Mrs. Jones asks her husband to pick up some groceries on his way home from work. Engrossed in his newspaper, he fails to hear her request. When he returns home in the evening without the groceries, Mrs. Jones complains angrily, "You never pay attention to what I say." A painful argument ensues.

Often couples are unable to share their most important feelings with each other. For years a husband and wife may appear to be living in perfect harmony, whereas in reality one of the partners is extremely unhappy, yet unable to communicate his frustration to the other. When he can stand it no longer, he suddenly declares to his perplexed mate that the marriage is not working and that he wants a divorce. At this point it is often too late to find a satisfactory solution to the problem.

The success of a family depends to a large extent on its ability to keep the channels of communication open. Social scientists have spent much effort in devising ways of teaching people to be better communicators. They developed various methods of sensitivity training and encounter group sessions. Particularly notable among the pioneers in this field are the National Training Laboratory Institute for Applied Behavior Science in Bethel, Maine, and the Esalen Institute at Big Sur, California. Employing their techniques can help to avoid crises not only in the family but also in schools, places of work, in government, and wherever people have to depend on each other to get things done successfully.

Poor communication is a frequent cause of family trouble, but it is by no means the only one. A family can be torn apart, physically and emotionally, by forces over which it has no control, such as the death or crippling illness of one of its members. War may deprive a family of the husband and father or of a son for a long period of time or permanently. Financial difficulties caused by unemployment, by a slump in business, or by poor management of the family income have often led to friction. And then there is the vast field of value and temperament conflicts, which threatens the peace within the family system.

THE FAMILY—A SOCIAL INSTITUTION

Several people may look at the same object, let us say, a lake, and each of them can see it from an entirely different viewpoint. A painter beholds its beauty, a fisherman sees it as a source of trout, and a water-skier longs to test its smooth surface. The family too can be investigated from different angles. From the sociologist's point of view the family is the oldest and most basic social institution. As mentioned before, let us beware of misunderstandings. In ordinary everyday language the word "institution" often suggests a mental hospital, school, or prison. Obviously this is not what we mean here. Rather social institutions are "complex norms or fixed procedures designed to preserve or to perpetuate life and to satisfy human needs."[4]

Let us illustrate this in terms of the family. Like other institutions, the family has a definite purpose. Well-known rules determine who can belong to it and how it should operate. Its fundamental purpose is procreation and the care of children. Rules, sometimes strictly observed and at other times publicly questioned, govern the sex life of the parents, their roles, their duties toward their children, the children's duties toward their parents, property, inheritance, and many other features.

Numerous customs have grown up around the daily life of the Western family. Of the many symbols that surround it we will only mention here the family name (which gives the individual his identity), wedding anniversaries, family reunions, the family pew in church, the family burial ground, and—in older times among nobility—the family coat-of-arms.

The family is also the most important *primary group*. The members of a primary group, which is always fairly small, have intimate face-to-face contact. They know each other by name. The primary group plays a very prominent part in our lives. It is where we belong. The other people in our primary group miss us when we are away, notice us when we are around. In the anonymous street crowd we feel lost, but upon returning to our homes we become Don, or Elsie, or Mom, or Dad, people who occupy a definite place especially reserved for them.

Throughout the history of mankind the family has proved to be the most durable, but not the only, primary group. Primary relationships also exist in a circle of close friends, a children's play group, a small village, or an immediate neighborhood where neighbors have known each other for a long time. One of the serious problems in our time is that so many persons, particularly in large cities, lose the opportunity for primary-group experiences. The result is loneliness and often despair.

You may also belong to a number of *secondary groups*. These are groups in which the members share a common interest. The interest may be occupational, political, religious, or relate to sports or ham radio operations. Some secondary groups may be quite important in your life, though it is impossible to have face-to-face contact with all their members. Think of such groups as the American nation, the Methodist church, the United States Navy, the Republican party, or the Teamsters' Union. Membership in secondary groups can cover wide territory and may even be world-wide. Membership in some secondary groups is voluntary. You make the decision whether to join the Elks, become a Catholic, or take out membership in the Izaak Walton League. You may also decide to end any such association. But when it comes to ethnic group or to nationality, you have little choice. Your membership in such secondary groups is a matter of fact. To switch from one to another that is more to your liking is difficult, and it is seldom done.

Family life and family character differ from place to place, from culture to culture, and they have differed from one period to another. Here we are discussing the modern American family, which is essentially *monogamous, nuclear,* and *patronymic.*

MONOGAMY

One woman married to one man: monogamy is the law of the land and the dictate of the church. Society reacts very strongly against any breach of this rule. Occasionally one reads stories about a truckdriver who has wives at both terminals of his overland route or of the ferryboat captain who maintains a family on each side of the straits. This is good comedy material, but if true and discovered, it would land the versatile truckdriver or captain in prison for the crime of bigamy.

During the past century the male members of the Mormon church used to marry several wives. A Mormon would keep all his women and children under the same roof, but each wife and her offspring inhabited a separate section with its own entrance. Bowing to outbursts of public indignation, the Mormon church eventually abandoned the practice. Monogamy proved to be too strongly ingrained in the American culture.

But as we move farther away from our cultural homegrounds, we are likely to encounter *polygamy* (having several mates), either in the form of *polygyny* (one man married to several women) or in the form of *polyandry* (one woman married to several men). (See Table below.) Biblical figures, such as Abraham, Jacob, and King Solomon, practiced polygyny. The Muslim religion allows its male members up to four wives, but today fewer and fewer adherents of the Muslim religion take advantage of this privilege. Women have become costlier and more demanding; so to have an extra wife or two is now frequently a status symbol, comparable perhaps to the acquisition of a costly limousine or a fancy yacht closer to home.

Forms of Marriage

Monogamy
    One husband and one wife

Polygamy
    Polygyny: one husband and several wives
    Polyandry: one wife and several husbands

Only rare instances of polyandry have been found. Best known perhaps is the situation in Tibet, a very rugged highland in Central Asia, where a woman would sometimes be married to a string of brothers. Under the Tibetan conditions of extreme climatic hardship it takes several males to support a family.

On the whole, monogamy seems to be becoming the dominant form of marriage throughout the world. Yet ironically with all our insistence on a single marriage partner, in Western societies we allow people to marry, divorce, and then marry again. Some have jokingly referred to this situation as "serialized polygamy."

The King of Akure, West Nigeria, with several of his 156 wives.
Marc and Evelyne Berheim from Rapho Guillumette Pictures

NUCLEAR AND EXTENDED FAMILIES

The necessities of urban industrial life have forced us to live in *nuclear families*, which consist of parents and children, rather than in *extended families*. (See Figure 7.) The extended family is not quite as easy to define as the nuclear family. It includes many more relatives, usually all descendants of one grandfather or great-grandfather with all their wives and children. Unmarried females and widows are also considered members of an extended family. Extended families were common among older rural societies and also in such civilized countries as China and India. With the coming of Western ways, industry, and urban life, however, the bonds begin to loosen. Where the extended family is still found, its members exhibit strong loyalty to each other. In some Asian and African countries, a man who becomes wealthy or attains an important government position is expected to take care of all his relatives. What we in this country would label corruption or graft is an expected and honorable duty in other places.

In the mountain regions of Southern Europe bloody feuds between extended families were carried on through many generations. A member of Extended Family A killed a member of Extended Family B. A B-member

the modern family

then had to avenge his relative's death on some A-member, and Extended Family A had to have its revenge in turn and so on.

Even in modern America it is not uncommon for members of an extended family to keep in touch. There are visits back and forth, and help is given in case of illness, poverty, or old age. But for the most part we grow up in one nuclear family, and when old enough, we break away and start a new one.

WHOSE NAME?

When Janet Brown marries William Green, she becomes Mrs. William Green. Chances are that she will be quite proud of both the new name and title. All her children will be Greens, and as long as they are male descendants, they will carry the same name. Our society accents the *patronymic* (name through the father) tracing of ancestry. The family members are identified by the name of the father, an indication that for a long time the male has been considered the dominant figure in the family.

Not all women are satisfied with this situation. *Feminists*, who demand full social and political equality for their sex, deplore the fact that a woman has to give up her name upon marriage and thereby lose part of her identity. In fact, many professional women who are, for example, writers and artists continue using their maiden names even after they have become wives and mothers.

These ladies might perhaps be sympathetic toward societies that

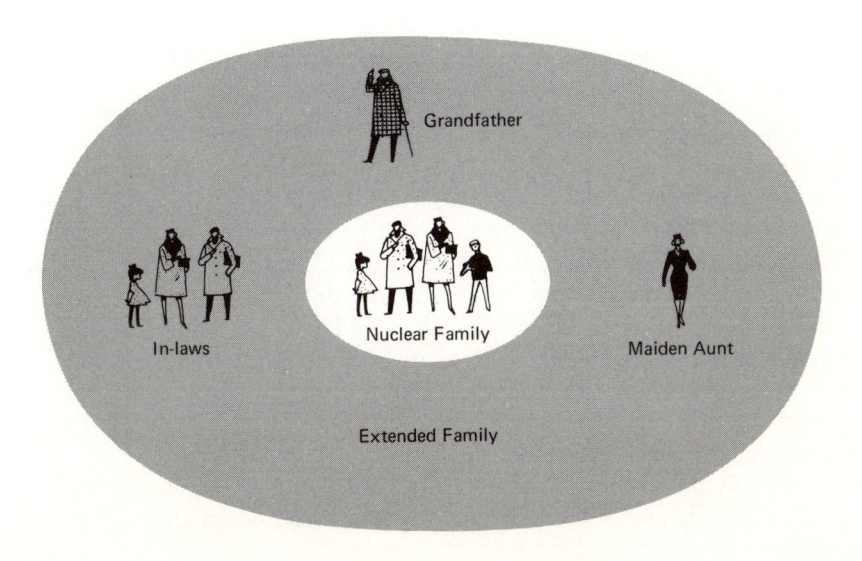

Figure 7
Nuclear and Extended Family

adhere to *matrilineal* (line through the mother) descent. When Bronislaw Malinowski studied the Trobriand Islanders of northwestern Melanesia fifty years ago, for example, he found that they did not realize that the husband had anything to do with the reproduction of children. They believed that only the mother's body figures in the reproductive process. As the children grow up, they consider their mother's brother their closest relative. The real father is not treated as blood relation at all. An investigator observed, "The father, in all discussions about relationship, was pointedly described to me as *tomakava*, a 'stranger,' or even more correctly, an 'outsider.' "[5]

FUNCTIONS

What is the family supposed to accomplish? What are its *functions*? The social scientist gives considerable thought to this question though it may seem obvious to the layman. The scholar tries to define these functions and observe what happens to them in our rapidly changing society. William F. Ogburn, a well-known sociologist, lists seven functions that the family has fulfilled in the past, and he concludes that "the dilemma of the modern family is due to its loss of function."[6] Now let us see what is happening to these functions in the age of the big city, the jet plane, and the computer.

Functions of the Family

1. Economic function
2. Status-giving function
3. Education
4. Protection
5. Religious function
6. Recreation
7. Affection and procreation

Source: William F. Ogburn, "The Changing Functions of the Family," in R. E. Winch, R. McGinnis, *et al.* (eds.), *Selected Studies in Marriage and the Family* (New York: Holt, Rinehart and Winston, 1953), p. 158.

Once, the members of most families worked together on farms with the father as a kind of foreman. Children were welcomed as an economic asset, because they provided needed farm hands. Nowadays, however, the father leaves his family in the morning and spends most of his day working away from the home. Often the mother does likewise, and as soon as the children are old enough, they follow suit as baby sitters and paper boys or work in various other part-time jobs. What is left of the family's economic function is that it still operates, to a large extent, as a *consumer unit*. But even here cracks begin to appear in the form of weekly allowances, separate savings accounts, and the motorcycle or car that belongs not to the family as a whole but to Tom, the oldest son.

Family membership automatically gives you your status and rank in society (see Chapter 11). It determines your racial designation. It makes you an Irish-American or a Japanese-American. In the past sons frequently followed their father's occupation, and daughters tried to marry into families equal in rank to their own. All of these factors are still of considerable importance, but more and more your social status depends on what you make of yourself in your work and in your associations with people outside your family. In the national elections of 1968, for example, both candidates for vice-president were the sons of rather poor immigrant families.

The task of educating and protecting the family now falls increasingly to schools, police, physicians, youth centers, and neighborhood play groups. Regular Bible reading is not practiced in many homes anymore. Religious observance is now mostly a matter of the church, inner-city missions, and religious broadcasts. In most cases children carry the same denominational label as their parents. Like their parents, they identify themselves as Catholics, Presbyterians, or Baptists, though they often question the religious beliefs expressed by father or mother.

In the field of recreation singing and playing games in a living room are crowded out by many available outside attractions that bid for family members' spare time, activities from dances to movies and bowling to watching professional football.

Ogburn maintains that in six of its seven functions the family has to contend with strong outside competition. "On the other hand, the family still remains the center of the affectional life and is the only recognized place for producing children."[7] This is true even when children are born out of wedlock. In one way or other, these children become members of a family even if the family does not include their natural fathers. They may be raised by their unwed mothers, by other relatives, or they may be adopted by couples who wish to have children. We associate the word "family" with the love between husband and wife and with the love parents lavish on the children they have brought into the world. Children need affection and also a set of rules by which they can live securely. Only so will they grow into stable adults capable of giving love in turn.

But even on this most private area the shadow of change is falling. Family life was less complicated when the father was the only breadwinner and the undisputed boss in the house. Wife and children obeyed him even when they did not like it. There was no other choice. Obedience was enforced with or without affection. Now the *patriarchal* (father-dominated) system is being challenged.

Beating his wife and children was once a man's undisputed right. Now it is not only unfashionable but, in many instances, illegal. Women have entered sports, politics, the professions, and the business world. They want to be equal partners with the man in the family, especially when they contribute to the family income. Children too demand the right to "do their thing." The adolescent, who is no longer a child but not yet an adult, learns in school about the principles of democracy, and he wants them to be practiced within the family.

The trend toward equality even extends into the once "top-secret" sphere of sex relations. Women were supposed to do their duty in the marital bed but not enjoy it or talk about it. Now matters of sex are being openly discussed. Both males and females expect sexual satisfaction. Wives rebel against the old "double standard" of morality in which it was considered acceptable for the male to step out with other women occasionally but not for his mate to do likewise.

THE UNHAPPY SIDE

Events in the larger world have brought unrest and tension into the world of the family. Once, the *roles* that family members played were well defined. Now they have become fuzzy and often conflict with one another.

A father sees his superior role threatened by other family members who demand a voice in decision making, especially in money matters. A mother is torn between her traditional role as housewife and her new roles as jobholder and participant in community affairs. At the same time she feels she should keep herself sexually attractive to her mate, which demands attention to dress and grooming.

Uneasiness about the roles to be played is a source of serious conflict in many homes. Even when a husband's income is sufficient, women find themselves increasingly dissatisfied with nothing but cooking and cleaning to fill their days.[8] This is especially true of housewives endowed with active minds and good educations.

A man, even if he has no objection to his wife's working, may become jealous of her success. If he is a blue-collar worker in industry and she qualifies to be a teacher, a nurse, or a social worker, she may outrank him in status because she is now a professional person.

Even children suffer from uncertainty about the roles they are to play in family life. An adolescent is admonished to listen to his parents, who have so much more experience and, at the next moment, he is told, "Don't act like a little child. Show some independence."

In some instances, especially among low-income minority groups, we can find a reversal of the patriarchal relationship into a *matriarchal* (mother-dominated) one. Sometimes this reversal involves a confusion of roles that takes on tragic proportions. In the days of slavery black mothers raised their children while the fathers were often sold elsewhere. Today the unskilled black male finds it more difficult to get a job than the unskilled black female. What is the consequence?

> Both as a husband and a father the Negro male is made to feel inadequate. . . . In a society that measures a man by his paycheck he doesn't stand very tall in comparison with his white counterpart. To this situation he may react with withdrawal, bitterness toward society, aggression both within the family and racial group, self-hate or crime.[9]

To keep a balanced view we should, however, remember that the middle-class black community leads a stable family life and that its membership is growing steadily.

Continued family tensions result in an alarming number of broken homes. The breakup of a home is not only hard on the individual family members, but it is also a danger to society. Family disorganization may be aggravated by poverty and discrimination, but it also contributes to poverty, deviant behavior, and mental maladjustment. It stunts the education of the young and may even affect the healthy development of their bodies. (This does not mean, however, that a home should never be broken up. Families where alcoholism, violent fighting, and sexual license persist need to be dissolved, especially in the interest of the children.)

The roots of family trouble are often deep and of long standing. A man and a woman enter marriage with conflicting ideas about what is right and wrong or with conflicting expectations of what constitutes marital happiness. Disagreements over money matters can become extremely bitter. So can arguments about the methods of raising children. A mother may expect her husband to be the disciplinarian. "Wait till Dad comes home," she warns her children. But during the few evening hours a father spends at home perhaps he doesn't feel like playing the role of disciplinarian; he may instead want to be a pal to his children.

The smallness of the nuclear family, as compared with the extended family, and the narrow living space afforded by some urban apartment houses make it difficult for family members to release tensions. Husband and wife lack the privacy that could make their intimate relations more satisfactory. There is no loving grandmother or aunt readily available to comfort a child whose parents are too busy at the moment to give him the attention he desperately needs. A trivial act, a harmless word, or gesture may rub another family member the wrong way and cause severe conflict.

A satisfactory sex life is part of a successful marriage. A wife who is frigid and rejects her mate's advances, a husband who is impotent or "just not interested" will bring about friction or at least disappointment. But we know now that unsatisfactory sexual performance can be the effect of some deeper cause. If a husband's job is threatened, or a wife was brought up to regard everything concerning sex as unclean and repulsive, the couple will carry their attitudes with them into the most intimate situations. What could be the crowning moment of a close and warm personal relationship then becomes a painful and frustrating experience.

Strains in family relations are not always visible to the outsider. Families may keep up a harmonious front, perhaps because their religion forbids divorce or because an open break might hurt the husband's career or bring loss of prestige. Such families may be nothing but "empty shells," as sociologist William J. Goode puts it. "People carry on their formal duties toward one another, but give no understanding, affection or support, and have little interest in communicating with one another."[10] The question may be asked whether it serves any good purpose to keep such families together.

DIVORCE

When two married people decide that they cannot even pretend anymore to live together harmoniously, they can obtain a *divorce*, which is a legal dissolution of their relationship. Once, divorce was something rare and sensational, and divorced women were considered scandalous. This is no longer true, and divorces can be found in all social classes in the Western world.

Divorce involves much more than just dissolving a household, dividing up furniture, and deciding who should keep the dog and who the cat. In solving one set of problems divorce creates a set of new ones. It cuts deeply into the pattern of day-by-day life to which a married man or woman has become accustomed. Loneliness and bewilderment can result. The ugly wrangling over possessions, the divided affections of the children, who are torn from one parent and may have to come to terms with a new stepparent, cause many tragic situations.

What does a divorced person do in the evening, on weekends, during vacations? Visiting is generally done by couples. Many other social activities are also for twosomes. Thus divorce breaks up patterns of long-existing friendships.

Add to this the confusion in our divorce laws, which are, in many instances, sadly outdated. You can obtain a "quickie" divorce in Nevada if you can afford to stay there a few weeks. In most other states obtaining a divorce is a difficult, costly, and long-drawn-out ordeal. Many courts accept adultery or similar serious offenses against the marriage vows as the only grounds for divorce. Thus, you must go through the motions of accusing your mate of some wrongdoing for which the judge then punishes the "guilty" party by issuing a divorce decree. All parties involved, husband and wife, court and lawyers, play out their roles, knowing very well that the two married persons primarily want to be free of each other. This situation is leading to growing demands that the laws pertaining to marriage and divorce should be updated and made more uniform throughout the country.

Against loud protestations that the whole institution of marriage will be killed by "instant divorce" several states have gone ahead with substantial reforms. In 1969, for example, the California legislature abolished all legal grounds for divorce except "incurable insanity" and "irreconcilable differences." The latter is a catch-all phrase meaning that a husband and wife cannot get along with each other. "The state will simply not bother to investigate the reasons for the divorce or seek to establish who is right or wrong. It will merely decide whether two people are incompatible."[11] This ought to eliminate much of the ugly wrangling and exchange of accusations that mar old-style divorce trials.

THE HAPPY SIDE

Despite the problems that the family faces, we can discover many hopeful signs in our changing world to indicate that the family as an institution is here to stay. Difficulties once considered hopeless can now be removed. New avenues to happiness and fulfillment can be opened.

To begin with, let's look at the basic function of procreation. Medical science can now help many couples who believe themselves unable to conceive children. Modern means of birth control make it possible for husband and wife to determine the number of children they want to raise and how to space new arrivals to fit overall plans of life. In this way the chances are increased that the children will be wanted and appreciated by their parents.

Fears have been expressed that making effective contraceptives, such as the birth control pill, so easily available will cause people to avoid having children altogether. Such fears appear to be largely groundless. The average married couple still wants to have offspring. Children not only enrich their lives and give them purpose, but they also enhance marital status. It is expected of married people to "have a family." Furthermore, childless couples show a higher divorce rate than those with offspring.

True, families are smaller now than they were in the days when a large portion of our population lived on the farm. We rarely find urban families with eight, ten, or more members, except in the poorest sections of the city. But couples are now having more children than in the depression years of the thirties, and there is no sign of a letup even though the child is an economic burden, rather than a helper, in an urban household.

Childless couples can adopt babies with the help of competent adoption agencies. This solves the problem for the couples, as well as for the babies which are usually illegitimate. Once branded for life as a "bastard," the illegitimate child now suffers less social discrimination. He encounters fewer obstacles in obtaining an education or in his quest for a gratifying occupational life. For example, illegitimate birth has not hampered Willy Brandt, the Chancellor of West Germany, from becoming one of the foremost statesmen of our time.

Of alarming concern lately are the catastrophic dangers of overpopulation. With this in mind perhaps childless couples will be praised as benefactors of mankind who are doing their share in keeping the planet from becoming dangerously overcrowded. We hear many admonitions to restrict reproduction to only one or two children per family, and the demands for easing of restrictions concerning birth control and abortion are taking on new urgency.

Sexual frustration is often caused by ignorance and by the reluctance to talk about sex openly. The whole topic has been, to a large extent, the preserve of pornographic literature and jokes. Now serious reading material, films, and tapes are available. Sex education is a matter of great concern to the teaching profession, though there is still much argument as to who should be responsible for it: the school, the church, the family, or all of them.

We should remember that desertion and divorce are not the beginning but rather the last step in the gradual decay of marital relations. The difficulties reach farther back. Skilled, understanding counsel, given in time, can frequently prevent the final breakup. Well-trained marriage counselors are available, but there are also ill-qualified quacks who try to cash in on marital troubles.

The clergyman has a unique opportunity to counsel couples both before they pronounce their marriage vows and afterward. Seminaries attempt to train future ministers, priests, and rabbis for this task. In many communities the legal machinery for granting divorces is being overhauled. New-style "family courts" try to save marriages rather than automatically handing out divorce decrees.

A growing number of parents take the business of bringing up children very seriously. It is a difficult task requiring skill and knowledge, yet society demands no proof of training, no diploma or certificate to testify to a person's fitness to raise children. Nevertheless, fathers and mothers eagerly seek advice by listening to lecturers and reading newspaper columns. Competent books on the subject are high on best-seller lists. (See "Suggestions for Further Reading" at end of chapter.)

As the work week becomes shorter and vacations become longer, working people can spend more time with their families. A father may say, "This summer I'll use my vacation to get acquainted with my children." Many popular hobbies and pastime activities lend themselves uniquely to family participation. A look at our public campgrounds or at various father-son gatherings sponsored by community organizations will furnish ample examples.

A big question is the fate of the family member who reaches old age. Once, grandparents used to live out their declining years in the homes of their grown children. But the size of the living quarters has shrunk, and different generations adhere to different styles of life. Men and women in their middle years are torn between the duties to their elderly parents and the much stronger obligations to their own nuclear families. Now society is assuming some of the burden of caring for senior citizens by providing Social Security, Medicare, and pension funds. But we are only just beginning to care adequately for them. Many still must live out their remaining years in shameful poverty and loneliness without seeing any purpose in the life that still lies ahead of them.

Main Ideas
1. The modern family shows many signs of disruption and disorganization.
2. Nevertheless, the modern family also shows signs of vigor, and it will, undoubtedly, survive.

3. The members of the family, like the members of other social groups, experience difficulties of communication.
4. Physical and emotional closeness may prevent communication of intimate feelings.
5. In the family, as in any other system, the parts are engaged in a continuous process of interaction.
6. Breakdown of communication occurs when incomplete or misleading signals are sent, when they are improperly decoded, or when the feedback is unsatisfactory.
7. The modern American family is an institution that features primary group relationships, monogamous marriage, nuclear composition, and patrilineal descent.
8. The modern urban family is losing some of its traditional functions but remains the socially accepted center for affection between the sexes and the procreation of children.
9. Husband and wife, parents and children, play conflicting roles in our changing society.
10. Role conflict strains and often breaks the family relationship.
11. Divorce reflects changes in our society; it has become accepted though it causes many painful problems.
12. The chances for a successful family life are being increased by the possibility of adoptions, the availability of contraceptives, and the increasing knowledge about problems of sex and of child education.
13. There is more time and opportunity for family activities.
14. Social legislation is beginning to relieve the family of the responsibility for its aged members.

Important Terms

Communication
Consumer unit
Decoding
Desertion
Divorce
Encoding
Extended family
Feedback
Feminist
Institution
Interaction
Matriarchal system
Matrilineal descent

Monogamy
Nuclear family
Patriarchal system
Patrilineal descent
Patronymic
Polyandry
Polygamy
Polygyny
Primary group
Secondary group
Socialization
System

Conclusion

Where is all this leading? We can only say: disorganization precedes reorganization. As the family of the 1970s is vastly different from its counterpart in the 1930s or the 1900s, so the family of ten, twenty, or fifty years hence will be different from ours. The competition of the school and of other social institutions for functions previously performed by the family will continue and probably increase. We seem to be moving toward more equality among family members and a greater stress on the individual within the family. In the meantime, husbands and wives, parents and children, would do well "to recognize each other's needs, learn to communicate with each other . . . learn to compromise . . . and not to demand too much of the other."[12]

Notes

1. W. J. Goode, "The Family as an Element in the World Revolution," in Peter I. Rose (ed.), *The Study of Society: An Integrated Anthology* (New York: Random House, 1967), p. 538.
2. John Wallen, *Emotions as Problems* (unpublished paper prepared for the Northwest Regional Educational Laboratory, Portland, Oregon, 1967).
3. James C. Coleman, *Personality Dynamics and Effective Behavior* (Glenview, Ill.: Scott, Foresman, 1960), pp. 35–36.
4. Jules Karlin, *Man's Behavior* (New York: Macmillan, 1967), p. 42.
5. Bronislaw Malinowski, "A Woman-Centered Family System," in Walter Goldschmidt (ed.), *Exploring the Ways of Mankind* (New York: Holt, Rinehart and Winston, 1960), pp. 233–239.
6. William F. Ogburn, "The Changing Functions of the Family," in R. E. Winch, R. McGinnis, *et al.* (eds.), *Selected Studies in Marriage and the Family* (New York: Holt, Rinehart & Winston, 1953), p. 157.
7. *Ibid.*, p. 158.
8. Mike Nawas, "Women in Role Conflict," in Fred McKinney (ed.), *Psychology in Action: Basic Readings* (New York: Macmillan, 1967), pp. 98–104.
9. Whitney Young, *To Be Equal* (New York: McGraw-Hill, 1964), p. 175.
10. William J. Goode, *The Family* (Englewood Cliffs, N.J.: Prentice-Hall, 1964), p. 101.
11. *Newsweek*, September 22, 1969, p. 110.
12. Richard A. Kalish, *The Psychology of Human Behavior* (Belmont, Cal.: Wadsworth, 1966), p. 226.

Suggestions for Further Reading

Albee, Edward. *Who's Afraid of Virginia Woolf?* New York: Atheneum, 1962. A play about the difficulties of communication between husband and wife.

Austen, Jane. *Pride and Prejudice.* New York: Dodd, Mead (Great Illustrated Classics Series), 1945. Novel about family difficulties.

Bossard, James H. *Why Marriages Go Wrong.* New York: Ronald Press, 1958. How to overcome the hazards of marriage.

Butler, Samuel. *Way of All Flesh*. New York: Modern Library, no date, first published in 1903. Novel about the conflict between a father and his children.

Cantor, Donald J. "The Right of Divorce," *Atlantic* (November 1966), pp. 67 ff.

Gesell, Arnold L. *Infant and Child in the Culture of Today*. New York: Harper, 1943. One of the popular books by the well-known child psychologist.

Gesell, Arnold L., Frances L. Ilg, et al. *Youth: the Years from Ten to Sixteen*. New York: Harper, 1956.

Ginott, Haim. *Between Parent and Child*. New York: Macmillan, 1965.

———. *Between Parent and Teenager*. New York: Macmillan, 1969.

Hartman, Sylvia. "Should Wives Work?" *McCalls* (February 1969), pp. 57 ff.

Hunt, Morton M. "The Rocky Road to Remarriage," *McCalls* (October 1966), pp. 126 ff.

Popenoe, Paul B. *Marriage Is What You Make It*. New York: Macmillan, 1950. A well-known expert on family relations speaks.

Spock, Benjamin M. *Baby and Child Care*. New York: Pocket Books, 1957. One of the popular books by the well-known pediatrician.

———. *Dr. Spock Talks with Mothers*. Boston: Houghton Mifflin, 1961.

*Does religion change with the times, or is it unchanging?
What is religion anyhow, yours as well as the various religions around the world?*

8 HALLOWED BE THY NAME
the need for religion

THE NEED FOR COMFORT

A short distance to the north of Mexico City stands the massive cathedral of Our Lady of Guadalupe. The cathedral's wide square is packed with pilgrims who have come from many parts of Latin America. Peasant women in colorful shawls and men with broad-brimmed straw hats are moving slowly across the square toward the church. They are down on their knees, and in this uncomfortable position they slide forward, one knee following another, murmuring prayers and fingering rosary beads. Groaning and aching, they work themselves up the marble steps and into the sanctuary. They try to get close to the high altar over which hangs the tapestry showing a picture of a brown-skinned woman in flowing blue and gray garments surrounded by golden rays of light. Through the smoke of innumerable candles and the haze of sweetish incense the gentle face of Our Lady of Guadalupe looks down upon her worshipers.

The pilgrims have come to Guadalupe seeking cures from illness or relief from extreme poverty. Barren women hope to conceive, cripples to become hale again. As they leave the cathedral, many are in a state of exultation, for they feel certain that Our Lady above the altar has heard their pleas.

From time immemorial man has turned to religion to seek comfort from fear and suffering. The caveman prayed to the threatening thunderstorm to keep the deadly bolts of lightning away from him and his family. Faced with drought or disease, primitive tribes offered to buy their safety with gifts to the dangerous forces of nature. On altars of stone priests sacrificed sheep and fowl and even other human beings. Tribesmen offered part of the roots and berries they had gathered, and after they had learned to farm, they offered the harvest's first sheaves of grain or the clusters of grapes as gifts of thanks and to ensure good harvests in the future. For ages soldiers have prayed before going into battle and sailors before entrusting their vessels to the unpredictable seas. The gods were invoked at the construction of a new house, at the coronation of a ruler, at the birth of a child.

Though religion has in the past, and still does today, acted as a pacifier for frightened and bewildered human beings, it does more than just offer comfort.

WHAT IS RELIGION?

The social scientist has a habit of trying to define what is already most familiar. Of course, you know what religion is. To you, for example, it may mean church on Sunday, grace before meals, the cross, Christmas, and so on. This is a true description, but only of *your* religion, of religion in your time and in the part of the world where you live. It may be something you cherish, something that your neighbors do, or something you were exposed to in childhood but have long since left behind.

But let us consider religion not only as you know it, but also as it is practiced in Chile, the Congo, Thailand, and Russia. Whatever else it may be, religion has been an important ingredient of man's culture and, in all likelihood, will remain so for quite some time.

For something so familiar religion is surprisingly difficult to define. To anthropologist E. Adamson Hoebel religion means belief in supernatural powers that must be appeased by prayer and sacrifice.[1] Hoebel has in mind mainly the religions of primitive cultures; and though primitive religions are different from each other, he finds in all of them a common feature. The natural objects that primitive man sees, the sun and the stars, trees, rivers and oceans, are manipulated by beings that he cannot see but that are far stronger than he is. He calls them by various names, such as spirits, demons, goblins, fairies, and ogres. They are everywhere and are capable of doing harm or good. So man must humor them and make friends—not enemies—of them.

Primitive religion has by no means ceased to exist, but it does not cover all aspects of modern religious life. More applicable to our times is Gerhard Lenski's statement that religion comprises (a) "a system of beliefs about the nature of forces ultimately shaping man's destiny, and (b) practices associated therewith shared by the members of the group."[2]

"Forces ultimately shaping man's destiny": this phrase leaves a great deal of leeway in interpretation. Lenski's "forces" could be any of an enormous variety of pictures that man's mind has created, ranging all the way from the fantastic half-man–half-beast creatures of ancient Egypt to the philosophical concepts of an all-encompassing world spirit or an impersonal creative force akin to the forces of gravity or electricity.

One more definition needs to be added here because it clearly designates the elements that have made religion such a durable part of man's past and present. J. Milton Yinger sees in religion "an attempt to explain what cannot otherwise be explained; to achieve power, all other powers having failed us; to establish poise and serenity in the face of evil and suffering that other efforts have failed to eliminate."[3] To Lenski's two elements that are present in all religions, namely, a system of beliefs and a system of practices, Yinger adds a third: a system of social relationships.[4]

We will now take a closer look at this three-paneled panorama of religion.

GODS

Thousands of years ago men were *animists*. As they saw it, the sun moved across the horizon because a spirit guided it. Spirits inhabited the innards of mountains, and in their anger they made the mountains erupt and pour fiery lava over fields and villages. The human body too was inhabited by spirits that continued to exist even after the body had died. Here perhaps is the origin of a concept that plays such an important part in modern religion—the human soul.

Spirits were also believed to inhabit such unseemly abodes as rocks, bones, or logs. Such an object, called a fetish, or totem, was then believed to have great power for good and evil and had to be treated with respect and veneration. A person today who carries a rabbit's foot or other charms for good luck is probably not aware that he is practicing *fetishism*, or *totemism*.

Not only certain objects but also certain persons and places were held to be sacred. These sacred persons, places, and objects had to be approached with time-honored ceremonies; their ability to cause harm and death or dispense generous blessings evoked fear and trembling. A sacred object was never supposed to be handled casually like an ordinary ax or an oar; a sacred place had to be avoided or entered with awe; and sacred persons, such as witch doctors, priestesses, and rulers who claimed to be related to the spirits, demanded unquestioning reverence and submission. A worshiper would stand anxiously in the presence of the sacred, never knowing how its power would affect him. For early man religion was not isolated from his daily activities. Sacred objects and the spirit world were all around him, in whatever he did, and in whatever was done to him.

As time went on human imagination shaped the various spirits into man's own image. It was felt that the powers that made day and night, life and death, war and pestilence, despite their great strength and longevity, looked very much like man himself, only more so. They were looked upon as the ideal of man—stronger, wiser, more beautiful than anything that could be found on earth in human shape. It was also assumed that these powers had feelings similar to those of their human worshipers. Man called them gods and described some of them as gentle and friendly, others as cruel and mischievous, characteristics to be found in his own neighbors. This belief in the existence of gods is called *theism*.

The gods were thought to be *anthropomorphous* (manlike), but they had certain advantages over real men. They were believed to be immortal and to have the power to become invisible or take the shape of animals or various human beings. This complicated man's life, for one could never be certain whether a stranger at the door or a beast in the woods was not in reality a god in disguise.

Since the gods were considered to be like humans, only on a larger scale, they could also act like humans. Stories, called *myths*, were told, first by word of mouth, then later in writing, about the numerous adventures, quarrels, and love affairs of the various gods. Collections of myths arose in every culture. Some of them, like those of ancient Greece, were sources of inspiration to poets, playwrights, and artists, whom they stirred to great accomplishments. Myths not only tell how the various gods spend their time but also explain natural events, such as the creation of the world or the changing of the seasons. Researchers have discovered startling similarities between myths that come from different parts of the world. Certain myths also seem to parallel some well-known Bible stories.

Concepts of the Supernatural

Animism
Fetishism (Totemism)
Theism
    Polytheism
    Henotheism
    Monotheism

The ancient Greeks and Romans worshiped many gods, as did many other nations; that is, they were *polytheistic*. Each god was thought to be a kind of specialist in a specific area, one for war, another for travel, a third for craftsmanship. One goddess could bestow fertility on man and on crops, another was the giver of wisdom. Even thieves had a god whom they invoked for success in their chosen occupation.

At times a tribe or a city selected one god as its particular patron, hoping that this divine being would always take its side in any conflict with other tribes or cities, who in their turn, also had supernatural patrons. This belief, called *henotheism*, was held by the Hebrews in their earliest days. They did not deny the existence of other gods, but Jehovah was their very own god. He was expected to look after their welfare, but in return he expected faithfulness from them.

Slowly the picture of Jehovah that the Hebrews carried in their minds became more and more powerful. The Hebrews pronounced the idea of *monotheism*, which then spread from Palestine to Europe, the Western hemisphere, and other parts of the world. Monotheism is the belief in one single God who has created the universe and controls all its happenings. Christianity in its many forms, Judaism, and Islam are the chief monotheistic religions.

But polytheism has by no means disappeared. The Hindus, for example, who number several hundred millions, assume the existence of numerous gods over whom preside three chief deities, Brahma, Vishnu, and Shiva. Hindu thinkers, however, reason that the many gods are in reality just different manifestations of the same universal deity, Brahma. This then actually comes quite close to monotheism.

What does God look like? What is his nature? What does he do? Men have argued such questions for ages, and today the discussions are more heated than ever among *theologians*, those scholars specializing in the study and explanation of religious beliefs and teachings.

Children often picture God as looking somewhat like their grandfathers. Many adults do the same thing. God dwells in a place, called heaven, where he spends his time listening to prayers and helping people out of trouble.

Many modern thinkers find this cozy picture of a grandfatherly God quite out of date. But even though they devise more sophisticated concepts of the deity, the Mexican peasant who goes on his pilgrimage and millions of people like him need a God to whom they can turn in their need and who, they feel, is interested in their problems and willing to listen.

Only a few centuries ago denial of God's existence could be punished by death. Today there is a much smaller risk involved in being a confirmed *atheist*, that is, one who does not believe in the reality of anything supernatural, including God. Some communist thinkers, for example, belong in this category. They are followers of Karl Marx, who taught that only the material world really exists. This, however, does not prevent thousands of Italian workers and peasants who vote for the Communist party from attending church faithfully every Sunday.

Whereas the atheist is sure that God is only a product of the imagination, the *agnostic* expresses doubt. "Nobody has ever seen or heard God," he argues, "and we will never know whether he exists or not." The agnostic considers God with the same attitude that the scientist shows toward the nature of man or animals. He will accept as true only what can be proved by observation or by logic, as we do, for example, when we prove that the square root of sixty-four is eight.

EXISTENCE AND DEATH

Whatever their beliefs about the nature of God, men have always felt the need to think about their own existence. We are curious creatures, and we like to ask such questions as: "How did we come into this world? Why are we here? What is the purpose of life, and in what direction are we moving?"

For a long time only religion came forward with answers to questions like these. But now it finds itself competing with modern philosophy and with the modern sciences, particularly astronomy, geology, and biology. Science as we know it has only developed in the last four centuries, and since its beginnings it has often clashed with religion. The Catholic church once imprisoned a man because he asserted, contrary to then held belief, that the earth moved around the sun. To this day some religious leaders still fight the scientific theory that the species of man evolved over millions of years from simpler forms of life.

Yet despite the differences between religion and science, we can say that both seek the same goal: truth. But they deal in different kinds of truth, and they use different methods. The scientist's methods are experimentation and reasoning, and his findings can be checked by other scientists; religion, on the other hand, claims to know the road to a higher truth that can neither be proved nor disproved in the laboratory or by statistics. Religious truth is presented as having been revealed by God to man in a miraculous way and as being stated authoritatively in divinely inspired writings.

Scientists can believe in God; in fact, many do. As long as both religion and science deal only with their special kind of truth, there should be no conflict. But this is not always the case. The *orthodox*, or *fundamentalist*, believer accepts all the teachings of his faith without question. If he is a Christian, his authority is the Bible. Whatever he reads in scripture, he believes is literally true whether or not it agrees with scientific findings. For him heaven and hell are real; angels, too, are real beings because the scriptures say so. He needs no eyewitness reports to confirm their existence.

Orthodox religion affirms belief in miracles, such as the virgin birth of Jesus, the parting of the Red Sea for the passage of the Israelites, or the visits of divine messengers with Mohammed. By their very nature miracles cannot be explained by the usual natural laws that scientists study. Scientists subject religion itself to critical investigations, something that the orthodox believer does not approve of. Astronomers, geologists, and anthropologists may find quite natural explanations for miraculous stories. They also discover great similarities between the sacred writings of the various religions and can demonstrate that, for example, the Christian Bible received much of its content from older spiritual teachings.

Inside and outside of all known religions there have always been some men who claim to have access to a truth that is neither scientific nor based on any authority, such as the Bible. These men are called *mystics*. Zen monks, Jewish Hassidim, Muslim Derwishes, and many Christian saints saw religion as mainly a mystical experience. The mystic *feels* that he has established a line of communication with the supernatural. This feeling is not a matter of learning. According to William James mysticism is a "state of insight into depths of truth unplumbed by the discursive intellect."[5] This insight is a profound emotional event that defies examination.

A mystical experience often comes in the form of a sudden *conversion*, when an individual is in solitude, as it came to Buddha when he was sitting in contemplation under a tree. After a long period of deepest concentration his mind was unexplainably filled with a new insight. He got up, and from that moment on until the end of his life he preached to the world his new message, the Buddhist message. Or the conversion may be triggered in the exciting atmosphere of a mass ritual, such as a revival meeting, when people are suddenly "saved" or "born again."

Man wants to live, and he fears death. Religion gives him hope that all will not end when he closes his eyes for the last time. The body dies, but the soul is immortal. Just what happens to the soul after it leaves its mortal abode is the subject of widely divergent ideas. The ancient Greeks believed that the souls of the dead were confined to a dreary place beyond a wide river. Muslims look forward to an afterlife in which a never-ending festive banquet is laid out for the virtuous and a fiery hell awaits sinners. Many Christians envision heaven as a place full of angels and heavenly music. Others expect a purely spiritual union with God though they may not be sure what this exactly means. Preachers and poets have used their vivid imaginations to paint hell as a place where legions of devils apply fiendish tortures to condemned sinners. Others contend that scenes like this are hardly consistent with the concept of a God who is all good and merciful. Older people who have to face the possibility of death soon are especially concerned with such questions.

The Bible states that God created the world and "saw that it was good." But many people see the world as a place full of evil and man as a basically sinful and unworthy creature who has contaminated God's work. Yet these people don't despair. On the contrary, they live in the hope of a blissful event that will bring salvation from suffering and guilt to all. Orthodox Jews still await the coming of a messiah who will deliver them from their sufferings; certain Christian groups await the Second Coming of Christ as the great turning point in human existence.

IMPORTANT MOMENTS

Religions don't simply present certain beliefs about life and death, about heaven and hell. They demand that their followers do something about these beliefs by following an immense variety of religious practices designed to meet almost every human need.

It is a Saturday morning—the Sabbath according to the Jewish faith. The synagogue, the place where Jews worship, is unusually crowded with men and women in their holiday garments. From the platform the cantor chants prayers in Hebrew. Beside him stands the rabbi clad in a black robe over which is draped a white prayer shawl with long fringe. They open the richly decorated, large "ark" and take from it an object wrapped in gold-embroidered red velvet and topped with a tinkling silver crown. The wrappings are removed. Underneath is a long parchment scroll rolled tightly over two staffs. It is a copy of the *Torah*, the sacred scripture of the Jews. The congregation stands reverently while the Torah is carried to a reading stand.

A boy of thirteen steps up and begins to read a portion from the holy book in a smoothly flowing singsong. He then delivers a little speech explaining what he has just read. The rabbi places his hands on the boy's head and blesses him. Afterward everybody crowds around to congratulate the young man.

This is the celebration of the *bar mitzvah*, which signifies that a boy has now completed his childhood and pledges to be a responsible follower of his religion. The rite of confirmation performed in Christian churches has a similar meaning.

The passing from childhood into adolescence is an important moment in an individual's life. We have a desire to lift such moments out of the day-to-day routine. Even people who otherwise give little regard to religious observances turn to the church to celebrate the birth of a child or the uniting of a couple in marriage. Religious ceremonies also give comfort during times of severe illness and death.

Like the individual, the whole community and the nation try to make important events more impressive with the help of religious gestures. A newly elected President of the United States takes the oath while his hand is on a copy of the Bible, and clergymen of different faiths invoke God's blessing on the new chief of state. Various communities inject moments of religious reverence into their meetings, be they lodge gatherings or high school commencements.

Part of the function that religious holidays serve is to gratify the desire for an occasional break in the monotonous succession of working days. Many old customs surround such days. Observers of religious holidays assemble in sanctuaries or march in solemn processions. Even the more indifferent ones decorate their homes and sit down to ceremonial meals.

Feast days commemorate events in history, or mythology, or in the lives of the spiritual leaders. Christmas and Easter are the most important festivals for Christians, Passover and the Day of Atonement for Jews. Muslims have their holy month of Ramadan, while Buddhists rejoice on

Buddha's birthday. Many of these festivals are older than the religions that observe them. In some instances they were originally colorful celebrations, either gay or solemn, of the ever-recurring cycle of the year, midwinter, the beginning of spring, and harvest time.

RITUAL AND CEREMONY

Each religion creates its own outward forms. There are sights for the eye, sounds for the ear, and even scents for the nose. Gods and spirits are approached through chants, dances, the beating of drums, fire and incense, and also by the dramatic enactment of their deeds. Some of the most magnificent music and poetry has been created in the service of the divine. The paintings of Leonardo da Vinci, the sculptures of Michelangelo, and great cathedrals and mosques testify to the depth of religious inspiration. For the poor, religious works of art have often been the only opportunities to experience beauty; therefore, they have not begrudged the temples and churches golden altars and bejeweled chalices, marble columns, and costly tapestries.

Ritual can be an expression of religion, or it can be an act of *magic*. Magic and religious rituals have much in common, since both attempt to establish contact with the supernatural. A woman who prays to Our Lady of Guadalupe for the recovery of her dying child is following religious ritual. When the same woman, back in her Indian village, retains a medicine man to perform certain rites that will drive the sickness from the child's body, she is taking refuge in magic. Religion appeals to the unseen powers and implores them to grant happiness and keep harm away. Magic, on the other hand, aims at controlling the unseen powers by using the right formulas. For example, this dance will bring rain; that chant will ensure victory in battle or success in the hunt; a certain plant picked at the full moon at midnight will make a barren woman conceive; and a powder made up of ground toads and other ingredients will keep away the plague. When drought threatens to ruin the crops, some people pray to their religious god for rain, while others use potent magical recipes to bring about rain.

Religion and magic are not always clearly separated, however. Pilgrims pray earnestly to Our Lady of Guadalupe, but they also feel that this particular picture of Our Lady has some miracle-working quality. Often believers wear religious medals or touch relics in the same spirit that prompts others to use magic amulets. Some people who consider themselves good Catholics keep good-luck charms on the dashboards of their automobiles, and many an old barn still displays a luck-bearing horseshoe over the door.

A strange mixture of religion and magic is the voodoo cult practiced by certain West Indian blacks. Voodoo combines long-cherished African rites with later adopted Catholic customs, and its followers express themselves in chants and dances and work themselves into ecstatic trances.

Not all magic is good, though, and there is evil magic that must be avoided. Walking under a ladder brings bad luck, and so does the number thirteen. These are examples of *taboos,* which often date back to old religious practices. But now we call them superstitions. Thus we can see that what is one man's religion may be another's superstition.

In magic, as in religion, a distinction is made between the layman and the professional. The expert in magic, be he shaman or witch doctor or medicine man, claims to know just the right way to get results. Many religions attribute similar roles to their priests. Through the priest's mediation and skill, prayer and sacrifice become more potent and the religious ceremonies are made pleasing to the deities.

RULES OF CONDUCT

"Thou shalt. . . ." With these words begin nine of the Ten Commandments, the foremost biblical rules of conduct.

Religion furnishes guidelines by which to live. These guidelines vary considerably among the different faiths. Catholics must go to confession at least once a year and are not supposed to practice most methods of birth control. Some Protestant sects do not allow smoking or dancing. Mormons refrain from coffee and tea, Muslims from wine and pork.

But with all this diversity there are common precepts regarding man's behavior toward his fellow-man. This brings us into the field of *ethics.* Almost universal are the commands to love your neighbor, practice charity, and exhibit compassion—commands more often ignored than heeded. *Liberals,* in contrast to orthodox believers, feel that ethical teachings are the most important aspects of religion, far surpassing in value ceremonial acts.

But morals, or ethics (the two terms have approximately the same meaning), are not always part of religion. A person may never enter a church or may even consider himself an atheist and still show as great a concern for his fellow-man as does a practicing Christian and sometimes even more. The ancient Greeks worshiped their powerful gods because they were afraid of them, but for ethical inspiration they turned to philosophers such as Socrates.

Today many church members in good standing go through all the motions of piety, pray loudly, and fill the collection plate, yet they are full of hatred and even advocate discrimination. Some of the most vicious racists consider themselves good Christians. Others would refer to them as *hypocrites,* people who only pretend to practice religion but violate its basic teachings. Yinger concedes that, on the whole, "correct belief and correct performance of ritual mark the religious man more certainly than does correct conduct."[6]

We find periods when ritual is emphasized over ethics and other times when the situation is reversed. The Hebrew prophets once thundered against the shallowness and hypocrisy of a priest-dominated religion.

They demanded more righteousness and less ritual. Later Jesus preached a similar message. And we can now hear again the cry from many pulpits, especially from the mouths of younger clergymen, that religion has become smug, that it should take up the cause of the poor, the neglected, the persecuted.

RELIGIOUS ORGANIZATION

Now we come to the third of Yinger's three religious elements: the social relationships.

Men dread being alone, and religion is a strong incentive to get together. When you enter your church, you most likely feel a common bond with all the other men and women you see in the pews. You become part of something big and important. "Men are disproportionally drawn to others who share their faith."[7]

In many societies the whole community acts together in matters of religion. Usually all the members of a tribe gather for ceremonies and festivals. In ancient Egypt and Rome, and later in Japan, the ruler was looked upon as a divine being, a living god. Loyalty to the government became synonymous with religious reverence. Priests played politics, and politicians officiated in the temples. Though living gods no longer run the affairs of state, there are still countries where recognized *state religions* exist. In Spain, for example, the Catholic church has a privileged position. It is supported from public funds, the laws are tailored to fit Catholic teachings, and the schools teach what the church prescribes. This dominant position of one single religion can be traced back to the times when rulers allowed their subjects no choice of faith. As the king prayed, so the people had to pray, or else. "Or else" could mean anything from exile to being burned alive.

But not even god-emperors and powerful kings could prevent the rise of new religious expressions. Religious innovators often organize themselves in the form of a *sect*. The small band of early Christians was a sect, as were the first followers of Buddha and the original Quakers and Methodists. Sects arise in protest against existing conditions. The members of a sect close ranks tightly against an outside world that they consider to be full of evil, of which they want as little part as possible. They set up strict rules of behavior that contrast sharply with behavior allowed outside. Violators are rigidly disciplined or expelled. Sects often rally around a charismatic leader who demands absolute loyalty and claims to speak with the voice of divine authority. Half-hearted members are not tolerated in the all-or-nothing membership of sects. The majority has often persecuted sects, but hardship has drawn the membership even closer together.

The Mennonites and the Hutterites, both typical sects, migrated from Germany to the New World to escape wholesale oppression, and their communities are still isolated islands in a strange social ocean. They avoid contact with the outside world as much as possible for fear that such contact will contaminate the young and cause them to break away from the group.

The Dukhobors are another tightly knit sect. Founded in protest against the Russian Orthodox church, which they accused of betraying the true Christian spirit, they were hunted as they fled from one Russian refuge to another. Finally Peter Verigin, a leader who commanded the worshipful loyalty of this sect, led them in exile to British Columbia, where they have built a strongly communal rural life. The world knows of them mainly through sensational news items about their way of objecting to government interference by stripping naked in public. More recently, young dissidents, in the world-at-large, protesting against the "power structure" have shown their disregard of established rules by a similar shedding of garments at their "happenings" and youth festivals.

We will mention only one more of the numerous sects existing in this country, the Jehovah's Witnesses. The members of this sect are awaiting a drastic upheaval in the world, which they predict by mathematical calculations from certain clues in the Bible. In the meantime they try to win converts by making house visits, often to the annoyance of those whom they visit. They also offend many by such practices as resistance to military service and refusal to pledge allegiance to the American flag. These practices have exposed them, especially in times of war, to angry attacks by outraged patriots.

Religious Organization

Tribal or national religion
Sect
Denomination

It was mentioned earlier that the Methodists began as a sect. In the eighteenth century small groups gathered around John Wesley for a more emotional, more mystical experience than could be found in the Church of England. Since then Methodism has attracted millions of followers, thereby losing its sectarian character and becoming a *denomination*. The large Protestant bodies in America, such as Baptists, Lutherans, Episcopalians, and Presbyterians, can also be considered denominations. By and large, a religious denomination is at peace with society as a whole. It is compatible with the mores of the society though individual members may not always be happy with them. When there are conflicts between religious demands and conventional habits, the denomination tends to compromise. Women may be dressed according to the latest fashion when attending church. Men may play golf on the Sabbath, something that would have been strongly frowned upon in the past.

The successful members of society, those who have "made it," feel at ease in belonging to a denomination; they would not be at ease in a sect.

On the other hand, those who feel strongly about the shortcomings of contemporary society will not join already established denominations but form new sects instead or become disgusted with organized religion altogether.

MANY RELIGIONS

If you are convinced by now that religion fulfills many important human needs, you might feel compelled to ask: "But why so many religions? Why not just one? Don't all men have essentially the same basic needs?" These sound like reasonable questions. Why indeed is there this proliferation of churches, denominations, and sects?

Social science finds that different religions are the expressions of different cultures. A faith tailored to one type of society may be incomprehensible or even repellent to another type of society. The Muslim religion was ideally suited to the desert tribesmen among whom it began. The inhabitants of Southern Europe are comfortable with the colorful pageantry of Catholic ritual, while the Puritans, hailing from Northern Europe, demanded simpler and more austere religious practices.

Not only did religion develop in many different forms, but churches have fought each other bitterly over the centuries. At times it was even considered a good deed, pleasing to the deity and guaranteeing salvation, to kill members of another faith. Every conceivable form of religious discrimination has been practiced, from name-calling to the most fiendish tortures, and all this in the name of a God who proclaims "peace on earth and good will toward men." (See also Anti-Semitism in Chapter 5.)

DRAWING TOGETHER

Of late we are finally beginning to recognize that the followers of different religions can live together peacefully and respect each other as human beings. Leaders of different religious groups are even finding out that they have much in common with one another. This feeling has led to the *ecumenical* movement; that is, Protestant, Catholic, and Jewish theologians are meeting for friendly discussions about religious unity. Instead of teaching what is wrong with other religions, churches now cooperate among themselves in many projects. Some have even merged to demonstrate the unity of all men of good will. In 1961, for example, three separate Lutheran denominations combined into the American Lutheran church, and currently discussions are under way by the "Consultation on Church Union" to unite nine different Protestant churches into a single body that would have about 25 million members.

One beloved personality who did much to further ecumenism was Pope John XXIII, who was the world-wide leader of Roman Catholics until his death in 1963. He held long friendly discussions with leaders of

Hinduism
Dancing God Shiva

Judaism
Star of David

Judaism
Tablets of the Law

Shintoism
Gate to Shrine

Judaism
Candelabra (Menorah)

Buddhism
Statue of Buddha

Islam
Crescent

Islam
Mosque

Christianity
Russian Cross

Christianity
Greek Cross

Christianity
Latin Cross

Figure 8
Some Religions of the World and Their Symbols

other religions, something that had never been done before, and he also created special bureaus in the Vatican to find ways of improving relations with other Christian bodies and also with Jews and Muslims.

Yet, despite such trends, it seems extremely unlikely that in the foreseeable future all religions will unite into one. Differences in culture and in types of personalities will probably continue to express themselves in different religious beliefs and practices.

AMERICAN RELIGION

There is no American religion in the same sense that Shintoism is a Japanese religion. Yet several new faiths originated in this country and have a peculiarly American character. Among them are the Mormon religion (officially The Church of Jesus Christ of Latter-day Saints) and Christian Science.

The great majority of Americans, however, are distributed throughout the older religious systems that originated in other parts of the world. About 66 percent are identified with Protestantism, which, in turn, is divided into more than 250 denominations and sects; 26 percent are Catholics, and 3.5 percent are Jews.[8] We also find smaller numbers of Eastern Orthodox Christians, Buddhists, and Muslims. Most white Americans adhere to the religion that they or their ancestors brought along with them as immigrants to this country. Most black Americans are Protestants (like their former slave masters).

Within the older religions differences arose concerning the problem of how to bring traditional forms and practices into line with the American situation. An outgrowth of such differences was the rise of Conservative Judaism. Up to about the time of World War I American Jews belonged to either Orthodox or Reform congregations, both of which had originated in Europe. Orthodox Jews tried to adhere strictly to the religious life they had lived before migrating to this country, while Reform Jews made radical changes until very little of the original traditions were left. A growing number of American Jews became dissatisfied with both of these branches, and so they formed a third one, Conservative Judaism, which occupies the middle ground between the two older forms. Conservative Jews preserve the traditional forms of worship to some extent, but they combine these forms with the customs of American society of which they are a part.[9]

Actually there is no special American religion, but observers note that religious life in the United States, no matter what label it carries, takes on a peculiarly American flavor. We almost try to make God a good American who upholds the righteousness of present American economic, social, and political ways.

Sociologist Robert Bellah speaks of the "American civil religion," which uses the symbols of various faiths to proclaim and honor the history and destiny of the American people.[10] George Washington and Abraham Lincoln, for example, have become more than just historical figures; their position in the American mind approaches that of sainthood. To speak irreverently about them is felt to be near blasphemy. Another example is Memorial Day and Mother's Day, holidays which originally had no religious significance but are now celebrated with sermons and special worship services and with a variety of religious symbolic gestures.[11]

Not many countries have such religious variety. Our Constitution safeguards religious freedom and forbids the government to interfere with religious matters. Therefore everybody is free to choose his own religious company, or to avoid any religion, or to start his own if he so desires. In contrast to countries where one religion predominates *pluralism* is the distinctive feature of religion in the United States. Some citizens even feel that our government has gone too far in its hands-off policy on several occasions, as, for example, when the Supreme Court outlawed reciting prayers in public schools. Others disagree.

On the surface "business is booming" in this country in the area of religious membership. In the last quarter of a century membership in various churches increased at a higher rate than did the general population (59.8 percent as compared to 28.6 percent). About 75 percent of all Americans now belong to a religious organization, and another 20 to 25 percent, though not on the membership rolls, are sympathetic bystanders.[12]

Until recently, the rate of church construction and the attendance figures at services and Sunday school were also on the rise. From the ranks of theology have come some of the most eminent intellectual leaders of our time, such as Reinhold Niebuhr, Martin Buber, Karl Barth, and Jacques Maritain. Their ideas are widely discussed even by people who are not regular churchgoers.

Yet deep shadows darken the well-filled churches, and many leaders show profound concern over the state of religion. They complain that the church is becoming more and more a recreation center or a country club and less and less a place of spiritual commitment and renewal. Well-fed and well-dressed churchgoers gather together in a good many sanctuaries to pat each other on the back, to pretend that everything is well in our society, and that God wants things as they are. The church tends to help preserve the *status quo*, or existing conditions, and is insensitive to the needs of the disturbed and the underprivileged. "Our preaching today," writes Harvey Cox, "is powerless because it does not confront people with the reality which has occurred."[13]

Cox and others express alarm that the churches neglect the misery of the modern city and of the minority groups that are crowded into the city's ghettos. When blacks move into an urban area and middle-class whites flee to the suburbs, the church usually moves with the latter and abandons the new inhabitants to some sort of patronizing missionary effort. "The church bows to the culture instead of resisting and reforming it."[14]

However, not all spokesmen of established religions take the easy way out. Cox himself speaks of significant experiments. Instead of the old residential parishes, we now find churches that minister to special occupational groups, such as the automobile workers in Detroit or artists in Manhattan.[15]

The voice of religion is also pleading loudly at last for racial justice, often against the strong opposition of the dominant group. While many economically successful church members want their clergymen to continue preaching in pious generalities, deeply concerned ministers feel that it is the moral duty of a sincerely religious person to correct injustice in day-to-day living. "We do not expect the country club to set standards of moral principle and practice, but we do await guidance from the church in both respects."[16]

The above statement is by Joseph H. Fichter, a Catholic sociologist and a Jesuit priest. Similar statements have also been made by Protestants and Jews. Priests and nuns, preachers and rabbis have marched and picketed together against racial discrimination and in behalf of other moral causes. Thus we can say that in America different religions are becoming more liberal, more alike, more distinctly American.

A high percentage of Americans are members of religious organizations.
George W. Gardner

In general though, religious practices have a tendency to be conservative. The hymns are old, and so are the vestments and rituals. The Bible is often read in a translation that dates from sixteenth-century England. Yet nowadays we notice efforts, both in the Catholic and Protestant folds, to update religious life. Catholic services are held in the language spoken by the people rather than in Latin, and Bible translations are available in modern English rather than in the English spoken 400 years ago. We can attend jazz masses and sing hymns to a rock-and-roll beat. Behind venerable stained-glass windows coffee houses for the young have been established. Discussion groups wrestle with many contemporary problems ranging from atomic war to the contraceptive pill, regardless of what church authorities may decree in such matters.

Protestants, Catholics, and Jews have similar goals that are typically American—good jobs, financial security, peace of mind. Many people feel that by practicing their religion they can reach these goals more easily. Religion becomes a means rather than an end; it is "good for you." So even when organ strains float over crowded pews, and collection plates grow heavy with good coin as they still do occasionally, the atmosphere inside the sanctuary is a heady mixture of spirituality and *secularism*.

SECULAR RELIGION

"Secular" is the opposite of "religious"; secularism deals with material things, or the world; religion deals with spiritual things, things not of this world. Preaching God's word is a religious occupation; teaching social sciences is a secular one. In older times religion played a much greater role in everyday life than it does today. Practically everything man did, whether he worked or played, was somehow related to religion. But ours is a secular age in which religion is relegated to a rather small role, perhaps an hour on Sunday morning or merely a short moment at Easter time. Many people never engage in any religious practices at all. But even those who never go near a church building are likely to use forms and symbols that are definitely derived from the world of religion.

Have you ever witnessed a Boy Scout honors court, a Campfire Girl assembly, or the solemn gathering of a fraternal lodge? If you have, you will recall hearing prayers and seeing gestures very reminiscent of those that take place in church. The participants wear colorful garments and carry staffs or other objects of special significance. Chains, badges, candles, and ritual pledges have symbolic and sometimes mysterious meanings. One would only have to change some of the words and give the performing officials different names in order to describe a full-fledged religious event.

From time to time groups that resist all existing forms of religion end up creating forms that are distinctly religious in character though not in name. Followers of the hippie movement (which aroused much public attention from 1965 to 1968) reject the society around them, including its religions; but hippie "happenings" show strong similarity to Oriental and American Indian religious forms. One of many short-lived semireligious cults has sprung up around the person of a bearded Indian mystic, Maharishi Yogi, who recommends something that he calls "transcendental meditation" as the cure-all for the world's ills.

We find people who are profoundly dedicated to helping their fellowman, yet God or any other supernatural existence has no place in their lives. We can refer to such people as secular humanists. Their goals are directed toward human beings rather than toward anything superhuman. In pursuing these goals they can be as strongly committed as anybody who worships God.

Communism, definitely a secular movement, is openly hostile to religion, yet it has its own creed, scripture, symbols, festivals, and even saints. On Red Square in Moscow stands the massive tomb of Lenin. Inside lies his embalmed body spotlighted by mysteriously hidden fixtures and guarded by motionless armed men in dress uniform. Like devout pilgrims, Soviet citizens daily file past the waxen figure in the dark business suit, as if it had some miraculous quality.

As the cross is the symbol of Christianity, so the hammer and sickle symbolize the atheistic faith of communism. In many communist states students are taught to believe unquestioningly in the teachings of Marx and Lenin—or Mao—as Christian youths are taught to believe in the truth of the Bible. In either case the teachers are not always successful.

Another very powerful substitute for religion is *nationalism,* the conviction that one's own nation is great and has a very special mission to fulfill. With its flags and songs, parades and sacred pledges, nationalism commands stronger loyalties than does religion in many parts of the world. Radical nationalists show the kind of enthusiasm, often even the kind of willingness, to sacrifice their own lives that was displayed by the religious martyrs of old. Both communism and nationalism are religions without a god, or "nontheistic religions" as Yinger would call them.[17] God has been replaced by an *ideology,* which is a group of ideas forming the program of a political or cultural movement.

Main Ideas
1. Religion fulfills man's need for comfort and security in a hostile natural environment.
2. Religion encompasses beliefs in supernatural powers, practices to appease and approach these powers, and systems of social relationships that provide a sense of belonging and serenity.
3. Among the various concepts of the supernatural developed by man animism, fetishism, polytheism, henotheism, and monotheism are most frequently found. The religions of Western civilization are mostly monotheistic.
4. Religion competes with modern science in explaining the nature of existence and in the search for truth.
5. Orthodox religion accepts religious authority without question.
6. The mystic claims to have an immediate and unexplainable insight into the nature of the supernatural.
7. Religion responds to man's fear of death and permanent extinction.
8. Religion furnishes opportunities to solemnize important moments in the lives of the individual, the community, and the nation.
9. Religion approaches the supernatural power with prayerful requests, whereas magic tries to control it.
10. Religious doctrines and organizations are important instruments in the control of human behavior.
11. Some more frequently found forms of religious organization are the tribal or national religion, the sect and the denomination.
12. The many existing religions are the expressions of different cultures, and they fill the needs of different types of individuals.
13. Religious pluralism prevails in America.
14. American churches are mainly middle-class establishments, yet

there is a demand for the church to take a stronger role in moral and social involvement.

15. Even outside the established religions, religious forms and symbols are widely used.

Important Terms

Agnosticism	Monotheism
Animism	Mysticism
Anthropomorphic gods	Myth
Atheism	Nationalism
Bar mitzvah	Orthodox
Conversion	Pluralism
Denomination	Polytheism
Ecumenical movement	Sect
Ethics	Secularism
Fetishism	State religion
Henotheism	Status quo
Hypocrites	Taboo
Ideology	Theism
Liberal	Theology
Magic	Torah

Conclusion

Religion has been an ingredient of man's life, probably since his beginning. Once it controlled practically every aspect of man's behavior. Today it battles with secular institutions that seem to increase in power with every passing year. Yet organized religion is not about to pass out of existence. On the contrary, institutionalized religion shows signs of renewed vigor. Churches are experimenting with new ideas and new forms. Though religion is no longer the final authority in many fields of knowledge, it remains a binding element in the realm of human association. Recent studies indicate that on the levels of personal friendship, social belonging, and sharing pastimes with fellow-men, people continue to seek out members of their own faith.[18]

Notes

1. E. Adamson Hoebel, *Anthropology: The Study of Man*, 3rd ed. (New York: McGraw-Hill, 1958), pp. 464 ff.
2. Gerhard Lenski, *The Religious Factor* (Garden City, N.Y.: Doubleday, 1961), pp. 298–299. This book is based on a Detroit area study of contemporary religious behavior, carried on in 1957–1958.
3. J. Milton Yinger, *Religion, Society and the Individual* (New York: Macmillan, 1957), p. 10.

4. *Ibid.*, p. 12.
5. William James, *The Varieties of Religious Experience* (New York: New American Library, 1958), p. 293.
6. Yinger, *op. cit.*, p. 24.
7. Lenski, *op. cit.*, p. 301.
8. Adapted from the figures in *Statistical Abstract of the United States*, 1968, pp. 41–42.
9. Marshall Sklare, *Conservative Judaism* (Glencoe, Ill.: The Free Press, 1955).
10. "A Civil Religion," *Newsweek*, February 3, 1969, p. 82.
11. W. Lloyd Warner, *The Living and the Dead* (New Haven, Conn.: Yale University Press, 1959), pp. 278–279, 343–345.
12. Will Herberg, *Protestant-Catholic-Jew* (Garden City, N.Y.: Doubleday, 1955), pp. 47–49.
13. Harvey Cox, *The Secular City* (New York: Macmillan, 1965), p. 122.
14. *Ibid.*, p. 159.
15. Joseph H. Fichter, "American Religion and the Negro," in Peter I. Rose (ed.), *The Study of Society: An Integrated Anthology* (New York: Random House, 1967), p. 747.
16. *Ibid.*, p. 748.
17. Yinger, *op. cit.*, p. 14.
18. Lenski, *op. cit.*

Suggestions for Further Reading

Ballou, Robert O. (ed.). *The Portable World Bible*. New York: Viking, 1944 (paperback). Selections from the scriptures of the major religions.

Bradley, David G. *A Guide to the World's Religions*. Englewood Cliffs, N.J.: Prentice-Hall, 1962 (paperback).

Cary, Joyce. *The Captive and the Free*. New York: Harper, 1959. Novel about a faith healer.

"A Chicago Catholic Asks: Where Does My Church Stand on Racial Justice?" *Look*, 30, November 1, 1966, 82–86.

"The Cool Generation and the Church," *Commonweal*, 87, October 6, 1967, 11–23.

Dimont, Max I. *Jews, God and History*. New York: Signet, 1964 (paperback).

Ellis, John Tracy. *American Catholicism*. Chicago: University of Chicago Press, 1956. History of the Catholic church in America from the earliest explorations to the 1950s and discussion of the problems that Catholics face in this country.

Fleming, E. D. "California Cults and Crackpots," *Cosmopolitan*, 146 (May 1959), 80–84.

Frazer, J. G. *The Golden Bough*. New York: Macmillan, 1922. Classic review of magic and religious practices.

Gaer, Joseph. *How the Great Religions Began*. Rev. ed. New York: Signet, 1958 (paperback).

Glazer, Nathan. *American Judaism*. Chicago: University of Chicago Press,

1957. History of Jewish settlement in America and of developments in the religious life of American Jews.

Gordon, Noah. *The Rabbi*. New York: McGraw-Hill, 1965. Novel about the problems facing a modern American rabbi.

"Jazz Goes to Church," *Ebony* (April 1966), pp. 76–80.

Lewis, John. *Religions of the World Made Simple*. Rev. ed. Garden City, N.Y.: Doubleday, 1958.

Lewis, Sinclair. *Elmer Gantry*. New York: Harcourt, Brace, 1927. Novel about a revival preacher.

Novak, Michael. "The Underground Church," *Saturday Evening Post*, 242, December 28, 1968, January 11, 1969, 26–29, 62–67.

Robinson, Henry M. *The Cardinal*. New York: Simon & Schuster, 1950. Novel about life and problems inside the Catholic clergy.

PART THREE THE WORLD OF WORK

Traveling businessman from New York to Pueblo Indian relaxing in the sun:
"Why aren't you working?"
"Why should I work?"
"To earn money."
"Why should I want to earn money?"
"So you can save it. Some day you can retire and won't have to work anymore."
"I'm not working now," says the Indian.[1]

9 WHAT DO YOU DO FOR A LIVING?

work—blessing or curse?

WHY WORK?

The Pueblo Indian relaxing in the sun makes sense, very good sense. Yet to the businessman from New York, he is an oddity, he is out of step.

Here is another case in point:

A friend of the author, a forester by profession, recently went to Nigeria, on a government project, to introduce modern logging operations in the tropical forest. Native workers were hired, but they invariably quit after a day or two. As soon as they had earned enough to provide their families with food for a while, they could no longer see any good reason to go on sweating and toiling. This seemed to them a perfectly sensible arrangement, but our American forester pulled his hair in desperation. How could he organize an efficient operation under such circumstances?

Now let's return from the jungle to more familiar ground:

It is Monday morning. The alarm clock rings. You yawn, rub the sleep from your eyes, and then reluctantly get out of bed. The pleasures of the weekend are but a memory. No more

163

leisurely breakfasts for a while, no more relaxed reading of the morning paper or slow strolling through the park.

Now it is time to rush to kiss the children good-bye, meet the fellows in the car pool, get on the freeway before it becomes too clogged with traffic, find a parking place, punch a time clock with barely enough time to spare before the whistle blows, work eight hours, and then once more struggle through the rush-hour homeward-bound traffic. The work week has begun, and you're back to the five-day routine.

What else would you want to do on a Monday morning? Or on any other morning between Monday and Friday, for that matter? Work is what the week is for. We find that life without work is hard to imagine, for we live in a *work culture*.

WORK—A CURSE

For our forefathers work was synonymous with long, hard, and often dangerous drudgery. In many parts of the world it still is. Hunting and fishing for survival, scratching the soil with primitive hoes that are in turn fashioned by back-breaking labor: this is the work that has filled endless days, that still drains the energy of people in underdeveloped countries. No wonder work has been regarded as a necessary evil like a foul-smelling medicine.

The Bible branded human labor as a divinely ordained punishment. When Adam and Eve dwelled in paradise they spent their days in idle happiness. The Garden of Eden had no shops, farms, or offices. But then the first couple sinned, and God expelled them from paradise with the curse, "In the sweat of thy brow shalt thou eat bread" (Gen. 3:19). Work has filled the waking hours of man from then till now, whether or not one accepts this religious explanation.

Work has been regarded as punishment by a great many people throughout the history of mankind. Leisure has usually been the privilege of ruling groups, work the curse of those that the privileged groups kept suppressed. In many societies men have made other men into slaves to work without limit at the pleasure of their masters. Prisoners of war frequently became the slaves of their captors. When this labor resource was too meager, slaves were acquired by armed raids into neighboring territories or were bought on the market from slave traders, men who were in the business for profit.

Slavery—that is, when one person becomes the "property" of another —existed in ancient Greece and Rome, in Africa and Arabia, in the Southern states of America, and in many other places. Although not all slaves led a life of continual misery, those who were put to work rowing galleys or laboring on plantations and in mines were treated as human machines that were operated until they wore out and had to be replaced.

Where slavery exists, the temptation to treat a slave as a tool rather than as a fellow human being is great.

Not much better off than slaves were the medieval serfs who plowed the fields, cut the forests, and built the castles in which the lords feasted unless they were busy fighting each other. What the serf produced belonged to the lord, who in turn let the serf keep barely enough to stay alive. Rennants of this system still survive in Latin America and the Middle East.

In some societies people were forced to work as a punishment for real or alleged wrongdoings, and this system endures in prisons and in forced labor camps. Men convicted to indentured servitude or those who volunteered to be indentured were among the first settlers of America and Australia. Not so long ago, the traveler could still observe chain gangs of convicts working on highways under the watchful eye of guards with shotguns.

Hitler rounded up people by the hundreds of thousands and herded them into the ammunitions factories of the Rhineland. Stalin too forced many people into the mines of Siberia. These are actual examples of twentieth-century slave labor on a giant scale.

THE VIRTUE

Now you are ready to protest: "I'm not a slave. I want to work, and I like to work. I do it of my own free will." Work has come to be regarded as a virtue. "It is the right thing to do." This attitude has also received the blessing of religion.

In the monasteries of the Middle Ages monks divided their waking hours between prayer in the chapel and work in the field or library. *Ora et labora* (pray and work), the rule laid down by Saint Benedict, was their guideline. In fact, they regarded their work, whether manual or mental, as another form of service to God.

Protestantism, which appeared in the sixteenth century, gave the strongest boost to the idea that work is the true Christian way of life. Its leaders, particularly John Calvin, taught that idleness is sin and that man has to merit his salvation by hard toil. If Christians applied themselves industriously, God would surely reward them with wealth and prestige even before they reached heaven. Thus wealth and prestige were signs of God's favor, and the rich could now rest assured that the Lord was on their side.

This new doctrine appealed particularly to the rising class of merchants and traders, who had always worked hard. Whereas the nobility had regarded work as something degrading, the new middle class found pride and religious comfort in the efforts and skills that brought its members material gains.

Christianity is not alone in praising work as a sterling virtue. The message seems to have passed from the believers to the nonbelievers, from West to East, from religion to communist atheism. In the Soviet Union, and more recently in China, children are taught that a good communist is a hard and dependable worker. Only by putting in long hours in a factory or on a collective farm can a person prove himself a worthy member of the party. He is constantly urged to work as hard as possible to meet quotas set by the state planners for factories, farms, and mines. Workers who outproduce their comrades are feted as heroes and rewarded with medals and free vacations. There have been propaganda stories of how boy meets girl in the tractor plant, but instead of wasting time on dates they decide to do overtime for the good of the state.

REWARDS OF WORK

What does man get out of work?

For the primitive hunter or fisherman the reward was enough food for his family. If he came home with more food than his family could have used, he might have traded off the surplus for something he needed. He might have *bartered*. This is the oldest form of commerce.

Peasants used to barter grain and fowl for tools and salt. Craftsmen, in turn, wanted food and raw material for the products of their skills: more leather to make shoes, flax and wool to make cloth. Merchants brought spices and tea from the tropics and exchanged them for furs and metal from other parts of the world.

Modern economic life is too complicated to utilize extensive bartering as a means of exchange. But little boys still enjoy engaging in intricate negotiations in which they exchange a candy bar for some marbles or a stick of chewing gum for a slingshot. And not only children continue to barter. What merchants have long abandoned, governments still practice to further their political or military goals. They conclude large-scale treaties with each other to barter wheat for machinery, oil for airplanes, and almost anything for weapons of war.

What men in advanced civilizations want for their work is *money*, for ours is a money economy. The dollar, the peso, and the franc are the media by which we exchange the products of our work for the things we need in order to exist. The paycheck of an employee, the profit of a merchant are the standard rewards for time, training, and ingenuity expended in work. Americans even rank people by the amount of money they are able to accumulate. A boy who starts his career by sweeping the floors of a bank and ends up as its president, a man who begins in a stockroom and rises to the position of owning a chain of department stores—these are the heroes of a money-minded society. We even speak of Mr. Jones being "worth half a million," as if the worth of a man could be measured by his bank balance.

Money is the most obvious compensation for services rendered, but it is far from the only form of compensation. Job satisfaction, that is, whether a person is satisfied with the work he does, depends on a number of other things besides the pay. In our work we seek fulfillment of various needs. Having an occupation gives us *identity*. We all identify ourselves as males or females, as strong or weak, but important too is our self-identification as students, mechanics, businessmen, farmers, nurses, and so forth. When you make a new acquaintance, one of the first questions you are likely to ask is, "What do you do?"

The type of work you do helps determine your social *status* (see Chapter 11). In James Michener's novel *Hawaii*[2] a very gifted child is refused admission to a private school because his father makes a living collecting refuse at night. The type of work that parents do even reflects on their offspring.

People often choose an occupation to achieve a certain kind of satisfaction. For example, those who find great enjoyment in traveling, or learning new things, or meeting interesting people may be attracted by occupations in the fields of science, education, journalism, or politics. The person who desires to create beauty or to be surrounded by it may want to be an artist, a poet or novelist, a musician, architect, interior decorator, or fashion designer.

Everybody seeks security and a sense of belonging. Work opens up the opportunity for *self-actualization*, which is the chance to apply whatever talents and interests one may have. A young person aims at a certain career because he feels he is the kind of individual who should do this type of work.

Satisfaction derives from the feeling of having done a good job, and most working people desire to do their best. Gratification comes to the craftsman and the artist from seeing a fine product taking shape under their hands, to the actor and musician from the applause of the audience, to the physician, nurse, and medical technician from the restored health of the patient. The gratitude of a client, a customer, or a student, the praise of a factory or office supervisor, or a well-earned promotion are cherished forms of recognition for work that is well done.

The hours we spend on a job give the day a definite pattern, which becomes a habit to us. We also get used to the company of our fellow workers. In many instances enduring bonds of friendship develop between the men who go out together to string power lines or among the women who type letters in the same office. The members of the work gang, the office team, the school faculty enjoy each other's company because they have a great deal in common, whether they swap ideas about their tasks or gripe about the boss. Those relationships are often sorely missed when workers change jobs or retire.

Lack of job satisfaction can cause deep depression. Work that may have looked fascinating at a distance can turn out to be dreary and monotonous. A technician finds himself unable to keep pace with changing procedures. A salesman does not reach his quota of required sales. Hostile fellow workers, a nasty foreman: when several such unfortunate experiences come together, grave personality disorders may result. The worker sometimes takes out his grievances on his wife and children, or on himself, or even on the family pet.

The obvious question arises: "If you don't like your job, why don't you move on to another one?" Many do just that. Ambitious workers, especially in the professions, rise from modest to more rewarding positions. There is, for example, a constant migration of college teachers from school to school to gain more prestige and higher salary as well as greater job autonomy.

But for many people better jobs are difficult to get. Older persons find it extremely difficult to relocate. Some employers close their doors to applicants beyond a certain age no matter how capable these applicants may be. Industrial workers depend on seniority for job improvement. Family ties, home mortgages, and sheer lack of initiative may also stand in the way of striking out for greener pastures in the job market.

WORK WITHOUT PAY

Not all work is done for money. In fact, throughout the ages some thinkers, such as Sir Thomas More,[3] have argued that love of money is the root of all evil. It fosters greed and brings out the worst in man. Sir Thomas More envisioned an ideal society, called *Utopia,* in which people work for the common good without any cash rewards.

From time to time small groups of enthusiasts have tried to form actual utopian communities. Such experiments in communal work have usually been short-lived, except when they were backed by strong religious convictions. For about one hundred years the Hutterites, a small Protestant sect, have inhabited small villages in the Middle West. Their farmland, houses, and livestock are owned collectively. They eat in a common mess hall, and their daily work is assigned them by an elected manager.

In modern Israel we find a similar type of settlement, called the *kibbutz*. The kibbutz may sell what its fields and orange groves produce, but the money received goes into a common treasury from which the members draw what they need in food, clothing, schooling, or travel expenses.

Although a Utopia today has remained a dream, in our society individual young men and women are trying to make it come closer to reality, at least for a year or two. They join such programs as the Peace Corps or VISTA (Volunteers in Service to America) to work for the poor and the backward with little or no financial return for themselves. Many others give of their spare time without pay to work for causes that they believe are valuable. Some are active in politics, others visit the sick, teach the illiterate, or help in the struggle against discrimination.

MONEY AND MACHINE

Having discussed work as punishment, work in collective communities, and the various labors of love undertaken without pay, we come to the most common kind of work situation in our society: people work to earn a living, and they work either for themselves, or they use their muscles and brains in the service of others.

The slaves and serfs that we discussed earlier were not their own bosses, but they worked for their masters and had little choice in the matter besides. But in some of the early communities of free men most working people used to be their own bosses. The peasant tilled his tiny plot with the help of his wife and children. In town the craftsman owned his little shop, including the back rooms where he ate and slept. During the day he fashioned shoes, saddles, oil lamps, or whatever was the product of his craft, and he then sold his products directly to the customer. The merchant offered his wares for sale from a stall in the marketplace or peddled them in a cart from door to door. Hired help was not much in evidence.

Two events changed this picture radically and divided most of the working force into two distinct groups: dependent and independent persons, or employees and employers. These two revolutionary events were the arrival of *capitalism* and *industrialization*.

Capitalism is roughly defined as the use of money to make more money. Some early merchants were so successful that they accumulated large amounts of gold and silver. Using these resources they hired others to work for them. A cloth dealer, for example, paid five, ten, or more weavers in cash for the cloth they had woven on their hand looms during the week; then he would attempt to sell the whole lot at a considerable profit.

Now add to this setup the use of mechanical power and machinery, and you have industrialization. A host of ingenious inventions replaced the old hand tools with labor-saving monsters of steel. Instead of human or animal muscle power steam, electricity, and the combustion engine were introduced. Today we are harnessing even more awesome sources of power. Besides using atomic energy, we may soon be able to use solar energy.

Machinery and mechanical power are put to use in the modern *factory*, a well-organized arrangement of technical devices and of the men who operate them. Engineers and efficiency experts constantly devise new ways of saving human labor and thereby increasing profits. In such large plants as the Ford Motor Company's River Rouge complex in Michigan workers are stationed along a continuously moving assembly line. As each uncompleted automobile moves by, each worker performs a single short task. All day long a worker may merely tighten the same few bolts or insert the same piece of tubing.

If industry as a whole had a motto, it might very well be: Be Efficient and Cut Production Cost.

BUSINESS

One in seven American working people is self- or family-employed. There were eight million American business units in 1970. All but a small fraction of them were tiny enterprises owned by a single person.[4] Many of these enterprises consist of businessmen who sell a product or a service.

Small business has experienced hard times in the present century. The little store and the owner-operated craftshop, which once dominated town life, are now retreating before big business. The neighborhood tailor cannot compete with the garment factory. The corner grocery store has to wage a desperate battle for survival with the supermarket on the next block.

Small operations can prosper these days, however, when they create highly specialized products: orthopedic shoes, personalized photographs, and so forth. They can also do well if they turn from production to service work. There is, for example, a great demand for television repairmen and other such skilled persons. Thus small business is not about to disappear, and the outlook is promising if owners are willing to adapt to the needs of the times. Over 80 percent of all businesses are in the hands of single owners, and most of them are small operations contributing less than 10 percent to the Gross National Product.[5]

A person trying to decide whether or not to go into business for himself would be well advised to weigh the advantages against the disadvantages.

Some of the positive reasons are:

1. Nobody can fire him.
2. All he earns (minus expenses) is his.
3. Nobody can order him around; he's independent.
4. He can put all his talent and know-how to use; he can express himself fully.

But there are also negative features:

1. Sucess depends entirely on my own work. I may not be able to quit after having put in an eight-hour day. When sickness strikes, the work may not get done.
2. When the business loses money, the loss is all mine.
3. Where do I get credit to hire help and to expand?
4. What happens when I want to retire or when I die?

To avoid some of the drawbacks of self-employment, other forms of business organization have been developed: the *partnership* and the *corporation*. In a partnership two or more owners share the work and the responsibilities. They also divide the profit and, when things don't turn out well, the loss.

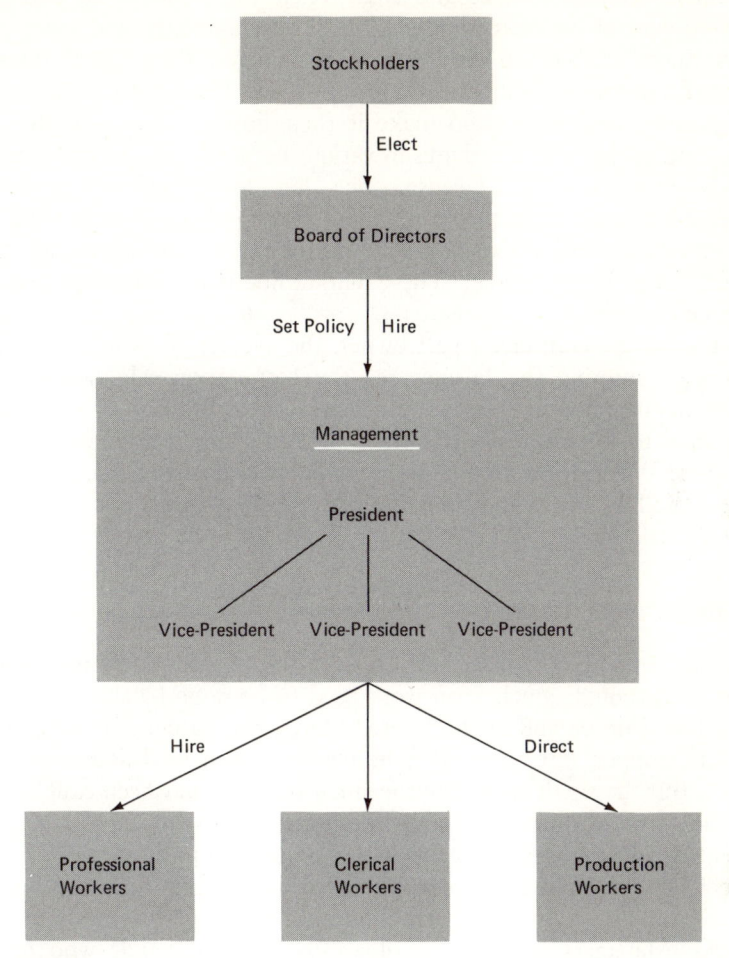

Figure 9
Structure of a Typical Corporation

Source: Reprinted by permission of the publisher, from S. D. Gordon and J. Witchel, *An Introduction to the American Economy* (Lexington, Mass.: Heath, 1967), p. 46.

Most typical of modern economic life is the corporation. Invariably large industries—chain stores, banks, insurance companies, transportation and communications firms—operate as corporations. Ownership is distributed among many people, often thousands of them, who have bought shares in the company. The profits are divided among the shareholders in the form of *dividends*—interest on their investments—unless they are used to enlarge or modernize the business. If the corporation loses money, the shareholder can only lose what he has invested; beyond that he is not liable.

Shares can be bought and sold. Their value moves up and down following general business trends, political developments, and many other factors. Speculators try to cash in on such changes. They "play" the stock market. Enormous amounts of money are made (and lost) by individuals and by investment firms who make it their business to watch the stock market and to buy and sell shares in various corporations. Actually theirs is not a business in the strict sense, since they do not sell any product or service. They only trade pieces of paper back and forth, indicating how much stock they own at the moment, and they try to take advantage of the ups and downs in the market. These market fluctuations are reported daily by our news media.

Though he is in fact a part owner, the average *stockholder* has little to do with running the business of the corporation. He hopes for an increase in the value of his investment and leaves the task of running the corporation to the *management*, which in turn supervises the corporation's employees. When there are many stockholders, a board of directors, which makes overall decisions and hires the managerial personnel, is elected (see Figure 9).

FARMING

What has become of the farmer? He is, after all, the oldest independent worker even though much farm work used to be done by slaves and serfs. In Western Europe and in the United States, the farmer may be a tenant or a sharecropper, but quite often he owns his own land and is proud of the fact. But the small farm, like the small business, has been caught up in the trend toward bigness. Today the most successful farms are those superenterprises that sell $25,000 worth of produce or more annually.[6]

Those enormous farms can be called agricultural factories. In fact, they are sometimes owned by corporations, just like steel mills or radio networks. Managers supervise small armies of farm hands who operate costly up-to-date machinery. Though the number of individual farms is steadily decreasing, the products of field and pasture are piling up in silos and warehouses. While millions go hungry on other continents, we have problems deciding what to do with the farming surplus.

Percentage of the American Labor Force Working on Farms

1900	37.6
1964	7.5
1967	2.1

Source: Reprinted by permission of the publisher, from S. D. Gordon and J. Witchel, *An Introduction to the American Economy* (Lexington, Mass.: Heath, 1967), p. 72.

The mechanization of the farm has changed the character of rural America. Because fewer jobs are available on the farm, young people are moving from rural areas into the city in a continuous stream, leaving behind an aging village population. The average farmer and farm laborer is five to nine years older than are male working people in general.[7]

In order to remain profitable family farms now need more land; otherwise the costly modern farm equipment could not be put to effective use. Lacking sufficient acreage, the head of the family is often forced to take a job in a nearby mill or factory and to do the farm chores during his off-hours.

Though fewer farmers are now needed to feed the nation, we cannot allow our rural areas to become completely deserted. In order to keep a necessary minimum number of farms producing, the federal government has introduced crop subsidies to control the number of acres under cultivation, and give all kinds of technical and scientific assistance. Farmers, many of whom are proud individualists, have openly resented this increasing interference by the government, but have grudgingly made use of its help, realizing that it was badly needed. The federal program of farm subsidies has come under much criticism. In order to keep prices for farm products up farmers are often paid for leaving their land uncultivated. This seems to be particularly unfair since the large landowners profit the most from this practice.

EMPLOYMENT

Most people work for other people, that is, they are employees. Together with those who are actively looking for jobs they constitute the *labor force*.

Labor Force in the United States

1919	42,000,000
1962	68,000,000
1968	79,000,000
1975	92,000,000 (estimate)
1980	100,700,000 (estimate)

Source: United States Department of Labor, *Occupational Outlook Handbook*, 1966–1967, p. 18; and 1970–1971, p. 11.

A growing population produces a growing labor force, and every year a new crop of 1.5 million young men and women knock at the doors of employment offices and personnel directors seeking jobs. Not only is the labor force growing constantly in size, but *productivity*, the output per worker per hour, is also increasing by leaps and bounds.

Who are the millions who make up the labor force? They do not constitute a faceless mass. Every member is an individual, yet some general statements can be made about the labor force as a whole—about age, for example.

Today the typical American employee is an adult male between the ages of twenty and sixty-five. This has not always been the case. In the early days of the factory children worked ten hours a day and more, women pulled carts in underground coal mines, and men stayed on the job till they broke down of old age or sickness. As late as 1890, one boy in four and one girl in ten at ages from ten to fifteen held steady jobs. Today child labor is mostly a thing of the past. Older workers retire at about the age of sixty-five.

A greater percentage of women than ever before hold down well-paying jobs. Women, in general, do not complain about this trend, since work is for them not a mark of oppression but, on the contrary, a symbol of social equality with men. Mothers and wives don't go down into dark mine shafts anymore but take their places alongside men in factories, offices, and stores, and not always in the lowest paid positions. About one-third of the total work force consists of females. The percentage of better-educated women who work is higher than that of less-educated women. Often the black woman finds it easier to get a job than does her mate.

Of course, most women have always worked. The housewife usually spent the whole day doing her chores; women working for people other than their own families as maids, cooks, and cleaning women, used to be a more common sight than it is today. But electric mixers and polishers, frozen and instant foods, and all kinds of modern gadgets have freed the housewife from much of her drudgery. And domestic service, since it pays so little, is no longer considered a desirable occupation. In fact, only 3 percent of working women still hold such jobs.

WHAT KIND OF JOB?

The *Dictionary of Occupational Titles*[8] lists about 25,000 jobs. And if this is not bewildering enough, some titles are becoming obsolete, while new ones are showing up. The demand for carriage makers or gas lamplighters has long since disappeared. Now the job of elevator operator is about to become extinct. On the other hand, the help-wanted call is out for computer programmers, punch card operators, and communications and rehabilitation specialists. These are occupations that hardly existed a generation or two ago. In fact, about half of today's employees are engaged in occupations that have only come into being in the last twenty years.

Here is a frequently used breakdown of the immense number of occupational titles into more manageable subdivisions:

1. Professional occupations (Physicians, lawyers, teachers, writers, and so forth)
2. Managerial occupations (Directors, supervisors, planners, comptrollers, and so forth)
3. Clerical occupations (Sales clerks, secretaries, bookkeepers, and so forth)

4. Service occupations (Domestic workers, waiters, repairmen, policemen, and so forth)
5. Skilled crafts (Printers, mechanics, electricians, and so forth)
6. Semiskilled occupations (Drill press operators, truck drivers, and so forth)
7. Unskilled occupations (Laborers, stackers of crates, and so forth)[9]

This list does not represent the only way of subdividing occupational titles. There are likely to be disagreements as to which occupation belongs to which category. But rather than making any new classifications, let's observe some general trends in the present occupational picture.

The professions require long training, usually at a university. Doctors, lawyers, and many creative artists are often independent agents who sell their services or products as do businessmen. Specialization steadily multiplies the number of professions. In the medical field, for instance, there are now specialists for practically every part of the human body and for every kind of disease. We find criminal lawyers, corporation lawyers, lawyers who specialize in tax cases, in divorces, and so on.

More and more people in various occupations are trying to raise themselves to the rank of professionals. This is true of engineers, social workers, nurses, and many others, though these people are more often employed than independent. The requirements for professional training are rising, and so are income and prestige. "The professions are being socialized, and the social and public services are being professionalized."[10]

This fact leads us to a quite recent development: the appearance of the *semiprofessional* occupations. Semiprofessional people aid the professionals who are usually in short supply. The technician assists the engineer, the medical technician the physician, the dental hygienist the dentist. These occupations require considerable training but less than the professions themselves.

Managerial people are the decision makers in corporations, government agencies, school systems, and in religious organizations. William H. Whyte, Jr., coined the term "organization man"[11] to describe members of this occupational category. He shows how many of these highly placed men are really "company men," that is, possessed, body and soul, by the firm for which they work. Though their pay is quite substantial, their working day often extends beyond the usual eight hours. Their social life too may be an extension of their office life. On the golf course and in the cocktail lounge the company seems to dominate their talk and action, and this control extends to the company wives as well. Both husband and wife are expected to display conventional behavior and to refrain from doing or saying anything that could cause raised eyebrows.

The organization man finds himself—and sometimes even his wife and family—in a highly competitive setup. In order to move up the ladder of promotion, he must please his superiors, who tend to judge him by their own standards. His situation can be compared to that of climbing up a pyramid: the higher he goes, the fewer the positions available and the fiercer the competition.

Managerial people working for a large enterprise or for a branch of government form a *bureaucracy*. Though we obviously cannot do without it, the bureaucracy must take a lot of critical lambasting. "The principal fault that gives bureaucracy a bad name is the ritualistic compliance with rules and procedures without realistic reference to goals to be accomplished and problems to be solved."[12] We often call this endless procession of meaningless rituals "red tape." In fact, complaints about time-consuming and seemingly senseless red tape frequently make good topics for discussion among friends and acquaintances.

> Frustrated clients can relieve their pent-up aggression in discussions of bureaucratic stupidity and red tape. Whereas the organization's ruthlessness, not its inefficiency, is the source of their antagonism, by expressing it in the form of an apparently disinterested criticism of performance, clients derive a feeling of superiority over the "blundering bureaucrats."[13]

Clerical workers may have been trained in high schools, business schools, or on the job. They are expected to dress conservatively and be well mannered, and they consider themselves as "white-collar" workers, a rather loose term that might include most of the occupations discussed so far. White-collar workers sometimes show contempt for blue-collar workers, who engage in physical labor, even though the man in the overalls may make more money than the man in the business suit. A female clerk in the front office of a factory was overheard boasting, "I don't care how much they make in the plant. My job is ten times better."[14]

The term "service occupations" covers a wide range of jobs. The only element that these various jobs have in common is that their holders don't fashion a product but help others to greater comfort and safety. This description fits the barber and the taxi driver, as well as the Federal Bureau of Investigation (FBI) agent. There is considerable variety in the skills required for this steadily growing list of occupations.

Skilled craftsmen are the elite of blue-collar society, proud of their competence and jealous of any intruders. They have usually completed several years of training, and in many instances—as happened to printers, welders, and others—they must retrain as technical advances make their skills partially obsolete.

Semiskilled workers are the privates first class of the industrial army, and they form the largest single group of employed people. Their training may last from a few weeks to a few months. Semiskilled workers usually do the routine jobs of factory work, which have a tendency to become monotonous. Here is a typical complaint: "The job gets so sickening—day in day out plugging in ignition wires. I get through with one motor, turn around, and there is another staring me in the face."[15]

There is little in the average factory job that gives the worker a feeling of accomplishment. His day is regulated by a time clock. He follows a set procedure with little or no variety in his task. As Simone Weil describes the situation, "Things play the role of men, men the role of things."[16]

However, we can also hear more optimistic accounts. John Kenneth Galbraith finds that factory work is becoming easier and more pleasant,[17] and that even factory surroundings seem to be taking on a more inviting air. Instead of the old soot-covered, smoke-belching monstrosities, the satanic mills that were the industrial plants of yesterday, architects now favor "dispersed one-story plants no more imposing than one of the new suburban shopping centers."[18] Some of the newer factories, hidden behind shrubbery and surrounded by landscaped lawns with fountains and picnic tables, could easily pass for vacation resorts. These are attempts to overcome the worker's distaste for his job.

The last occupation on our list is that of the unskilled worker. Workers in all categories discussed so far are in short supply, and even greater shortages are forecast. But the outlook darkens as we come to the last group. Once, the overwhelming majority of working people had no skills. Many never learned how to read and write. Schoolchildren were told to study or else face a career as a ditch digger or street sweeper. Today, however, ditches are dug and streets are swept by huge machines with a single man at the controls. The ranks of unskilled labor are thinning rapidly because their jobs are disappearing.

Yet concerned observers claim that, given the necessary public interest and funds, even unskilled people can be put to work to perform much needed services. An immediate need exists for the jobs shown in the following table, all of which require only very simple skills and which would contribute immeasurably to the public welfare.

Where Help Is Needed

Aides in medical and health services	1,200,000 needed
Aides in educational institutions	1,000,000 needed
National beautification work	1,300,000 needed
Welfare and home care	700,000 needed
Public protection	350,000 needed
Urban renewal and sanitation	650,000 needed

Source: Reprinted from *Commentary*, by permission; Copyright © 1966 by the American Jewish Committee. Reprinted by permission of Robert Lekachman.

FINDING A JOB

Next to selecting a partner for marriage, choosing an occupation is perhaps the most important decision a young person has to make. Yet careers are often selected in haphazard ways. Many adolescents "fall" into jobs without seeking information about the work situation in either their home community or in other locations.

Few people know during childhood what they want to do with their lives. In earlier times a son would follow his father's occupation. The cobbler's son became a cobbler, and the young nobleman followed his ancestors into a military or diplomatic career. In some places even the position of executioner was hereditary. There are still instances of sons following their fathers into politics, or the ministry, or other careers, but in most cases the young now make their own choices. Middle-class parents especially encourage their children to aim for a higher occupational level than their own generation has achieved.

America has often been called the land of unlimited opportunities. This was more true of our country in earlier times when the population was smaller and much land was still unsettled. But even then only the luckiest or the most ruthless individuals rose from the humblest beginnings to the top. Today opportunities seem to be rather limited. True, ambitious men climb in increasing numbers from the lower classes to high positions in the professions or in business. But for the vast majority of people placement in society is determined by the position of their parents. Many of our foremost businessmen are the sons of businessmen, while the children of low-income families continue to fill low-income jobs. These last lack the education that middle-class families can provide, and they doubt the chances of improving their lot substantially.

How does one find a job? Obviously you can only seek jobs that you know about, and thus your choice is limited by your lack of knowledge. To match job vacancies with job seekers is the task of state employment services, private employment bureaus, youth opportunity centers, and the placement services of various schools and colleges. Also of help are civil service listings and the want ads in newspapers.

Trained vocational counselors give help in schools and in various public agencies. The counselor is familiar with available job opportunities, and he can describe the nature of specific jobs. Sometimes his descriptions help clear up an applicant's misconceptions about certain jobs. He can also guide the young person in assessing his own strengths and weaknesses. Is the job seeker better fitted for a job requiring manual dexterity or for one that demands lots of patience under intense pressure? Is a woman who wants to be an engineer or a man who is considering a nursing profession willing to play a role not commonly associated with their respective sexes? It is the counselor's task to help the job seeker make intelligent choices that will prevent disappointment and failure. Elaborate tests are often used to support such vocational advice.

The professions have careful screening processes for candidates as they move through their years of intensive training. Likewise industries and business enterprises have elaborate techniques and specialized personnel officers to select promising employees and to place them in the job for which they appear to be best suited.

work—blessing or curse? 179

AUTOMATION

The large pulp factory is filled with the steady hum of machines. On crowded panels mysterious lights flash on and off. The rhythmic pulse of utmost efficiency animates the unending process of production. But something is missing, and it takes the visitor a while to put his finger on the missing element: people. Once, the factory would have been crowded with busy men and women. Now only one or two important-looking individuals in white coats walk around checking instruments and reading gauges. *Automation* has invaded the factory.

What gives an automated plant a ghostly appearance is the scarcity of human beings. In the old-style factory men or women labored side by side. In the automated factory they are gone, and instead a few technicians push buttons, move levers, or watch dials. These technicians control the operation of machines that, in turn, operate other machines. So far, only some

Figure 10

Copyright 1969 Saturday Review, Inc. Reprinted by permission of Ed Fisher and *Saturday Review*.

"*Sorry, boys, you're being phased out of the technology.*"

of the largest industrial plants have been automated. Human hands are still needed to turn out goods, but the trend is toward fewer hands and more electronic circuits.

The computer is the latest such triumph of man's ingenuity, an intricate electronic device capable of controlling assembly lines, turning out payrolls and bills by the millions, scoring school examinations, and compiling sales statistics. It has a memory and can perform many thought functions faster and more accurately than the human brain. And it does not get tired, or grumble, or require coffee breaks.

Automation is undoubtedly causing some hardship, and because of it, not just individual workers have been laid off, but whole job classifications have been eliminated, apparently for good. As with the first machines in the early days of industry, workers resent the new monsters threatening their livelihood. (See Figure 10.) However, mechanization has become a part of our way of life, and automation likewise seems destined to take its place. Automation is something we must learn to live with, and we are beginning to find out that it has some beneficial effects. It takes over the drudgery, the dulling routine that heretofore has been the companion of most human labor. Man is freed for more challenging, more creative tasks, provided he has the necessary abilities and opportunities. Furthermore, automation is creating a number of new occupations, from the scientists and engineers who devise these technical wonders to the men and women who operate, repair, and program them.

There is an old German legend about a sorcerer who could make a broom sweep and a bucket carry water all by themselves. The sorcerer's apprentice was once left alone to clean the house by his own labors, but he used instead his master's formula to make the broom and bucket do his work for him. But the apprentice soon discovered that he did not know the formula to make the broom and bucket stop. By the time the master returned, the house was flooded.

If automation is to be a blessing rather than a curse on our society, we must be in the position of the sorcerer, not the apprentice. Much thought has already been given to the need for restructuring our social and economic life to meet the challenge of automation. Some proposals have been made for a much shorter work week, others for earlier retirement and a guaranteed annual income. These proposals are based on the assumption that, in the future, much less human work will be required to produce everything we can possibly use. Strong efforts need to be expended to retrain workers whose jobs have become obsolete because of automation. Such people can, to a large extent, be redirected into other occupations that will be in demand for a long time to come. In many types of service occupations, for example, manpower is in very short supply.

The whole Protestant concept of work as the primary virtue and idleness as the primary vice may be in for a thorough reshaping. In the meantime government and business can do much to slow down the tragic consequences of sudden automation by introducing changes gradually and by giving displaced workers a chance to retrain for other jobs.

UNEMPLOYMENT

"Everyone has the right to work." This terse statement can be found in the Declaration of Human Rights, a very significant document drawn up by the United Nations. It means that anyone anywhere in the world who wants and needs to work should be given the opportunity.

Once, it was widely held that those who did not work were lazy freeloaders on decent working people. British police used to round up beggars and haul them to jails or "workhouses" that were hardly a shade more comfortable than the prisons. Today we know that being out of work is rarely a sign of laziness. The factors causing unemployment are most often beyond the control of the job seeker. We have mentioned automation, but there are a number of other possible causes, such as a shift in public taste. The fact that many men now wear no hats during a good part of the year cut deeply into the ranks of labor in the hat industry. A change in the ownership of a business or an economic slump may also reduce payrolls. The older generation still remembers vividly the general depression of the 1930s, which idled millions who were only too eager to work.

In the 1960s the American unemployment rate never exceeded 5 percent. This is not a high figure compared to earlier times and to other parts of the world; still it gives little comfort to those who are affected. Among the hardest hit elements of our population are school dropouts and some minority groups. Their rate of unemployment is two or three times the average. Open discrimination combines with low skill levels and lack of seniority to victimize these people.

The loss of his job can come as a profound shock to a worker. One day he feels he is a secure human being with plans for his future and that of his family. Then he receives a sometimes completely unanticipated notice to leave his job. In addition to suffering a financial crisis, he has suddenly lost his sense of security, he sees his plans for the future clouded, and he misses the friends and routine of his old job. On receiving the dreaded slip telling him he need not report to work until further notice, he feels like an outsider; everything is gone: the friendly feeling among the members of the car pool, the lunch crowd, the jokes exchanged by the watercooler.

In a work culture being unemployed can also be a shattering, humiliating experience, especially to the male who sees himself deprived of his traditional role as the breadwinner. Deviant behavior of all kinds, even suicide, can sometimes be the consequence. When unemployment rises to huge proportions, it threatens the inner peace of the community and the nation. When the Nazi regime came into power in 1933, millions of desperate unemployed Germans were counted among its followers.

Finding jobs for the unemployed is a task fraught with many difficulties. One of them can be a man's attachment to a particular place or to a way of life. In West Virginia many coal mines have closed, but the older miners refuse to leave for regions with better opportunities.

In some communities the lot of the jobless is being eased by unemployment compensation and welfare payments. These aids may alleviate suffering somewhat, but they don't restore the pride and self-esteem that are lost when a job no longer exists.

WORK ORGANIZATIONS

People who do the same kind of work usually feel close to each other. In medieval times the merchant and craft guilds were tightly organized bodies that controlled not only the occupational but also the private lives of their members. All the nail makers or wool merchants of a town often lived on the same street, worshiped in their own church, and found entertainment in their own guild hall.

Examples of Modern Work Organizations

National Association of Manufacturers
United States Chamber of Commerce
American Medical Association
National Education Association
Teamsters Union
American Federation of Labor and Congress of Industrial Organizations

Modern occupational organizations are established mainly to provide for the economic welfare of their members. But they also set up training standards and codes of ethical behavior. Individual work organizations expend much effort to represent a favorable image of their particular trade or profession to the outside world.

Labor unions developed with the rise of industry. At one time employers and government tried to suppress them with brutal means. Since then they have not only become recognized but have also attained vast power. Unions are strong among manual workers, especially in the fields of manufacturing, construction, transportation, and mining. They have been less successful in rural areas, small towns, and generally in the Southern states.

Unions were formed to improve the lot of the worker, and there can be no doubt that, in this, their success has been spectacular. Once overworked, underpaid, and made to face unsafe and degrading conditions, the laboring man has become a proud and stable member of society. Unions have not only wrested higher wages, paid vacations, and other benefits from employers but have also used their influence to advocate many general welfare measures, such as social security, minimum wage, and child labor laws.

What labor unions must now realize is that new kinds of underdogs have appeared in our society—blacks, the poor, the unskilled—who want to find a place at the table that has been set for the union members. Organized labor has been under attack for practicing racial discrimination. Shipbuilding and railroad unions, for example, restrict the membership of blacks, and without joining the unions black applicants cannot obtain jobs. Those who are now deprived of the coveted union card demand that "grandfather clauses" be abolished. Such clauses practically limit membership in some unions to sons and other relatives of older union members. These and other restrictions are typical of the craft unions, while the more recently established unions of factory workers, such as the United Automobile Workers (UAW), are much less exclusive and discriminatory.

Some critics maintain that unions have become too powerful. A strike called by a large union can seriously cripple the economic health of the nation. In some instances bigness has brought corruption and bossism, as it does occasionally to large organizations, whether they deal with business or politics. While many countries have labor parties with radical political goals, American unions are comparatively conservative. Their intention is not to overthrow the capitalistic system under which they have prospered but rather to concentrate on winning the "next round" of economic benefits for their members.

Though labor unions are now fully accepted, their future is somewhat clouded. Automation is taking a heavy toll on membership rolls despite increased production. Leaders are trying to make up for the losses by unionizing white-collar workers, public employees, and farm workers. These groups have a possible membership pool of about 27 million. The stakes are high. To date, union organizers have not had too much success with farm laborers, but among public employees some groups have managed to form strong organizations and have forcefully presented their demands for better income and working conditions. In the spring of 1970, postal workers across the country carried out a much publicized strike. School teachers, once known for their meekness, have walked out of classrooms in a number of places in order to emphasize their demands.

Trends in Union Membership

Year	Number of Members	Percentage of Nonfarm Workers
1950	15,000,000	31.9
1960	17,000,000	31.5
1966	17,800,000	28.8

Source: *Business Week,* April 12, 1968, p. 158.

The labor movement can only function effectively in a free society. Under dictatorial regimes, whether communist or fascist, unions either don't exist or else are mere extensions of the ruling machine without the right to strike or bargain collectively.

LEISURE

We have discussed many elements about the nature of work, but we have yet to define what work really is. It is practically impossible to find a definition that would encompass all types of work, manual and intellectual, repetitive and creative, the work of leaders and that of the followers.

Let us simply state, "Work is what needs to be done to keep alive and be comfortable." This statement is quite general but covers all the various categories of work; furthermore, it clarifies the main reason why we work so many hours of the week: work is a necessity.

If a carpenter builds a desk, it is work. If a lawyer does the same in his spare time, we call it a hobby. Painting, writing, music, photography, gardening, and almost any task, except the most undesirable ones, can be considered either work or recreation. The need for recreation is increasing as jobs require less and less working time. The work day is shrinking, while vacation and free time are lengthening. Since 1850 the full-time worker has gained twenty-five hours of free time per week,[19] and the end is not yet in sight.

What are we to do with all this extra time? "It will destroy us unless we learn how to use it."[20] A century ago the prospect of a little more leisure time seemed wonderful to the overworked laborer. Today we hear older people attribute rising juvenile delinquency, drunkenness, and other social evils to the fact that too many youngsters have too much time on their hands. Whether they are right or not, the question remains: Will our work-oriented society go to pieces under the stress of not working?

Many people can find nothing besides work to fill their waking hours. As the work week grows shorter, they turn to "moonlighting" (working on a second job) to fill the idle periods and to have more spending money. Others join the steadily growing army of do-it-yourselfers. Garages and basement shops resound with their hammering, sawing, and chiseling. They are kept busy with something resembling work, even though there is no financial reward, except the savings on repair bills.

Even when playing, some Americans find themselves unable to relax. They work as hard and competitively around a bridge table or in a bowling alley as they did from 9 A.M. to 5 P.M. in their stores and offices. Community centers and vacation resorts organize "activities," so that the patrons can do something even when they are "supposed" to do nothing. Whole new professions have arisen, such as that of recreation director, to help fill this need. There is a hectic rush not to miss out on the fun.

Boredom has become a frightening menace, because bored people sometimes seek outlets in dangerous and destructive thrills. When reprimanded for acts of vandalism or for wild joy rides, teen-agers have been known to reply with a shrug of the shoulders, "Nothing else to do."

To enjoy the ever-increasing hours of leisure, individuals must find something to do. We must develop new interests, which many are already doing quite successfully. Musical ensembles, for example, are springing up all over the country. Classes in painting, ceramics and weaving, discussion groups, and hobby clubs enjoy growing patronage. Outdoor recreation on land and water, in the mountains and on beaches, in summer and winter, attract swelling multitudes. Almost 500 million visitors are clocked annually at the entrance gates to our national and state parks, and American tourists have visited just about every place in the world.

On the other hand, one can also observe a growing "at-homeness," especially in middle-class suburbia. Living and family rooms receive plenty of use, and so do patios and backyards, weather and climate permitting. Nine out of every ten American households contain television sets.

The question of how to fill idle hours is asked with great urgency by those who are retired. The retired person faces a dreary succession of empty five-day stretches. Medical science has increased our life span, while social pressure and technological progress have forced us to stop working with many years of life still ahead of us. At a time when the threat of poverty forced aging men to keep on working till they dropped, the dream of a carefree retirement was likened to a vision of paradise. Now many dread the moment when the co-workers give a departing gift, say good-bye, and return to their own daily tasks.

Many times, as the door closes behind a newly retired worker, he realizes with a shock that old bonds of friendship have been broken and the feeling of being appreciated has vanished. The senior citizen must learn, however, to do more than sit in idleness and wait for death. Retirement can be a time when he can read the books he never had time to read, learn skills he had to neglect up till now, talk with people at leisure, travel, take walks in strange parts of the city, and do a hundred other fascinating things. Middle-aged workers are now urged to prepare for retirement as they once prepared for holding a job.

Main Ideas

1. For the most part, human work has been hard and has at times, therefore, been regarded as punishment.
2. Christian, as well as communist spokesmen, have praised work as the foremost virtue.
3. Work brings many rewards, among them financial returns, identity, self-actualization, and the satisfaction derived from having done a good and valuable job.
4. The rise of capitalism and of industrialized production have, to a large extent, determined the present occupational picture.
5. Independent business and farming enterprises show a tendency toward bigness. The typical business organization of our age is the corporation.

6. The job market of today indicates a great demand for professional, semiprofessional, managerial, clerical, and service occupations, as well as for skilled and semiskilled craftsmen; but the opportunities for unskilled labor seem to be on the decline.
7. Automation is causing hardship by lessening the need for human labor, but it also frees man from dull routine work and makes it possible for him to turn to more creative tasks.
8. Unemployment is a tragedy, since it damages an individual's self-esteem.
9. Labor unions have gained spectacular success and power in our society but are threatened with loss of membership due to automation.
10. Selecting an occupation is a very important decision for the young person. Various agencies and trained personnel are available to assist in this task.
11. Since the work week is becoming shorter, our society must learn to make proper use of the increased leisure time.

Important Terms

Automation	Labor force
Barter	Management
Bureaucracy	Money
Capitalism	Partnership
Corporation	Productivity
Dividends	Self-actualization
Factory	Semiprofessionals
Identity	Stockholder
Industrialization	Utopia
Kibbutz	Work culture

Conclusion

Once most work was done for physical survival. As man became more efficient in providing for his physical needs, he could devote more and more working time to creating beauty, discovering the unknown, and searching for knowledge. Unfortunately he also used his increased skills to create more powerful tools of destruction and warfare (see Chapter 19). Work is necessary, not only to provide us with food, clothing, and shelter, but also to give us a sense of worth and a place in the community with our fellow-men. We try to make work as pleasant, creative, and meaningful as possible. We have ample time for leisure, but we must be prepared to get full enjoyment out of our leisure time.

Notes

1. Stuart Chase, *The Proper Study of Mankind*, rev. ed. (New York: Harper Colophon, 1963), p. 99.
2. James A. Michener, *Hawaii* (New York: Random House, 1959).
3. Thomas More, *Utopia* (first published in 1516 in Latin).
4. Paul A. Samuelson, *Economics*, 8th ed. (New York: McGraw-Hill, 1970), p. 77.
5. S. Gordon and J. Witchel, *An Introduction to the American Economy* (Boston: Heath, 1967), p. 43.
6. E. Hunt and J. Karlin, *Society Today and Tomorrow* (New York: Macmillan, 1967), p. 336.
7. Joel M. Halpern, *The Changing Village Community* (Englewood Cliffs, N.J.: Prentice-Hall, 1967), pp. 112–113.
8. U.S. Department of Labor, *Dictionary of Occupational Titles*, 3rd ed., 1965.
9. Simplified list adapted from U.S. Department of Labor, *Occupational Outlook Handbook*, 1966–1967.
10. Dick Bruner, "Why White-Collar Workers Can't Be Organized," in S. Nosow and W. H. Form (eds.), *Man, Work and Society* (New York: Basic Books, 1962), p. 193.
11. William H. Whyte, Jr., *The Organization Man* (New York: Simon & Schuster, 1956).
12. Wilbert E. Moore, "The Organized Individual," in Peter I. Rose (ed.), *The Study of Society: An Integrated Anthology* (New York: Random House, 1967), p. 228.
13. Peter M. Blau, *Bureaucracy in Modern Society* (New York: Random House, 1956), p. 103.
14. Bruner, *op. cit.*
15. M. Weinberg and O. E. Shabat, *Society and Man*, 2nd ed. (Englewood Cliffs, N.J.: Prentice-Hall, 1965), p. 388.
16. Simone Weil, "Factory Work," in Nosow and Form, *op. cit.*, p. 455.
17. John Kenneth Galbraith, *The Affluent Society*, college ed. (Boston: Houghton Mifflin, 1958), p. 336.
18. D. Riesman and W. Blomberg, "Work and Leisure: Fusion or Polarity?" in Nosow and Form, *op. cit.*, p. 38.
19. Sebastian de Gracia, *Of Time, Work and Leisure* (New York: Twentieth Century Fund, 1962), p. 70.
20. Nels Anderson, *Dimensions of Work* (New York: McKay, 1964), p. 90.

Suggestions for Further Reading

Bell, Daniel. *Work and Its Discontent*. Boston: Beacon Press, 1956. The effect of mechanization and hierarchical organization in industry on the worker.

"Big Business, Big Labor and Big Government," *Senior Scholastic*, 90, April 7, 1967, 4 ff.

"Employing the Unemployable," *Fortune*, 78 (July 1968), 29 ff.

"Got the Itch to Change Jobs?" 21, *Changing Times*, 21 (February 1967), 31–32.

Hawley, Cameron. *Executive Suite*. New York: Ballantine, 1966. Novel on the tactics that a business executive uses to get ahead.

Hoppock, Robert. *Occupational Information*. 3d ed. New York: McGraw-Hill, 1967. Textbook for occupational counseling, containing much valuable job information.

"Latest on Career Opportunities for Young People," *U.S. News*, 64, May 20, 1968, 101 f.

Lowe, J. R. "Race, Jobs and Cities; What Business Can Do," *Saturday Review*, 52, February 22, 1969, 32 f.

Ryscavage, P. M. "Changes in Occupational Employment over the Past Decade," *Monthly Labor Review*, 90 (August 1967), 27–30.

Sinclair, Upton B. *The Jungle*. New York: Harper, 1951. Novel about working conditions in a Chicago packing plant.

Smitter, Wessel. *F.O.B. Detroit*. New York: Harper & Row, 1938. Novel about life in a mass production automobile factory.

Steinbeck, John. *The Grapes of Wrath*. New York: Viking, 1939. Novel about the hard lot of migrant farm laborers in California a generation ago.

Tyler, Gus. *The Labor Revolution: Trade Unions in a New America*. New York: Viking, 1967. An important union official describes the role of unions in the age of automation and of growing racial equality.

U.S. Department of Labor, Bureau of Labor Statistics. *Occupational Outlook Handbook* (published every two years). Gives employment information; discusses over 700 occupations.

Wilson, Sloan. *The Man in the Gray Flannel Suit*. New York: Simon & Schuster, 1955. Novel about the life of an upper-middle-class suburban executive.

Zola, Emile. *Germinal*. Garden City, N.Y.: Dolphin, 1961. The famous French novelist describes life and work in a coal-mining town.

Zugsmith, Leane. *A Time to Remember*. New York: Random House, 1936. Novel describing a strike of white-collar workers in a large department store.

Friday Special
Great White Sales
Travel now, pay later
America's most distinguished car—
a silhouette with streamlined trimness

10 MONEY COMES—MONEY GOES
income and consumption

Television commercials assault you. Neon signs blink on and off through the night. Appealing leaflets are placed behind the windshield wiper of your car. And on Friday, payday, these invitations to spend your money seem especially tempting.

The work week is over. Men and women cash their paychecks. Big shopping centers are crowded. Cash registers jingle as coin and slips of paper are converted into steaks or hamburgers, milk or beer. A worker's salary may at various times mean a fishing trip, a visit to the opera, rent for an apartment, or a United States savings bond.

Whatever its final use, it is money that we are speaking of here.

MONEY

What is money? One cannot eat it, nor does it give warmth or shelter, but it can be converted into things that we want; that is, it is a *medium of exchange*. Thousands of years ago man decided that it was more practical to use money rather than rely only on barter. Imagine the difficulty you would have trying to find something to barter for a hamburger or a Coke every time you feel hungry or thirsty.

When a society decides to use money, it settles on some particular medium of exchange that all its members consider valuable. Gold, silver, and other rare metals have been frequent, but by far not the only choices. The Romans, for example, used square pieces of leather. In early America white traders gave Indians beads and tobacco in payment for furs. A beaver skin was worth a certain number of pounds of tobacco. In other cultures goods were exchanged for whale teeth, shells, goats, or cattle. Where wives were offered for sale, a wife could sometimes be bought for a certain number of cows.

Money has value only as long as there is something that can be bought with it. A trunkful of money will not keep you from dying of thirst in the desert or from freezing in the Arctic if nobody is around to sell you beverages or fuel. According to an ancient legend, when King Croesus, who possessed fabulous wealth, was vanquished in war, his enemies killed him by pouring molten gold, his own gold, down his throat. All the wealth in his possession could not even buy his own life for him.

In our own society gold and silver coins have become quite rare, and we have ceased using them as the main medium of exchange. In addition they are impractical. Can you imagine paying $20,000 in gold or silver coins for a house?

So for convenience we use folding money, pieces of paper worth nothing in themselves, and we only carry coins for small change. Paper money and coins make up our *currency*, which is issued by the federal government. Americans now hold about $39 billion in currency,[1] printed or minted by a government agency and made available to the user through the *Federal Reserve Banks*, which in turn supply approximately 40,000 commercial banks with currency.

Twelve Federal Reserve Banks are distributed over the various regions of the country. They supervise the activities of all large banks and impose certain standards. They regulate the supply of credit and influence interest rates that represent the "cost" of money to the borrower. Another important function of the Federal Reserve System is to act as banker to the federal government, which constantly collects and pays out gigantic sums of money.

Even paper money has become too cumbersome in our vastly complicated financial system, and so about 90 percent of all payments are actually made through checks on a bank. Now this procedure too is being simplified. We can carry credit cards and thus save ourselves the trouble of writing checks, except at the end of the month.

Money does not automatically bring happiness, but with it we can buy material goods, such as food, drink, and clothes; money may also aid us in the attainment of intellectual and *aesthetic* goals, as for example, when we purchase books or paintings, travel, or pay for an education.

Ours is a strongly money-minded society. Some people become so obsessed with the acquisition of money that this becomes an end in itself.

They forget the original purpose of money, and instead of converting it into goods or services, they use it to make more money or hoard it in bank vaults. To such people having money is more enjoyable than the pleasures that could be derived from spending it.

What do we expect from our money?

1. It should be easily exchangeable for the goods and services we desire, without much delay or red tape.
2. It should easily and quickly indicate the value of a thing we want to own, be it a shirt, a motor scooter, or a cruise to Tahiti. The price tag must be visible.
3. We should be able to store it and have it accumulate for later use, whether under a mattress, in a vault, or through *investments*.
4. It must be generally acceptable. You may own bundles of Confederate money or bills issued by the Russian czars, but you will get very little or nothing for them, except perhaps as collection pieces.
5. The value of your money should be stable so that it may buy about the same in a year from now or in ten years as it does now.

INFLATION

The requirement of stability presents problems. The dollar is not passing this test very successfully. The Consumer Price Index shows what we have to pay in stores, gas stations, doctors' offices, and so forth. It indicates that an item that cost $100 in 1957–1959 was priced at $120.40 in 1968. In 1968 alone food prices rose 3¾ percent, while doctor and hospital bills increased a whopping 7½ percent.[2] The dollar buys less than it ever did before. For what it costs a college student today to see a movie his parents could have seen two or three. This weakening of buying power is called *inflation* (see Figure 11).

Inflation occurs when too much money is competing for too few goods and services. When doctors or mechanics are in short supply, they demand higher returns for their work. When fewer houses or apartments are available than are demanded, prices and rents go up. Furthermore, new and more expensive public tastes stimulate inflation. The buyer of a house wants more than one bathroom; car owners want their cars to be equipped with cigarette lighters and radios. Political developments, such as war or the threat of war, also tend to push prices upward.

Ours is a controlled inflation. The value of the dollar does not drop suddenly—at least it has not so far—and we are able to predict its approximate value next year. The government puts brakes on inflation by siphoning off spending money through increased taxes and by using the Federal Reserve Banks as floodgates to regulate extensive buying. Even with governmental controls the steady rise of prices is hard on people who live on limited fixed incomes, such as the retired, and also on the unemployed

192   An Introduction to Social Science

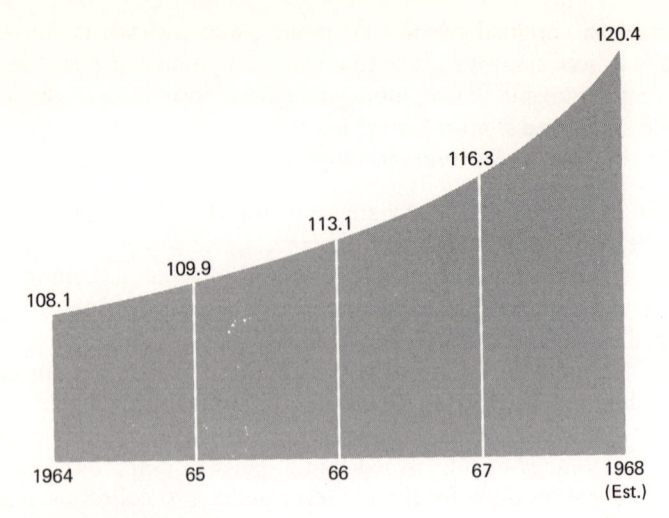

```
                                                        120.4

                                         116.3
                               113.1
                    109.9
         108.1


         1964       65         66         67         1968
                                                     (Est.)
```

Consumer Price Index
Yearly Averages : 1957-1959 = 100

Figure 11
Inflation Raises Prices

Source: *The New York Times Student Weekly,* December 9, 1968. © 1968 by The New York Times Company. Reprinted by permission.

and on unskilled workers with low-paying jobs. And when attempts are made to halt the run-away flow of inflation, the poor are again hardest hit by increased taxes and by rising interest rates on small loans, the kind mostly given to the people who earn the lowest incomes.

Comparative Cost of Living Increases in 1968 over 1957–1959*

United States	23%
West Germany	26
Canada	27
United Kingdom	37
Italy	41
France	52
Japan	67

* In all seven of these countries the cost of living increased substantially between 1957–1959 and 1968 because of inflation. But during this period the United States was much less affected than the other countries. In order to determine the cost of living the government selects a number of items consumed by the average family and then observes how the cost of these items rises or falls from year to year.

Source: *Wall Street Journal,* January 20, 1969, p. 1 ("Outlook"). Reprinted with permission of *The Wall Street Journal.*

However, upper- and middle-class Americans seem to live more comfortably than ever before despite the disappearance of the five-cent Coke and the ten-cent milk shake. Many other countries, including those with sizable industries, have suffered much more severe inflation. Runaway inflation can turn into a catastrophe. It can drive prices up to such a height that even necessities like food and fuel are out of reach. It can wipe out savings overnight and crumble whole social structures, as happened, for example, in Germany after World War I.

INCOME

How do you obtain the money you want to spend? Since manufacturing money is forbidden by law, you must earn it by working or by investing the fruits of your work. In the United States 70 percent of all personal income is from wages and salaries.[3] The other 30 percent represents business and farm profits, rents from property, interest and dividends on investments, pensions and social security payments.

The general picture in this country is one of rising incomes. Payments for all kinds of services are steadily increasing. The earnings of businessmen and independent professionals are also increasing. Labor unions successfully negotiate higher wages for their members. Their main arguments have been the rising cost of living and growing productivity of the individual worker. If an individual turns out more goods and services per hour, they reason, he is entitled to more pay.

The trend toward higher earnings is also reflected in the minimum wage laws that protect most industrial workers. In 1938 the minimum wage fixed by Congress was $.25 per hour; in 1950, $.75; in 1956, $1; and in 1968, $1.60.[4] Actually the hourly earnings of workers throughout the country in March 1969 averaged $2.98.[5]

Legislation establishes a floor for the earnings of many individuals; this floor represents a level below which income is not supposed to fall. But there is no ceiling on earnings. Given the right skills, opportunities, and good fortune, you can take home pay that is many, many times more than the legal minimum.

The range of incomes is tremendous. An employer pays his factory workers or clerks the "going rate," that is, the customary wages paid for doing a certain job in a certain town or section of the country. The going rate sometimes varies from town to town or section to section. Rural wages, for example, generally lag behind city wages. Women, older people, and minority groups generally have smaller earnings.

One would expect that the people doing the most undesirable and the most dangerous jobs would receive the highest pay. This is perhaps true of movie stunt men. Loggers, who have to mount and cut giant trees, also earn fairly good salaries, but their jobs are seasonal. In general, however, the highest paid jobs are the cleanest and most pleasant.

There are people who do quite well financially though they have spent little time in classrooms or libraries. But, as a rule, income rises with length of training unless it is kept down by discrimination or other handicapping factors. Education is a good investment in future income, as the table below clearly indicates.

Lifetime Average Income

Education Attained		Expected Lifetime Income
High school	1–3 years	$283,718
High school	4 years	$340,520
College	1–3 years	$393,969
College	4 years	$507,808
College	5 years or more	$586,905

Source: United States Office of Education, 1966. Based on Census Bureau statistics.

Particularly handsome is the immediate payoff for professional graduates of top schools in scarce fields. In 1968 several major Wall Street law firms raised the salaries for starting lawyers from $9,000 to $15,000, and some graduates of Harvard Business School were offered $11,300 for their first jobs.[6] Many physicians now earn in excess of $30,000 a year, while at the opposite extreme are a considerable number of agricultural workers who make $1,700 or less during the same period.

Not all highly trained persons, however, draw correspondingly high incomes. A high-school teacher earns about one-fourth as much as a physician. Teachers and librarians have long complained about being underpaid (see Chapter 12). In 1959 25.3 percent of all real-estate agents and 10.1 percent of all locomotive engineers earned $10,000 or more, but only 5.7 percent of high-school teachers and 3.3 percent of grade-school teachers in the ten largest cities earned as much.[7] Since teaching careers are less desirable financially for men, especially for those with families to support, the schoolroom has traditionally attracted large numbers of women.

The highest incomes from salaries are drawn by persons who are able to do what few others can do and who attract large paying audiences. Athletes and entertainers obtain incomes way out of proportion to their skills. A baseball pitcher, for instance, may collect in excess of $100,000 annually, in many cases augmented by endorsement fees from advertisers. Many movie stars and popular singers also take in fantastic sums. As long as athletes and entertainers are in top demand, which may only be for a short time, managers and directors compete for their services, which drives their wages way up.

On the whole, more Americans enjoy comfortable incomes than ever before, and their number is on the rise. In 1947 the *median* family income was $3,104; by 1966 it had risen to $7,803.[8] (Median means halfway point; half the families had higher and the other half lower incomes.)

Despite inflation this has meant that there was not only more money available to spend on food, clothing, housing, and medical care but also more for pleasure and education. Here is one compelling reason for calling ours a middle-class society, a society of people who, as a whole, are neither poor nor very rich. (See Chapter 11.) But we must remember that as incomes go up for the majority, those who are left behind become increasingly bitter about their deprivation. With rising prosperity the gap between the poor and the well-to-do widens, and cries of discontent become louder.

Family Income Distribution

Percentage of Families

Income	1950	1965
10,000+	7%	25%
7,000–9,999	13	24
5,000–6,999	20	18
3,000–4,999	30	16
3,000 and under	30	17

Source: William Bowen, "The U.S. Economy Enters a New Era," *Fortune*, LXXV, 3 (March 1967), 113. Reprinted by permission. Parios Studios for *Fortune* Magazine.

THE CONSUMER

Today people rarely keep their money in stockings or under mattresses. Hiding money this way was more common in former times, when gold and other valuables were often buried in yards and fields for safekeeping.

Chances are that you don't do any of these things with your money. You use your money to buy something, you *consume*. Purchasing a new hat or a bottle of French perfume means buying *goods*; having a medical examination or taking a course in a dance studio means buying *services*. Even when you put money into a savings account, buy life insurance, or acquire shares in a uranium mine, you are buying something: security for the future. When you pay taxes, you probably complain that money is being taken away from you, but actually you are buying fire and police protection, the use of schools, highways, and many other services that only governmental machinery can provide. You are a consumer, and as you consume your money is channeled back into the production process. In a smoothly running economy production and consumption flow constantly, one into the other.

Let us look at an example. Gary is a chef in a good restaurant. While working he calls himself Gaston, since customers like chefs to have French-sounding names. He earns $1,200 a month by cooking appetizing dishes. Having pocketed his paycheck, he now becomes a consumer. Some of the taxes he owes have already been withheld from his gross pay and diminished his take-home pay. The same is true of his Social Security payments, contributions to a retirement fund and perhaps to a medical insurance plan. Of what is left he will save, let us say, $100 by adding to his credit union or other investment shares. With the remainder of his pay he will purchase goods and services that others are producing. He may not want to eat in restaurants too often, but he will have to pay the mortgage on his house, make installment payments on his car, and meet the costs of all the other items he and his family will need till the next payday comes around.

196 An Introduction to Social Science

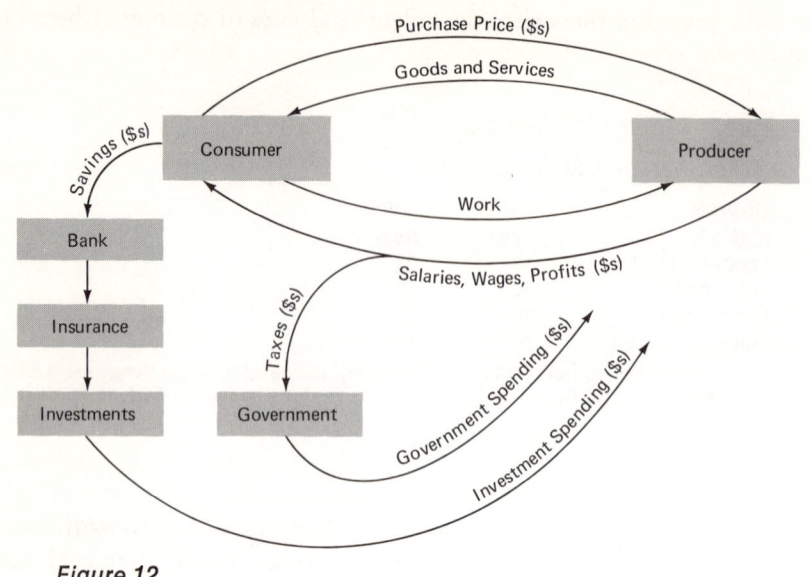

Figure 12
Flow of Income and Consumption

The flow of money in our economy can be compared to water being pumped through a network of pipes, returned to its original station, and re-used in a continuous circular movement. Figure 12 illustrates this system. Workers produce goods and services in factories, shops, and offices; consumers buy the goods and services with money; this money is then returned to the producer in the form of salaries, wages, and profits. The producer in turn uses part of his salaries, wages, and profits to become a consumer himself. As a consumer himself now, he purchases food, clothing, and shelter for himself and his family and perhaps makes deposits in a savings account, buys insurance, or invests in stocks. Another part of the money earned by the producer is paid to the government in the form of taxes. The government returns the money into the pipe line in the form of purchases, and so do banks and insurance companies as they make further investments.

CONSUMER HABITS

Much of what you buy is used up quickly. Food is eaten; last week's haircut is losing its shape; and an evening spent at a movie or night club is but a memory. But other things you purchase remain permanently or at least for a long time in your possession. They become part of your *assets* and may include your home, household furnishings, and tools. Count among your assets also your automobile, works of art, and jewelry that you may have bought or inherited. Finally there are such items as life insurance and pension reserves, savings accounts and shares of stock, which also constitute forms of saving.

Americans save an average of 7 percent of their income. This gives everybody except the poor a safety cushion against the dangers of severe illness and the needs of old age. It is part of the long-range plan for the education of the children or the enjoyment of things that cost too much to be purchased right away, such as a cabin in the mountains or a trip abroad.

When income is very small, everything must be spent for immediate necessities, and nothing can be saved. Supposedly we can choose how to spend our money, but actually the choice is limited. Only the extremely rich don't have to choose one purchase over another; they have sufficient money to avoid postponing satisfactions.

If families are in debt—and this is true of many with low, as well as high, earnings and of many men with "middle incomes"—interest and debt payments must be met before anything is consumed. The same goes for taxes on income and on property. Only after these expenses are taken care of can the consumer decide how to spend the rest of his income.

Your choice depends on your personal tastes and interests, but to a large extent it is determined by the habits of the society around you. For instance, many a Swiss citizen of ample means lives frugally and deposits a large part of his income in the bank, whereas Americans, even if not financially stable, often insist on owning high-priced automobiles. The culture that surrounds you has a decisive influence on what you buy and how you dispose of your income. What and how you buy is further influenced by changing social tastes and habits. What was considered a luxury yesterday may be considered a necessity today, as, for example, electric clothes dryers, air conditioning in the Southern states, or two years of college.

How does the average American spend his income (see table below)? Actually the so-called average American does not really exist. Social scientists use the phrase, nevertheless, as a concept or point of reference in order to make generalizations for discussion and study.

As wages, salaries, and profits increase, the family spends a smaller proportion of its total income on the basic necessities. After the expenses for food, heating, repairs, commuting to work, and so forth, are taken care of, there is still some income left. This leftover income is used for less urgently needed items, such as personal grooming and spare-time activities. It is an indication of financial well-being when you can afford things that you like but don't necessarily need.

On the sales floor the consumer is king, and the seller must bow to his wishes. If enough consumers want gold-colored automobiles or tasseled sports coats, manufacturers and merchants will provide them. But as a consumer you cannot fully employ this power unless you have a great amount of money to spend. It is the middle- and higher-income groups—

even though they are not the majority of consumers—that wield the most influential consumer power.

Outlay of the Average American Household in 1962, Compared with 1956

	Percentage of Income Spent	
	1956	1962
Food	29%	25.4%
Home operation	19	14
Home furnishings and equipment	9	13
Transportation	14	12.6
Clothing	12	9.9
Medical and personal care	5	13.4
Recreation	5	6.1
Other	7	5.6

Source: Nels Anderson, *Dimensions of Work* (New York: David McKay, 1964), p. 99, and S. D. Gordon and J. Witchel, *An Introduction to the American Economy* (Lexington, Mass.: Heath, 1967), p. 177. Reprinted by permission of the publisher.

A family with a minimum of funds to spend must buy the least expensive food, rent the smallest apartment, and furnish it in a modest fashion. When a family has more cash available, it can select more expensive meats, trade in the better furniture stores, and follow the latest fashions in buying clothes. If even more cash is available, a family can visit swanky resorts or give champagne parties at home.

HOW MUCH CHOICE DO YOU HAVE?

If you are lucky enough to have your pockets stuffed with folding money, you can make quite a few buying choices. A night out on the town, clothing, books, a trip, music lessons, a down payment on a sports car: these are only a few of the possibilities. But don't conclude that, just because you have cash, you can always decide what is to be sold to you and at what price. There are important limitations.

In the Orient one finds streets filled with colorful bazaars where merchants line up before their tiny stalls to offer you their wares. You stop at one stall, bargain, and then move on to the next stall. Traders try to attract you by lowering their prices until finally, feeling that you are getting a good bargain, you make a purchase.

This is an example of *free enterprise*. The sellers compete with each other for the buyer's purchase, and the buyer gets the benefit of better merchandise at lower prices. This kind of *market* operates in favor of the consumer.

Sometimes we hear or read about the American free-enterprise system, a system that allows us to sell or buy goods and services as we choose. How free is this system really? Whatever articles you decide to buy in this country, about 70 percent of them have been mass produced by a handful of giant corporations.[9] Actually not the many thousands of stockholders who own shares in these large businesses but a small corps of managers determines what is to be produced, in what quantity, and at what price.

It is much easier to haggle over the price of a brass table or a woven rug in Istanbul or Bangkok than to bargain for the price of a camera or a tape recorder in Milwaukee or Atlanta. The price tag that one large business puts on its product resembles very closely that of the business' competitors. When General Motors raises its charges for new automobiles, Ford and Chrysler are likely to follow suit. The automobile industry tends to attract consumer dollars, not with lower prices, but with snob appeal and concentrated advertising campaigns.

The consumer's freedom of choice is also curtailed by the growing role of government in our economy. Federal, state, and local governments operate numerous enterprises, from the postal service to municipal parking lots. Many private businesses depend on substantial government contracts, especially in the areas of national defense and space exploration. In the last sixty years America has participated in four wars. In addition we have given assistance to a number of nations involved in other wars. Thus government in this country has become a giant producer and consumer of goods. What it does and plans to do have a great impact on what the ordinary consumer will see in the store windows and showrooms of his hometown.

Big business—often in cooperation with big unions—and big government have decisively altered the old free-enterprise system. Prices tend to become fixed, and the consumer's choice is, to a large extent, limited to a choice between two equally expensive brands or between buying and not buying.

In an ideal free-enterprise system a comparatively large number of moderately sized capitalistic enterprises compete for your patronage. On the other hand, if you lived in a communist country, such as Russia, you could only patronize government products, since the state is the only producer and seller of goods. You would buy in the state-operated store and pay state-determined prices or not buy at all.

The economies of the United States and a number of European countries seem to move toward a middle ground. Competition exists to some degree, and private capitalists do rather well. But the heavy hand of the government is felt quite strongly, and some powerful corporations vie with the government in wealth and influence. In fact, one such industrial giant in this country is wealthier than twenty-one of the states combined.[10]

BUDGETING

The very rich can satisfy nearly every whim without considering the expense. They can travel often and at the same time maintain several city apartments and country homes if they wish to do so. But unless you belong to this group, you must try to match your finances to your desires. In other words, you have to *budget*.

Budgeting means planning ahead. Even the millionaire keeps and increases his millions by careful budgeting, although he does not have as great a need to do this as others. You ask yourself, "What will my income be during the next week or month or year?" Then you blueprint your expenses, first for necessities and then for the things that you would like to have if enough income is left. A budget will help you to decide whether to buy a new suit this month or wait until the refrigerator is paid for, whether it will be feasible to take up skiing this winter or leave it for another year. A budget does not make financial decisions for you, but it helps you make wise and realistic ones.

Newlyweds will find budgeting a must. A couple establishing their first moderately comfortable home in an unfurnished one-bedroom apartment has to expend about $2,000 before they even begin their housekeeping.[11] A family must consider outlay for food and other necessities, as well as some reserves for possible illness or unemployment, for the education of the children, and for old age. By careful budgeting people can often "afford" things they might not otherwise have, for example, a second car or the down payment for a house.

Unfortunately, many adults find themselves poorly prepared for spending their own income. If you are in this position, consider taking a course in personal finance. Books, pamphlets, and a number of magazines are available to assist the consumer (see Suggestions for Further Reading). You can also turn for help to the community Better Business Bureau and the Chamber of Commerce.

"But why should I worry so much about budgeting?" you may argue. "I can buy what I want on time and pay a dollar a week or twenty dollars a month." True, installment buying is an important feature of our economy and a great help to the consumer. You can enjoy the comfort of a home or the elegance of a new car long before you have the total purchase price. But if handled unwisely, buying on time can bring grave hardship. Should you become unable to continue paying your installments, you may lose everything you have paid up till now and also the very things you wanted to acquire. In most states you will also be held liable for the remainder of the payments. The repossession rate of automobiles bought on time is alarmingly high.

The consumer must steel himself against the temptations offered by eager salesmen. And if he is planning to buy through an installment plan, he should carefully study the conditions of the purchase, including the fine print in any contract, and be aware of the extra costs to the buyer.

The buyer who needs it least is the one who can purchase the easiest credit at the lowest cost. Banks and stores compete with each other for the privilege of making loans, extending charge accounts, and performing all kinds of services to the well-to-do. It is the poor and people of little means who find it difficult meeting installment payments or borrowing small amounts; and when they do borrow money, they are often penalized with higher interest rates and all sorts of special charges because they are poor credit risks. Often they also pay for their ignorance in financial matters and for the inability to obtain competent advice.

Sensible installment buying is acceptable in our culture. To acquire what one could not pay for immediately was once considered slightly dishonest, something that a stable and respectable citizen would not do. The American consumer today must find a middle ground between this attitude and the habit of indiscriminate and irresponsible buying on time.

Your *credit rating* is an important part of your personal record. Special credit bureaus make it their business to keep track of your financial behavior. They know how reliable you are in paying your debts, and they give this information to those from whom you want to buy or to borrow. There is probably more known about you, especially how you handle your money, than you might be aware of. In fact, some members of Congress have become concerned over the amount of information collected by private agencies about American citizens. The question arises whether this is not an invasion of a citizen's rights.

ADVERTISING

The ring of the cash register is sweet music to the ears of the merchant. Factories and stores, insurance companies and airlines: all compete for your dollar. All are only too happy to offer you easy credit. To get your attention they use advertising.

Businessmen place ads in newspapers and magazines, buy time on radio and television to present commercials, erect signs along highways, and send leaflets through the mail. Advertising itself is big business. Highly trained experts in this field devise promotion campaigns and think up special sales, contests, lotteries, and many other "gimmicks." The more expensive campaigns are preceded by intensive research to determine how to entice the consumer to spend the most.

Advertising is a by-product of the free-enterprise system whereby many different stores, many different brands of merchandise compete for our patronage. Even in communist countries, state-owned stores put up their modest signs and window displays.

Much has been said for and against our advertising practices. Ads inform the public of what goods are available, where, and at what prices. You can compare and select. You become aware of items that you never heard of before but that can be useful to you. Perhaps you learn that aluminum roofing has certain advantages over asbestos shingles. You discover interesting places to spend an evening or a weekend.

But advertisers also face strong criticism for high-pressure tactics. They are accused of trying to sell you things that you don't need. Clever advertising sometimes aims at creating new needs. For example, with glamorous new cars flashing at you from magazines and television tubes, with the implication that you are not "with it" unless you drive one, you suddenly feel humiliated because your car is six years old. To impress his acquaintances, many a young—and not-so-young—man rushes to buy a more expensive vehicle that he can often ill afford. As the buyer twists and turns under the credit squeeze, it is of little help to him that he can blame part of his predicament on the enticing ads and commercials.

Middle-class young people have more money to spend than those of any previous time, a fact that has not gone unnoticed by manufacturers of sportswear, records, and motorcycles, who in their advertising cater to this market. Advertising can make it appear that one brand of aspirin or toothpaste is far superior to others though most brands may actually contain the same ingredients. Sometimes the only difference is in the attractive packaging and in the mind of the consumer.

Two techniques used by advertisers have been particularly criticized: the appeal to man's interest in sex even when nonsexual products are offered and the testimonials of celebrities or bogus experts. The critics feel that scantily dressed beauties are appropriately used in ads in which ladies' lingerie or bathing suits are offered. But in ads for spark plugs or cigars they only attract the male viewer's eye without necessarily saying anything about the quality of the product. The fact that a particular aging movie star uses certain pills of supposed rejuvenating power does not make them more effective nor do the assertions of an actor dressed as a doctor or chemist.

Some television viewers object to the poor taste of advertising in which an overabundance of commercials deal with bad breath, body odor, stomach acid and similar troubles. These kinds of commercials can be a disagreeable background to many viewers, especially during dinner time, but apparently advertisers feel that scenes of human discomfort help sell products nevertheless.

The excess ardor of salesmen and advertisers has prompted a countermove for *consumer protection*. We have laws that protect the consumer by prohibiting the sale of unwholesome foods and unsafe drugs. It is forbidden for advertisements and commercials to make false claims about the effects of medicines, cosmetics, and other merchandise. Labels on cans and packages must indicate the true weight of the contents. Cigarette advertising, car safety, and car insurance have become subjects of legislative investigation.

Consumer organizations and labor unions demand more protection, while representatives of business, especially in the advertising field, vigorously oppose such interference in their activities. But even among businessmen themselves voices have been raised calling for much-needed self-regulation.

LIVING STANDARD

We eat about twenty pounds more meat and two pounds more cheese per person per year than we did ten years ago, but our consumption of butter and foods made from flour has gone down. More of us than ever before are concerned not about eating too little but too much. These are sure indications that our *living standard* has been moving upward, though, unfortunately, a substantial minority of Americans has had no part in this rise.

The living standard is the rate of consumption beyond the subsistence level, the absolutely necessary minimum. It indicates how comfortably we live, how much we can afford of the pleasures, the beauty, and the thrills of life. Surveys indicate that in 1951 an urban family of four needed $3,730 per year to maintain a modest living standard. The corresponding figure for the present is $9,191.[12]

Part of this rise in the cost of living is due to inflation, but even with prices moving upward the consumer is still ahead. In late 1968 consumer prices were 4.75 percent above the previous year, but the earnings of workers had risen 6.3 percent in the same time.[13]

If we want to compare the living standards in various countries, we should not look mainly at very rich people. Multimillionaires live in luxury and abundance whether you find them in Miami, Athens, or Calcutta. The poorer the region, the more appalling is the contrast between the wealth of a few and the misery of the overwhelming majority.

In order to recognize differences in living standards we must look at the middle- and lower-income families in the countries being compared. A skilled American worker drives to the plant in his own car; his Russian counterpart pedals a bicycle. Few repairmen in Mexico City own the pleasure boats, campers, or vacation trailers that are a common sight in the driveways of even some of our modest homes. A village craftsman in Spain would probably never think of sending his children to college, but many students at our state universities, community colleges, and local institutions of learning are the sons and daughters of workingmen.

All of these comparisons indicate that our standard of living is the highest in the world.[14] However, the blessings of the American living standard are not evenly distributed among all the inhabitants of this country. There are pockets of dismal poverty in the midst of plenty, of inferior housing and nutrition in the midst of comfort and abundance of food and drink. As far as the even distribution of life's finer things is concerned, Sweden, Norway, and Denmark are far ahead of the United States, even though the living standards of these small Scandinavian countries are lower than ours. These people consume less costly goods and pleasures, but at the same time they seem to be more successful than we in overcoming the disturbing contrast between wealth and poverty.

As individuals and as a society we generally assume that raising the standard of living is a worthwhile goal. We take pride in being able to afford now more expensive pleasures than we could afford in earlier years. Even in sports we display this tendency. There was a time when golf, hunting, and tennis were customarily enjoyed by a small privileged upper class. In many parts of the world this is still the case, but in America these sports have become favorite pastimes for working people in the middle-income group.

Other nations, such as Japan and the West European countries, are becoming wealthier, and as they do, they tend to adopt some of the same habits of increased consumption for which Americans are criticized.

Among our severest critics we find Americans themselves, especially the younger generation. Are we seeking only *materialistic* values? Are we too much concerned with the size of the engine in our car or the number of visits to the beauty shop, and not enough with love, friendship, and real beauty? Do we acquire things because they enrich our lives or rather because the Joneses down the block have also acquired them? Is "surpassing the Joneses" a goal worth striving for?

Despite the soaring living standard our society faces grave difficulties. In fact, some difficulties seem to increase with our growing *affluence*. The struggle against organized crime, racial discrimination, and against the decay of the big cities goes on, and what is perhaps hardest to understand, especially while the nation grows weathier, is that there still remain ugly pockets of poverty. The gap between "haves" and "have-nots" is wider than ever.

POVERTY

What does a poor man look like? He may walk around clad in rags; he may be skinny and pale. But as he walks past you, he may also be indistinguishable from his more fortunate fellow citizens.

Millions all over the world live on the edge of starvation. Many die young. We are accustomed to hearing such news come from distant continents, but it sometimes is a shock to learn that even in America, the land of plenty, stark hunger and ruinous malnutrition exist. Local officials in several states succeeded for a long time in hiding these dire facts from the nation, but in news reports and congressional inquiries during 1968 and 1969 the ugly truth has begun to surface.

Hunger is terrible, but it is not the same as *poverty*. Poverty generally means being hungry, but this isn't always the case. "Poverty exists when the resources of families or individuals are inadequate to provide a socially acceptable standard of living."[15] Therefore, what constitutes poverty depends on what is the acceptable living standard in a particular society. To be poor then means different things to different people and nations. In America a family may live in an apartment with electricity, a refrigerator, and an indoor flush toilet and still be considered poor. Thousands of Southeast Asians who sleep in the streets because they lack any kind of housing would call this luxury.

Who are the poor? They are not only a statistical figure, they are individuals suffering from individual hardships. Michael Harrington calls them the inhabitants of "The Other America."[16] Many are nonwhite.

Blacks form a large reservoir of poverty, but the American Indian is possibly even worse off. White Americans forced the Indian off his old hunting grounds and onto reservations that were usually located on poor and remote land. Here the Indians were left to live in tatters, often with hunger as their daily companion, unable to maintain their tribal economy, and excluded from full participation in the white man's culture.

Poverty exists among the unemployed, among rural sharecroppers and migrant farm workers, among the unkempt residents of skid row in our cities. Poverty is often a companion of old age, too. What we like to refer to as the "golden years" are years of misery for at least one-half of the aged, especially for many widows whose poverty is paired with loneliness. People who are old and poor "are literally cut off from the rest of America."[17]

One can study the geography of poverty. The run-down sections of our cities, the urban slums, are marked by poverty. We can also pinpoint rural slums in various stages of decay. Certain pockets in regions such as Appalachia and the Ozarks have been by-passed by general material progress, and poverty is widespread there.

So far we have mentioned sizable poverty-stricken groups. We also find isolated unfortunate individuals who are poor because they are plagued by physical or mental illness, alcoholism, family breakup, or involvement in crime. Here we deal with *case poverty*. Poverty is more than just peeling plaster and patched clothes—it is a feeling of hopelessness, the conviction that "nobody cares," that pervades the subculture of the poor. Only too often the poor are bitter, and they have given up trying to better themselves. Their children, who are exposed to this attitude, come under its influence, and so poverty extends from generation to generation.

FIGHT AGAINST POVERTY

During most of human history the rich have been in the minority, and the poor have been in the majority. Even as recently as fifty years ago, most unskilled people had barely enough to eat. Like old age and death, poverty was accepted in earlier periods of our history as something unavoidable. Still the plight of the poor disturbed the consciences of some of the more fortunate.

Most religions command charity toward the poor. The ancient Hebrew farmer left the corners of his field unharvested so that the needy might collect a few sheaves. In early Christian society monasteries fed the poor, and beggars waited at church steps for the coins of the pious worshipers.

In some cultures though poverty was once felt to be a divine punishment for laziness. In our country even today this attitude has not completely died out. The British Poor Laws, enacted in the nineteenth century, decreed that beggars should be rounded up and put into poorhouses. The novels of Charles Dickens describe these places as veritable hellholes in which people lost the last shred of human dignity.

Shocking as the conditions in the poorhouses were, the laws at least indicated that governments were becoming aware of poverty and felt that something ought to be done about it. Today few citizens deny that public agencies should be concerned about the poor in our midst. It is generally agreed that the poorhouse of old is not the solution, but there is still much debate on methods of attacking the problem.

The fight against poverty is now being waged by government on both local and national levels. Since government dispenses public funds, it must define poverty in terms of money. Because of the general inflation, the "poverty line," or point at which a person or persons are considered poor, has had to be moved upward from time to time. In 1966 the poverty line for an urban family of four was set at $3,000, up $1,000 from 1946. The line extends from $1,560 for a woman over sixty-five living alone to $5,440 for a family of seven or more. Included in these poverty figures are 29,700,000 Americans, or 15.4 percent of our population.[18]

It is encouraging to note, however, that poverty in the United States is decreasing (see Figure 13). In 1959 the number "below the line" was much higher: 38,900,000 individuals, or 22.1 percent of the population. But white Americans find it easier to climb upward than members of minority groups, and so the income gap between the races is widening. Between 1959 and 1966 only about 1 million nonwhites crossed the poverty line, compared to 8 million whites.

Poverty remains an ugly scar on the national body though it may not be visible to a person driving through the verdant countryside or strolling past abundantly filled store windows. It has long been obvious that in a society as complicated as ours poverty cannot be eliminated by the handouts of private individuals or groups, however generous they may be. Society as a whole, through its public institutions, must shoulder the responsibility of caring for those who cannot care for themselves. What efforts have been made in this regard?

Those of the poor who don't have jobs need them, and those who have work are often very poorly paid. Attempts are being made to attract business and industry into the urban poverty pockets to create new jobs. Public agencies, churches, and private foundations encourage various self-help schemes by which people can find a new sense of worth as they work their way out of poverty.

But such measures take time. Meanwhile, financial help must be given where the need is most urgent. This is the task of various public assistance, or, more commonly called, "welfare" programs.

Welfare agencies have received much criticism both from the poor who are on the receiving end and from the citizens who provide welfare money through taxes. Taxpayers complain about people who live off welfare money rather than work, and the recipients protest that they have

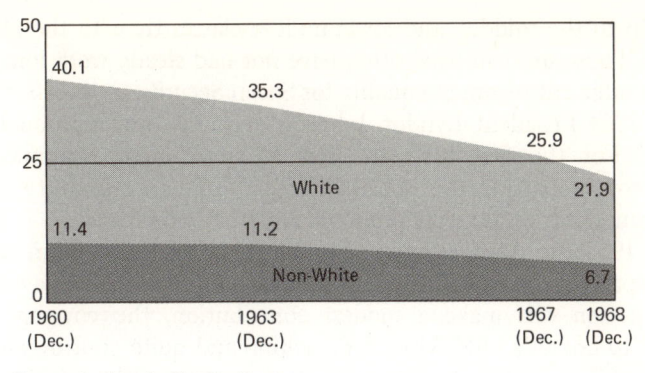

Poverty in America Has Declined...
(Millions of poor persons)

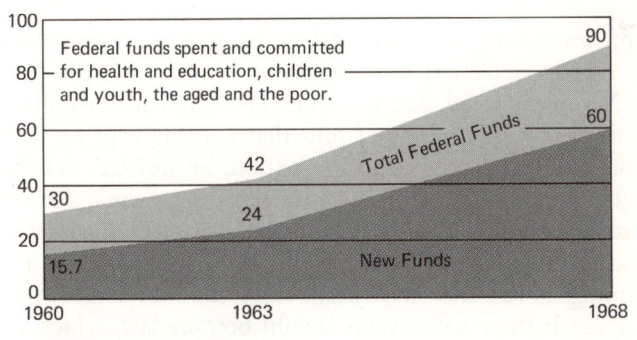

- 1960 (Dec.): White 40.1, Non-White 11.4
- 1963 (Dec.): White 35.3, Non-White 11.2
- 1967 (Dec.): White 25.9
- 1968 (Dec.): White 21.9, Non-White 6.7

...As Social Welfare Spending Grew
(Billions of dollars)

- 1960: Federal funds spent and committed for health and education, children and youth, the aged and the poor: 30; New Funds: 15.7
- 1963: 42; New Funds: 24
- 1968: Total Federal Funds: 90; New Funds: 60

Figure 13
Fight Against Poverty

Source: Department of Health, Education, and Welfare. Appeared in *The New York Times Student Weekly*, January 13, 1969. © 1969 by The New York Times Company. Reprinted by permission.

to submit to checks and inquiries that offend their self-respect. There is also resentment of the fact that welfare measures are actually least helpful to those who need help most, because of many unfair restrictions.

Welfare payments throughout the country are uneven. They vary from state to state and from community to community. "It is much better to be poor in New York City than in Montgomery County, Ohio, and better to be poor in almost any place than in Mississippi."[19] Knowing this, many poor people migrate to places where higher payments await them, thereby creating worse slums and more misery.

About 90 percent of all employed persons are covered by Federal Old-Age and Survivor's Insurance, commonly called Social Security. But here again the most needy are often left out. Monthly payments average $80, hardly enough when no other resources are available. Social Security is of more help to the middle- and lower-middle classes than to the poorest of the poor. Those most in need often have not had steady work long enough and with sufficient income to qualify for Social Security payments.

In 1964 President Lyndon Johnson declared "unconditional war on poverty." For the first time the federal government committed itself strongly to combatting this social disease. Various antipoverty programs were begun, many others were proposed and widely discussed.

In 1965 the *Medicare* law was enacted. Medicare is an insurance program paying hospital and nursing home expenses for the aged. If the insured person can make a modest contribution, the coverage can be extended to doctor's bills. More far-reaching and quite controversial is the proposal of a guaranteed minimum income for everybody. "Its benefits would cover all those in need and would be paid automatically, thus eliminating expensive and unnecessary bureaucracy and its degrading forms of means tests."[20]

As of this writing, however, nothing has yet been done about guaranteeing everybody in America a minimum income. But in August 1969 President Nixon proposed that the federal government guarantee payment of $1,600 a year to each family of four that is being kept on welfare rolls. As he submitted this proposal to the nation, he insisted that he did not want to guarantee money to those who refused to work. He wanted his measure to be referred to as a "national floor under incomes" and suggested that payments should be made only to people willing to accept work or job training, unless they were disabled or the mothers of preschool-age children. Even if these suggestions should become law, which is far from certain, they would still leave millions of Americans below the poverty line.

The war against poverty goes on, but its progress is sluggish and uneven. We still have not developed a successful strategy to reach the "hard core" of our poor population. Some social scientists feel though that, for the first time, perhaps in all history, poverty could be completely eliminated because we can afford to eliminate it. According to John Kenneth Galbraith we could provide every family in the United States with a minimum living standard and still meet our obligations to the rest of the world. We could give every poor child a good education to prevent poverty from being self-perpetuating. "In the contemporary United States [poverty] is a disgrace."[21]

Main Ideas

1. Money is a medium of exchange used to convert income into consumer goods and services.
2. Inflation occurs when too much money is available to buy too few goods and services; the buying power of the dollar drops.
3. The average income that Americans receive for their work is increasing.
4. On the whole, the more education the worker has obtained, the

higher will be his income; but some people draw payments out of proportion to their training and skills.
5. In a well-functioning economy production and consumption flow constantly into one another.
6. A person's assets consist of the goods that remain in his possession for an extended length of time.
7. The higher a consumer's income, the more choice he has in how to spend it.
8. The more limited an income is, the greater is the necessity of budgeting.
9. Installment buying is an important aid for the individual and for the economy but must be handled with care.
10. Advertising is a necessary tool of marketing and is of help to the buyer; but advertisers have been criticized for misleading statements and high-pressure tactics.
11. The rate of individual consumption beyond the subsistence level determines the living standard.
12. Americans have the highest living standard in the world but face grave social difficulties, nevertheless, because of uneven distribution of income and lack of adequate care for the underprivileged.
13. Poverty still exists in America, though it is decreasing.
14. Poor people lack the income to provide a living standard acceptable to the society in which they live.
15. Public agencies on various levels and also private organizations are engaged in efforts to wipe out poverty in America, a goal that some now consider possible.

Important Terms

Aesthetic goals
Affluence
Asset
Budget
Case poverty
Consumer protection
Consumption
Credit rating
Currency
Federal Reserve Bank
Free enterprise
Goods

Inflation
Investment
Living standard
Market
Materialistic values
Median
Medicare
Medium of exchange
Poverty
Productivity
Services

Conclusion

In our complex society the visible and countable reward for production is money. Money is not valuable in itself but only as payment for consumer goods and services. Though vast differences exist from person to person and from place to place, everybody has some kind of income, and everybody is, in some measure, a consumer. Our incomes, in part, depend on our skills, our inherited social positions, and society's demand for what we can do. As consumers we are limited by our financial situation and also by the tastes and values of the society to which we belong.

Notes
1. George L. Bach, *Economics: An Introduction to Analysis and Policy*, 5th ed. (Englewood Cliffs, N.J.: Prentice-Hall, 1966), p. 99.
2. U.S. Department of Labor, Bureau of Labor Statistics, *Monthly Report* (January 1969).
3. R. E. Glos and H. A. Baker, *Introduction to Business* (Cincinnati: South-Western, 1967), p. 43.
4. *United States Code* (Washington, D.C.: Government Printing Office), vol. 7 (1964), p. 6314, and Supplement 5 (1965–1969), p. 2375.
5. U.S. Department of Labor, *op. cit.*
6. *Wall Street Journal,* February 8, 1968, p. 14.
7. Leon H. Keyserling, *Goals for Teachers' Salaries in Our Public Schools* (Conference on Economic Progress, Washington, D.C., 1967), p. 28.
8. U.S. Department of Commerce, *Statistical Abstract of the United States* (1968), p. 325.
9. Robert L. Heilbroner, *The Worldly Philosophers,* rev. ed. (New York: Simon & Schuster, 1961), p. 268.
10. *Ibid.,* p. 259.
11. *Changing Times* (March 1969), pp. 24–28.
12. *Wall Street Journal, op. cit.,* p. 14.
13. U.S. Department of Commerce, 49, *Survey of Current Business,* 27–28.
14. Bach, *op. cit.,* p. 23.
15. Harry G. Johnson, "Unemployment and Poverty," in Leo Fishman (ed.), *Poverty Amid Affluence* (New Haven, Conn.: Yale University Press, 1966).
16. Michael Harrington, *The Other America: Poverty in the United States* (New York: Macmillan, 1964).
17. *Ibid.,* p. 109.
18. U.S. Department of Commerce, *Statistical Abstract, op. cit.,* p. 329.
19. Harrington, *op. cit.,* p. 111.
20. Bach, *op. cit.,* p. 544.
21. John Kenneth Galbraith, *The Affluent Society,* college ed. (Boston: Houghton Mifflin, 1960), p. 333.

Suggestions for Further Reading
Bagdikian, Ben H. *In the Midst of Plenty.* Boston: Beacon Press, 1964. Vividly presented case studies of poverty in the United States.

Changing Times; Consumer Reports; Consumer Research Bulletin. Monthly magazines giving consumer advice.

Donaldson, E. F., and Pfahl, J. K. *Personal Finance.* 4th ed. New York: Ronald Press, 1966. Textbook on how to manage one's money.

"Lord, I'm Hungry," *Newsweek,* 70, July 24, 1967, pp. 22–24. A Senate subcommittee investigating hunger tours the Mississippi Delta.

MacClellan, Grant S. *The Consuming Public.* New York: H. W. Wilson, 1968. Discusses consumer needs and activities of government in the consumer field.

"Meet Ralph Nader," *Newsweek,* 71, January 22, 1968, 65 ff. Mr. Nader crusades for automobile safety and other consumer needs.

Moscowitch, E. "Finding Jobs for the Poor," *New Republic,* 155, November 5, 1966, 16–19.

Public Affairs Pamphlets. Social Problems Series. No. 39, "Loan Sharks and Their Victims"; No. 61, "Installment Selling—Pros and Cons"; No. 221, "When You Invest—the Role of Investment Companies"; No. 362, "The Poor Among Us—Challenge and Opportunity."

*Who are the people you envy?
Is it the editor of the school
newspaper? or the girl who dates the
captain of the football team?
or the owner of that fast Jaguar?
or the man just elected Exalted
Ruler of your lodge?*

11 HOW DO YOU RANK?
status, caste, and class

On television the President of the United States is seen draping a blue ribbon around the neck of a young marine. Suspended from the ribbon is the Congressional Medal of Honor. A thousand miles away, in a crowded lodge hall, a boy of fourteen has a similar-looking symbol pinned to his green uniform. His parents sit in the audience beaming with pride as he is pronounced an Eagle Scout.

The wife of a newly promoted assistant bank manager is deliriously happy. She has received her first invitation to the exclusive sewing circle that meets every Tuesday afternoon in a member's home. At the same time, in a cheap waterfront bar, a bedraggled panhandler tells his friends that he has just collected over thirty dollars for a half-day's work on the streets of the downtown section. The other derelicts are awe-struck by this tale of supreme begging skill.

STATUS

The medal winner and the Eagle Scout, the lady who was accepted into the sewing circle and the derelict who claims to be the best beggar in town: all have achieved a *status* higher

Something to believe in.

BUICK MOTOR DIVISION

    This is what happens when Buick mixes excitement with craftsmanship.
    This is the 1970 Buick Skylark Custom.
    Exciting? If looks alone don't get you, consider the standard equipment.
    A 260 horsepower, 350 cubic inch V8 is standard. It runs on regular gas.
    Fiberglass belted tires that provide longer tire life and better traction are standard, too.
    So are hidden windshield wipers, and a radio antenna that's concealed in the windshield for uncluttered, unbroken styling. Deep foam-cushioned seats and wall-to-wall carpeting are standard as well.
    The result? More comfort and more beauty.
    But excitement aside, never forget that this is a Buick. Built with traditional Buick craftsmanship and product integrity. That's the reason behind Buick features like side guard beam construction for more strength and confidence and an Acrylic lacquer finish that's put on six coats deep for shimmering beauty that lasts and lasts.
    The 1970 Buick Skylark Custom. Built to make it a pleasure to drive. Built to give you something to believe in.
    Wouldn't you really rather have a **Buick.**

A new car is a means through which many people achieve status.
Reproduced courtesy of McCann-Erickson, Inc.

than the one they had previously. Status is a person's position or rank as compared with other persons. We are proud of high status and look down with either pity or contempt on those who have failed to achieve it. Status fills our need to shine, to be noticed.

We expect people to strive for higher status and to be proud when they attain it. Status fills a need to be noticed, and we find the search for it "normal"; status-seeking is a trait of our culture. Yet there are societies in which status is not a desirable goal. The Zuñi Indians, who live in our southwestern states, have only contempt for a member of their community who is trying to raise himself above his companions. Zuñis want to live quietly without arousing much attention. When tribal leaders or officials are needed, somebody has to be almost forced to take such a job. If a man tries to assert himself, he is suspected of witchcraft and may bring much trouble on himself. Even in sports, winners are disliked, and rather than being acclaimed, they may be barred from future contests.[1]

Practices like these are in sharp contrast with the ways of most Americans. We want our associates to see the medal or merit badge, the former club president's gold pin or the brass discus thrower that was awarded as first prize at an athletic meet. We cherish these *status symbols*, which tell the world, "Look, this man or this woman is somebody."

A status symbol is not necessarily something that you wear. There are many other distinctions, such as sitting at the head table during a banquet, being asked to serve on the church board, or being able to afford taking your date to a high-class night spot.

Those possessing the highest status in a society form the *elite*. An elite is found in almost every walk of life, even among criminals. The Wild West outlaw of movie fame who was the "quickest on the draw" has his counterpart in the modern specialist who can crack even the most intricate safe. To "make" the "Ten Most Wanted" list of the FBI might even be considered a high point in a wayward career. The men whose faces greet us from post office walls have entered the elite group of the professional lawbreakers.

Status involves *rating*. We rate other people, and we are in turn rated by them according to the values of our society. People desire high status because it brings them all kinds of rewards. If they are rated high in status, their neighbors and associates show them respect. They are likely to have power, leadership, and privilege. High-ranking statesmen are addressed as "Your Excellency," high-ranking Catholic clergymen as "Your Eminence." If you enjoy high status, exclusive clubs and cliques tend to seek your membership. You may be envied, and, openly or secretly, people strive to be like you.

We often avoid contact with those whom we rate as being low in status. "He is not our kind," we say. "Don't play with Pete," Mother warns. "His folks aren't any good." A girl suddenly finds herself shunned by her former friends, who whisper with outrage, "Nancy goes out with the wrong kind of boys."

The striving for status is as old as mankind. In primitive societies that depended on hunting and fishing for a livelihood, the most successful hunter or fisherman held the highest status. He could not keep more of his catch than he and his family could eat; so the status symbol became the amount of food that he gave away.

The *potlatch* of the Pacific Northwest Indians was a festival in which the host lavished presents on his guests. Cheerfully the members of the tribe competed in their generosity. The more bountiful the presents, the higher rose the status of the giver.

We often envy persons who donate large amounts to charities and educational and cultural causes, since their gifts are indications of their wealth. Aside from possessions, however, we also rate people by their occupation, education, and even by the status of the schools they have attended.

HIERARCHY

A person who tries to flaunt his status is often called a *snob*, an uncomplimentary term. A snob will also try to acquire symbols of a status higher than the one he really possesses. Though we may laugh about such vanity, merchants and advertisers use it. They know what items have "snob appeal," and they gear their markets and advertising to the status seekers.

Real-estate businessmen, too, recognize the importance of a desirable address to the status seeker. A country house becomes a château and a farm an estate. Roads are called boulevards, drives, terraces, or cliffs. Houses built on hills often bring higher prices. There is status in being able to look down upon one's neighbors as a king looks from his throne on his subjects.

When status is distributed in a definite order, ranging from very high to very low, we speak of a *hierarchy*. Good examples can be found in the military, in the Catholic clergy—where the term "hierarchy" is used officially—and in college faculties. The hierarchy in these three examples can be compared to rungs on a ladder: in the army generals are on the highest and privates on the lowest rungs; in the Catholic clergy the range extends from pope to priest; and among college and university teachers the range extends from full professors to instructors.

In all these examples status is easily recognizable by definite sets of symbols: clothing, stars and bars, titles, and the form of greeting expected from those of lower rank.

Elsewhere hierarchies may not be as obvious, but they exist nevertheless. Government employees or business executives don't wear uniforms, and one may look not too unlike the other. But as they climb in rank and responsibility, certain symbols indicate the rise. Their offices become larger, wall-to-wall carpeting appears, and at some point a man on the rise may even win access to the executive dining room. If he continues to advance, he might eventually be given an official car and a personal chauffeur or other status symbols.

In our minds we arrange occupations in some sort of hierarchy. In a 1947 survey of the National Opinion Research Center people were asked to rate fifty occupations. Supreme Court judges and physicians were rated as having the highest prestige, while janitors, street sweepers and shoeshiners were rated as having the lowest. In 1964 it was found that most people still held the same opinions in this regard.[2]

How do the people of lower rank feel about their position? They too have a desire for higher status. One way of satisfying this desire is to create new status symbols by giving their tasks more elegant titles. The janitor becomes a "maintenance engineer," the policeman a "peace officer," the garbage man a "sanitation worker," and the caretaker a "building superintendent." Society as a whole often accepts these new titles; it doesn't cost anything to do so.

ASCRIBED AND ACHIEVED STATUS

In France, when a king died, the herald blew his trumpet from the palace steps and then solemnly proclaimed, "The king is dead. Long live the king." The one whose long life was being heralded was the king's oldest son, who automatically ascended the vacant throne. He had neither to seek employment nor compete with other candidates in an election. His status was determined by his birth into the royal family: that is, it was *ascribed*. The advantage of this was that everybody knew who would hold this momentous position. But the drawback was that not everyone born into the royal family necessarily made a good ruler. In fact, history has shown us numerous poor rulers among royal families, but there was little done about the situation.

In this country some people eagerly trace their family trees back through many generations. They often hound libraries for books on *genealogy*, hoping perhaps to find an ancestor who came to America on the earliest boat or who fought under George Washington.

Your ascribed status, then, depends on the family into which you are born and on the ethnic and religious group to which your family belongs. In a society in which class lines are drawn sharply and permanently ascribed, status is all-important. This is not the case in a society in which the cultural picture changes rapidly and old ways become outmoded. Here *achieved* status—the status that comes with personal success based on strength, skill, possessions, beauty, or sheer luck—becomes most desirable. Achieved status belongs to the Homecoming Queen, to the champion pool player in the local recreation hall, to the businessman who started as a stockroom clerk and now owns his own company.

STRATIFICATION

Status applies not only to individuals but also to whole groups. Belonging to a high-status group usually assures its members greater *prestige*. Such groups try to be exclusive and erect barriers to keep outsiders from joining.

A society that has such status groups is *stratified*. That is, the groups are arranged either above or below one another like the geological layers (strata) of rock that form a mountain. Stratification can range from strict formality to informality. Informality, for example, pervades the *cliques*, the tightly knit groups of friends, of high-school students.

In 1961 August B. Hollingshead published a study of an American community that he named Elmtown. His findings indicate that high-school students are very careful about the people with whom they "run around" and "go places." They form cliques, which Hollingshead calls "prestige groups." The author distinguishes three types of cliques among high-school students:

> *Elite*: its members consider themselves the leaders and the cream of the student body.
> "*Good kids*": this middle-ranking group comprises about two-thirds of the student body.
> "*Grubby kids*": these are students who have not made it into accepted youth society. They live "on the other side of the tracks," don't behave in acceptable ways, and are not held worthy of trust or friendship by most of the other students.

In Elmtown boys mostly dated girls of the same level. Hollingshead concludes: "Adolescent clique and dating patterns are a reflection in large part of the adult social structure."[3]

In every stratification system large layers break into smaller layers: strata contain *substrata*. Craftsmen of old, who represented a stratum of society, divided their ranks into masters, journeymen, and apprentices. Within the nobility, the highest status group of the Middle Ages, counts ranked above barons and dukes above counts. Modern organized rackets have intricate hierarchies from big bosses down to enforcers who kill or rough up their victims on orders passed through the ranks.

CASTE

When stratification is extremely rigid and when it is permanent and hereditary, we speak of a *caste system*. The society of India is often given as the prime example. For many, many generations Hindus belonged to four main castes, each broken into numerous subcastes. The system was so complicated that only people living in the same region could understand how it worked locally. At the top of the ladder were the Brahmans, or priests; on the bottom were the Sudras, or laborers; and below all these castes existed many millions, the outcastes, or untouchables, a mass of people condemned to a life of sweeping refuse and cleaning toilets.

The Indian caste system is interwoven with the religious concept of *reincarnation*. Hinduism teaches that at death the soul enters another body. For having performed good deeds the soul is rewarded with the body of a higher caste person. As a punishment for improper behavior, on the other hand, it must inhabit the body of a person of lower caste.

As India struggles to become a modern industrial country, the caste system is beginning to collapse. Caste discrimination has been outlawed by the government. The old rules forbidding lower castes to eat with higher castes as well as even forbidding the shadow of an untouchable to fall upon a Brahman, are no longer feasible to maintain in factories, at universities, or on airplanes.

Main Hindu Castes*

Brahmans	(Priests)
Kshatriyas	(Warriors)
Vaisyas	(Traders, craftsmen, farmers)
Sudras	(Laborers, servants)
Pariahs	(Untouchables)

* These were originally also occupational groups but are less so today.

In traditional terms a caste is a part of society to which a person belongs for life. He is born into it, and he dies in it. A man must marry a woman of his own caste (*endogamy*). He cannot hide his caste because he is marked by the color of his skin, his garments, or some other visible sign.

Medieval Europe also had a kind of caste system; it allowed, however, a very limited amount of mobility. People were born as either nobles or commoners. The nobles ruled from their castles and engaged in fighting and hunting. The commoners farmed, traded, and worked in shops. These two groups are often referred to as *estates,* a division somewhat less rigid than the Indian caste system. Occasionally the ruler elevated a commoner to noble rank as a special favor. There was also a third estate, the clergy. Since priests were not supposed to have children, men were not born into the clergy but had to enter it from one of the other two estates. Remnants of the division into a landholding nobility and a suppressed peasantry still exist in many countries.

In the United States the relationship between the races has some features of a caste system. Some whites consider themselves superior to blacks, Indians, Puerto Ricans, Mexican-Americans, and, to a lesser degree, Orientals. In the Southern states especially, blacks have been socially ostracized. The symbols of rank and privilege have been carefully preserved by the white ruling group, which has traditionally held the positions of power and demanded strict obedience from blacks. Segregation, discrimination in jobs, and laws against intermarriage have added to the problem. Any attempts by blacks to disregard these restrictions have brought swift revenge in the form of lost jobs, assault, and even murder. Now blacks are showing a strong determination to change or completely destroy the system, while the ruling caste tries hard to maintain it.

CLASSES

The wife of a plant manager speaking about the wife of a plant worker might say, "She is not in our class." The worker's wife would probably say the same of the lady married to the boss. *Classes* differ greatly in status, and yet there is mobility from class to class. (Classes are unlike castes in this respect.) The plant manager's father may have been a worker himself. Depending on your own effort and personal luck, you can move from class to class. The class system is characterized by *fluid ascription*,[4] which means that different class labels can be attached to the same person during different phases of his life.

THEORIES OF CLASS

What are the classes that make up a society? How do they differ from one another? Should there be any class structure at all, and if so, what kind? These questions have fascinated economists, political scientists, and philosophers for a long time.

Plato, an ancient Greek philosopher, envisioned an ideal society. In this Platonic society members of the community would not be equal but would be divided into three classes, differing in their functions and also in their rights. In the highest positions would be the guardians, trained to rule and understand what life was all about; next, the warriors, charged with the duty of defending the country; and finally, the workers, charged with producing food, clothing, and shelter for the whole community. Each member of the community would do the task for which he was best suited. Plato's ideal society definitely involves a hierarchy but one that depends on talent and ability rather than on birth.[5]

Hundreds of years later Christian theologians, such as Saint Augustine, observed, as did everybody else, that some men were rich and powerful while many more were poor and wretched. Yet the theologians felt that God apparently wanted it so. Though life was hard for the majority, everybody had an equal chance of getting to heaven. In the meantime, those who lived in abundance were bound to practice charity and give to those who had little or nothing.

It was not until the eighteenth century that writers began to question the justice of class privileges. But they were less concerned with possessions than with the basic equality of all men before the law.

With the Industrial Revolution came big cities and factories. Bleak tenements for the working people and luxurious mansions for the wealthy were built. In such closeness the contrast between luxury and misery became more obvious and formed an explosive mixture. Now critics began seriously to consider the problem of social classes.

The economist Adam Smith had much to say about the problem in his book *The Wealth of Nations,* published in 1776.[6] He saw two classes sharply divided in purpose and privilege: the employers and the laborers. The employer seeks profit, and the more profit the better. The laborer sells the employer his time and strength, but he does not determine the price of his labor and has nothing to say about the conditions under which he works. The employer regards him as a piece of machinery that is to be kept operating at the lowest possible cost. Wages will, of necessity, be at or near the absolute minimum to keep workers alive and producing. Smith paints a grim picture, especially for the laborer, who is condemned to spend his life as a member of a rather miserable class.

Others, not content with the plight of laborers, raised their voices, and among them was Karl Marx, who has had a profound influence on social theory. In the communist world his writings are a kind of official bible. From East Germany to the People's Republics of China and North Korea, statesmen quote him and students study him as one might study a religious prophet.

Marx learned from Smith but went far beyond him. He taught that human beings have been engaged in an eternal class struggle involving two main classes—one at the top and one at the bottom—the exploiters and the exploited. At different periods in history these two main classes have had different names: slaves and free Romans, serfs and barons, and so on. But no matter what their names, one class worked and was suppressed while the other practiced the suppression and reaped the fruits of the laborers' work. In his theory Marx did not condemn the upper classes. They were not motivated by maliciousness but were just fulfilling the role that destiny had thrust upon them.

Marx saw the class struggle of his own nineteenth century as a clash between the *bourgeoisie,* his term for the owners of factories and businesses, and the *proletariat,* his term for poor people, especially factory workers. He vividly described the terrible living conditions of the workingman in the early days of industry. He foresaw an inevitable, violent confrontation between bourgeoisie and proletariat. (See Figure 14.) The lot of the worker will worsen, he predicted, as better machines take over more workers' jobs and as the bourgeoisie makes the remaining laborers work harder and for less money. The rich will become richer, the poor poorer, and the middle class will be ground up between the two groups. Eventually the proletariat will become so desperate that it will rise up in a world-wide revolution and destroy the bourgeoisie. "The proletarians have nothing to lose but their chains. They have a world to win."[7] A *classless society* will then follow, a kind of paradise on earth without exploitation of man by his fellow-man. Everybody will reap the full reward of what he produces, whether it is a product of his hands or his mind. But Marx did not say how this classless society would operate. He left no blueprint.

For Marx classes were large groups of people doing the same kind of work—that is, if they worked at all—and having approximately the same kind of possessions, one class having very much and the other very little.

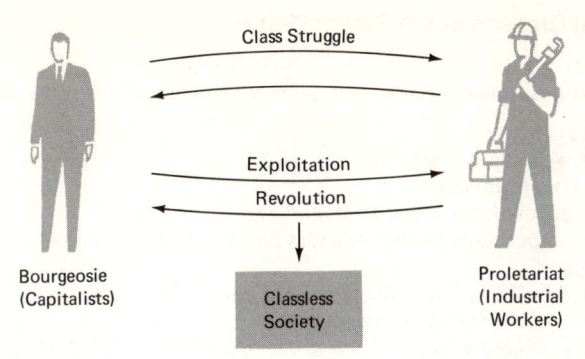

Figure 14
Marx's Prediction of the Outcome of the Class Struggle

Marx felt that economic conditions were the most important consideration.

Now, more than a hundred years after Marx made his analyses, some serious flaws have become apparent in his forecasts. In many countries, including ours, the worker is much better off than ever before. He thinks little of revolution; in fact, rather than destroying the present system, he tries to gain more advantages from it.

The role of the bourgeoisie has also changed. J. Pierpont Morgan, an immensely rich banker and industrialist, once said, "I owe the public nothing." Since then owners of automobile or appliance factories have learned that only a public that is fairly well-off can afford to buy cars or refrigerators. Marx's prophecy about the disappearance of the middle class has also been proved wrong, at least in technologically advanced countries. Today the middle class is stronger than ever.

How have Marx's ideas fared when tested? He had predicted that the proletarian revolution would begin in the most industrialized countries, such as England and the United States, and then spread from these countries across the world. Instead the revolution occurred in Russia, where there was very little industry. Moreover, what actually developed out of the Russian Revolution was by no means Marx's classless society but rather a new system of classes.

Despite his errors Marx was an intellectual giant. Not only is he the absolute authority in the communist world, but his teachings have made a deep impression everywhere, even where they are not fully accepted. The subject of social classes has remained foremost in the minds of scholars ever since. We will mention here only two of the more recent voices on the subject.

In 1899 Thorstein Veblen wrote *The Theory of the Leisure Class*.[8] He distinguished among the different classes not only according to their possessions but also their way of life. The lower classes work and pride themselves on doing a good job while the upper classes contemptuously

Social Classes in the Soviet Union

Upper Class
Highest government, party, and military officials; all educated party members

Middle Class
Writers, scientists, astronauts
Urban skilled workers
Clerks, accountants, lower bureaucracy
Well-to-do peasants (high producers on best collective farms)

Lower Class
Ordinary peasants (on ordinary or poor collective farms)
Forced labor (inmates of camps)

Source: "Social Classes in the Soviet Union" from *The Study of Sociology*, by Joseph S. Himes. Copyright © 1968 by Scott, Foresman and Company.

---

scorn work and spend their time in leisure. Veblen did not mean by this that rich people sit in idleness or sleep all day. Rather they do things that are not absolutely necessary but that they consider "beautiful and ennobling in all civilized men's eyes." For example, they breed race horses, study foreign languages, or practice strange cults. Any chosen activity is suitable as long as it is not productive work or a needed service. Rich people may have golden faucets in their bathrooms, not because golden faucets work better than ordinary faucets, but because they are costlier. This is a display of wealth for its own sake.

Like Marx, the German sociologist Max Weber (1864–1920) described classes as economic groups.[9] But he also spoke of "status groups," which overlap the classes. A status group follows a certain style of life. The members feel close to each other and like one another's company. A waiter who happens to be the son of a Russian count belongs, economically, to the working class but likes to associate with people of aristocratic background. A former logger who is now wealthy shuns the refined upper circles and feels more comfortable in a tavern or lodge hall with his former buddies.

CLASSES IN AMERICA

Do we have social classes in this country? At first impulse many students may answer with a resounding No. Having social classes at all somehow seems to conflict with our ideals of equality and democracy. Many cite the fact that most Americans dress in the same fashion, watch the same television programs, and attend the same motion pictures. Nevertheless, social scientists do not conduct their work through the use of slogans, and they find that people "deny the existence of classes directly, but act as if classes exist."[10]

Although to admit the existence of classes may seem to conflict with our democratic ideals, we also see that we need not spend our whole lives in one class. Many of us change classes and move mostly upward. Together with the countries of Western Europe the United States shows a high degree of social *mobility*. The sons of farmers seek jobs in the city; those who work with their hands try to see that their children exchange overalls for the business suits or white jackets of office and professional personnel. Automation and other innovations in the industrial and business world have created a tremendous need for more "white-collar" workers, and this situation gives children of lower classes an opportunity to climb higher on the occupational ladder than their parents had been able to do. But there are other young people, especially at our universities, who, while not denying their middle-class background, are far from happy about it. They accuse the middle and upper classes of being the Establishment that keeps itself in power by suppressing the majority of our citizens. These critics want to see a revolution take place, somewhat along the lines of Marx's ideas, that would right these wrongs and bring about a just society. Once these young people gain positions of leadership in various fields, we might witness considerable changes in our political, social, and economic situation.

Before looking at social classes in our own society, we need a working definition. Marx's concept does not adequately describe our mobile class situation. Let's try this definition: a *class* is "a group within a society whose members hold a number of distinctive statuses in common and who . . . develop an awareness of their like interests as against the unlike traits and interests of other groups."[11] As we examine the American class picture in more detail, this definition will become clearer.

In daily conversation we commonly use the terms "upper class," "middle class," and "lower class." This author has frequently asked his students to which class they think they belong. Almost without exception, these children of merchants, small farmers, factory and service workers declared themselves to be from the middle class, as if this were the only respectable choice.

Obviously, if we have a class system, there must be more than one class, and not everybody can belong to the same class. Experts have not been able to agree on the number of classes that exist in this country. To find the answer teams of researchers have investigated numerous American communities. Especially since 1945 such projects have become more numerous and more elaborate. Some have taken nearly two years for the investigators to thoroughly familiarize themselves with the habits of the people being studied along with their thoughts about themselves and about their neighbors.

After analyzing the results of their interviews and observations, the researchers obtained a picture of the class system in a particular community, hoping that their findings would also apply to other small and medium-size communities around the country. The situation in the large cities, such as New York and Los Angeles, is much more complex and also far more difficult to observe.

224 An Introduction to Social Science

The studies show that the class that you belong to is not determined solely by your income. Other classification factors must be considered, such as the type of work you do, where you live, the organizations you belong to, your political attitudes, how you raise your children, and so on.

The previously mentioned report on *Elmtown's Youth*, which concerns itself mainly with high-school students, made the following point:

> The lower class boys and girls do not have access to the Country Club and, in large part, they cannot attend lodge dances because few of their parents belong. They could participate in high school dances, but they are not "comfortable" there. . . . The boys and girls who attend the dances at Morrow's Hall or Scrugg's Tavern would be uncomfortable at the Country Club because experience has not prepared them to go to the Country Club in any capacity other than as caddy, waitress, janitor, garbage collector or workman. Conversely the "Country Club crowd" would be morally outraged to be invited to a dance at Scrugg's. The net effect is the segregation of the young people along class lines at the private clubs, semi-public and public dances.[12]

Obviously not all high-school student bodies are as rigidly segregated. In fact, educators often make strong efforts to bring young people from different class backgrounds together for various activities.

FROM UPPER UPPER TO LOWER LOWER

How many classes then are there in our society? Social scientists have no single answer, but they seem to agree that the old division into upper, middle, and lower classes oversimplifies reality. They frequently mention instead the idea of six classes ranging from an "upper upper" to a "lower lower" class.[13] We cannot describe all six divisions in detail, but a brief glance at some may be in order.

Classes in a Modern American Community

Upper Upper
  Old wealthy families (not found in newer communities)

Lower Upper
  New wealth

Upper Middle
  Business and professional people ("backbone of community")

Lower Middle
  White collar, small merchants, skilled workers

Upper Lower
  Semi-skilled, unskilled workers ("poor but honest")

Lower Lower
  Shiftless, unsteady jobs, in need of relief or charity

Source: Adapted from W. Lloyd Warner and Paul S. Lunt, *Yankee City Series*, 4 vols. (New Haven, Conn.: Yale University Press, 1941–1947).

To the untrained observer there may not seem to be too much difference between the upper upper and lower upper classes. Both comprise wealthy people, but the former group considers itself superior because wealth has been in the family for many generations. Families of the upper upper class belong to exclusive clubs; their names are listed in the social registers of large cities; they stress "good breeding," a way of behavior that is learned in expensive schools. "Attendance at a proper private school is virtually mandatory for the girl who hopes to make a real debut. . . . The students learn how to dance and dress and comport themselves."[14] The "debut," a girl's first formal introduction to society, takes place as a costly formal ball.

A well-known verse pokes fun at the snobbery of "proper" families, particularly those of New England:

And this is good old Boston,
The home of the bean and the cod,
Where the Lowells talk to the Cabots,
And the Cabots talk only to God.

There is also an amusing story about a young Bostonian who wanted a job in a Chicago bank. When the bank asked a Boston firm for a reference, back came a long glowing recommendation stating that the young man was descended from the Cabots and the Lowells and a host of other "first families." Whereupon the Chicago bank replied that the young man was not exactly what they were looking for. "We were not contemplating using Mr. —— for breeding purposes."[15]

"Social climbers" from the lower upper or the upper middle classes who want to enter exclusive cliques are sternly put into their place, especially if they violate highly valued rules of dress, speech, and general behavior. "Violation of the social code appears to be a vastly greater sin than violation of the Ten Commandments."[16]

At the other end of the scale both lower classes live on very little money; but in the upper lower class we find the steady worker who, mostly through physical labor, ekes out a modest living, whereas the lower lower class depends on occasional jobs and handouts. All the others tend to look down on this group at the bottom of the class system as outside the confines of respectable citizenry.

European immigrants of the nineteenth and early twentieth centuries usually possessed no money or useful skills when they first came to this country. But they did possess something very important—they had strong backs. Therefore the Irish, East European Jews, Italians, and others joined the lower lower classes. Eventually, however, many of them or their descendants were able to work themselves up the class ladder. On the other hand, racial minority groups have been held down on the class ladder by discrimination, and they are still found there in large numbers despite some improvements in recent years. It should not be surprising that this is particularly true of the South, where black people were prevented by many means from improving their position.

Class Structure in a Southern Town

	Percentage of the Population	
	White	Negro
Upper	4.1%	.3%
Upper Middle	20.7	1.6
Lower Middle	35.7	9.2
Upper Lower	29.1	25.9
Lower Lower	10.4	35.2

Source: Adapted from M. C. Hill and B. C. McCall, "Social Stratification in 'Georgia Town,'" *American Sociological Review*, 15 (December 1950), 726. Reprinted by permission.

UPPER—MIDDLE—LOWER

Now, for a final look at the ways of the different classes, we will return to the simplified three-point list that is most generally used in everyday language. On the whole, to be accepted into the upper class requires a high income, but there are exceptions. Promising or well-known artists, even with meager incomes, are sometimes welcome in wealthy circles, and the same is true of clergymen, especially Episcopalian priests.

In Europe a rich man will often hide the fact that he has very humble origins, whereas the American "self-made" man is rather proud of the fact. Biographies of powerful industrialists dwell at length on how such individuals began at a workbench or in a stockroom, and candidates for high political office find it advantageous to point out modest family origins. This attitude shows the impact of a younger and more democratically minded society.

Religion and sex too are related to the class system. We find that some people choose their churches along class lines, although most follow the religion of their parents. A Catholic parish takes in a complete geographic area, and so if you live within its boundaries you automatically belong to the parish. But even in this case, parishes in poorer sections have predominantly poor parishioners, and those in the suburbs serve wealthier people.

Protestants have the choice of many denominations. The upper and middle classes seem to prefer Episcopal, Congregational, and Presbyterian churches. It is noteworthy that three-fourths of the weddings involving prominent New York families take place in Episcopal churches, according to the announcements in *The New York Times*.[17] The Methodist, Baptist, and Disciple of Christ congregations attract mainly middle-class worshipers, while the lower classes frequently find their spiritual homes in the numerous Pentecostal and Holiness sects.[18]

These are overall observations, and we could cite many exceptions. Some sects have a tendency to move upward on the social scale as their members become more successful. Many Baptist churches, for example, were once comprised mainly of small farmers but have since attracted urban worshipers of substantial means.

One would think that sexual practices would be the same no matter what the class. Yet, on the whole, the lower classes approach sex more straightforwardly and matter-of-factly than the upper classes, who show more restraint and also more frustration.

Lower-class young people marry earlier. In their sexual relations they are less likely to use contraceptives. Youths from the middle and upper classes, especially when they attend college, delay marriage. They are more reluctant to engage in premarital sexual intercourse and therefore practice petting as a substitute to a much greater extent than young working-class people. On the other hand, upper- and middle-class young people *talk* more and more openly about sex, and in their serious discussions they demand greater sexual permissiveness than the older generation is willing to grant.

The middle class seems to furnish the model of what is usually called the "typical American." It keeps the churches, service clubs, and most other organizations operating, for middle-class Americans are avid "joiners," ambitious for themselves and, even more so, for their children. Education is important to them. Their sons and daughters are taught to lead interesting lives, and parents urge their children to climb a notch higher than they themselves have been able to do.

Middle-class parents spend much time with their children and, on the whole, devote much attention to training their children in character and cleanliness. Mothers devote a great deal of energy getting their children to and from ballet and piano lessons, scout meetings, and Little League games. Fathers exert themselves trying to be "pals" to their sons.

When asked about their occupations, middle-class people will usually name the type of work they do. They will say, for example, "I'm a certified public accountant" or "I'm the school superintendent"; the blue-collar worker, on the other hand, is more likely to answer, "I work for Acme Pulp and Paper," without indicating what his particular job is, since it is likely to be less creative and confer less status than some middle-class positions.

The lower-class worker often feels uncomfortable with persons of higher status. Therefore he does not join many organizations, except trade unions and certain lodges. Much of his social life consists of visiting back and forth with "the folks." His taste in entertainment runs to Western movies and to Western music that is often produced by a jukebox and enjoyed in his favorite tavern. Not many books and magazines are found in the home, but the television set is usually on. While he may not be too interested in national and international politics, he is often well acquainted with the standing of all big-league baseball players. On the whole, the lower-class working man has a conservative outlook. If he is white, he often shows strong racial prejudice. While he tends to complain about the rich and the bosses, he is against radical and violent change and not at all inclined to support a revolution such as Marx predicted.

Whatever else may have been said about class differences, let's not forget that the class structure, especially in our own society, is something vague and fluid. Rather than thinking of strict dividing lines between classes, we should visualize our class structure as a continuous stream that expands at certain points into large lakes. Many occupations can be named that would be difficult to place in a particular class. Where do we put, for example, professional athletes, writers, independent cab drivers, and teachers?

The American class picture shows contradictions. We find a hardening of the class lines and, at the same time, growing mobility from class to class. In our cities and suburbs new housing developments are built to be sold to specific income groups, a practice that tends to keep the members of one class together. The poorer person decides that the training he needs to advance himself is out of his reach on account of the cost. Thus he resigns himself to his fate and to his class.

But we also see many examples of children of manual workers moving up into white-collar ranks and farmers' sons going into the cities for work. An estimated one-third of the younger generation forgoes their fathers' assembly-line jobs in favor of clerical, managerial, or professional positions.[19]

As class lines become blurred, old status symbols are taken over by newcomers. The prestige groups have to scramble for different symbols that will help distinguish the "ins" from the "outs." Some millionaires, for instance, begin to buy small deserted islands in the Caribbean. Professional people go to India where some holy men initiate them into mysticism, while working people carry swords and call themselves knights in the rituals of their fraternal organizations.

To the casual observer people seem to be becoming more and more alike. At a political rally or a PTA meeting one would have difficulty distinguishing between those whose incomes are $5,000 a year and those who draw ten times as much. Even different class homes contain many of the same items of furniture and equipment, differing only in quality and price.

Main Ideas

1. People rate each other according to the values of their society. This rating determines their status.
2. In a hierarchy people are ranked in a rigid pattern, and their ranks are indicated by certain symbols.
3. Ascribed status is determined by birth, whereas achieved status comes with personal success.
4. A caste system is an extremely rigid system of social stratification.
5. Up to the early nineteenth century the division of society into classes was held to be inevitable.
6. Marx saw history as an eternal class struggle. He predicted the

coming of the proletarian revolution followed by the establishment of a classless society.

7. Whereas Marx believed that social classes were only determined by their economic standing, modern scholars feel that several other factors also determine the class to which a person belongs.

8. Some social scientists see American society as being divided into six classes, but we commonly speak only of three: the upper, middle, and lower classes.

9. The middle class sets the pattern for life in American society.

10. In some ways the class lines in American society are hardening, while other factors indicate growing mobility from class to class.

Important Terms

Achieved status
Ascribed status
Bourgeoisie
Caste
Class
Classless society
Clique
Debut
Elite
Endogamy
Fluid ascription
Estate
Genealogy

Hierarchy
Mobility
Potlatch
Prestige
Proletariat
Rating
Reincarnation
Snob
Status
Status symbol
Stratification
Substrata

Conclusion

It was once believed that status derived mainly from *objective* features, such as birth, wealth, and occupation. Now, especially in regard to class standing, the social scientist gives more consideration to the *subjective* side; he inquires about how people rank themselves and others. The American class structure once formed a broad-based pyramid, the great majority forming the bottom layer, a small middle class above it, and an even smaller upper class on top. Now the structure resembles a diamond, with the middle class occupying the largest area and the upper and lower classes at either end.

Notes

1. Ruth Benedict, *Patterns of Culture* (New York: Penguin Books, 1946), pp. 90 ff.
2. Melvin M. Tumin, *Social Stratification* (Englewood Cliffs, N.J.: Prentice-Hall, 1967), p. 37.
3. August B. Hollingshead, *Elmtown's Youth* (New York: Wiley, 1961), p. 242.

4. Peter I. Rose (ed.), *The Study of Society* (New York: Random House, 1967), p. 326.
5. Plato, *The Republic* (New York: Modern Library, 1941).
6. Adam Smith, *Enquiry into the Nature and Cause of the Wealth of Nations* (New York: Barnes & Noble, 1950).
7. Karl Marx and Friedrich Engels, "The Communist Manifesto," in Arthur P. Mendel (ed.), *Essential Works of Marxism* (New York: Bantam Books, 1961), pp. 13 ff.
8. Thorstein Veblen, *The Theory of the Leisure Class* (New York: Crowell, 1913).
9. Max Weber, *Essays in Sociology* (New York: Oxford University Press, 1946).
10. Hollingshead, *op. cit.*, p. 83.
11. E. Adamson Hoebel, *Anthropology: The Study of Man*, 3rd ed. (New York: McGraw-Hill, 1958), p. 402.
12. Hollingshead, *op. cit.*, pp. 306–307.
13. W. Lloyd Warner and Paul S. Lunt, *Yankee City Series*, 4 vols. (New Haven, Conn.: Yale University Press, 1941–1947).
14. Vance Packard, *The Status Seekers* (New York: McKay, 1959), p. 236.
15. Joseph B. Gittler, *Social Dynamics* (New York: McGraw-Hill, 1952), p. 151.
16. Hollingshead, *op. cit.*, p. 89.
17. Packard, *op. cit.*, p. 196.
18. Liston Pope, "Religion and the Class Structure," in R. Bendix and S. M. Lipset (eds.), *Class, Status and Power* (Glencoe, Ill.: Free Press, 1953), pp. 316 ff.
19. S. M. Lipset and N. R. Ramsøy, "Class and Opportunity in Europe and the U.S.," in Rose, *op. cit.*, pp. 339 ff.

Suggestions for Further Reading

Lawrence, D. H. *Sons and Lovers.* New York: Viking Press, 1968. Novel about working-class life, set in a British mining district.

Lewis, Sinclair. *Babbitt.* New York: Harcourt, Brace & World, 1949. Novel depicting middle-class life in a small town.

Lynes, Russell. "Highbrow, Lowbrow, Middlebrow," *Harper's Magazine* (February 1949). Tastes and activities of various social strata.

Major, G. "New Image of the Socialite: Negro Woman Socialite," *Ebony*, 21 (August 1966), 63 ff.

Marquand, John P. *Point of No Return.* Boston: Little, Brown, 1950. Novel presenting social stratification in a New England town.

Mayo, Katherine. *Mother India.* New York: Harcourt, Brace & World, 1928. Insight into the Indian caste system.

Michener, James. *Hawaii.* New York: Bantam Books, 1961 (paperback). Novel on the history of Hawaii; gives a good picture of stratification in Hawaiian society.

Moraes, Frank. *India Today.* New York: Macmillan, 1960.

Morley, Christopher. *Kitty Foyle*. Philadelphia: Lippincott, 1939. Novel about Philadelphia's upper and middle classes.

Tyrmand, L. "Upper Class in Eastern Europe," *The Reporter*, 38, January 11, 1968, 14–19.

How good are our schools?
What are schools supposed to accomplish?
Is school the only place where education occurs?

12 TRAINING FOR WORK AND LIFE
education

Dan decided to drop out of high school. "I wasn't getting anywhere in school," he explained to his friends, also dropouts. "The teachers were bugging me for every little thing. Classes bored me stiff—just a lot of words without meaning."

There are many dropouts like Dan. Lately, every year 100,000 more young people disappear from classrooms than in the previous year. Presently the number who leave high school without finishing has reached a yearly high of about 700,000.[1] Many dropouts have been "turned off" by the way schools are operating.

Clearly American education is not completely fulfilling the task it is meant to fulfill. What is this task, and what is the purpose of education in general?

WHAT IS EDUCATION?

No society could exist for long unless it provided some means of passing on what it considers important from generation to generation. As a new discovery becomes part of our culture, it must be transmitted from the old to the young. Culture is a vast storehouse that constantly receives more items to store, not only facts like the temperature on the moon but also techniques for working, eating, handling finances, and ideas about what is right and wrong, proper and improper.

We have many means of transmitting information about all these items. We record and store information in books, on tape and slides, and in computers, so that it can be retrieved when we need it. Thus no person needs to retain more than a small portion of the available knowledge.

But books and slides and computers are worthless unless a sufficient number of people learn how to use them. The same is true for tools. People must also learn about manners, tastes, and behavior in general. All this is accomplished through the process of education, which involves far more than classes, teachers, credits and diplomas, though we commonly think of it in these terms. Education, aiming at the socialization of the child, existed long before there were schools. The school, whether a one-room cabin or a university campus spread over a hundred acres, encompasses only one phase of education, namely *formal education*. But every human being, even though he may never have gone to school, has been exposed to a much older phase, *informal education*.

INFORMAL EDUCATION

Prehistoric man had no textbooks. And today, where nonliterate cultures still survive, youngsters receive their training not in classrooms but through participation in adult activities. By watching and imitating their mothers young Samoan girls learn to weave, light fires for cooking, climb a coconut tree, and break open a coconut with one well-directed blow of a knife. By the same method a girl also learns to sing old songs, honor the chief, and take responsibility for watching smaller children.

Young American Plains Indians learned the art of survival in the wilderness from their elders. The priests imparted to the braves the religious and moral ideas of the tribe. By the time a boy reached puberty he knew everything a full-fledged member of his society needed to know. Then came his initiation as a warrior, a kind of final examination, measured not in words but in actions. His flesh was pierced, and sticks were thrust into the wounds. He had to dance around a fire without betraying any pain. Thus he demonstrated the desirable qualities of an adult, and he could now be depended upon to do a man's job in peace or war.

Informal education is by no means restricted to nonliterate societies. Every child learns informally from the day he is born just by living with other people, especially the members of his family. We have seen (Chapters 6 and 7) that the first years of our lives leave a strong imprint on our character, on the way we react to the world around us. As a child grows, his informal education continues through associating with playmates, friends, and co-workers, through watching, traveling, participating.

Modern means of mass communication have vastly increased the range of informal education. We learn something every time we read a newspaper, magazine, or book. Our minds are constantly attuned to the sights and sounds of radio, television, records, and motion pictures. We are educated, often without having the slightest intention of being so. Many companies that operate radio and television stations or publish magazines and books carry on the business of mass communication mainly to make a profit for the owners and stockholders. But since what they communicate has such great impact on the minds of everyone, especially the young, the public takes considerable interest in the content and quality of mass communication. Parents and educators are concerned about the strong doses of violence and sex presented by the media. However, psychiatrists are divided in their assessment as to how harmful these influences really are or whether they are harmful at all. In a democratic society this concern over what is made available to young minds poses a delicate problem: we want to see our children protected from what some authorities judge harmful, yet we also find censorship repugnant, whether exercised by government or by the media themselves, since it is contrary to our concept of free expression.

Fear of public criticism can have ridiculous effects. A few years ago a radio and television station banned a song called "I Saw Mommie Kissing Santa Claus." An official defended the ban on this song "in which children describe parents' misconduct; it implies an insult to Santa Claus and to the sacred occasion of Christmas."[2]

The motion picture industry has, in the past, made several attempts at self-censorship, with limited success. In 1968 the censorship idea was abandoned in favor of a rating system, and films now receive classification letters. Those that might possibly have an injurious effect on the young are rated "X" (nobody under sixteen years of age admitted), "R" (no admission under sixteen years of age unless accompanied by an adult), or "M" (for mature audiences). These film ratings are made public as a guide for parents.

As the disputes over movies and television programs indicate, not all members of our society welcome informal education. Parents are often shocked when they hear their children using "bad language." But in certain groups four-letter words and other "objectionable" terms are bandied about quite freely. As a person comes into close association with a group, he learns, among other things, its language. In the same way, through informal education a young boy learns to think and act like the members of the violent gang that he has joined. A newcomer to a neighborhood learns how the people living there dress, talk, and behave toward each other. All these examples are part of the on-going process by which an individual becomes a conforming member of his group.

FORMAL EDUCATION

Formal education is carried out by specialized personnel, called teachers, usually within the confines of a specialized institution, called a school. Historically, formal education was originally only available to a small minority and was not related to training for work.

The philosopher Socrates, who lived over 2,000 years ago in ancient Greece, was one of the greatest teachers of all time. He gave no grades and had no formal classroom. While strolling about the marketplace of Athens, he engaged the idle sons of the well-to-do in conversation. Through skillful questioning he led them to think about the purpose of life and about the value of goodness.

Since the time of Socrates education has been concerned with such broad questions. Good teachers have always tried to inspire their students to ponder the goals of man and the world in general. They attempt to have students honor outstanding personalities and noble deeds; they instill in them a love of beauty and dignity.

For some 1,500 years formal education in the Christian world was restricted to young men who planned to enter the priesthood. The universities taught mainly the *humanities* (classic languages, history, literature, and philosophy), and they taught all subjects in the Latin language. Those who reached the university level of education looked with contempt upon the overwhelming majority, who were unschooled and had never learned to read and write.

Similarly, before the nineteenth century formal education in the Far East was mostly restricted to the study of philosophy and literature, represented mainly by the writings of Confucius and his disciples. After successfully passing examinations in those fields, students were then eligible for positions in the governmental bureaucracy.

Muslim children of the Middle East and North Africa received their education in a mosque, a house of worship. Here they learned to read and memorize passages of the Koran, the holy scriptures of Islam. Some of the mosque schools in the larger cities developed into universities in which Muslim law and even, in a few instances, botany, chemistry, and medicine were taught.

In the past in Europe most people were peasants who needed no special training for the back-breaking job of tilling the soil. Nor did the future craftsman attend any formal school. A boy who was fortunate enough to live inside a walled town tried to apprentice himself to a shoemaker, weaver, or glass blower, for example. For several years then he lived in the master's household learning the trade. If fate put him in the care of a cruel master, he was whipped when he was clumsy.

Schools in the modern sense were slow in developing. The concept of free *compulsory* education for every child, rich or poor, is scarcely 200 years old. It was eighteenth-century King Frederick the Great of Prussia who first opened elementary schools for all his subjects. These schools were crude and primitive by our present standards. Slowly other European countries adopted the idea of free schooling for everybody. In colonial America where schools were private or run by churches, teachers were satisfied when their pupils could read the Bible, though the pupils often did not understand what they were reading. In 1852 Massachusetts enacted the first compulsory school attendance law. Since then the idea that every child in the United States should attend school has been generally accepted.

Even today, millions of children in Asia, Africa, and Latin America never see the inside of a schoolhouse. Others come only for a very short time. The teachers in these countries are often without sufficient education or training themselves.

AMERICAN SCHOOLS

Modern American education is big, complicated, and costly. One-fourth of the population is comprised of either teachers or students, which makes education the largest "industry" in the country. It takes more than $5 billion annually to pay for the cost of education, a gigantic sum indeed but still less than the sums we spend for either alcohol or tobacco.

Whatever yardstick we use, we can measure continuous rapid growth of the educational enterprise in every direction. The school year has lengthened by one-third in the last fifty years. During the same period the number of teen-agers in high school grew from 60 percent to 90 percent. Early in the century perhaps 4 percent of Americans between the ages of eighteen and twenty-four were in colleges; now the figure is roughly 45 percent.[3] In 1967 nearly 7 million students attended institutions of higher learning.[4]

Structure of American Schools

Type of School	Age of Students
Nursery school	3–4
Kindergarten	4–5
Elementary school	6–11 or 6–13
Junior high school	12–14
High school	14–17 or 15–17

Type of School	Years Needed for Completion
Junior college	2
Four-year college	4
Graduate school	1–5

Once children went to school for only a few short years of their lives. Now a person may enter nursery school at the age of three or four and continue to go to school for more than twenty years. Students who prepare themselves for the professions often don't receive their final credentials till they are in their late twenties. Many engage, beyond this point, in postgraduate studies.

ADULT EDUCATION

School is no longer a place for children and young people only.

It is 7 P.M., a time when the school building used to be quiet and empty. But this is not the case anymore, for the classrooms are brightly lit, and adults swarm through the doors to beat the bell that signals the beginning of evening school.

Every year 26 million adults return to school, and the number is growing constantly. Who are these new students? Their ages range from seventeen to seventy-five years. Quite a few are the dropouts of yesterday. Among the students are: a mother of five children, whose husband is babysitting while she prepares herself to be a kindergarten teacher; a welder who comes to relearn his trade, which has undergone massive technological changes; a salesman who is taking public speaking courses; a clerk who must learn how to operate new office machines; and a factory foreman who has been advised to study some psychology. But not all are interested in better jobs. A physician, for instance, is taking a course in Greek literature, and a nurse is learning the elements of ceramics.

Los Angeles schools offer 3,000 adult classes annually, covering 500 subjects, among them parent education, seamanship for boat owners, retirement planning for the elderly, and foreign languages such as Arabic, Chinese, Hebrew, and Swahili. Besides all these offerings many industrial and business concerns train their own employees. On-the-job course offerings have become so elaborate that we can speak of school systems inside factories. Seventeen billion dollars are spent annually for this purpose.

HOW SCHOOLS ARE RUN

Most children are enrolled in the public school system, but a substantial number attend private schools. Some private schools cater to the wealthy and emphasize the manners and the pastimes of the very rich. Many more promote the ideals of certain religions. Among these are the Seventh Day Adventists, Lutherans, and Episcopalians, who operate their own schools. But the largest private school system in the United States is under the direction of the Catholic church, which enrolls over 10 million pupils every year. Despite the size of the system Catholic schools face great difficulties, and some have already been forced to close their doors. Finances are severely strained, and religious teaching orders that have traditionally made up the faculties are in short supply of new members.

The question of whether parochial schools, like public schools, should receive financial aid from the federal government has been heatedly debated in the past. "Send your children to public schools like the rest of us," argued the opponents of financial aid, "and you won't need those funds." "We are saving the public school systems large amounts of money by sending the children to parochial schools," countered the defenders of the parochial school system. "We are entitled to some aid from our government. We pay taxes like everybody else." Lately the discussion over parochial schools has quieted down considerably.

Catholic parents once feared that the public schools were hostile to their faith. This fear has largely disappeared, and we can foresee close cooperation between public and parochial schools in the future. In many communities they already share laboratories and other facilities. Athletic contests, festivals, and club activities also bring the student bodies together.

There are many ways to operate a public school system. France, long one of the most enlightened and culturally advanced countries, is dedicated to *centralization*. From his office in Paris a minister of education runs the system. He and his staff determine what should be taught and how, who should be a teacher and what he should be paid. It has been said that if one walks into any French classroom at a given time, the chances are good that the children will be studying the same material as in any other French classroom. At the end of the school year the graduating pupils all over the country take the same examinations. A few years ago some copies of such a test were stolen just before examination day. The whole country was shaken by the scandal.

Guarding the secrecy of examination questions is not the only problem facing a centralized educational system, especially when it extends from grade school to the university level, as it does in France. The bureaucracy entrenched in the ministry of education is slow to respond to changing conditions and often sadly unaware of the needs young people have in the different sections of the country. Such a system tends to be rigid, outmoded, and unwilling to experiment with new ideas and techniques.

Several countries follow France's example, but the United States is not one of them. Here most schools are under *local control*, even though we find instances of state-wide tests (New York State Board of Regents) and also of nation-wide examinations (National Merit Scholarship) given to high-school students. About 60,000 elected school boards make decisions that concern the running of our grade and high schools (see Figure 15).

Both systems have their advantages and their drawbacks. Under local control the citizen in the community may have some voice in the matter of how his own children are being educated. He is likely to be much more interested in problems of the school than he would be if some remote governmental agency made all the decisions.

On the other hand, students who move to a new community location

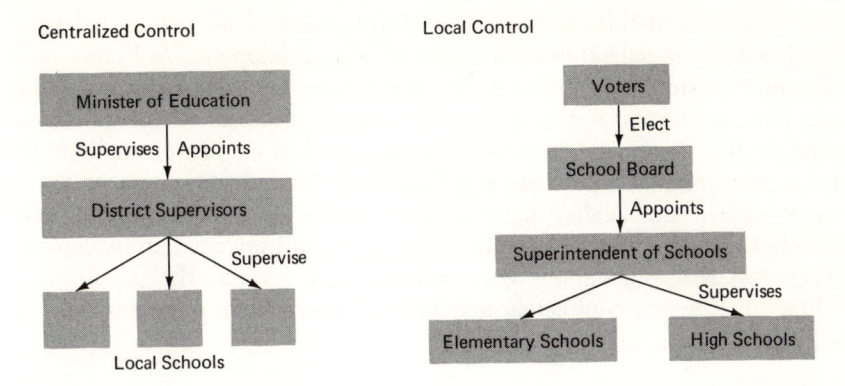

Figure 15
How School Systems Are Controlled

may find it difficult to fit into a different curriculum and study under differently prepared teachers. School systems across the country vary greatly in quality, depending on the character of the local community.

Most persons who run for school board positions are sincerely interested in education. But they aren't always in agreement as to what good education is all about. Some board members are more concerned with a winning basketball team than with competent teachers. One board member may have a personal ax to grind, while another feels that what was good enough for him when he went to school is good enough for students today, or he may feel that education today should not cost more than it did a generation ago.

School boards strongly reflect the thinking of the middle class, while the voice of the lower classes is heard only very faintly. According to the United States Office of Education business owners and officials comprise 34.5 percent, professional persons 27.4 percent, and farmers 12.4 percent of the school board membership throughout the country. But only 6.7 percent of the board members come from the ranks of skilled workers; 1.8 percent are semi- or unskilled workers, and 0.9 percent are service workers.[5]

Who pays the bills? Education has become so costly that the local community by itself has long been unable to cover the expenses. State and federal government must support it too, and this brings on heated political controversies. The question of federal aid to education has caused especially lively debates. One side feels that only the federal government can provide an equal chance for the children of the poor. For example, New York state spends almost three times more on education per child as the poorer state of Mississippi. Federal funds should make up for such glaring discrepancies, the advocates of federal aid to education say. Many of them also maintain that our national leadership should force the Southern states to end racial segregation by withholding money from the schools if they don't integrate.

The foes of this kind of aid to education are afraid that with federal funds will come federal control of the schools, as happened in France, and this they definitely don't want. Bureaucrats in the nation's capital, they maintain, are too far removed to understand the needs of schools in a local area. So the arguments are presented, and in a democracy we usually settle for a compromise. But as the price tag for public education continues to show higher and higher figures, educators become increasingly disenchanted with the present uncertain and haphazard financial arrangements. They feel that our various governmental agencies and the people as a whole must take a completely new look at the problem of paying for our schools.

Some Roles of State and Federal Government in Education

State Government
- Outlines courses of study
- Certifies teachers
- Approves building plans
- Distributes state and federal funds

Federal Government
- Finances vocational education
- Finances school lunch program
- Finances training of veterans
- Finances training in sciences and foreign languages
- Runs military academies and schools for Indians
- Job Corps
- Head Start

CURRICULUM

What are the schools teaching? The "three Rs" (Reading, 'riting, 'rithmetic) were and still are basic. They provide the instruments of communication by which knowledge can be transmitted.

When Socrates taught, he did not worry about how his Athenian followers would earn their bread, for they were a privileged group who had slaves to do all their work for them. As long as schools received students only from the ranks of the privileged few, the *curriculum* was comprised of subjects that were not necessary in making a living but that were highly valued as the mark of a distinguished and refined gentleman. Even today the humanities are still part of the curriculum in many schools and colleges.

Today schools also offer courses in physics, chemistry, geology, and biology. But it was only in the past two centuries that the door was opened to the study of these natural sciences. Previously, very little was known about them, and it was also considered unworthy of a gentleman to dirty his hands in a laboratory. This was too reminiscent of work, something reserved for the lower classes.

The study of the social sciences came into the classroom even later. America leads in this respect, while European schools still offer little in sociology, anthropology, economics, and similar subjects. The European high-school student learns mostly about the theories developed by early social scientists, whereas a detailed study of modern research methods and findings takes place mainly at the graduate schools of the European universities.

Today, when people speak of education, most of them think primarily of training for an occupation. You go to school to become a secretary, draftsman, teacher, or physician. This is *vocational education* in the widest sense. In a more limited way we refer to vocational education as training in the crafts and in technical skills.

The medieval universities can be considered the first vocational schools. They produced clergymen and, later, doctors and lawyers. Since then a host of professional and semiprofessional occupations have arisen, all requiring special schools or college departments. Modern universities train veterinarians, pharmacists, engineers, journalists, hotel managers, and many others. If you are planning for a military career or want to be a model, a commercial artist, or a mortician, you can usually find schools exclusively devoted to each purpose.

Even the craftsman of today needs more than the old-style on-the-job training of the apprentice. He handles costly and often dangerous machinery and must keep acquainted with rapidly improving techniques. Only in the classroom can he learn to meet the demands of his field.

The same is true for the farmer and rancher. The struggling farmers and peasants of old have been transformed into modern agricultural technicians who must have a knowledge of chemistry, mechanics, and economics if they want to be successful.

Today vocational and "general" education have become thoroughly intertwined. Beginning in grade school, children are taught good work habits and the proper use of simple tools. They are cautioned to observe safety rules in their own interest and that of their classmates.

Students in high schools and especially in colleges readily recognize the value of courses that are directly related to their future occupations, such as drafting for the draftsman and typing for the secretary. But many students show a tendency to resist learning about matters that seem further removed. Does a future physician need to study sociology? How does an engineer benefit from studying economics or political science? Will a businessman profit from knowing something about geology? These questions lead us to another question: What are the ultimate goals of education?

GOALS OF FORMAL EDUCATION

It is not easy to agree about what the task of the schools should be. Few objections will be raised to the assertion that the schools of today try to introduce the child to the significant contributions of civilization, art, literature, and history, and to the secrets of life and the inanimate world around us.

Other goals of education are open to more dispute. Besides knowledge should the school also impart moral values, and if so, what kind? It is felt that in a democratic society the student must be encouraged to think for himself, to be a contributing but critical member of his community. Yet there are those who would rather *indoctrinate* him in a single point of view—be it religious, political, or moral—that he is to accept uncritically.

Should it be the goal of the schools to combat prejudice, for example? We know that children are not born prejudiced against other races, religions, or classes. Prejudice is learned through the process of informal education. If a society wants to reduce prejudice, its schools must counteract the prejudicial influences of the home and neighborhood. A racially integrated school not only provides better education for minority children, it also offers the dominant group a very valuable learning experience in getting along with others. Where children from different social backgrounds are taught together, they learn to respect each other as equal companions. Often they discriminate far less than their parents do, something that the young may even teach their elders.

Combating prejudice will only be accomplished, of course, if school and community leaders are determined to make integration work. They must make minority-group children feel welcome in newly integrated schools. Special and competent training must be given those who lag behind in reading and other skills.

Although part of the function of the school is to perpetuate the culture in which it exists, educators cannot help trying to change this culture according to their own ideals. Like other citizens, they are critical of the ways we work, play, and act toward each other. They feel morally bound to impart their critical attitudes to their students.

Education must change with changing times or become stale and outmoded. But to prepare the young for a tomorrow that is uncertain is quite a task. How quickly should schools replace the old with the new? If changes come too quickly, much of what is valuable might be discarded. Some years ago, for instance, high schools cut back severely on the teaching of mathematics and foreign languages. We came to regret this change when we found communist countries were turning out much better-trained youngsters. Now foreign languages and large doses of mathematics are back in high-school curricula.

On the other hand, schools can be too reluctant to change. We still have three months of summer vacation, a custom dating back to the time when most children had to help with harvesting the farm. Objections are raised against introducing sex education though much evidence exists that youngsters need guidance and information in this area.

Besides being slow to adapt themselves to the needs of today, schools are even slower in adapting for tomorrow. High schools often expend their greatest efforts in behalf of college-bound students but often neglect the needs of the other students, some of whom may not even stay to receive a diploma. This is especially true of schools located in the ghetto sections of our cities.

In many instances vocational courses are offered for the students who are not college bound, but in this age of rapid technological progress such instruction is frequently out of date. Automation may even cause a young person to prepare himself for a job that will no longer exist by the time he is ready for employment. To answer these needs we are learning new ways of improving the work of our schools. Well-trained specialists are able to help slow learners and poor readers so that such students will not regard themselves as failures. Counselors, if they are available in sufficient numbers, assist the child with his personal problems. Schoolwork becomes more interesting and meaningful when teachers have access to modern teaching machines. Our curricula and teaching methods need constant updating, which puts a great strain on available money and on the imagination and flexibility of educators.

We hear demands that the schools should instill more patriotism, more compassion, more international understanding in their charges. Others are against such emphases. Opinions are divided as to whether schools offer enough or too many social and athletic activities, whether stricter discipline or more informality is needed.

A persistent demand is often raised for a more intellectual climate in our high schools. James S. Coleman describes the adolescent subculture as one that requires lots of energy-consuming group activities. This abundant energy is now expended in the gymnasium, on the football field, at dances, and at various other "activities" encouraged by faculties and school administrations. Learning sometimes seems to conflict with all these nonacademic activities. But high-school activities could be organized in such a way "that their adolescent subcultures would encourage rather than discourage the channeling of energies into the direction of learning."[6] Perhaps the "College Bowl" program on television is a step in this direction. Young people enjoy competing in teams and bringing glory to their schools. Now they can do this not only by engaging in sports but also in contests of quick recall of knowledge.

Previous chapters have shown how other institutions, mainly the family and the church, are giving up some of their traditional functions. It is the school that is being asked to assume these functions whether it wants to or not. The school must see that the growing youngster keeps his body healthy and his ideals high. It is expected to provide entertainment for Friday nights so that romance may blossom and young people can be "kept off the street." The new roles that schools play are certainly a dramatic change from old days when the role of the school in teaching the three Rs was considered sufficient.

THE TEACHER

Any school is only as good as its teachers. Once, teaching was a monopoly of the priesthood. The priest transmitted traditional values that were considered sacred. He was not necessarily interested in imparting anything new. Much of what he knew, he kept a deep secret; it was not meant for unworthy ears. In the ancient Near East, the priesthood knew a lot about the orbits of the stars and the seasonal life cycle that occurs in nature. But it was only to apprentice priests that this knowledge was imparted. The people in general stood in awe before those wise men who could seemingly miraculously predict the annual flooding of the rivers and make highly accurate calendars and sun dials. The student's critical examination of what was taught to him was definitely discouraged; in fact, this could be extremely dangerous for the examiner.

Things have changed considerably. Teachers are now vitally interested in passing on what they know in the most effective way possible. Much of their training deals with this effectiveness. Yet, except for a few high-ranking university professors, the teacher's position on the social ladder has remained rather low.

In pioneer days not many able-bodied men could be spared for the classroom. To this day the typical American teacher, especially in the lower grades, is female, though the boys especially need male teachers with whom they can identify. The teaching profession's lack of status and low pay often causes the brightest and most promising young people to turn to other careers. Those who elect to teach must begin teaching almost before they have had a chance to learn much more than their pupils. Though the training of educators has gradually improved, because of a severe teacher shortage, not all parts of the country have the requirement of a four- or five-year college education for teachers.

Low status and corresponding low pay are not the only reasons why many young people avoid the teaching profession and why others who have already entered it drop out to seek positions in business or industry.

Teachers resent restrictions on their personal lives. Until quite recently, especially in rural areas, they were often forbidden by their school boards to smoke, attend dances, have dates, or even to be out after a certain hour. Women were dismissed when they married. Such rules are now less frequent.

In general, the last few years have witnessed the beginning of a change in the teacher's position. Like other occupational groups, educators now form increasingly stronger organizations that demand not only higher salaries but also a louder voice in determining how the schools are to be run.

Teaching is becoming an increasingly difficult task. The old-time schoolmaster drilled his pupils by having them do much memorizing, and he kept discipline with the help of a stout paddle. Now the child is regarded more as a human being in his own right. Psychologists study his needs and the methods by which he learns best. The teacher is expected to apply these psychological findings in the classroom. He is to respect the child's feelings and aspirations, which requires not only skill but deep insight and an ability to establish rapport.

When a child enters school, the teacher replaces his parents, to a large extent, as a model and as an authority. The teacher sets standards of personal behavior. Therefore what he does or fails to do is carefully observed by the pupil. Should a teacher be seen drinking after he has discussed the dangers of alcohol? Disappointment in unsatisfactory teachers can be a shattering experience for a child.

The moral commitment that goes with his job puts the teacher under far greater stress than most other people encounter. The stress is heightened by his lack of freedom. Unlike doctors and lawyers, teachers have many authorities over them: principals, superintendents, and lay boards,

Teachers are increasingly displaying their new activism.
UPI

plus parents and self-appointed guardians of particular beliefs. They all look over his shoulder and often criticize without clearly understanding what his problems are.

According to their outlook and way of life most teachers belong to the middle class. Many have stepped up from the working backgrounds of their parents in joining the profession, which makes them especially conscious of middle-class values. Proper behavior and language oftentimes becomes very important to them, and the stress on propriety clashes at times with adolescent fads and fashions. This may lead to directives on how long a boy's hair or how short a girl's skirt ought to be, rules that are often resented by students.

In schools that draw heavily from low-income and minority groups the middle-class values of a teacher may hinder his ability to communicate. If a teacher expresses shock rather than sympathy, he remains an outsider, and he becomes disgusted with his work. "They smell terrible," said a teacher in a ghetto school to a visitor in front of his class. "They always smell that way, just like little animals." (The classic answer to this statement is: "Johnny ain't no rose; learn him, don't smell him!")

Often teachers consider assignment to an inner city or ghetto school as a kind of punishment. This attitude, of course, does not enhance their performance. It has been suggested that the best and most effective teachers be sent into the ghettos and that they receive encouragement by certain privileges, including higher pay.

SCHOOL AND THE MINORITY GROUPS

School leads the child to the starting line of the race. The winner's prize is the chance to play as successful an adult role as his ability allows. In theory everybody begins the race at the same starting line, but reality does not bear this out. A long-standing tradition of racial discrimination has prevented blacks, Puerto Ricans, Mexican-Americans, and Indians from being properly educated.

The situation is improving though not fast enough to satisfy the minorities, especially the black community. A 1969 survey of ninety-eight state universities and colleges showed that of 1,268,185 full-time undergraduate students 67,309 were black Americans; this is only a little over 5 percent. The black enrollment in graduate and professional schools was even more disheartening; it stood at 2.94 percent.[7] These numbers become even less impressive when we realize that many of the degrees were earned at colleges in the South with a predominantly black enrollment. Such institutions have, until very recently, been financially starved and have therefore often lacked in quality.

School segregation has been an established practice in the Southern states. Though outlawed by the United States Supreme Court in 1954, the situation remained largely unchanged for the next decade due to the

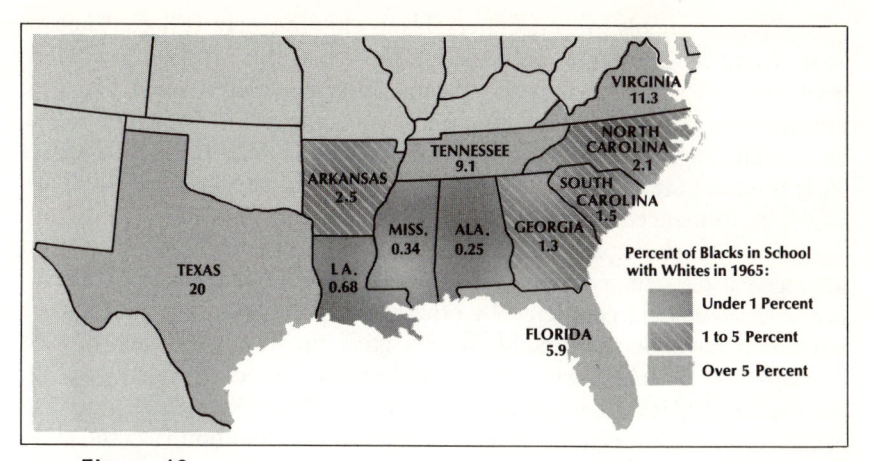

Figure 16
The Progress of School Desegregation in the South

Source: *The New York Times.* © 1966 by The New York Times Company. Reprinted by permission.

stubborn resistance of the Southern white Establishment (see Figure 16).

Outside the South education is officially integrated; in practice, however, schools in many Northern cities have either a predominantly white or black enrollment. This comes about because the members of each racial group tend to live only with other members of the same race in different parts of the city. Add to this the fact that some prejudiced school boards use artificial districting means to concentrate all white children in certain schools and minority children in others. Furthermore, white middle-class children who live in the inner city are often enrolled in private schools. All these facts contribute to the existence of elementary and high schools with an almost completely black school population. The parents of the black children who attend these schools complain about the continued humiliating effects of being practically segregated. They are also angry when they observe that their children are sent to overcrowded schools located in rundown, poorly equipped buildings. What they demand is an end to inferior education for the children of the ghetto.

Under the pressure of mounting black protest a number of remedies have been tried. In several communities children are *bussed* to schools located outside their immediate neighborhood. This should give pupils an opportunity to associate with youngsters of another race even though they may live farther away. In New York City the giant school system has been broken up into smaller neighborhood systems with their own school boards, administrators, and faculties. Though this measure does not alter the racial composition of the student body, it gives black parents some say in the way their children are being educated.

Where schools are integrated, black children may still continue to suffer from disadvantages, unless they are part of the middle class. Their textbooks describe a way of life that is often completely alien to them. Poverty at home often means absence of encouragement. Poor homes lack books and magazines. Poor parents are less apt to take their children on trips, to museums, or to the zoo, all of which has an effect on the children's school performance.

Some psychologists claim that black children generally score lower on intelligence tests than whites and are therefore inherently less intelligent. But such claims are countered by others who point out that the tests are slanted in favor of those children who grow up in a white middle-class environment. Teachers who are themselves prejudiced will gladly accept the idea that black students lack intelligence. "Poor teaching is protected in the American educational system through the assumption that the child doesn't have the ability."[8]

THE DROPOUT

Now let's return to Dan, the dropout whom we encountered earlier. After Dan left school, he set out to seek employment. At one personnel office he was asked to fill in an application blank. When the interviewer saw the eighth grade circled on the paper, he shook his head, "No, I am afraid we can't use you." It was the same story at a department store that needed an elevator operator and at an office that was short a messenger.

Obviously a boy can run an elevator or carry a message without having acquired a high school diploma. Requiring one is merely used as a screening device. When there is more than one suitable applicant for a job, the insistence on an official-looking piece of paper makes it easy to select among them, and the procedure has the appearance of being fair and impartial. "We evaluate people not on the basis of performance, but on the basis of credentials."[9]

The insistence on paper credentials is a hardship on working-class youths. The same is true of many of the tests given by personnel officers to job applicants. Such tests are usually composed by middle-class professionals, and they "discriminate against thousands of American workers."[10]

So Dan continues his search for employment, and he is having a rough time like many other dropouts, especially urban youths who are black or belong to other minority groups. Some seek help by joining the Job Corps, a federal project that was designed as part of the government's war on poverty. The Job Corps leads dropouts back into the classroom, but in a situation in which the young people live and learn together. The emphasis is on vocational training, and the teachers try, by their attitude, to convince the students that life still holds the promise of fulfillment. A seventeen-year-old boy, when asked why he had joined the Job Corps, answered, "Because it is my last chance."[11] Unfortunately the Job Corps has not made much headway, and it has been unable to help many of those who most need this kind of assistance. For reasons of political expediency its funds have been severely cut back. This experimental venture has not been given an opportunity to correct initial mistakes and work out the problems that are likely to arise in such new, untried projects.

The odds are that Dan will eventually find a job. In all likelihood it will be unskilled work of some kind, and he won't mind it very much, as long as he earns enough money to have a good time after hours. The dropout who needs work is not, in many cases, ambitious. His main interests lie outside the confines of his job.

Why did Dan drop out of high school in the first place? Apparently he saw little connection between school and his own life experience. What went on inside the school building had little relevance for him. The subjects taught and the activity going on were based on a middle-class value system alien to him. It is this value system that stresses staying in school and going on to college as a prime duty, and it is the teacher who presents these values to the student. The teacher who usually embraces middle-class values quite strongly has little understanding of the student who rejects them. "The lower the position the child's family occupies in the social structure the less his chances are of being helped by a teacher, and, equally important, of accepting the help if it is offered."[12]

Most students who drop out today would never have been in high school fifty years ago. This was not part of the ambitions implanted in them by their upbringing. The son of the working man or small farmer was expected to go out and seek work as soon as he was physically able to do so. The same was true of the daughter unless she was needed at home to help with the housework. Anyhow, it was felt that, as a future housewife and mother, a girl did not need much formal education.

The high dropout rate does not speak well of our educational system. For a sizable portion of our youth education fails to do what it is supposed to do. But for society as a whole the effects of dropping out are not all bad according to some observers: "Today's dropouts are, perhaps fortunately, pretty skeptical kids; if they all believed that the school could deliver them to a brighter economic future, we would soon have unemployed IBM operators and technicians hanging around the way India and Africa have lawyers."[13] So it is the specter of spreading automation that casts its shadow on the dropout problem as it does on many other aspects of our lives.

THE GENERATION GAP

It is often found that the dropout is not only at odds with school, but he is also disgusted with the whole adult society, of which education is a part. This is especially true of dropouts from middle- and upper middle-class backgrounds and especially for those who leave colleges and universities before completing their studies. Of this last group there are others who prefer not to leave but to express their disenchantment through protests and demonstrations, which have become common in recent years. On some campuses demonstrations have become violent; buildings have been stormed, office material burned, and the teaching process brought to a standstill.

Recently events on our college campuses have become first-rate news items. On television screens helmeted police can be seen charging into the protesters with clubs and tear-gas canisters. The mood of many adults, including governors and congressmen, is turned against such demonstrations, and school administrators are pressured to discipline any disturbers of the peace sternly. But some educators realize that many times the protests are justified, even though they are unhappy about the violent methods employed. At a number of universities reforms have begun. Student representatives are receiving a greater voice in the shaping of campus life. Black studies programs are being introduced, and attempts are being made to keep students, professors, and administrators in closer contact with each other.

Once universities were removed from the bustle of the outside world. In their "ivory towers" scholars read and wrote and lectured with little regard for the problems of the village or the city or the nation or even the world. All this has changed drastically, and today students and faculty alike have become involved with the many social issues facing us.

One root of the present difficulties lies in bigness. In 1930 our colleges and universities enrolled 1,101,000 students. By 1966 the figure had climbed to close to 6 million. The total population included 95,000 college graduates in the year 1900 but will include 3,515,000 college graduates in 1975.[14] This has brought on the expansion of campuses to huge "multiversities" where the individual feels he is nothing more than a number on a punch card. Deans, counselors, and professors are not accessible to students who need guidance.

The university is now very much involved in the efforts and also in the controversies of the world around it. Research is carried on for warfare, space travel, marketing, and industrial improvement. Professors act as consultants for government and private industry. This involvement is criticized by those who do not agree with official political and economic positions.

Young people are the most radical critics, and, to a large measure, the schools have helped to bring this about, since they operate in a strongly youth-centered society. The student attacks his school because it has serious faults, but also because it is the institution of society that affects him most directly every day. But school only symbolizes the whole generation of adults, which, he feels, has failed him. He sees that generation unable to adequately handle the most pressing problems of international stability, poverty, racial conflict, pollution, and the deterioration of our cities, and he asks, "How can that generation present itself as a model for us to imitate?"

Students know that they are needed, as soon as they graduate, to keep the machinery of government, business, and industry turning, but they question the value of the whole setup; they wonder whether it is worth the effort. In their humanities courses they study great moral ideas but watch them being discarded in practical life. This hypocrisy, the gap between what we profess to believe and what we actually do, is the main target of student disenchantment. One student protester declared, "It is not as despisers of democracy that we demonstrate. We protest because our faith in the democratic dream which leaders of [an older] generation bequeathed to us has been betrayed."[15]

Unrest among university students is an old story in many parts of the world. Oftentimes they have stood in the forefront of violent opposition to the political order. In the spring of 1968 students fought pitched battles with the police in the streets of Paris and almost brought down the government of Charles de Gaulle.

In the United States an important segment of academic youth has only recently become concerned with the faults of society. Previously some of the boys had expended their exuberance and surplus energy on such stunts as pantie raids and contests in goldfish swallowing. Adults tried to shield them from the real world as long as possible, and the students went along with this strategy. The great change did not become apparent till the 1960s.

Only a small portion of American students engage in protests and an even smaller portion in riots. Yet the feeling of disillusionment is far more widespread, even among the majority who faithfully attend their classes and prepare themselves to take their places in the social system that they find faulty.

Main Ideas
1. Education transmits culture from one generation to the next.
2. Informal education occurs as the child associates with the people around him and is exposed to the communications media.
3. Formal education occurs in a specialized institution, the school.
4. American education is available to the student from early childhood on.
5. American public schools are basically under local control but receive financial aid and some direction from the states and the federal government.
6. School curricula are made up of the humanities, the natural sciences, the social sciences, and the subjects required for vocational proficiency.
7. Formal education has the conflicting goals of perpetuating the

existing culture and attempting to change it according to the moral values of the educators.
8. Teachers have occupied a rather low status in America, as compared to other countries.
9. American teachers generally espouse middle-class values.
10. Despite court decisions and other official acts many children of minority groups still receive inferior education.
11. Student unrest at colleges and universities indicates dissatisfaction, not only with the educational system but with the practices of adult society in general.
12. The high dropout rate indicates that many young people consider school irrelevant to their own life experience.

Important Terms
Bussing
Centralization
Compulsory education
Curriculum
Formal education
Generation gap
Humanities
Indoctrination
Informal education
Local control
Socialization
Vocational education

Conclusion
Our schools operate under great difficulties. They are faced with skyrocketing costs. As in every field, quality products are more expensive than shoddy, outworn goods. "We want the best for our children," we proclaim, but we have difficulty meeting the cost of education.

Educators are uncertain how to respond to the quick pace of social change, and students struggle to find in the offerings of their schools relevance to their personal aspirations. Political pressure and lay control make it difficult for the educator to experiment with new and unconventional ideas.

But the picture is not completely bleak. The generation gap is not a new phenomenon. It has occurred before in different forms and has prevented the older generation from becoming too set in its ways. Even though opportunities are not yet equal for all American children, the United States compares favorably with other parts of the world, even with such advanced countries as England. In the British Isles less than 20 percent of the sixteen- and seventeen-year-olds still attend school, as compared with more than 80 percent in the United States.

America provides twelve years of schooling for all children through its public education system. To offer more nearly equal opportunities beyond high school, we have introduced community colleges and set up scholarships. Many young people are being assisted in "working their way through college." Yet the opportunity gap still exists, and much remains to be done till education will take everybody as far as his ability allows him to go.

Notes
1. Edmund S. Muskie, "What Happens When Peace Breaks Out?" *Saturday Review*, May 24, 1969, p. 14.
2. G. A. Lundberg, C. C. Shrag, *et al.*, *Sociology* (New York: Harper, 1954), p. 482.
3. *Time*, November 7, 1967, p. 33.
4. *World Almanac*, 1969, p. 344.
5. "Local School Boards," *U.S. Office of Education Bulletin*, 1962, No. 8.
6. James S. Coleman, "The Adolescent Subculture and Academic Achievement," in Peter I. Rose (ed.), *The Study of Society* (New York: Random House, 1967), p. 677.
7. *Higher Education and National Affairs*, American Council on Education, Washington, D.C., 18, May 16, 1969, p. 8.
8. W. H. Boyer and P. Walsh, "Are Children Born Unequal?" *Saturday Review*, October 19, 1968, p. 78.
9. S. M. Miller, "The Outlook of Working-Class Youth," in Rose, *op. cit.*, p. 406.
10. *Agenda*, 4 (January/February 1968), p. 13.
11. *Dialogue on Poverty* (Indianapolis: Bobbs-Merrill, 1967), p. 90.
12. August B. Hollingshead, *Elmtown's Youth* (New York: Wiley, 1949), p. 331.
13. R. Perrucci and M. Pilisuk, *The Triple Revolution: Social Problems in Depth* (Boston: Little, Brown, 1968), p. 449.
14. *Statistical Abstract of the United States*, 1969, p. 121.
15. Richard Poirier, "War Against the Young," *Atlantic Monthly* (October 1968), p. 67.

Suggestions for Further Reading
Conant, James B. *Slums and Suburbs: A Commentary on Schools in Metropolitan Areas.* New York: McGraw-Hill, 1961. The former president of Harvard University reports on his survey, which reveals severe shortcomings.

Harris, Mark. *Wake Up Stupid.* New York: Knopf, 1959. Novel about an unusual college professor.

Hentoff, Nat. *Our Children Are Dying.* New York: Viking, 1966. Observations on the failings of education for minority-group children.

Hersey, John R. *Too Far to Walk.* New York: Knopf, 1966. Novel about boredom and rebellion among undergraduates in a New England college; follows the traditional theme of Dr. Faustus and the Devil.

Hilton, James. *Goodbye, Mr. Chips.* Boston: Little, Brown, 1934. Novel about an old-time dedicated schoolmaster.

Holt, John C. *How Children Learn.* New York: Pitman, 1967.

Kaufman, Bel. *Up the Down Staircase.* New York: Avon, 1964. Humorous novel set in a high school with mostly underprivileged pupils.

Kozol, Jonathan. *Death at an Early Age.* Boston: Houghton Mifflin, 1967. A shocking account of racial discrimination and brutality in the Boston public schools, written by a former Boston school teacher.

Lineberry, William P. (ed.). *New Trends in the Schools.* Reference Shelf, XXXIX, No. 2, New York: Wilson, 1967.

McClellan, Grant S. *America's Educational Needs.* New York: Wilson, 1958. Material for high-school debate and discussion.

Patton, Frances G. *Good Morning, Miss Dove.* New York: Dodd, Mead, 1954. Novel about an old-fashioned but lovable spinster school teacher.

Sanford, Nevitt. *Where Colleges Fail.* San Francisco: Jossey-Bass, 1967. Colleges fail wherever they treat the student as less than a person.

"Student's Rights: Academic Freedom in the Secondary Schools," *Education Digest,* 34, December 1968, 19–22.

Woodring, Paul. *A Fourth of a Nation.* New York: McGraw-Hill, 1957. Critical look at American public-school education and at the training of public-school teachers.

Do you like your job?
Is it what you had expected?
Do the people you work with like you?
What can you do to be liked?

13 GETTING ALONG
human relations at work

Sally has just landed her first job as a salesgirl at the local Penney's store. "I'm so thrilled," she reports to her friends, "but I'm also scared."

She is thrilled because she has finally accomplished what she set out to do when she began answering ads, calling the employment office, and making the rounds of the local stores. To her the job means money to buy some of the things she had been needing for a while, more independence from her parents, and the satisfaction of knowing that the store manager was so favorably impressed with her. All in all, the prospect of holding down a job gives Sally the feeling that she is an adult.

But getting the job is only the beginning. As in the case of marriage, the test of success comes afterward.

SATISFACTION OF NEEDS

In order to keep her job, Sally will have to please her employer. How well she succeeds and how long she wants to stay with Penney's hinges on how well the work will satisfy her needs. What, then, does she *expect* from the job? She probably needs

255

income, as do most people. Besides she hopes that she will like her work and be proud of her achievements.

The kind of work people prefer to do depends greatly on their personalities. Some are perfectly happy with routine factory jobs, while others find them very boring. A mortician may be quite satisfied with his business, while certain of his friends would not enter this line of work even if they had to face starvation. Many skilled craftsmen, artists, and professional people are sincerely devoted to their occupations regardless of the financial rewards. Salesmen who "like people" go about their tasks with zest and vigor.

But money, the feeling of competence, and enjoyment of the activity are not the only factors that contribute to job satisfaction. There are others. An obvious way of finding out what helps create a healthy work situation is to ask the people who are working. A number of studies have used this approach, especially with employees in large firms. One such study involved 1,128 employees in the city of Oslo, Norway.[1] The results showed that workers wanted to have some voice in decision making in their company. The workers felt that their bosses should not only give them orders but should consider them as partners in a common enterprise as well.

A great number of jobs are routine.
George W. Gardner

Similar feelings were expressed in interviews with a large number of American automobile workers. "A good foreman," explained a press operator, "makes you feel like somebody, not just like another machine."[2] The workers also expressed dislike of assembly-line jobs that dampen personal initiative or personal freedom and that have to be performed under constant close supervision according to a rigid timetable. Many would have preferred driving a truck, not because it paid more money, but because "you aren't pushed or crowded like on production."[3]

Another research project indicated that persons who draw a salary seem to be happier, on the whole, with their work than those who are paid by the hour.[4] Of course, salaried employees often hold jobs of higher status though not necessarily with higher income.

When asked to evaluate their work, college graduates tend, on the whole, to place less value on pay and job security than do blue-collar workers, though they often consider themselves underpaid. On lower occupational levels workers hold pay to be much more important, but they are more likely to be satisfied with what they receive. It comes closer to their own expectations since they had not aimed much higher to begin with.

The rate of employee turnover seems to be a good indication of satisfaction. If Sally changes jobs half-a-dozen times a year, we can assume that the work she has been doing does not meet her expectations. Satisfied workers will hold on longer to their positions.

What needs then do people hope to satisfy through their work? Much of what we do, whether on the job, at school, at home, or during leisure hours, is done to support the picture we have of ourselves, our self-concept (see Chapter 1). The closer we come in this attempt, the better we feel. The self-concept of most persons demands, among other things, a fair evaluation of the work we do and the respect and appreciation of those with whom we work.

HUMAN RELATIONS

Most types of work involve frequent contact with others. In factories, offices, and stores cooperation among many persons is a necessity. Students have to get along with teachers and teachers with students. The success of salesmen, welfare workers, counselors, and many others depends, to a large degree, on their ability to relate to customers and clients.

Do you find it easy or difficult to meet people and become acquainted with them? Do your associates like to talk with you? Do they enjoy your company?

What social science has discovered about the nature of human relations may be used by counselors, teachers, clergymen, and therapists to assist people with their personal problems. Scientific findings are being applied to give advice that may be helpful in day-to-day situations. Such advice may also be found in books, articles, lectures, and courses. Here are a few suggestions that you may want to consider:

> 1. Be conscious of the other person and note what he does. Talk about the subjects that interest him and he will think of you as a person with an interesting personality. . . .
> 2. Assume that people like you. If you show that you want people to talk to you, they will respond warmly. . . .
> 3. Build up the other fellow's feelings of self-worth. Note things about which he feels inferior. Offer him sincere compliments which prove that he has better qualities than he thought he had. . . .
> 4. Admit your own defects. You need not deliberately make an ass of yourself but, when you have acted as one, let others make humorous remarks at your expense. It makes them feel superior and keeps your personality more flexible. . . .
> 5. Practice use of the word YOU and avoid I.[5]

Following this and similar advice may not bring startling results in a day or even a week. But continued practice should eventually be rewarded with increased satisfaction with work, school, family, and any other group relationship.

MORALE

Your satisfaction at work is not only important to you but also to your employer. In the past the boss saw to it that the worker turned out a good product and that he did not loaf on the job. There was little concern on the part of the owner, supervisor, or foreman about the feelings of the workers. In many places this is still the case, but more and more employers realize that high *morale* among their employees can be of invaluable benefit to them. Satisfied workers not only produce better, but they also give the company a more favorable image toward the outside world, that is, they help improve public relations.

It is true that the employer may have a purely selfish reason for treating his worker as a person rather than as a machine. It is good for business, an important factor in the capitalistic system. But in this case, what is good for the company or the boss is also good for the employee. It is finally being realized that the interests of the two don't necessarily have to be opposed to each other.

One means of adding to the contentment of the worker is to make him physically comfortable. To this end modern plants install good lighting, heating, and air conditioning. Coffee breaks are provided, some places furnishing free coffee. Music is piped in, and food is made available at reasonable prices in company cafeterias. But man needs more than physical comfort.

A psychologist inquired of a drill-press operator, "Joe, how's the food in the plant cafeteria?"

"Food's okay, but the prices they soak us with are terrible."

"Aren't they less than you'd have to pay outside?"

"Maybe so. But with the company able to buy in quantity, they must get everything cheap. Us guys figure they're making plenty of dough right out of the food they serve us."

Later the same interviewer found out from the president of the company that the cafeteria was operated entirely for the convenience of the workers and was losing about $50,000 a year. Clearly here is a case where management has failed to explain itself to labor and has been entirely unaware of the workers' antagonism.[6]

Much attention has been given a pioneering study undertaken between 1927 and 1932 as a joint project of the Western Electric Company's Hawthorne plant and Harvard University.[7] Six girls were chosen to work in a test room. They were told to work "as they felt," not to make any extraordinary effort. An observer was stationed with the girls, and careful records were kept on production, conversation, the health of the girls, and other related factors.

As the experiment progressed, the girls developed common interests and loyalties. They took over their own discipline from the supervisor and supervised themselves. Group pressure made them stick to the job and avoid unnecessary breaks. Working conditions were changed a number of times. The number of working hours was increased and then lowered; the lighting was alternately dimmed and brightened. Some of these changes were repeated. Yet throughout the whole experiment, there was an almost steady increase of production.

Clearly it was not the changes in physical working conditions that made the girls work harder, but the fact that they had been chosen for the experiment, the feeling that what they were doing was significant and of great interest to many important people. Many lessons have been drawn from this experiment and from others that followed. Suggestion boxes appeared near typewriters and machinery. Some companies made a habit of taking newly hired workers on a tour of the whole plant and explaining to them how their particular job was an essential part of the whole production process.

The author knows of a personnel officer in a large aluminum plant whose job it is to help employees with any kind of problem even though the problems may not be at all related to the job. He spends considerable time advising workers on financial difficulties and explaining points in their medical-insurance program. Often the problems involve members of the family rather than the employee himself. This kind of service gives the worker the feeling that someone on the management level really cares about him. Although he is in a mass employment situation, the individual retains his sense of identity.

All such innovations have their origin in the fairly recent discovery that job satisfaction depends not only on good pay, reasonable working hours, and physical comfort but also on (1) supervisors and fellow workers who show interest in how the individual is getting along and respect his complaints and (2) opportunities for the worker to participate in making decisions concerning his work.

According to Daniel Bell even changes based on such discoveries are not enough.[8] True, pleasant material working conditions and improved "human relations" may make the worker feel better for a time, but Bell doubts whether, as the Hawthorne experiments seem to indicate, employees really don't mind tedious and repetitive labor. Despite all well-intentioned managerial efforts the worker remains harnessed to the dehumanized process of mechanization. Bell suggests a whole new approach to work organization. The prime objective should be the emotional welfare of the man on the job and not increased output. If dull jobs cannot be avoided, they ought to be rotated. Management must see to it that work is made challenging and personally gratifying. This, of course, could only be accomplished if the pressure on owners to show immediate profits were relieved.

It has also been found that employee discontent and poor performance of a business or a public agency often result from a failure of management to clearly outline job standards and responsibilities. A worker who does not know exactly what is expected of him will fail to satisfy his co-workers and his superiors. Lack of recognition will cause him to become disgruntled. He may even be fired without really knowing why. The so-called management-by-objective approach stresses very detailed descriptions of job duties and work standards, such as given in the table entitled "The Successful Secretary."

The Successful Secretary—an Example of Job Description and Standards

Major Job Segments	Job Duties and Work Standards
Dictation I	
A. Oral	1. Takes dictation at normal talking speed.
B. Dictating Machine	1. Operates dictating equipment used by Supervisor.
Typing II	
A. General	1. Types from dictation or longhand.
	2. No visible erasures on typed work.
	3. No errors in spelling or grammar.
	4. Proofreads all material before giving to Supervisor.
	5. Work is completed by time requested.
B. Letters, Memos, Reports	1. Always types 1 yellow carbon for writer and 1 green carbon for chronological file.
	2. As requested, types white carbons for others and green carbon for department reading file.
C. Mats	1. Gives to Supervisor for proofreading before running.
	2. Types requisition form to accompany it.
D. Forms, Handouts, Requisitions	1. Types as directed.
	2. Personally takes requisitions to Purchasing and explains what is needed and when.
Filing III	
A. Correspondence File	1. Green carbons are filed in monthly folder by date.
B. Outside Seminars and Conferences	1. Bulletins are filed in subject folders as categorized by Supervisor.
	2. Files are cleaned of program bulletins once every two months.
	3. Separate files are maintained of evaluation sheets of programs attended.
C. Subject Files	1. Materials are filed in appropriate folder as indicated by Supervisor.
D. Handouts, Pamphlets, Forms	1. Appropriate files are maintained.
E. Visual Aids	1. Films and other aids are kept in cabinet in neat and orderly arrangement.
	2. Record is kept of the locale of all aids. (Loaned, etc.)

F. General

1. All items are filed within a week of receipt.
2. Any filed material can be found within 3 minutes.

Mail IV

A. Incoming

1. Does not stamp or read mail marked "Personal and Confidential."
2. Opens, stamps, and reads all other incoming first class mail.
3. Opens but does not stamp or read third and fourth class material. (Bulletins, advertisements, etc.).

B. Outgoing

1. Uses Special Deilvery, Air Mail, and class of postage as indicated by Supervisor.

Machines V

1. Operates thermofax, verifax, dictation transcribing machine, calculator, and any other equipment necessary to perform job.

Telephone VI

A. Own Phone

1. Answers promptly and courteously.
2. Limits personal conversation to 10 minutes per day.

B. Supervisor's Phone

1. Answers promptly and courteously in his absence.
2. Answers immediately after the 2nd ring when Supervisor is in office. Explains to caller that "He has someone in his office; can he call you back?"
3. Places calls as requested.

General VII

A. Conducts Tour

1. Conducts Tours of A.C. when requested by Public Relations and approved by Supervisor.

B. IMC Chorale

1. Handles arrangements and correspondence as requested.

C. Assembling

1. Assembles or arranges for assembling of materials and booklets as requested.

D. Supervision

1. Supervises work of an assistant when assigned help.

E. Arrangements

1. Makes arrangements for conference rooms, equipment, etc., as requested.
2. Checks on arrangements prior to meetings.

F. Appearance

1. Personal appearance is neat and pleasant.
2. Desk and work area are neat at all times.
3. Desk and work area are cleaned and typewriter covered each evening before leaving work.

G. Communications

1. Freely offers suggestions to Supervisor on any phase of her own work, the work of Supervisor, or others in the department.
2. Asks for clarification when not sure what is to be done.
3. Asks for work when not busy.
4. Tells Supervisor when cannot complete work by time requested.

H. Other	1. Carries out other assignments as directed by Supervisor or Skokie Personnel Manager in absence of Supervisor.
2. Performs overtime work as requested or approved by Supervisor.
3. Completes time sheet at the end of each week.

Source: *Management of Personnel Quarterly* (University of Michigan), Vol. 4, No. 4, 1966, p. 4. Reprinted with permission.

It has been suggested that an ideal situation could be created if the employee considered himself a co-owner of the business that employs him. In fact, this approach has been tried with great success. A number of companies encourage their employees to purchase company stock by contributing part of the cost as a bonus. Among the many large corporations that have developed stock-purchasing plans for their employees are Procter & Gamble and American Telephone & Telegraph with its subsidiaries.

In another form the workers actually own the entire business and only those employed in it can be stockholders. In a sense, they "buy" their jobs by purchasing a portion of the company. In such a setup the employees take over the total responsibility for major policy decisions and also for the hiring of management personnel. Profits are shared; the worker receives the satisfaction of being his own boss though he voluntarily follows the orders of his supervisors. He now refers to his company as "we," and the interest of the company becomes his own interest.

THE GROUP

Most work is done in groups. A large factory may employ many hundreds of workers, but the shapeless mass is usually divided into smaller units under a lead man, foreman, or supervisor. Similar group organization prevails in office buildings that employ the staffs of insurance companies, banks, or governmental agencies.

Road repair, running a railroad or commercial airline, and various outdoor electrical installations are carried out by small groups. The success of the work depends not only on the skill of the individual member but, to a large extent, on the cooperation among members of the group.

Much attention has recently been given to the study of *group dynamics*. The problem is: What makes one group strong and unified while another is divided by bickering and antagonism? Obviously the strongly unified group functions better, and its members receive a high degree of satisfaction. They take pride in the record of the whole group; they look out for each other's welfare; they become a *team*.

It is well known how important team spirit is in competitive sports like football and in military organizations. During battle the life of the individual soldier often depends on the actions and attitudes of his fellow soldiers.

Perhaps you have heard the expression *esprit de corps*. It is a French term meaning "group spirit" and was originally applied to military units. The famous French Foreign Legion, heralded in stories and films for its valor, was credited with a high degree of esprit de corps. The chief allegiance of this motley conglomeration of soldiers who came from many parts of the world was not to a country or to an idea but to the outfit. The legionnaires fought for the Foreign Legion and for nothing else. In our own country the United States Marines have sometimes been praised for having a similarly high team spirit.

In civilian life too it is not difficult to find out whether or not a working group has a positive or negative attitude toward its task and toward the whole organization. This is true of road gangs, as well as school faculties, police forces, and sales personnel in a store.

If group attitude is positive, we speak of *cohesion*, "the quality of a group which includes individual pride, commitment, meaning, as well as the group's stick-togetherness, ability to weather crises, and ability to maintain itself over time."[9] Cohesion and productivity are definitely related to each other but not always in the same way. High cohesion may lead to high productivity, but, under certain circumstances, it can also result in very low productivity.

In one incident, for example, a man worked for a while in a manufacturing plant and became a member of a small group that spent much time griping about the management. At first the man could not understand the reasons for the complaints, which definitely repelled him. But soon he experienced a change of attitude. He too became convinced that the bosses were incompetent and had no personal interest in the employees. Like the others of this group, he made no effort to work beyond the absolutely required minimum and refrained from showing any kind of initiative.

One job, for instance, required the rolling of heavy barrels down a set of rollers that formed a kind of conveyor belt. The barrels had been freshly treated with a preservative, and the rollers soon became coated with the sticky substance, making it very difficult to move the barrels along. The resulting slowdown could easily have been avoided if the workers had periodically halted the movement of the barrels and cleaned the rollers; but the workers would not do anything unless instructed by the foreman. Needless to say, this plant was not a very pleasant working place, nor was its productivity rate very high.

This is not the kind of cohesion personnel managers and efficiency experts have in mind. They think rather of the strong team spirit that pervades the scientists and technicians who work in the space program. These people are strongly motivated. They know very well that they are bringing extremely valuable knowledge and skills to the enterprise. Their interest in the success of the project is exceedingly high, and they are also aware that not only their immediate superiors but practically the whole world follows their efforts with sympathy and attention.

Although not everyone can work for a project as glamorous as the space program, a high degree of positive group cohesion can be achieved in other places as well. Success depends to a large extent on the group leader.

LEADERSHIP

The old-style factory foreman was a cousin of the old-style army drill sergeant. Both knew a good deal about the mechanics of their jobs but very little about what makes human minds tick. Both liked to bark out orders and punish offenders, often by subjecting such offenders to ridicule before the whole group. Both considered unquestioning obedience the prime duty of their charges.

Hard-boiled drill sergeants and foremen are beginning to disappear because the results of their methods have proved to be less than satisfactory and also because our respect for the worth of the individual human being is rising. People in supervisory positions are being selected not only for their ability to run a linotype press or to assemble a machine gun but also for their understanding of human needs.

Let us examine the following case:

A new truck has been assigned to a crew of eight men. The foreman must decide who will drive the truck. If he arbitrarily selects one of the men, the other seven are likely to resent it. They will find all sorts of reasons as to why they are more entitled to the coveted vehicle. What is worse, most of the grumbling will occur behind the foreman's back. If the foreman becomes aware of his crew's resentment, he may perceive it as a threat to his authority and react with unreasonable harshness. The net result could very well be prolonged tension and bitterness.

A foreman more skilled in human relations may recognize the danger of assigning the truck to a man of his own choice. Perhaps he would call the whole crew together, explain the problem, and then ask the men to help him make the decision. Each man would then feel that he has a part in the decision, which would result in an entirely different feeling toward the foreman and also toward the worker finally selected to drive the new truck. What is perhaps most important, the foreman would be communicating his belief in the worth of each member in the crew. It has been said that "supervisors who can develop democratic work teams by encouraging their employees to participate in supervision have few production and morale problems."[10]

Bradford and Lippitt, whose statement is quoted above, identify four different types of leaders:

1. The hard-boiled autocrat who rules with an iron hand
2. The benevolent autocrat who encourages his employees to be dependent on him and to follow his orders out of loyalty
3. The *laissez-faire* (French for "let do") supervisor who leaves everything up to the employees and places no restrictions on the actions of the individual

4. The democratic leader who shares the decision-making process with his employees whenever possible and is careful to explain any decision he must make himself

Experiences in industry, in the classroom, and even in the armed services indicate that the type of leader described in 4 is the most desirable. Highly autocratic leaders may produce cohesion but of the negative variety. "Frustration, failure, and insecurity," say Bradford and Lippitt,[11] are the consequences of a laissez-faire type of leadership, but under a democratic leader productivity and constructive cohesion are highest.

A cohesive group must have well-defined goals. In industry each person needs to see how his work fits into the overall purpose of the organization. Only when the members of a group have a good idea where they are going can they evaluate their success in reaching their goals. People must feel they are moving forward; otherwise they will not experience satisfaction with their work.

In order to be successful a group should be neither too large nor too small. A commander who issues orders to a large crowd through a loudspeaker will not bring about much team spirit. The restlessness of students at our large universities has been caused, to a great extent, by a lack of democratic leadership (see Chapter 12). How does one achieve cohesiveness at an institution of 25,000 or more where lectures are given to 500 listeners at a time?

On the other hand, to lead a group of two or three may likewise prove to be an extremely difficult task. Instead of leadership, a struggle for power can develop. Often competition rather than cohesion is then the very destructive result. Research seems to indicate an *optimum size* of four to seven members for a work group in the charge of one leader.[12]

Some teachers, supervisors, military commanders, politicians, or street-gang chiefs have been called "born leaders." They inspire loyalty and enthusiasm. Those leaders who possess charisma (see Chapter 3) have no trouble getting the group to expend its best effort or endure hardship with cheerfulness. Their understanding of human needs and expectations seems to be instinctive.

Such exceptional leaders are assets to our society, but we cannot wait for chance to supply them for business, industry, or public service. We must train them. Leadership training has become an important effort in many segments of society, but unfortunately it has not been extended to politics. No formal leadership training is required to occupy even the most vital political positions.

But many companies now feel the need to provide special leadership training for their supervisory personnel. Courses in various aspects of human relations are offered right at the plant, or else foremen and supervisors are encouraged to enroll in colleges and evening schools. At periodic conferences people in positions of leadership meet to exchange ideas. They present problem cases and listen to various opinions of how to handle them. Occasionally experts from university campuses or research institutes may be called in as consultants.

A very stimulating learning technique is *role playing*. Supervisors improvise little plays in which they enact different roles. One may pretend to be a new worker who is scared of a machine or suffers from being the target of his teammates' practical jokes. How can the foreman handle the situation? The player is forced to think in terms of the character he pretends to be.

Earlier in this chapter we mentioned the problem of a foreman who had to assign a new truck to a member of his crew. This situation can be dramatized through a technique that has been used by the Detroit Edison Company.[13] A large number of supervisors gather in one room. They divide into groups of six. One member of each group is assigned the role of foreman. The other five are repairmen, each caught in a different set of circumstances. One pretends that he has been with the company for twelve years and has been driving a five-year-old Dodge truck. Another plays the role of a newcomer who has to struggle with a much older and more dilapidated vehicle, and so on.

Each group of six enacts its little play. For half an hour it is debated whether the new truck should go to the man with the higher seniority, to the man with the less satisfactory vehicle, or to somebody else. Then all participants assemble again, and each group reports on its role-playing session. The result is that almost all groups have reached a decision and that the great majority of would-be repairmen are satisfied with it because their opinion has been sought and they have had a hand in resolving the issue.

Role playing involves putting oneself in the other fellow's shoes and looking at a problem from somebody else's vantage point. This brings new insights. The dramatization might help overturn old habits and prejudices more quickly and thoroughly than hearing a lecture could.

Main Ideas
1. A worker will be satisfied with his job if it meets his personal needs.
2. These needs include not only satisfactory financial rewards and comfortable physical working conditions but also a role in the decision-making process and a feeling of being appreciated as a person.
3. The worker can contribute to his own satisfaction by establishing a good personal relationship with his co-workers and supervisors; he does this by exhibiting a sincere interest in other people, without engaging in flattery or self-belittling.
4. High morale in the working force is of great advantage to the employer.
5. Management has learned the value of explaining its actions to the worker and of giving him a feeling of importance.

6. Group cohesiveness can have positive or negative effects. Positive cohesion brings about team spirit and high productivity.
7. The leader determines to a large extent the spirit of the working group. Democratic leadership seems to assure the best results.
8. Leadership training is becoming an important concern of management in business, industry, and public service.

Important Terms
Cohesion
Esprit de corps
Group dynamics
Laissez faire
Morale
Optimum size
Role playing
Team

Conclusion
The job seeker will do well to look for the organization that is most likely to satisfy the greatest number of his needs. You should try especially to find an employer who will give you consideration as a person; you should then make a determined effort to show appreciation of the people with whom you come into contact at work. Chances for job satisfaction will be most favorable where group cohesion exists and where democratic group leadership is encouraged.

Notes
1. Harriet Holter, "Attitudes Towards Employee Participation in the Company Decision-Making Process," *Human Relations,* 18 (1965), 297–321.
2. Ely Chinoy, *Automobile Workers and the American Dream* (Garden City, N.Y.: Doubleday, 1955), p. 73.
3. *Ibid.,* p. 72.
4. S. D. Saleh, E. P. Prien, *et al.,* "The Relations of Job Attitudes, Organization, Performance and Job Level," *Journal of Industrial Psychology,* 2 (1964), 59–65.
5. H. W. Hepner, *Psychology Applied to Life and Work,* 3rd ed. (Englewood Cliffs, N.J.: Prentice-Hall, 1957), pp. 177–178.
6. A. Corning White, "Auditing Employee Relations," *Dun's Review* (March 1949).
7. F. J. Roethlisberger and W. J. Dickson, *Management and the Worker: An Account of a Research Program Conducted by the Western Electric Company, Hawthorne Works, Chicago* (Cambridge, Mass.: Harvard University Press, 1939).
8. Daniel Bell, *Work and Its Discontent* (Boston: Beacon Press, 1956).

9. Clovis R. Shepherd, *Small Groups: Some Sociological Perspectives* (San Francisco: Chandler, 1964), p. 88.
10. L. P. Bradford and R. Lippitt, "Building a Democratic Work Group," in *Leadership in Action* (Washington, D.C.: National Education Association, National Training Laboratories, 1961), pp. 52–61.
11. *Ibid.*
12. Shepherd, *op. cit.*, p. 118.
13. N. Maier and L. F. Zerfoss, "MRP: A Technique for Training Large Groups of Supervisors and Its Potential Use in Social Research," *Human Relations* (University of Michigan), 5 (1952), 177–186.

Suggestions for Further Reading

Ballard, Virginia and Ruth Strang. *Ways to Improve Your Personality*. Rev. ed. New York: McGraw-Hill, 1965. Highly readable book, aimed at young adults.

Carnegie, Dale. *How to Win Friends and Influence People*. Rev. ed. New York: Simon & Schuster, 1939. Well-known book of advice on how to be successful.

Chapman, Elwood N. *Your Attitude Is Showing*. Chicago: Science Research Associates, 1964.

How to Get and Hold the Right Job. Washington, D.C.: U.S. Department of Labor, Public Employment Service (pamphlet).

Laird, Donald A. and E. C. Laird. *The Techniques of Handling People*. Rev. ed. New York: McGraw-Hill, 1954.

Levinson, H., C. R. Price, *et al*. *Men, Management and Mental Health*. Cambridge, Mass.: Harvard University Press, 1962. Short, lively, and rich in examples.

Nunn, Henry L. *Partners in Production: A New Role for Management and Labor*. Englewood Cliffs, N.J.: Prentice-Hall, 1961. A former industrialist reports on his philosophy and his experiences.

Sartain, Aaron Q. and A. W. Baker. *The Supervisor and His Job*. New York: McGraw-Hill, 1965. Textbook for a course in supervision.

Whyte, William H., Jr., *The Organization Man*. Garden City, N.Y.: Doubleday, 1956 (paperback).

PART FOUR **YOUR COMMUNITY**

*Do you know your next-door neighbor?
Or do you recognize him only by the sound
of his snoring through the apartment
wall?
Can you see your neighbor's house
from your window?
Or is it hidden behind a wooded hill?*

14 FROM HAMLET TO MEGALOPOLIS
the community

THE PLACE WHERE YOU LIVE

So far we have dealt largely with the groups into which you are born: family, race, caste, and, to some extent, also class and status groups. The community that you belong to, on the other hand, depends upon the place where you live. It is made up of people who have found shelter, for a short time or for life, in a certain spot. Living in one place gives people many common interests. They must cooperate for their own good, and they show similar attitudes and ways of behaving. A community may be tiny or huge. The American nation is, in some ways, an oversized community, and we have even begun to speak of the world community, though cooperation among the inhabitants of the world is not widespread or consistent.

Men living close together have always tended to form some kind of unit, known as a band (or by a variety of other names) to work for the common good, to defend themselves against common danger, and to help each other with the task of survival.

Early man could not stay permanently in one place. As long as his food supply depended on hunting or fishing or gathering what the woods and meadows had to offer, he had to move whenever the supply was exhausted. Thus he was a *nomad*.

When men learned to domesticate sheep, cattle, and other animals, they often continued their nomadic ways. Such communities can still be found today. The Bedouins of the Middle East roam with their herds from grazing place to grazing place along the edge of the desert, or they stop temporarily by an oasis. Northern Asiatic tribesmen drive their herds southward in winter and return to their northern home grounds for the short summer when the surface ice melts and gives way to a lush green ground cover. Since food is rarely overabundant, such roaming bands cannot be very large, and they number anywhere from only a few dozen to a few hundred men, women, and children.

Traveling Gypsy groups, with their wagons and horses, which have been a familiar sight in many parts of the world for ages, follow the nomadic way of life. Their alien language and seemingly strange moral ideas have often aroused irritation and suspicion among more settled populations.

When, in the New Stone Age, man finally learned to till the soil and to build more permanent dwellings, he wanted to remain in one place. Having planted a crop, he wished to harvest it, store the surplus for the harsh winter, and plan for a long future. The farmer became deeply attached to his homeplace, and with others whose fields and pastures adjoined his own he formed a more stable kind of community, which we call a *rural* community.

THE RURAL COMMUNITY

Traveling the narrow hardtop or gravel roads that lead off the main highways, the American motorist traverses forest and open land, broken here and there by a cluster of homes surrounded by plowed fields. Each cluster is a *hamlet*, and some hamlets carry such names as Pumpkin Hollow, Spring Valley, or Brush Prairie.

What is it like to live in Pumpkin Hollow? A more relevant question would actually be, "What *was* it like when grandfather was a young farmer?" because rural society is undergoing rapid and massive changes.

Many hamlets used to be quite isolated and had to carry on their own community life. Others were within walking distance or a horse ride away from other hamlets or from single farms; together these formed a neighborhood community. Once, everybody in such a community did farm work, except perhaps for the owner of the general store at the crossroads. People almost always stopped to chat with one another when they met at the store or on the road. Aside from such occasional meetings they saw each other at weddings, funerals, and a few festivals where there was singing, dancing, and general merrymaking. Relatives and neighbors visited back and forth on Sunday afternoons. Community life centered around the church, the one-room schoolhouse, and perhaps also the Grange hall, where the farmers' organization used to meet.

The neighborhood formed a primary group (see Chapter 7). Mem-

Many people are deeply rooted in their rural communities.
Ted Spiegel from Rapho Guillumette Pictures

bers shared many similarities in thought and behavior. It was almost impossible to keep a secret in Pumpkin Hollow. Everybody understood clearly what was expected of him in the way of correct speech and action. Stepping out of line usually incurred general disapproval, and the culprit became the target of gossip, was reprimanded, and found himself excluded in many painful ways.

Although such a way of life may seem stifling to many, there were advantages to it. Neighbors were willing to help each other in case of fire, sickness, or death. This gave the individual a feeling of security; he thought in terms of "we" instead of "I." His world seemed to him to be an island isolated from the big and dangerous outside world. Most residents had deep roots in the neighborhood. Generation after generation had continued living in the same house and working the same farm. Though Pumpkin Hollow had problems, the memory of this rural scene took on the glow of a happy dream the more it faded into the past.

What made Pumpkin Hollow typically rural was its smallness, its preoccupation with farming, the open spaces that gave everybody enough elbowroom, and the spirit of unity among its inhabitants. Although these traits have not completely disappeared, Pumpkin Hollow is no longer what it used to be. The impact of the growth of large cities has reached into the quiet countryside. First came the railroad, then the automobile, and finally the airplane. Together with telephone, radio, and television they have penetrated Pumpkin Hollow's isolation.

Now the farmer goes to the state capital to attend a convention and to the campus of the state college for a refresher course in agriculture, while his wife watches the same television serial that moves an urban organization man's wife to tears. The farmer's wife shops from a national mail-order catalog, or she drives to the nearest town, where she uses her credit card in a modern department store.

Rural and urban people used to eye each other with distrust and mutual contempt, and the distinctions between them produced such terms as "city slicker" and "country yokel." Now the once sharp dividing lines have become fuzzy. The insurance man planting in his backyard resembles a farmer and the farmer could just as well be taken for a building contractor when he goes to church or visits his lodge.

The Pumpkin Hollow store has added a gas station. As the men stop to have their cars and trucks fueled, they discuss the World Series or the speed races that they have been watching on television. The young men enter military service or attend colleges or vocational schools in other towns and cities. Many decide to move to more exciting places where they hope to find high-paying jobs, fabulous entertainment, and, generally, a life of high adventure awaiting them. Pumpkin Hollow is gradually becoming a neighborhood of older people.

This is the trend in rural communities not only in the United States but also in Belgium, the Netherlands, and in countries where modern technology and speed play havoc with accustomed ways. Tepoztlàn, once a sleepy village south of Mexico City, is rocking giddily under the tide of urbanism surging from the capital. Most villagers have given up the native Indian dialect in favor of Spanish. Peasants now ride the bus to their fields, and the young *paisanos* (farmers) are restless. They sneer at the old ways and wait impatiently for a chance to make more money to buy more factory-made gadgets.[1]

TYPES OF RURAL COMMUNITIES

Not all rural communities are as small as Pumpkin Hollow, which is *unincorporated*—that is, this cluster of about a dozen houses has no recognized government of its own. Instead it is one of several *subcommunities* that, in a widespread net, lies on the outskirts of a *village* or a small *town*. More and more the town becomes the center for trade, entertainment, and general social life for the rural inhabitants of the outlying neighborhoods.

The tiny country church and the schoolhouse with outdoor pump and privy may now be boarded up or in various stages of decay, unable to compete with the town churches and the consolidated schools that can easily be reached by car and bus. The town has other attractions, too, among them the weekly newspaper, a movie house, a clinic, a bank, and a number of specialized stores and services.

Depending on how close you want to be to your next neighbor, you can choose between living in an *open-country neighborhood* or residing in a village (see Figure 17). A village may, in time, grow into a town. The difference between the two is mainly one of size. According to the United States census of 1960, villages ordinarily have populations ranging from 250 to 2,500 and towns from 2,500 to 10,000.

Figure 17
Rural Communities

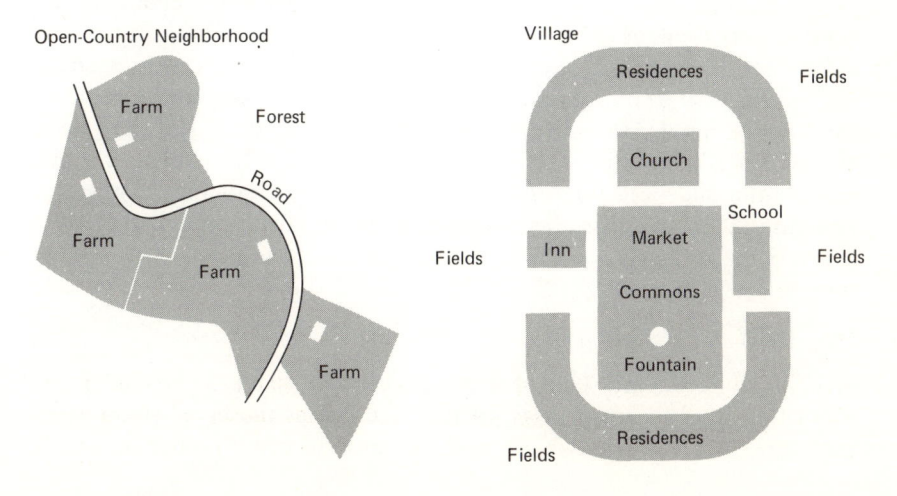

In rural Central and Eastern Europe and also in parts of New England the village type of community prevailed. The houses were crowded close together, much as the little chicks crowd around the mother hen. Before the advent of the automobile and of instant communication the pace of village life was slow. Daily routine was seldom interrupted, and what interruptions occurred were caused mostly by natural events: birth, death, illness, drought, storm, or flood. In the morning the farmer of yesterday walked or drove his wagon to his piece of land, which might be at quite a distance. In the evening he returned home to rest or to socialize in the village inn. The women used to meet by the fountain and exchange news while they filled their water jugs. Once or twice a week, farm produce was sold at the central marketplace, which then became crowded with people who bargained loudly with the stall keepers. Thus the village or town afforded neighborliness and also provided protection in unsettled times. Various versions of this old form of community life are still very much in evidence.

In the American Middle West and Far West, where immense stretches of prairie and forest are found, the open-country neighborhood is more typical. Houses are situated on farmland, and each one is often quite remote from the house of the nearest neighbor. Much of what the family needed to sustain life used to be produced right on the farm, and trips to town for shopping or entertainment were rare before the coming of the motor vehicle.

Though rural life is rooted in the farm, there are towns in which agriculture plays only a minor role. The colorful mining towns of the Old West are the setting for many daring adventure stories. During gold-rush days they were the scenes of great activity, but some have since deteriorated into abandoned towns called *ghost towns*. Several have been sold, but others have been turned into tourist attractions. In others industries, organized annual pageants, and communities for the retired were established.

The small town is not vanishing from the American scene; only the old rural way of life is in retreat. As it fades away, imagination turns it into a lost ideal. Many urban dwellers take pride in their rural ancestry or speak with nostalgia of a youth spent on the farm, where the air was invigorating and life was simple. The wickedness of the city is contrasted to the "clean life" and neighborliness of the country. City people who rarely see a live cow admire the peaceful rural scenes painted by Grandma Moses and sometimes decorate their homes with outdated rural furnishings that have now become antiques.

THE CITY

In 1790, when the first United States census was taken, 5 percent of our population lived in urban areas. In the 1960 census the figure stood at 70 percent. But this is not the whole story. Of the remaining 30 percent only a small portion still farms for a living; and even these few farmers are strongly affected by the influence of the city. The whole nation is in the process of rapid *urbanization*.

What is a city, or an urban area? (*urbs* means "city" in Latin.) It is a community where a large number of inhabitants live together in a comparatively narrow space. It is a center of commerce, manufacturing, learning, and a great variety of services, from marriage counseling to diaper service. People engage in many different occupations. Entertainment facilities cater to every appetite. Schools, theaters, concert halls, museums, and libraries feed the intellect and the desire for beauty. Churches of all denominations abound, and if none satisfies your spiritual needs, you will also find, in some cities, devotees of Zen or Yoga or other mystic cults. There are organizations for practically every special interest and walk of life. In tall buildings are housed the headquarters of banking, business, industry, government, publishing, and advertising.

Characteristics of the City

Large size	Anonymity
Specialization	Mobility
Segregation by class and ethnic group	Impersonality
Heterogeneity	Formality of relationships

The history of the city goes back at least 5,000 years. Splendid ruins of the earliest examples of cities are found in the valley of the Euphrates and Tigris rivers and on the banks of the Indus River. Athens and Rome were the hubs of brilliant ancient civilizations. Medieval merchants and artists brought world-wide renown to Constantinople, Venice, and Florence. At the same time the Mayas and the Aztecs in Mexico built magnificent citylike centers in the New World. At every age the city has been the place of progress, the point from which man's inventiveness reached out to make the seemingly impossible a reality.

However, not everything that has taken place in the city has merited praise. In the amphitheaters of ancient Roman cities men and wild beasts fought each other to death for the pleasure of the onlookers. In the narrow confines of medieval cities devastating fires were frequent, and plagues often raged unchecked and claimed a frightful toll in human lives.

Today the large city is a place of air pollution and traffic jams. People jostle each other on packed major streets as they rush from place to place. Blinking neon signs assault the eye. The rich parade their wealth extravagantly, while abject poverty is rampant around them. As thousands of people mill about him, the city dweller can often be the loneliest man on earth, suffering agonies while nobody around him pays the slightest attention.

ORIGIN OF CITIES

Why does a particular location invite the rise of a city? In many instances cities originated when traveling merchants found a spot that made a good resting place during a long journey—possibly a crossroads, a natural harbor, an oasis along the caravan route, or a shallow spot where a river could be forded. In these places traders rested, displayed their wares, and exchanged them for other goods. They also paused to worship at local religious shrines, where they prayed for a safe return.

Cities were places of refuge in time of war and unrest. Thick walls often surrounded the innermost sections, and within them the peasants from the surrounding countryside found temporary shelter. The Acropolis of Athens and the Kremlin of Moscow were such central fortresses around which large cities sprang up.

Government was needed to keep order among the citizens and to organize defense. Many older cities were, for a long time, city states, independent from each other, having their own rulers, armies, and navies. Later they were to become the capitals of kingdoms and empires.

Special circumstances prompted the growth of certain cities. Oxford, England, grew around a noted university; Wiesbaden, Germany, and Vichy, France, were widely known health centers. In our own country a number of small towns rose to importance as state capitals, and because of its attractiveness as an amusement center, Las Vegas has mushroomed.

Estimated Population of Leading Old Cities

Athens, 5th century B.C.	120,000–180,000
Florence, 14th century	90,000
Venice, 15th century	190,000
Antwerp, 16th century	200,000

Source: Kingsley Davis, "The Origin and Growth of Urbanization in the World," *The American Journal of Sociology*, 61 (March 1955), 430–437. Reprinted by permission of the University of Chicago Press. Copyright 1955 by the University of Chicago.

By present standards cities were small before the coming of industrialization. But things changed drastically under the impact of the factory with its sooty smokestacks and rows of steam-powered machinery. The mammoth city, as we know it today, was born. In 1750 Manchester was a sleepy British town of 17,000 inhabitants. Then the textile manufacturers moved in, and a hundred years later the population had swelled to 400,000.

The textile factories and steel mills of the nineteenth century had to be located near coal mines, which were the sources of fuel for steam power. Workers lived within walking distance of their work place, so sprawling districts of ugly tenement houses sprang up within earshot of the factory whistle. Taverns, stores, and warehouses also sprang up. Later these were followed by railroad depots, schools, hospitals, and dance halls. Populations grew to tremendous proportions.

Largest Modern Cities and Their Approximate Populations*

Tokyo, New York	c. 11 million
Paris	c. 10 million
London	c. 8 million
Moscow, Mexico City, Shanghai, Los Angeles, Chicago	c. 7 million

   * These figures are subject to dispute. They depend on how much of a densely populated area is included. For example, if all surrounding towns and suburbs are counted as part of New York City, the population figure would be closer to 15 million.
    Source: *World Almanac*, 1969, pp. 578–579; *Statistical Abstract of the United States*, 1968, p. 19.

HETEROGENEITY AND MOBILITY

The masses in American cities are not alike as were the farmers of the old hamlet. The populations of our cities are *heterogeneous*. For example, there are people living in Los Angeles who came from every state of the Union. The poor and oppressed of Russia, Italy, Greece, and Ireland migrated to New York, Boston, and Chicago, bringing with them conflicting habits and ideas.

The range of wealth, status, and education among our urban populations is wide, from multimillionaire to beggar, from scholar to illiterate, from the "jet set" to "winos" on skid row. The big city is the home of the generous philanthropist and the idealistic VISTA worker but also of the racketeer and the pickpocket.

Numerous *voluntary organizations* bring together citizens of the same national origin or even immigrants who came from the same Polish, Russian-Jewish, or Finnish province. Other organizations devote themselves to politics, sports, hobbies, and various causes ranging from planned parenthood to the preservation of barbershop quartets.

People who live in cities are highly *mobile* (Latin for "on the move"). They frequently move *horizontally*—that is, from place to place. Many live in apartments that they change for more or less expensive ones as their pocketbooks get fatter or slimmer. Many move into new apartments when they need more space. Even one-family homes in urban areas change owners frequently. People who move from job to job may move in and out of a community. Furthermore, the city offers numerous opportunities for *vertical* movement, that is, movement up—and sometimes down—the status ladder. With luck and perseverance workers and employees gain seniority and advancement, and businessmen become more prosperous. But city living also involves greater risks of unemployment, business slumps, and impairment of physical and mental health.

The pace of city life is hectic, with people usually in a nervous hurry. We hear gloomy voices predicting the downfall of our whole civilization and blaming all the evils of our time on the city. Lewis Mumford is among those who loudly decry the filth of city streets, the foulness of city air, and the lack of warm neighborliness in the urban community. "Vital conditions for social continuity and personal integrity have been breaking down in both the central metropolis and its outlying areas; and they have most completely broken down among the lowest-income groups."[2]

Less pessimistic observers point out that cities are and will continue to be the seats of economic and political power and of learning and art, which set the tone for the conduct of life all over the country. Cities produce the necessities and refinements of life: women's apparel and stereo sets, rock-and-roll sessions and symphony concerts, pulp magazines and college textbooks. Each city has its own special atmosphere that attracts people of similar tastes. Los Angeles is known for its informality in dress and manners, while San Francisco, in the same state, stresses Old World elegance and formality. New York City is a place of stark contrasts. It houses the very rich and the dismally poor. It is the nerve center of the nation's artistic, scholarly, and economic life, but it is also the headquarters for organized crime and the hunting grounds for an army of lesser criminals. Within the city limits of New York live millions of average citizens leading ordinary lives. But the same city also attracts every conceivable type of nonconformist.

ECOLOGY OF THE CITY

Despite its size a city is a community. It has a city-wide government. There are many city-wide services, such as fire and police protection, street repair, garbage collection, and so on. But the population is far too large for one inhabitant to have face-to-face contacts with all the others.

We know that man desperately needs the intimacy of primary-group relationships, and much has been said about the loneliness of city life. Yet a good many Bostonians, Seattleites, and Philadelphians don't feel particularly lonely. They create their own primary contacts. Obviously, compared to the total population of his city, one Cincinnatian knows few others and never sees all of them together. But he still gets to know quite a few people in his own neighborhood or subcommunity. The *ecologist* furnishes insight into the number and character of these urban neighborhoods.

Ecology is the "study of the mutual relations of groups of organisms and their environment."[3] The term was originally coined by biologists studying life in the swamp, the desert, the alpine forest, or some other well-defined natural setting. Now social scientists apply ecology to the relationship of people within a certain area.

Urban ecologists speak of the central city, the main shopping district, industrial areas, lower-, middle-, and upper-class residential areas, slums, and suburbs. These subdivisions are not only measured by blocks and square miles but also described in terms of economic standards and the cultural climate.

Ecological theorists provide us with several typical maps of city neighborhoods. We cannot say that one of these theories is correct and that all the others are wrong. Rather, all apply to different types of cities that grew under different physical and historical conditions.

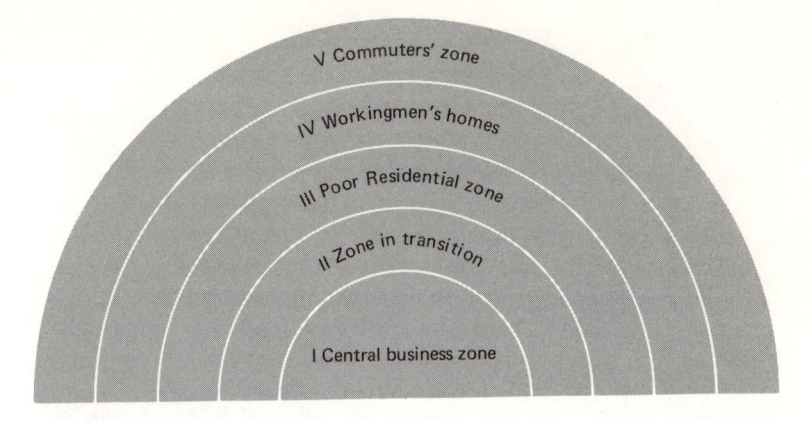

Figure 18
Urban Ecology: Concentric Zones Theory

Source: Ernest W. Burgess, *The City* (Chicago: The University of Chicago Press, 1925), pp. 47–62. Reprinted with permission of the publisher.

According to the theory of *Concentric Zones*[4] the oldest part of the city is the central district (see Figure 18). Around it the city expands in a pattern that resembles the layers of an onion. Though this theory was proposed as early as 1925, recent studies confirm that it still applies to many cities.

According to the *Sector* theory[5] once a certain zone establishes itself near the central district, it tends to grow outward so that the ecological structure eventually resembles a pie sliced into wedges (see Figure 19).

Figure 19
Urban Ecology: Sector Theory

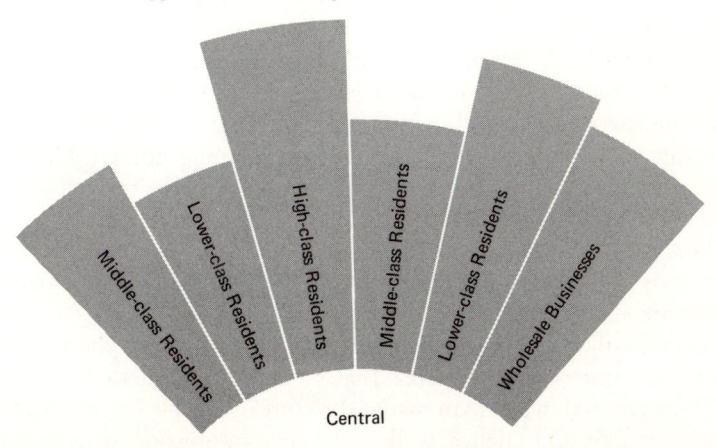

Source: Homer Hoyt, *Structure and Growth of Residential Neighborhoods in American Cities* (Washington, D.C.: U.S. Government Printing Office, 1939).

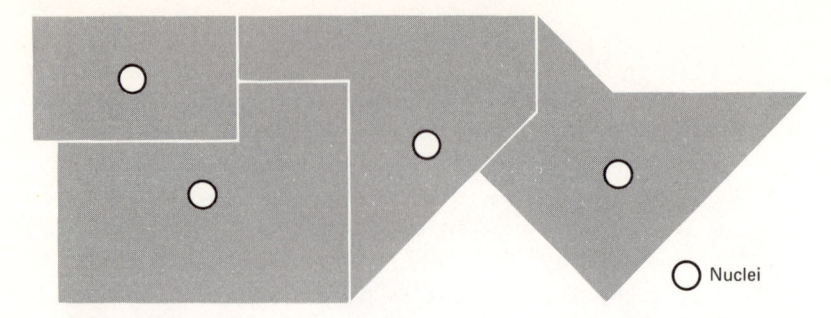

Figure 20
Urban Ecology: Multiple Nuclei Theory
Source: C. D. Harris and E. L. Ullman, "The Nature of Cities," *Annals*, 242 (November 1945), pp. 14-15. Reprinted by permission of the authors and The American Academy of Political and Social Science.

The theory of *Multiple Nuclei*[6] holds that a large city is put together like a jigsaw puzzle. Originally there were a number of separate centers (*nucleus* is Latin for "center," or "core") often belonging to different towns. As the city grew, they were swallowed up and formally annexed. Roxbury, Massachusetts, for example, was once a small rural town but is now one of many neighborhoods inside the city of Boston. This theory is illustrated in Figure 20.

SLUMS

A trip "downtown" leads one into the most glittering part of the city. Along the crowded, brightly lit main thoroughfares the visitor finds elegant stores, first-run movie theaters, and luxurious hotels teeming with vacationers and convention guests. This is the "central city," which is a major concern of ecologists.

The central city is not just an accumulation of towering skyscrapers and glittering marquees. It is also a place of sharp contrasts. Only a few blocks from the elegance and extravagance old men in shabby clothes may sit listlessly in the doorways of broken-down rooming houses. The flotsam of society congregates in cheap taverns. At its nightly revival services a missionary in a ramshackle storefront calls on sinners to repent.

This is the blighted part of town. Depending on the ecological theory applied, it is shaped like a ring or a wedge. It may be the only area of its kind, or it may have duplicates in other sections.

As you walk away from the hotel and theater district, you enter other parts of the "inner city," an area that is densely populated and almost completely covered with man-made structures, except for an occasional piece of greenery. On such a walk, your first impression may be one of dismay or even disgust. But closer inspection reveals the interesting variety of social groups that are the occupants of the inner city. They are the people who actually live there year-in, year-out, whereas the office skyscrapers are only filled with humanity by day and the amusement places by night.

Herbert J. Gans distinguishes among five types of inner-city residents:

1. The *cosmopolitans*. These are young adults who are writers, artists, or students. They have little money but a great deal of contempt for the ways of the majority. In their "Latin Quarter" they live by their own rules and create their own nonconforming subculture.
2. The unmarried or childless. Many intend to move away from the inner city as soon as they marry and can afford a family.
3. The "ethnic villages." Here immigrants or their descendants try to preserve the ways of the old country.
4. The "deprived." These are those who are too poor, too confused, or too defeated to leave the blighted streets.
5. The "trapped." These stay behind when their neighborhood is invaded by minority groups or poverty-stricken whites. Often they are small businessmen who are reluctant to leave a source of income that they have built up through many years of effort.[7]

The neglected parts of the city are generally called *slums*, and they have caused grave concern, not only on the part of city dwellers but of society in general. In our Northern and Far Western cities slum streets are fronted by solid rows of aging tenement houses with little or no open spaces, except dusty or overgrown empty lots. Sidewalks and alleys are littered and dirty. The bulging population suffers from high rates of crime, disease, and child mortality.

These districts have seen many different types of residents come and go. Some of the structures were at one time the spacious homes of the well-to-do. As the original owners moved away, the homes were partitioned off into small apartments. The more apartments to a building, the more rent could be collected.

Into these dwellings moved the masses of immigrants who landed on our shores up to the time of World War I. New arrivals moved into neighborhoods where their native language was spoken, hoping to find help and understanding. Thus were created the Little Italys, Chinatowns, Greek sections, Jewish sections, and many more ghettos.

Ghettos were once picturesque sections within the city that made newcomers welcome and gave them a feeling of belonging and an atmosphere of home. Walking through certain streets, a newcomer would be greeted by the aroma of old-country home cooking. He could read the signs over the stores and the newspapers sold on street corners. Relatives were close to one another and celebrated the familiar festivals in accustomed ways. But as time went on, the ghettos deteriorated into slums, the ugly neglected eyesores that dot our urban areas.

Slum life is not desirable for an indefinite length of time. Those who live there are either on the way up the ladder of success or on the way down. Most immigrants arrived poor and without skills. For many years they provided cheap labor for America's budding industries. But as their savings grew and they acquired new skills, they left the slums for more pleasant surroundings. Only the memory of the old-country ways remained, and they cherished it by gathering together, outside the slums, in numerous clubs and organizations.

As these quarters were vacated by early immigrant groups, they were taken over by blacks, Puerto Ricans, and Mexican-Americans. These people are migrant groups too, not from abroad though, but they are people trying to escape a life of sharecropping hunger, and Jim-Crow humiliation. This nonwhite migration is still swelling the population of our inner cities, while the proportion of whites there is decreasing. In 1930 almost three-fourths of the residents of Washington, D.C., were white. Currently more than one-half of the residents are nonwhite,[8] and over 90 percent of the pupils in the public schools are black.

Today the black ghetto is a place of frustration and trouble. The conditions of squalor are worsening, and blacks are being held down by discriminatory practices based on the difference in color. This difference is visible to all, and although, hopefully, the discriminatory practices may be done away with in time, the difference will not disappear as did the handicaps of European immigrants.

Ghettos, as we know them today, differ from other neighborhoods in that their inhabitants feel no pride in their homes, their blocks, or their streets. A ghetto dweller wishes to be somewhere else; he feels trapped in an atmosphere of poverty and degradation. Though ghetto apartments in many cases do not even meet minimum health standards, the rent is higher than in other sections. The ghetto resident is forced to pay these unjust prices, since barriers of discrimination prevent his moving to other neighborhoods. Private agreements exist between realtors and property owners not to sell or rent dwellings outside the ghetto areas to certain racial groups. Congress and the courts have outlawed such practices, but discrimination continues because the rules of fair housing are difficult to enforce.

Where black and white neighborhoods meet or overlap, violent resentment is not uncommon. Ethnic groups that have only recently moved up from the slums themselves are grimly determined to keep the blacks from following them. On the other hand, whites who remain behind, especially Jewish merchants, suffer from black bitterness.

Not every ghetto dweller is poor, but even the middle-class black may find himself tied to the slums because discrimination makes it difficult for him to find housing elsewhere. So he becomes part of the general disaffection that makes the street a meeting place by day and night, filled with easily excitable crowds.

SUBURBIA

Driving along in heavy traffic, you pass a sign that reads "Cleveland—City Limits." You continue beyond the sign, but the sights along the highway do not change. The city has grown beyond its official limits. As you drive on, tenements make way for neat one-family homes. Yards surround them, many adorned with slides, swings, and outdoor barbecues. You have arrived in the *suburbs*.

The suburb is a by-product of financial well-being and of the automobile. The great age of the suburb dates from the end of World War II. Young families whose income was rising wanted to combine the advantages of the city with the tranquility and friendliness of the country. The result is neither Broadway nor Pumpkin Hollow. The suburb has some rural features, but its life is mainly controlled by the city to which it is attached.

Suburbs are, to a large extent, "dormitory villages." Jobholders usually commute to the offices and factories of the city. During the working day suburbia is mostly a community of women and children, though wives are taking on jobs in increasing numbers. The streets are quiet until school is out, but here and there bustling new shopping centers with large parking lots interrupt the calm. Even small industrial plants have recently come to suburbia to stay. With these additions the cluster of homes is on its way to becoming a *satellite city*.

The critics of city life level their verbal guns especially at the suburb. They decry the snobbery of upper middle-class society. Families of equal status tend to keep together in neighborhoods with houses of equal cost. The urge to conform is very strong. Idle women meet for "coffee klatsch" to talk about trivial matters. The hilarity of evening cocktail parties is sometimes artificial. Some best-selling novels have made it appear as if alcoholism and wife swapping were common in suburbia.

Commuting is time consuming and nerve racking, and when the head of the household has finally put his car into the garage, he cannot relax because the lawn has to be mowed and the flower bed weeded. Appearances must be kept up, or the neighbors would talk.

More impartial observers of suburban life are far from dismayed. Dormitory villagers spend much time in their homes. They lavish attention on their children and on the schools that their children attend. These schools are often better staffed and better equipped than city schools. Neighbors are warm and friendly, exchanging visits informally. Car pools and shared baby-sitting make socializing easier.

Levittown, New Jersey, is a suburb near Philadelphia that was developed by a single builder and has since become the model for many similar communities. According to sociologist Herbert J. Gans, who lived there and studied its inhabitants thoroughly, Levittowners lead, for the most part, full and satisfying lives. A friendly atmosphere prevails, and there is much "neighboring" and mutual help; but conformity and competition for status symbols are not particularly strong. Rather than mindlessly copying each other, these suburbanites remain distinct individuals and follow their own interests. "To be sure, social life in Levittown has its costs, but these seem minor compared to its rewards."[9]

The suburb is growing at a faster rate than the general population of the United States, and it seems to have a magic attraction for young adults. When several hundred seniors at twenty universities were asked where they wanted to live, most named the suburbs even though living in the inner city would have meant more and quicker success in their careers.[10]

People don't overhaul their thoughts and feelings radically as soon as they move to the suburbs. They are very much the same people as they were in the city. "People who are family-oriented and value neighboring are attracted to the suburbs."[11] It is not the suburb—as is mistakenly thought—that makes them so.

Suburbia has ceased to be an exclusive playground for the white-collar middle class. Better-paid workingmen have left the cities and formed their own suburban communities. Bennett M. Berger studied a California suburb, inhabited mostly by workers in a Ford Motor Company plant nearby. He found that "their tastes and preferences seem untouched by the images of 'suburbia' portrayed in the mass media."[12] They like to watch Westerns and sports programs on television just as before. They are not "joiners" to a great extent, nor do they entertain much, even though they now live in more comfortable homes.

Actually there is no sharp dividing line between the outer residential sections of the city proper and its suburbs. Those city districts were the suburbs of yesterday, and present suburbs may become part of the city of tomorrow.

MEGALOPOLIS

A central city with all its suburbs forms a *metropolitan area*. Rapid population growth has resulted in many strange situations. The Chicago metropolitan area covers more than seventy-five communities, some within and others outside the city limits. As a city spreads, it makes suburbs out of rural communities and city districts out of suburbs. A sizable city may suddenly find itself demoted to being a suburb of an even bigger one. This is how Newark, New Jersey, was drawn into the shadow of New York City and Long Beach, California, became a satellite city of Los Angeles (see Figure 21).

The central city is stable or declining in population. Many citizens move outward because of congestion and the high cost of living. At the

Figure 21
Metropolitan Area

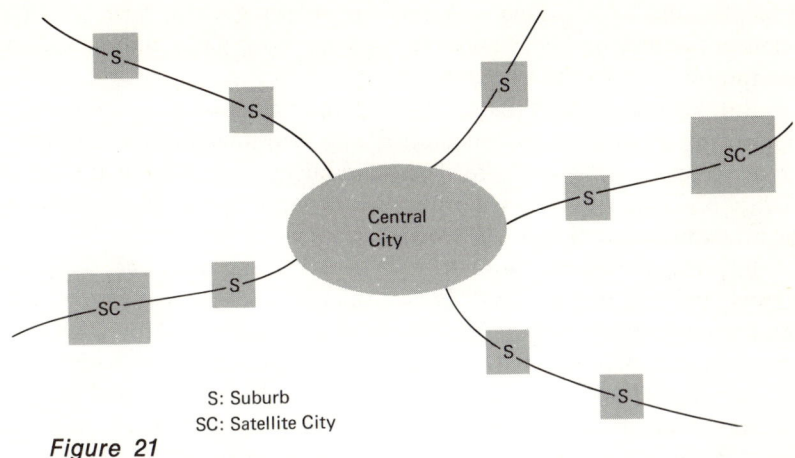

S: Suburb
SC: Satellite City

same time the metropolitan areas as a whole keep adding to the number of their residents. Between 1950 and 1960 the population in the central city grew by 9 percent, whereas that in the suburbs jumped by 48 percent.

The traveler today is unable to see where one metropolitan area ends and the next begins, and the result is *megalopolis*. (*Mega* is a Greek word meaning "huge." Scientists use it to indicate 1 million, as in megatons or megacycles.) The metropolitan areas blend into one another with hardly a break of open country. Villages, farms, and orchards succumb to the bulldozer and make way for housing developments linked by expressways and interchanges.

A prominent example of a megalopolis is the coastal strip from north of Los Angeles to San Diego. Another hugs the southern end of Lake Michigan from Milwaukee to Chicago, Gary, South Bend, and beyond. But the most formidable megalopolis extends along the Atlantic Coast from southern Maine to northern Virginia. It contains some 35 million people and includes the metropolitan areas of Boston, New York, Philadelphia, Baltimore, and Washington, D.C. Writers have referred to it as the "Main Street of America."

PLANNING

The more people that make up a community and the closer they live together, the more complications are likely to arise. To deal with urban problems—or, even better, to anticipate them before they arise—is the task of the planner.

Washington, D.C., the nation's capital, is a city that was planned before it was built. More recently, some suburban settlements and retirement communities have been totally planned before construction. If the job of planning is well done, it allows for orderly growth, takes into consideration the flow of traffic, and sets aside space for parks and recreational areas and for shopping and service areas.

But most cities existed long before planning became a possible means of improving them. Now we are saddled with foul-smelling waterfronts and narrow streets dating back to horse-and-buggy days. Industrial plants spewing obnoxious odors are interspersed with family dwellings, and unsightly junk heaps disfigure the roads.

In such situations planning can cure existing ills, but this is an extremely difficult undertaking. *Zoning* rules have to be worked out, often against the strong opposition of those who profit from existing conditions. The most commonly adopted zones are: central business, subbusiness, light and heavy industrial, multiple dwelling, and single family zones. In properly zoned cities factories and warehouses are located close to docks and railroad terminals. Apartment buildings where many elderly and single persons live are not far from the city center or from public transportation, and the homes of young families are grouped together in quiet districts where heavy traffic does not endanger the lives of children.

An extremely important phase of city planning is *urban renewal*, which attempts to rescue the blighted parts of the city. This means salvaging or replacing run-down slum buildings, adding playgrounds and medical facilities, and, together with these material improvements, developing among the residents a new pride in their neighborhood. Unfortunately urban renewal does not always accomplish what it sets out to do. In many instances it has replaced slum dwellings with high-rise apartment or office buildings without providing adequate new housing for the poor who have been displaced.

Planning in megalopolis involves cutting through innumerable boundaries of cities, towns, counties, and even states. It calls for the updating of building codes and labor-union restrictions, which often stand in the way of more efficient construction methods. Private efforts and public projects must be combined so that people of all income groups can live together in decent surroundings. This is a comparatively new endeavor that daily takes on added urgency. City and regional planning has become a very important profession that combines engineering skills with a sense of beauty and an understanding of human needs and relations.

Main Ideas
1. Bands of food gatherers and nomadic herdsmen formed the oldest communities.
2. People engaged in farming form rural communities.
3. Rural life is characterized by primary-group relationships.
4. Under the influence of modern technology the rural community is taking on features of urban life.
5. Types of rural communities are the open-country neighborhood, the hamlet, the village, and the town.

6. The city is a large community that offers specialized services and products of all kinds.
7. Comparatively small cities have existed for thousands of years, but the giant city of today arose with the coming of industrialization.
8. The city contains a heterogeneous population that is highly mobile.
9. Several ecological theories help account for the existence of different city districts that contain different social segments of the population.
10. In the blighted areas of the city, usually called slums, live socially disadvantaged people, belonging mainly to minority groups.
11. During the last quarter century there has been a tremendous rise in the suburbs, which are located within commuting distance of the central city.
12. Suburbanites try to combine the advantages of the city with the pleasures of rural life.
13. The large cities with their suburbs and satellite cities form huge metropolitan areas.
14. In several parts of the United States several metropolitan areas combine into a megalopolis.
15. City planning attempts to ensure orderly growth and satisfactory living conditions in the city.

Important Terms

Concentric Zones theory	Satellite city
Cosmopolitan	Sector theory
Ecology	Slum
Ghost town	Specialization
Heterogeneity	Subcommunity
Hamlet	Suburb
Horizontal mobility	Town
Megalopolis	Unincorporated community
Metropolitan area	Urbanization
Mobility	Urban renewal
Multiple Nuclei theory	Vertical mobility
Nomad	Village
Open-country neighborhood	Voluntary organization
Rural community	Zoning

Conclusion

Megalopolis will remain for some time to come. Increasingly it dominates society and gives direction to life in the nation and the world. Americans are attracted by the excitement and the opportunities of the city, yet they retain in their imaginations an idealized picture of rural peace and serenity. Therefore the continued migration into the suburbs and the rush into campsites and wilderness areas would appear to be an attempt on the part of the urban American to try to recapture some of the lost simplicity of rural life. Urban planners are searching for practical ways to combine the urban values that relentlessly impress themselves upon us with the rural values that are in retreat.

Notes
1. Joel M. Halpern, *The Changing Village Community* (Englewood Cliffs, N.J.: Prentice-Hall, 1967), pp. 9–12.
2. Lewis Mumford, *The Urban Prospect* (New York: Harcourt, Brace & World, 1968), p. 254.
3. John Sirjamaki, *The Sociology of Cities* (New York: Random House, 1964), p. 192.
4. Ernest W. Burgess, *The City* (Chicago: University of Chicago Press, 1925), pp. 47–62.
5. Homer Hoyt, *Structure and Growth of Residential Neighborhoods in American Cities* (Washington, D.C.: U.S. Government Printing Office, 1939).
6. C. D. Harris and E. L. Ullman, "The Nature of Cities," *Annals* 242 (November 1945), 14–16.
7. Herbert J. Gans, "Urbanism and Suburbanism as Ways of Life: A Reevaluation of Definitions," in Peter I. Rose (ed.), *The Study of Society* (New York: Random House, 1967), pp. 309–310.
8. Leo F. Schnore, *The Urban Scene* (New York: Free Press, 1965), p. 269.
9. Herbert J. Gans, *The Levittowners* (New York: Pantheon, 1967), p. 154.
10. David Riesman, "Suburban Attitudes," in C. E. Elias, J. Gillies, *et al.* (eds.), *Metropolis: Values in Conflict* (Belmont, Cal.: Wadsworth, 1964), p. 72.
11. Sylvia F. Fava, "Contrasts in Neighboring: New York City and a Suburban County," in Roland L. Warren (ed.), *Perspectives on the American Community* (Chicago: Rand McNally, 1966), pp. 161 ff.
12. Bennett M. Berger, *Working-Class Suburb: A Study of Auto Workers in Suburbia* (Berkeley and Los Angeles: University of California Press, 1968).

Suggestions for Further Reading
Aumente, J. "Ghetto Is People: Involving the Community in Planning," *Nation*, 205, November 27, 1967, 555–557.

"Can Today's Big Cities Survive?" *U.S. News*, 63, November 6, 1967, 54–58.

Cozzens, James Gould. *By Love Possessed.* New York: Harcourt, Brace & World, 1957. Novel portraying the social texture of an entire American community.

Dougherty, W. H. and J. A. Norton. "Urban Redoubt," *Saturday Review*, 51, January 13, 1968, 34 ff.

Ferry, W. H. "Blacktown and Whitetown: The Case for a New Federalism,"

Saturday Review, 51, June 15, 1968, 14–17. Discusses the need for black communities to establish their own institutions.

Isenberg, Irwin (ed.). *The City in Crisis*. Reference Shelf, Vol. XL, No. 1, 1968. Excerpts from newspapers, magazines, and speeches referring to the problems of slums and ghettos.

Michener, James A. *Caravans*. New York: Random House, 1963. Novel set in the nomadic society of Central Asia.

Mumford, Lewis. *The City in History: Its Origins, Its Transformation and Its Prospects*. New York: Harcourt, Brace & World, 1961.

Moore, Ruth. *The Walk Down Main Street*. New York: Morrow, 1960. Novel about small-town life and the importance of high-school athletics to the community.

Steinbeck, John. *East of Eden*. New York: Viking, 1952. Novel depicting country and small-town life at the turn of the century.

Whyte, William F. *Street Corner Society: The Social Structure of an Italian Slum*, 2nd ed. Chicago: University of Chicago Press, 1955.

> *For forms of government let fools contest;*
> *Whate'er is best administer'd is best.*
>
> —ALEXANDER POPE,
> An Essay on Man, 1733.

15 CAN YOU FIGHT CITY HALL?
how the community is run

LOCAL GOVERNMENT

What should we do about Red China? Can America feed the hungry millions of Africa and Asia? How many billions should we spend on the exploration of outer space?

These are fascinating questions to debate over a Coke or beer, on a picnic or by the warmth of a fireplace. They often sound more stimulating than an argument over whether or not a new sewer should be constructed across town or where a needed bridge should cross a river. Yet sewers and bridges, water mains and traffic lights, though less glamorous, affect you directly and personally every day. They are the concerns of local government (see Figure 22).

Local government means that decisions affecting the local community are made by the members of the community themselves. The federal government is farthest removed from the local scene. To many citizens it is represented as Uncle Sam, a nebulous busy distant relative who has very little time for his numerous nephews and nieces. The state capital is closer, but the local man still feels, "*They* are in charge, not *we*."

But whether the resident of the local community realizes it or not, state government has a great influence on the local scene. In the United States it is the privilege of the state legislature to *create* local governments and determine what they can or cannot do. Originally the state formed counties, granted and revoked city charters, and passed *ordinances*, which are the

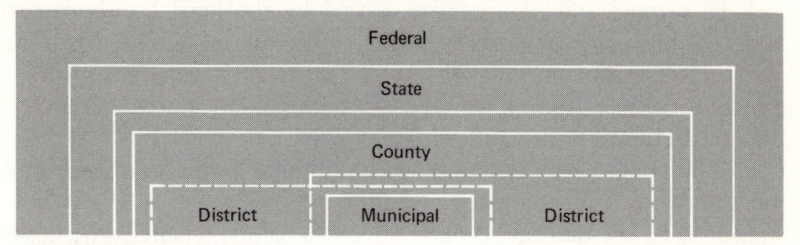

Figure 22
Areas of Government

legal rules by which a community operates. Only since the end of the last century has local government assumed an increasingly independent role, and state officials now seem less likely to interfere with town or city business.

America is a big country, and its great size has provided it with many advantages. But size has its disadvantages too. In the 1968 presidential election 73,186,819 votes were cast. This is a vast number of votes. In a mass society such as ours the individual may, at times, feel that he doesn't count. "What difference does it make," you may ask, "whether I vote or not? Why bother to express an opinion at all?" This attitude is not a responsible one in a democracy, but it is understandable considering the masses of people around you.

Personal involvement is difficult on the national level. But when you have complaints about the police department or about confusing street signs, it is comparatively easy to see a local official about the difficulties. You may even know some of these officials personally, and you can attend open hearings or public council and commissioners' meetings. Thus it is in the local community that the citizen can more easily retain a sense of participation. His voice can be heard. In many a neighborhood election a few votes, even a single vote, have determined the outcome.

WHAT LOCAL GOVERNMENT DOES

Your daily routine is affected by the actions and rulings of local government, and the more urban your area of residence is, the more rules there are. As we rush through our activities, we are hardly aware of these rules unless something goes wrong.

The house or apartment building where you live was constructed according to standards that your city or county required the builder to meet. *Building codes* vary from one community to another. The differences result from the various attempts to reconcile the safety and comfort of the tenant with the financial interests of the builder.

The pleasure of eating out in a restaurant may be heightened by your knowledge that certain health standards must be maintained in the kitchen and dining room. Local government checks the quality of the food and the sanitary conditions of the kitchen. Eating places that fall below standards will be warned and, if necessary, closed by the local health department unless public officials are lax in enforcing the rules. Likewise, when we turn on a faucet, we assume that the water that runs out is safe for drinking. It probably comes from a county or metropolitan water system that is supervised by the health authorities.

If a street becomes bumpy with potholes, local officials will probably be showered with complaints, and, sooner or later, a repair crew will appear to fix the damage. Broken sidewalks will be repaired whether or not the property owner consents, and the cost of the repair is then *assessed* against the property that borders the sidewalk.

Fire and police protection have long been the responsibility of local government. The more motor vehicles there are congesting our streets, the more traffic control has to be exerted. Many cities maintain *municipal* parking lots and employ specially trained *traffic engineers.*

So many instruments in home, office, and factory are now powered by electricity that life virtually comes to a standstill when electrical current ceases to flow. Many cities operate their own electrical systems, or the current is provided for several communities by a *public utility district* that has its own elected governing board.

Often, when you apply for a job, you must show a birth certificate. Proof of age is also required when you register to vote or when you want to obtain a driver's license. The clerk's office in the county courthouse is where you must go to get a certified copy of your birth certificate. The courthouse also keeps records of property sales, supervises elections, and issues licenses to drivers and to those who operate businesses or practice certain professions.

These are only examples of the many activities in which local governments engage, and the list seems to be growing as our culture becomes more urban and more complex.

TYPES OF LOCAL GOVERNMENT

On a Sunday drive into the quiet countryside you are likely to pass signs such as this:

```
FOUR CORNERS
UNINCORPORATED
POP. 123
```

When a neighborhood like Four Corners grows to a more imposing size, it will petition the state for a *charter,* which, in legal terms, makes it a *municipal corporation.* The charter grants permission to set up some kind of local self-government.

We have already encountered the terms "village," "town," and "city" (see Chapter 14). These terms denote different types of communities according to the size of their populations. Several states (Pennsylvania, Connecticut, New Jersey, and Alaska) call their municipal corporations *boroughs*.

In most states the *county* is the major unit of local government. One difficulty in studying local politics is that a term may have different meanings in different parts of the country, and various names may be applied to the same units. Louisiana calls its counties *parishes*, and in the New England states counties are less important than towns as areas of local government.

Our needs have become so many and complex that the traditional county and municipal governments cannot fill them anymore. Almost everywhere in the United States we now find, in addition, special district governments. Best known probably is the local school district, which may extend over one or several communities. An elected school board makes the decisions.

A list of all the special districts that perform certain services would be very lengthy. There are drainage districts, weed-control districts, dike-improvement districts, library districts, cemetery districts, and many more. Clark County in the state of Washington, which is a medium-sized county with a population of 125,000, has 45 governmental units supervised by 227 elected officials.[1]

TYPES OF CITY GOVERNMENT

Since the major social problems of our time seem to be concentrated in the city, the quest for the best-functioning and most up-to-date form of city government is an extremely vital one.

Do you really know what goes on in City Hall? Not too many people do. And it is unusual to find the person who is familiar with the make-up of government in neighboring cities. The fault lies not so much with the ignorance of the individual citizen as with the bewildering variety of governmental systems. "There are probably no two cities in the United States that have exactly the same structure of government."[2]

The *mayor-council* form of city government is the most commonly found type. It appears in two main variations, the *strong* and the *weak* mayor-council systems. When the mayor, like the President of the United States, is the only elected official who has the power to appoint and dismiss his assistants, we speak of a strong mayor-council type.

In cities having weak mayor-council governments, the voters elect some officials, while the city council appoints others. Often the council members select one from their own midst to act as mayor. In this case the mayor is not much more than a moderator at meetings and a figurehead, who cuts ribbons and welcomes visiting celebrities.

When large cities have strong mayor-council governments, the mayor often becomes a nationally noted political figure. In more than one instance the mayoralty has been used as a stepping stone to higher political positions.

The *commission form*, which provides for the election of a city council that forms the legislative body, seems to have declined in popularity. But besides being legislators, members of the city council also act as commissioners; they direct various administrative departments such as the departments of public safety, public health, parks and recreation. Thus they combine executive with legislative functions.

More and more political scientists agree that running a governmental

Figure 23
Types of City Government

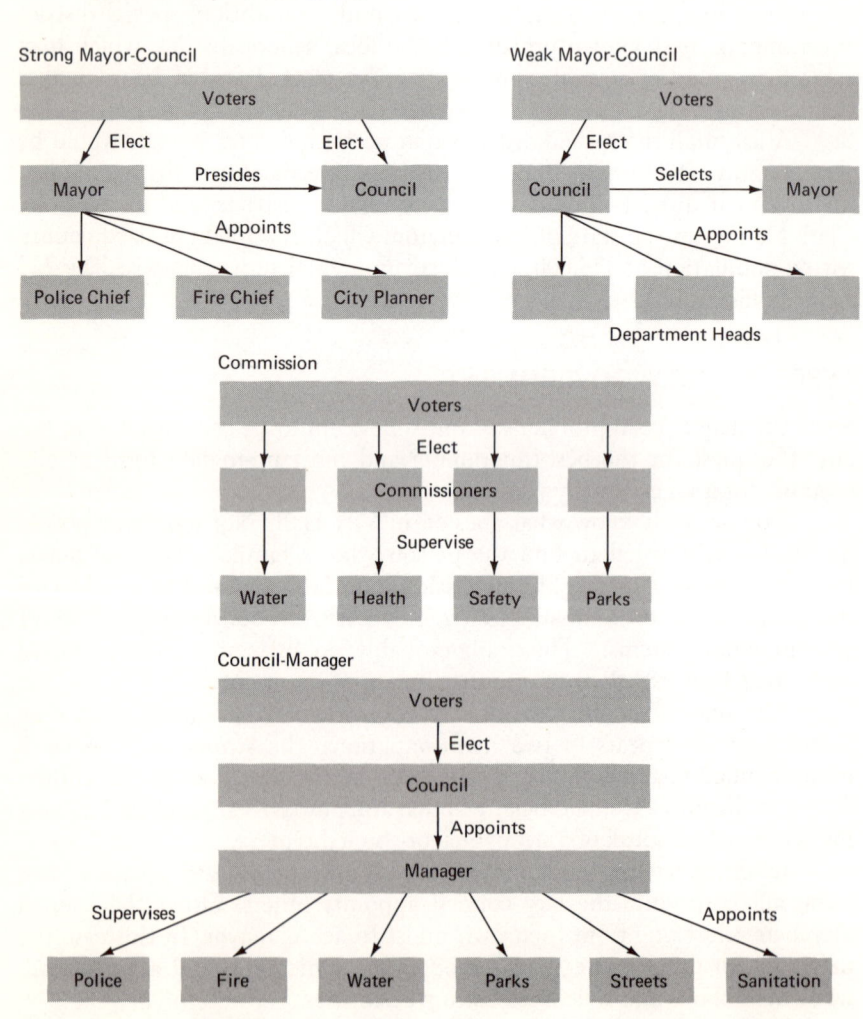

unit requires professional training. When a city council is elected and a specially trained executive is hired, the result is the *council-manager* form, which has become increasingly prevalent in recent decades. The legislative body, which is the elected city council, makes overall decisions and hires a city manager to carry them out. The city manager also supervises all other employees of the city.

Compared with the city, the county seems to have more difficulty in modernizing its governmental practices. Usually the county government is in the hands of an elected board of commissioners or supervisors. Following the pattern of the city, counties are now beginning to use county managers, who are appointed by elected officials to whom they must answer in performing their jobs. Figure 23 illustrates the three main types of city government.

PROBLEMS OF LOCAL GOVERNMENT

Local government is becoming increasingly complex. Difficulties arise faster than cures can be found. This trend is reflected in the huge number of books and articles being published on urban problems. Even many universities and colleges have introduced special programs on urban affairs.

The overlapping of governmental agencies is especially a headache, because it duplicates human efforts and costs the taxpayer unnecessary money. "Such fragmentation is sapping the strength of local government. No citizen, no matter how civic-minded, can inform himself of the affairs of a dozen or more local governments."[3] The responsibility of dealing with urgent issues, such as traffic congestion and air pollution, is divided, and needed action is subsequently slowed down. Government that is complicated and split "cannot respond to major problems which ignore its boundary lines. Time, energy and money are being wasted."[4]

It has happened that a sprawling city has completely surrounded patches of unincorporated county land. Several such unincorporated "islands" can be found deep inside Los Angeles. The residents of these bypassed areas use city services, but their property is taxed at a much lower rate. The taxpayers inside the city limits have to make up the difference.

The burgeoning suburbs contribute to the financial plight of the inner city. Suburbanites use city streets and city transportation. They read in city libraries and attend city concerts, but they pay taxes only to their own suburban governments. On the other hand, slum dwellers living in the city cannot afford the high taxation that is needed to provide funds for rebuilding slum neighborhoods.

Different *ordinances* apply to different areas. This segmentation hampers planning, and sometimes it also allows criminals of all kinds to avoid prosecution by simply crossing some local boundary line. Often gambling and prostitution rackets foil the urban police by operating unhampered beyond the city limits.

Such loopholes could easily be plugged if a whole metropolitan area were to function under a single governmental structure. This has been widely advocated and even attempted in a few places, for example, in St. Louis, Miami, and Cleveland. A unified metropolitan government would need only one mayor, one chief of police, one chief planner, and so forth. An obstacle to this reform is that none of the numerous little town and county officials are eager to give up their jobs and imposing titles. "Rarely are any units of government, elected positions or political jobs eliminated."[5]

What about "crooked politicians," who are the objects of much anger on the part of citizens? Probably the average holder of a political job is just as honest as the average jobholder in other walks of life, only the temptations in his line of work are more numerous. Most of us will leave a coin at the unmanned corner newspaper stand even when nobody is around to watch us. But quite a few will use the opportunity to get something for nothing. Among public officials too we will find freeloaders here and there; only in their case the take is higher than a free newspaper. It may amount to substantial gifts for seeing that the contract for a road-repair job is awarded to a friend, that a liquor license is granted a particular restaurant owner, or that some offense against the building code is conveniently overlooked. But in contrast to the private chiseler the public officeholder who accepts graft must face exposure by the press and ultimately by the public if he is caught.

In the past public servants had to be independently wealthy because public office paid very little or nothing. This made politics the privilege of a few. Low pay is no longer a problem, to a large extent, but traces of it still linger in the comparatively low salaries of local officeholders. Many state legislatures pay their elected representatives no salary but only *per diem* (Latin "for the day") expenses while the legislature is in session. Most able and honest people cannot afford to leave their jobs and run for public office.

Of those who do choose politics some fall victim to corruption. City governments have been known to come under the influence of special interests, in a few instances, even that of organized crime. The voter becomes disillusioned when his needs are neglected. He sadly resigns himself to the conclusion that "you can't fight City Hall." Most students of the political scene feel that we have better and more honest government today than ever before but that the situation is far from ideal. Part of the incentive in attracting competent people to serve efficiently in the public interest is to make the income high enough to be worth their time and training.

Low income is not the only deterrent for a man with political ambitions. Should he want to run for an elective office, he must consider the expenses of campaigning long before he has any chance of drawing a salary. And these expenses are mounting continuously.

When the student body of a school or the membership of a local club holds an election, the candidates don't have to buy time on television or space in the newspaper. They can present themselves to their voters free of charge. But a candidate for the office of sheriff in Montgomery County, Maryland, estimated the cost of his campaign would run close to $25,000, more than a year's salary.

Compare this with the conditions in an earlier period: "In 1846, Abraham Lincoln's friends gave him $200 to finance his campaign for Congress. The victorious Lincoln was able to return $199.25. His entire expense had been seventy-five cents for a barrel of cider."[6] Today a race for Congress may cost in the neighborhood of $100,000 and very often much more. That makes it hard and sometimes impossible for good people of modest financial means to run for public office.

Several foreign countries have laws limiting the amounts that political candidates may spend on their campaigns. We also have federal, as well as state-wide, restrictions, but too many loopholes remain.

THE FIFTY STATES

If City Hall is much closer to the people than the state capital, then, by the same reasoning, the state government is closer than the federal government. There was a time when the major loyalty of the American people was to their states and only vaguely to the Union. Even today feelings run high on the issue of states' rights. Some people express exaggerated pride in their state, and this attitude has given ammunition to innumerable jokes. For example, the fictitious Texan of cartoons and quips is convinced that his state has wider deserts, richer millionaires, faster horses, and more dangerous outlaws than any other place.

Though the federal government has steadily expanded its power and taken over many functions that once exclusively belonged to the states, such as supervision of the foods and drugs we consume, state government today is more important than ever. It is engaging in new activities that are increasingly felt in the daily lives of its citizens.[7] State troopers police our highways and try to make safe drivers out of the men and women behind the wheels. State parks beckon to picnickers and campers, and state schools teach the blind, the deaf, and the retarded.

Each state has a constitution of its own. Strangely enough, the state constitutions are frequently less flexible than our Federal Constitution, a condition that handicaps the smooth functioning of the state governments. Many state constitutions are unnecessarily long; for example, the state constitution of Louisiana is over thirty times longer than that of the federal government. Their length indicates that these documents go into minute details that become easily outdated. But once a constitution has been adopted, it is very difficult to amend or replace it. The procedures for such steps are costly and complicated.

Another very serious problem that the states must face is the unevenness of representation. Not every member of a state legislature represents the same number of citizens. When these lawmaking bodies were first established, America was a rural country. The populations of the various voting districts were then about equal. But as large cities arose and the voting districts remained the same, the densely populated urban areas were easily outvoted in the legislative halls of the state capitols by the representatives from the countryside. Rural politicians have fiercely resisted any redistricting for fear of domination by city-run "machine politics." In Tennessee the district boundaries were not changed between 1901 and 1961 with the result that "37% of the voters elected 61% of the senators, and 40% of the voters elected 64% of the representatives" to the state legislature.[8]

In 1962 an attempt was finally made to remedy iniquities such as this when the United States Supreme Court ordered state legislatures to *reapportion* legislative districts. But it is not easy to eradicate old injustices. Some legislatures have been in the habit of drawing district boundary lines in such a way that most opposition votes were concentrated in one area. The ruling party could then easily win in the surrounding districts. By means of this method, called *gerrymandering,* a minority of voters actually elected a majority of representatives. This scheme has also been used to keep racial minority groups from having equal representation.

The states have various elected officials. Their number and kind varies from state to state. The voters usually elect a governor and lieutenant governor, an attorney general, a treasurer, an auditor, and, in many instances, a state superintendent of schools. State judges are also elected, often on a *nonpartisan ballot,* that is, without regard to party affiliation.

More and more the governor emerges as the prime mover of action in the state. He is assuming greater power and increased responsibility, and he rules over a complicated bureaucracy.

FINANCING STATE AND LOCAL GOVERNMENT

As families need to budget their incomes and expenditures, so must governments. People are demanding more services from their city and state governments, all of which cost money. We pay for these services with our taxes.

Types of Taxes

Income tax	Inheritance tax
Property tax	License fee
Sales tax	Tolls
Occupation tax	Fines
Corporation tax	

The most common source of revenue on the local level is the property tax. Taxes on real estate are very common, but other kinds of personal property are also subject to taxation, depending on the particular locality. One community taxes boats, another pianos.

Thirty-eight states, the District of Columbia, and a number of cities—as well as the federal government, of course—levy income taxes. A resident of Flint, Michigan, for example, pays income taxes to the city, the state and the federal government. Income tax is labeled *progressive* when it is based on an individual's ability to pay. The higher an individual's income is, the greater his rate of taxation. Many men in politics consider this the fairest method of exacting revenue from taxpayers.

Sales taxes, however, which are levied by most states and by many communities are criticized as *regressive*, which means they hit the poor harder than the rich. A 4 percent tax on the purchase price of clothing or shoes takes a bigger slice out of the laborer's pay than out of the executive's salary.

When pinched for income, public officials find more items to tax. Corporation, business, and occupational taxes are now fairly common. So are taxes on liquor, cigarettes, and gasoline. The license fees required of automobile and dog owners and the tolls collected from the users of bridges and expressways are also taxes. When a small community sets up a "speed trap" for unsuspecting motorists, collecting the imposed fines is another way of boosting the town finances.

Like going to the dentist, paying taxes is unpleasant but necessary. The inevitable grumbling of the taxpayer can be kept to a minimum though if he is satisfied that his money is being spent wisely and honestly and that he is being taxed fairly and equitably.

VOTING

In a free society all governmental action should, in the final analysis, depend on the vote of its citizens. This is a principle with which not many of us will argue. Yet the democratic process depends, to a large degree, on the mechanics of voting.

How is voting carried out? Who is entitled to vote? Who counts the votes and by what method? Only by having the answers to these questions can we determine whether a truly democratic spirit prevails in the more than 91,000 government units found in the United States.

State and local governments collaborate in carrying out the voting process. The states determine the requirements for voting; however, the counties handle voter registration, actual voting during elections, and counting of the ballots.

In 1965 Congress intervened in local voting procedures by passing the Voting Rights Act, which was designed mainly to protect the right of black citizens to the ballot. Up to that time most Southern blacks had been prevented from registering as voters. Violence or the fear of violent reprisals, poll taxes, and tricky examinations designed to trip would-be voters, had kept the black population away from the polls. With the help of the new law civil-rights volunteers encouraged the frightened blacks to register for the first time. In subsequent elections the impact of the black vote began to make itself felt. This brings us closer to the realization of the idea that all citizens must be able to participate in elections.

Still some restrictions exist and will probably continue to exist. One concerns having a criminal record, another the length of residence of a citizen.[9] Convicted felons lose the right to vote, and newcomers to a community in a different state don't gain the right to vote until they have lived in the state or community or both a certain length of time. To get on the voters' roll in the state of Washington, for example, a citizen must have resided one year in the state and six months in one particular community.

A much debated question is that of the minimum age required for voting. Shouldn't a young man who is old enough to fight for his country also be allowed to cast his ballot? In most states a person cannot vote until he has reached the age of twenty-one. This figure seems arbitrary, but it is accepted not only in the United States but also in many other countries. Recently the pressure for the lowering of the voting age has been growing as young people have become more involved in the political process. In 1970, eighteen-year-olds in England voted for the first time, and in 1972, eighteen-year-olds in this country will vote for federal officials.

What is the voting procedure? The membership of a club can be polled by a show of hands. If this becomes too cumbersome, slips of paper are distributed and then counted by hand. Some electoral districts still use this slow and expensive method. In the nineteenth century several days were required to obtain final election returns. Today we have voting machines, and most recently a computerized punch-card system has been introduced to speed up the balloting.

Today we take secret voting for granted. Actually this method of safeguarding electoral freedom is of fairly recent origin. Australia led the way in 1856 by making sure that nobody could check on how a particular person voted, and the "Australian ballot" was quickly adopted in America.

Compare the freedom of our voting booths with the situation in Russia. A ballot with only one name is distributed, and this is what happens:

> . . . if the voter wishes to do so, he can retire to a partitioned area, cross out the candidate's name (he is not permitted to write in another name), fold his ballot so that no one can tell what he has done, and drop it in the ballot box. If he approves of the candidate on the ballot, he merely drops his ballot in the box.[10]

In the view of Americans or others accustomed to the democratic process, Russians don't have enough opportunity to indicate their choice through voting. But we also hear complaints about too much voting—that is, when citizens are asked to decide on too many issues and too many

"Board of Elections Meets Here"
Laurence B. Fink from Nancy Palmer Photo Agency

candidates at the same time. "In one case a ballot was twelve feet long and contained almost five hundred names."[11] No wonder we refer to such a ballot as a *long ballot*. It is an arduous task to mark such a sheet, which may contain the names of candidates for federal, state, county, city, and various local offices in addition to perhaps a dozen tax measures and a sizable number of initiative and referendum decisions. The *referendum* and the *initiative* enable the voter to approve or disapprove or initiate laws through his ballot. They are instruments of direct democracy (see Chapter 16).

The job of choosing among the various candidates and issues on an excessively long ballot is frustrating and confusing to say the least. It becomes almost impossible to make intelligent and meaningful choices. How can the average citizen know which candidate would make the best sheriff, coroner, judge, assessor, park superintendent, tree warden, and so forth? Many voters do not have the slightest notion of what qualifications are required by some of these offices, nor do they know whether Mr. Brown is better qualified than Mr. Green. Yet county governments in particular have kept the long ballot, using the justification that the more officials that are directly elected by the people, the more democracy we have.

Most political scientists, however, believe in the superiority of the *short ballot*. They believe that officeholders who must make policy decisions should be elected by and be responsible to the people. But sheriffs, coroners, assessors, and other officials who must carry out policy decisions might better be chosen by the elected policy makers according to their professional skills.

Main Ideas

1. The actions of local government vitally affect the life of every citizen.
2. The citizen has many opportunities to influence the functioning of local government.
3. Some of the functions of local government are concerned with the supervision of construction, eating places, street traffic, fire and police protection, water supply and electricity, and with the keeping of records.
4. The types of local government vary from place to place. It is becoming increasingly prevalent for elected officials to hire trained professionals to carry out administrative work.
5. Local government suffers from the overlapping of political boundaries in metropolitan areas.
6. The high cost of campaigning and the low salaries paid to public officials offer temptations to corruption.
7. Difficulties in the governing of states arise from outdated state constitutions and from the unevenness of representative districts.

8. Increased government services must be financed by a growing list of taxes, license fees, tolls, and fines.
9. Good government distributes the tax burden fairly among its citizens.
10. The democratic system aims at a free and secret vote for all eligible citizens.
11. The short ballot seems to be more meaningful than the long ballot; it enables the voters to elect the policymakers who, in turn, hire competent administrators.

Important Terms

Assessment	Municipal corporation
Borough	Nonpartisan ballot
Building code	Parish
Charter	Per diem
Commission form of government	Progressive tax
Council-manager form of government	Public utility district
County	Reapportionment
Gerrymandering	Referendum
Initiative	Regressive tax
Long ballot	Short ballot
Mayor-council form of government	Traffic engineer

Conclusion

The nature of local and state government is changing. Blacks and other minority groups are demanding—and getting—a voice in making governmental decisions. Issues, such as unemployment, urban renewal, and riot control, are of direct concern to these groups. In 1965 when Robert C. Henry was elected mayor of Springfield, Ohio, he became the first black mayor of a fair-sized American city in this century. Similar election victories have taken place in Cleveland, Ohio, Gary, Indiana, and Newark, New Jersey. Strong efforts are being made to come to grips with community problems on the local level. Reform is difficult and slow, but changes are taking place. Local and state governments are most responsive to the needs of the people when they are aware of what government can do and what it is supposed to do. Each individual citizen should be informed, interested, and actively participating in the political life of the local and the wider community.

Notes

1. *Clark County, Washington, Directory*, 1968–1969, Foreword.
2. Charles R. Adrian, *Governing Urban America* (New York: McGraw-Hill, 1955), p. 173.

3. Michael N. Danielson, *Metropolitan Politics* (Boston: Little, Brown, 1966), p. 128.
4. *Ibid.*, p. 129.
5. *Ibid.*, p. 155.
6. W. Ebenstein and E. W. Mill, *American Government in the Twentieth Century* (Morristown, N.J.: Silver Burdett, 1968), p. 259.
7. A good discussion of local government can be found in Ebenstein and Mill, *ibid.*, pp. 514–595.
8. "Baker v. Carr, 1962," in John Vanderzell (ed.), *The Supreme Court and American Government* (New York: Crowell, 1968), pp. 29–30.
9. H. A. Bone and A. Ranney, *Politics and Voters*, 2nd ed. (New York: McGraw-Hill, 1967), pp. 6–8.
10. Austin Ranney, *The Governing of Men*, 5th ed. (New York: Holt, Rinehart and Winston, 1966), p. 306.
11. J. M. Burns and J. W. Peltason, *Government by the People*, 6th ed. (Englewood Cliffs, N.J.: Prentice-Hall, 1966), p. 339.

Suggestions for Further Reading

Adrian, Charles R. *Governing Our Fifty States and Their Communities.* New York: McGraw-Hill, 1967. Good discussion of federal, state, and local government.

Book of the States. Chicago: Council of State Governments. Published biannually. Current information concerning organization and activities of state government.

Danielson, Michael N. (ed.). *Metropolitan Politics: A Reader.* Boston: Little, Brown, 1966.

Municipal Yearbook. Chicago: International City Managers' Association. Published annually. Excellent source of information on local government.

Vanderzell, John (ed.). *The Supreme Court and American Government.* New York: Crowell, 1968. A collection of the most important Supreme Court decisions.

Wilson, James Q. "A Guide to Reagan Country," *Commentary*, 43 (May 1967), 37–45. Witty and informative study of the political culture of southern California as contrasted with northern California and other parts of the nation.

Much insight into the working of local government can also be gained through local newspapers and local radio and television reports.

A democracy is the worst possible form of government; except for all the others.
—WINSTON CHURCHILL,
Politics and Politicians

16 WE, THE PEOPLE
the democratic community

"Politics is not for me." Statements to this effect are heard all too often. Usually they are coupled with some unkind words about "politicians," a nasty species of crooked, lying, and grasping individuals. Actually, the men in politics are as varied as the members of any other group. And politics *is* for you, whether you want it or not. It is for you, for your neighbor, for everybody in the local community and in the nation.

Politics is everywhere. It is in your daily newspaper, on radio and television. It comes as a notice in the mail from your draft board, a bill for back taxes that you owe the government, or as a check from the welfare department. Because politicians are at work—and provided they are effective and honest—you can be reasonably sure that the food you buy in a grocery store is not poisonous and that a glue factory will not be built across the street from your home.

In short, politics influences our lives day in, day out. We are invariably affected by the multitude of laws and ordinances that are passed and by the way they are enforced. To study the mechanism and principles of politics and the way in which political power is distributed is the task of the *political scientist.*

Elements of Democracy
Rule of law
Guaranteed individual freedom
Participation
Majority rule with respect for minorities

WHAT IS DEMOCRACY?

Most Americans pride themselves on their democratic system of government but would find it difficult to give an exact definition of *democracy*. Probably the best short and very general description would be Abraham Lincoln's famous words from the Gettysburg Address, "Government of the people, by the people and for the people."

Democracy (Greek for "rule by the people") was practiced more than 2,000 years ago by the Athenians, but Plato and Aristotle, the great Greek thinkers, found fault with it. Plato described democracy as "a state in which the poor, gaining the upper hand, kill some and banish others, and then divide the offices among the remaining citizens equally, usually by lot."[1]

Obviously Plato's description of democracy is not what modern defenders of the idea have in mind. Even today the term is subject to much abuse. Dictators, such as President "Papa Doc" Duvalier of Haiti, often justify their brutal authoritarian rule by retaining a few democratic trappings for show. Dictators who rig elections or put a parliament of yes men through the motions of approving their edicts hardly ever fool anybody. This is not democracy, for the term clearly means that the people must have some voice in the way they are governed.

Plato is by no means the only spokesman of an older time who distrusted the democratic idea. In fact, during most of history, the idea that the very few were born to dictate and the vast majority to obey was seen as natural. In the seventeenth century King Louis XIV of France is reputed to have proclaimed, *"L'état, c'est moi"* ("I am the State"). He, like most contemporary monarchs, was an *absolute ruler,* and he justified his unrestricted power by the idea of the "divine right of kings." The right to rule was derived directly from God. Crowned heads were responsible only to God for their actions, not to any human law.

During the eighteenth century the divine-right idea was shattered by new ideas that were pronounced by a number of forward-looking writers who named their time the Age of Enlightenment. The Frenchman Jean Jacques Rousseau and the Englishman John Locke stated that all government is based on a contract between the ruler and the ruled. Each party to the contract must live up to his obligations. If the ruler does not live up to his obligations, he breaks the contract, and the people are no longer bound by it. The people then have the right to create a new government that will adhere to the contract and consider the welfare of the citizens. Soon these ideas were put to the test in two revolutions that shook the world. The American Revolution (1775–1781) laid the foundation for the independent United States of America, and the revolution in France (1789–1799) toppled the absolute government that arrogant kings had created.

The founding fathers of the revolutionary movement in America were determined to get away from the absolute rule of one man, whatever his title. Moved by the ideas of Rousseau, Locke, and others, they wanted to try out new forms of government that came closer to the ideal of democracy. The Declaration of Independence (1776) states: "We hold these Truths to be self-evident, that all Men are created equal, that they are endowed by their Creator with certain unalienable Rights, that among these are Life, Liberty, and the Pursuit of Happiness . . ." After the revolution had achieved its goal, the Constitution of the United States was written. It begins with the words "We the People . . ." This indicates the ideal. Now what about the practical application? Who are "the people" of whom, by whom, and for whom government is supposed to exist? In 1787, when the Federal Constitution took effect, "the people" meant mainly white adult males who owned property; and even their rights were not clearly spelled out. Democracy in the new country was only skin-deep.

As America gained more experience in shaping its own destiny, the democratic character of the nation was gradually strengthened. This process is not yet completed. The continuing democratization of our political life is expressed by the twenty-five amendments to the Constitution, enacted between 1791 and 1967, and in various acts of Congress.

The first ten amendments, usually called the Bill of Rights, ensure the personal freedom of the citizen from arbitrary and oppressive governmental interference. Amendments Thirteen, Fourteen, and Fifteen prohibit slavery and grant every American political equality, regardless of "race, color, or previous condition of servitude." It was not till 1920, with the enactment of the Twentieth Amendment, that women also received the right to vote.

Despite constitutional guarantees of political equality various minority groups have been kept from exercising their rights as citizens. It required the special Civil Rights Act, passed by Congress in 1964, to reaffirm in no uncertain terms that black citizens also had the right to vote. Slowly and against strong opposition the principle of democracy is being translated into actuality.

When we try to pinpoint what democracy *is*, we should not forget to state what it is *not*. Democracy, which is a political system, is often confused with an economic system, such as *capitalism* or *socialism*. Great Britain's economy is partially socialistic. Coal mines, railroads, and one of the radio and television networks are owned and operated by the government. In our country these economic activities are in the hands of private enterprise, though they are subject to various forms of governmental supervision and regulation. The two countries' economic systems differ, but the British political system is at least as democratic as ours. We must keep in mind that a wide variety of economic practices can exist under a democratic regime, and democracy itself appears in many different shapes and forms.

TYPES OF DEMOCRATIC SYSTEMS

If you belong to a club or to a religious or civic organization, you know that certain rules are needed to carry on the business of the organization. These rules, or guidelines, concern the making of decisions, selection of officers, handling of finances, and so forth. Often these guidelines are written down, but in many instances they are simply understood by the members.

A nation embodies such rules in a constitution.

> Every state, regardless of its form of government, must operate under some kind of basic or constitutional rules. Without such rules, a state would be torn apart by *anarchy* or paralyzed by total uncertainty as to where authority lies and what the limits of individual action are.[2]

The British constitution is unwritten. There exists no single document comparable to the American Constitution. England draws its rules of government from several great documents of the past, such as the *Magna Charta*, and also from parliamentary and court decisions and from customs handed down through the generations. Customs are often as important to nations as written charters.

The written constitutions of many Latin American countries are beautiful statements of ideals, but the actions of the leaders are not based on them. A democratic constitution does not always guarantee a democratic government. Russia grants its citizens freedom of expression on paper but often imprisons writers who criticize the country's leaders.

A government, whether democratic or not, can be *federal* or *unitary*. In a federal system, such as we have in the United States, the political power is divided between the national government and the various levels of local government: state, county, and city. A unitary national government has total power; it may or may not grant some power to local units as it wishes. The governments of France and Denmark exemplify the unitary system (see the discussion on the differences between local and centralized control of schools in Chapter 12).

Democracies may be *monarchies* or *republics*. They can also favor either *presidential* or *parliamentary* rule. A monarchic government is headed by a king who inherits his office by being born into a royal family. Great Britain, Sweden, and Norway are monarchies, but they are also parliamentary democracies. The monarch is a figurehead or national symbol with little or no political power.

In a republic we find either a presidential or a parliamentary system.

the democratic community **313**

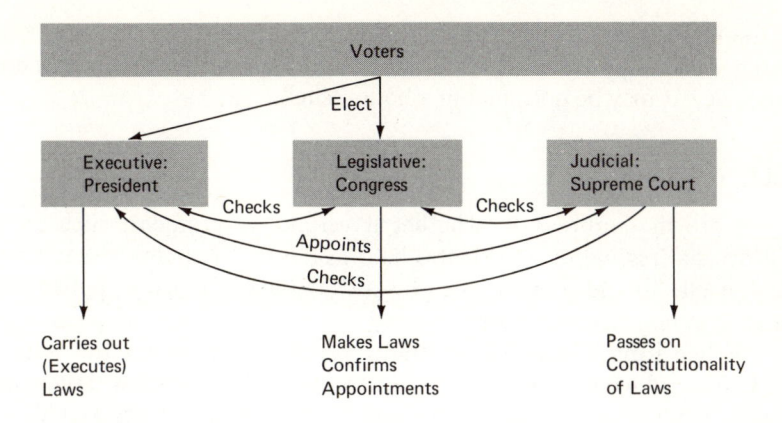

Figure 24
Presidential System

[Diagram: Voters Elect Executive: President, Legislative: Congress, Judicial: Supreme Court. Congress Checks Executive. Executive Checks Congress. President Appoints Supreme Court. Supreme Court Checks President and Congress. Executive Carries out (Executes) Laws. Legislative Makes Laws, Confirms Appointments. Judicial Passes on Constitutionality of Laws.]

The United States has a presidential system in which the *executive power* is separated from the *legislative power*. In this country the *judicial power* is also separate, and the three branches of government operate under an arrangement of *checks and balances* (see Figure 24).

Great Britain, Canada, and West Germany provide examples of the parliamentary system. The voters elect the members of a parliament that combines both the legislative and executive functions. The chief administrator of the government, called a *prime minister* or *premier,* usually heads the majority party and is an elected member of parliament. He must answer to parliament for his actions. Often the judicial function is also under the supervision of the lawmakers (see Figure 25).

One should not be deceived by names. In many countries, such as Spain, East Germany, and Russia, we find what appears to be a legislative body, whether it is called parliament or congress or Supreme Soviet. However, some of these bodies are often nothing but a captive audience

Figure 25
Parliamentary System

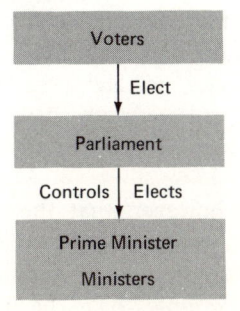

[Diagram: Voters Elect Parliament. Parliament Controls and Elects Prime Minister and Ministers.]

for the real leaders. "Their function is to listen rather than debate."[3] The existence of a supposedly representative assembly is not a sure indication of democracy; it may be nothing but a hollow shell.

RULE OF LAW

If you are in doubt as to whether a certain government, such as the controversial regime of President Thieu in South Vietnam, is democratic, ask yourself, "Is the country ruled by law? Is the law equally applied to all citizens? Who makes the laws?"

When King Louis XIV of France claimed that he was the state, he should have added that he was also the law. Historians doubt whether Louis actually made these famous statements, but these assertions would have fitted him and every other absolute ruler of the past, as well as every totalitarian dictator of the twentieth century. An absolute ruler can make his every whim the law of the land. He can have people arrested and executed, hand out government jobs and also take them away again as he pleases, and ignore existing law when it gets in the way of something he wants.

In a democracy everybody, king and beggar, general and private, must obey the law. The law is higher than any individual or special group. But this is not enough. Democracy also requires *equality before the law*. Solon, an Athenian statesman (640–558 B.C.), recognized this and drew up what was perhaps the first code of "equal laws for the noble and base." His name has since become the term for lawmaker or legislator.

Not only must laws apply equally to black and white, friend and stranger, they must also be *enforced* equally. When police and courts fail to do this, many citizens lose confidence in their leaders.

Not all laws are good or just. Rules of behavior become outdated as times change, but legal codes have a way of persisting long after they have outlived their usefulness. Also, in a democracy the majority decides, and the majority is not always fair or wise. Majorities have been known to have trampled, at times, upon the rights of weaker minorities. However, a constitution such as ours guarantees everybody certain rights that even the majority cannot abridge unless it has power enough to change the constitution itself. A small group, for example, or even a single individual may practice a religion that irritates the majority, yet, according to the Bill of Rights, "Congress shall make no law respecting an establishment of religion, or prohibiting the free exercise thereof." Nor may government, even when supported by a majority of citizens, deny a person the right to be against any religion.

This does not mean, however, that the conduct of Americans has always been modeled on the principles laid down in our Constitution and laws. Citizens are guaranteed freedom of religion, but in some places Jehovah's Witnesses, for example, have been mobbed because, in accordance with the commandments of their faith, they refuse to salute the flag and pledge allegiance to it. Time and again, people have been harassed by law-enforcement agencies or have had their careers shattered and their names blacklisted because they held opinions that were unpopular with the majority. To grant the minority the right of free expression requires tolerance, self-discipline, and a deep commitment to the democratic ideal.

The problem of minority rights in a democratic society is not a new one. The Frenchman Alexis de Tocqueville, who traveled widely in this country during the early part of the nineteenth century, admired our democratic system but feared the "tyranny of the majority which could crush diversity and compel conformity."[4]

PARTICIPATION

In a well-functioning democratic society all people must be free to participate in political activity. This includes voting, running for office, campaigning, holding meetings and demonstrations, writing letters and articles, and, generally, expressing oneself freely on all questions confronting the public. Freedom must be accompanied by the willingness to participate in the political process and by the knowledge of what the participation is all about. Many political scientists believe that a highly educated electorate is an absolute requirement for a successful working democracy. "The higher one's education, the more likely one is to believe in democratic values and support democratic practices."[5] However, small violent groups of students, such as the Weathermen, must be excepted from this general statement.

Where ignorance and illiteracy are widespread, an elite group tends to emerge and monopolize political power. Often the educated few dominate politics and use it to their own advantage. In some of the new African states, having attended a missionary school or a college abroad "has endowed the educated African with an exaggerated sense of superiority and special legitimacy. Politics has been permeated with the presumably uncontestable assumption that the educated have a divine right to rule."[6]

Where the electorate is uninformed, *demagogues* may spellbind the masses easily. They present themselves as saviors who, seemingly, will wave a magic wand to conjure away all misery. The people soon vote away their freedom and install the demagogue as dictator. Germans, in large numbers, voted Hitler into power in 1933. Early in the last century Napoleon was likewise hoisted to the position of dictator by the enthusiastic French voters. From the elected position of First Consul, for life, Napoleon then elevated himself to the more exalted title of emperor.

Freedom to participate must be linked with the will to make use of this privilege. To emphasize this obligation, Australia levies a fine on nonvoters, as do some parts of Switzerland. Americans are not forced, but they are strongly encouraged to go to the polls. At election time vigorous campaigns are carried on to "get out the vote." Transportation and baby-sitting services are offered to those who have a difficult time getting to the polling places. Even so the American voter turnout is disappointingly low, except for presidential elections.

MAJORITY RULE WITH RESPECT FOR MINORITIES

Democratic government is based on the concept of *majority rule*. When a class wants to decide what kind of party to have, the students usually vote on the question, and the choice of the majority decides. Similarly clubs and civic organizations make decisions on their programs, membership fees, and officers. This is done during a meeting of the whole group.

Political decisions can also be made in meetings of all citizens if the group is small enough. Ancient Athens required all free men to assemble in the marketplace, where debates took place and decisions were made. It was not only a right but the duty of every free Athenian to participate. In early New England the *town meeting* served a similar purpose. Even today we find other examples of *direct* democracy (see Figure 26) in some of the smaller Swiss cantons (states). At certain times of the year all males in those cantons converge on an open ground to hear speeches and vote on the questions raised.

Where the number of voters has grown very large, direct democracy becomes too cumbersome and makes way for *representative* democracy. The student body of a large high school or college elects a student council. The fate of a big corporation, like General Electric, or of a national organization, like the American Legion or the AFL-CIO, is determined by an elected board of directors. The actions of these representatives may or may

Figure 26

Drawing by Ed Fisher; © 1968 The New Yorker Magazine, Inc.

"All right, all right! I promise you you'll have a bigger say in the running of the flock!"

not reflect the opinion of the majority. The membership then has the privilege of not reelecting them to office when their term is finished.

Representative, or *indirect*, democracy is the governing principle by which the affairs of our cities, states, and the nation are, or ought to be, run. Some democratic countries make strong efforts to ensure that all minorities, except the tiniest ones, are represented.

Forms of Representative Democracy

Multiple-Member Election Districts	Single-Member Election Districts
Proportionate Representation	
Multiple-Party System	Two-Party System
Less stability?	More stability?

Denmark has perhaps the most complicated system for allowing the voice of the minority to be heard. *Proportionate representation* is the rule for elections to the Folketing, the Danish parliament. The country is divided into *multiple-member election districts*. The votes each party receives in each district are added together, and the seats in the Folketing are divided among the parties in proportion to the national totals. In this way political opinions, even though they may have gained only a small following, have a good chance of being expressed in parliament.

The Radical party in Denmark, for instance, which is not especially radical, polled only 7.3 percent of the votes in 1966 but received 13 of the 179 seats in the Folketing.[7] This explains why the Social Democrats, the largest party for half a century, have never held a majority of seats. Therefore this party has had to govern the country with the help of a *coalition*, a group of cabinet ministers belonging to different political parties.

By contrast, in the United States we have *single-member election districts* for elections to the House of Representatives. The one who receives the most votes in one district is the winner; all the other candidates are eliminated. It is possible, but extremely unlikely, for all members of the House to be Republicans, elected by only 50.01 percent of the vote in each congressional district. The other 49.99 percent of the voters would have no person of their choice to represent them.

Critics maintain that our system does not provide fair representation because minorities have difficulty making their influence felt. But there are some political scientists who see a great advantage in the single-member district idea. It seems to favor the *two-party system,* which is typical not only of America but also of Canada and Great Britain. Here third parties have found it very difficult competing with either Republicans or Democrats. This, so the experts argue, gives our political life stability.

The point can be debated. It is true that the United States, Canada, and Great Britain have not had revolutions for a long time. Nor have they been the scenes of *coups d'état,* attempts at violent overthrow of the government. But the same can be said of Sweden and Denmark, which have a variety of parties and still show remarkable stability.

DEMOCRATIC TRADITION

Why do judges wear black robes when they perform their duties? They could function as well in business suits. Why do men hold doors for women? They certainly don't do so because most ladies are too weak to do the job themselves.

These are traditions. We are reluctant to go against them. We follow them without questioning whether or not they still make sense. Many traditions concern the political life of society. For several hundred years it was customary among British noble families for the oldest son to run for a seat in Parliament, while the next son went into military service and the youngest son entered the church.

Democracy works best where there exists a long-standing democratic tradition, involving a willingness to obey the law, to compromise with opposite points of view, and to participate actively and intelligently in the affairs of the community. Many new countries, such as Ghana and the Congo, find it difficult, if not impossible, to operate effectively under democratic rules. Nothing in their colonial traditions has prepared them for such a task. On the other hand, British democracy is functioning though it lacks the checks and balances that, in America, prevent individuals or groups from becoming too powerful. The British system appears extremely vulnerable to the antics of a would-be dictator, but its democratic tradition acts like a shield against totalitarian control. Though "Parliament is legally supreme, the key to its actions lies in responsible self restraint. . . . The first defense of the constitution lies in the force of tradition and public opinion."[8]

DEMOCRACY AND FREEDOM

Democracy cannot exist without freedom. But what is freedom? The word has suffered much abuse. Even the most brutal oppressors have proclaimed that they operate in the name of freedom. Disregarding the various distortions of meaning, we find that there are two sides to freedom: we desire (a) freedom from interference by somebody else, for example, a policeman, a censor, or a bully, and (b) freedom to do what we want, to go where we wish, to say what we feel.

Obviously, total freedom is impossible. You are not free to throw a brick through your neighbor's window or to drive at sixty miles per hour through a downtown street. Your neighbors and the pedestrians have the right to be protected *from* your inconsiderate actions. They also need protection in case you should misuse your freedom of speech by slandering them. Freedom requires a balance of responsibility and control. Most people act in a responsible and controlled manner, not out of fear of the police but under the impact of the mores that our society has developed (see Chapter 4). But we still need constitutions and laws to reinforce the mores, make them universal, and ensure protection for everyone.

The Bill of Rights, as we mentioned earlier, guarantees freedom of speech, religion, and other basic rights—some of which we tend to take for granted. It omits certain human rights that are considered very important by other countries. The Russian constitution, for example, lists the right to work. It states that society owes every citizen a job, in line with the often-quoted communist maxim, "From each according to his ability, to each according to his need." Since the government is the only employer in Russia, it is supposed to furnish employment to all Russians.

A democratic government must be subject to *limitations* of its power, but it must also be aware of its *obligations* to the citizenry. Our Constitution lists mainly the limitations of our government, while the obligations are left to action by the lawmakers.

Limitations and Obligations of Our Government

*Some Limitations**
Freedom of religious worship
Freedom of speech
Freedom of the press
Freedom of assembly
Freedom to petition the government
Prohibition of slavery
Guarantee of "due process" of law
Guarantee of speedy and public trial

Some Obligations†
Minimum wages
Unemployment assistance
Social Security
Prohibition of child labor
Public assistance to education
Public assistance to recreation

* These freedoms and guarantees are included in the Federal Constitution; the government cannot limit them.
† These are obligations enacted by law.
Source: Adapted from a compilation in Austin Ranney, *The Governing of Men*, rev. ed. (New York: Holt, Rinehart and Winston, 1966), pp. 158–159. Reprinted by permission.

One of the rights that are basic to any democratic society is *universal suffrage*, the right of everybody to vote according to his choice. Yet this right has been slow in being extended to all American citizens. Women did not gain it until 1920. It took a number of decisions by the Supreme Court during the past two decades to wipe out some other glaring injustices. These court decisions have "expanded constitutional protections for the politically weak, the socially disliked and the criminally suspect."[9]

At the moment when we enter the voting booth or pull the lever on the voting machine all Americans are equal; that is, every vote has the same weight. But otherwise, the citizens of a democratic community are far from being equal. Certainly this is true of the American people. We differ greatly in wealth, status, political and economic influence, and also in talent and opportunity. Yet observers, such as Seymour M. Lipset, find that, especially in our social relations, we stress equality more than other nations, for example, England, from which so many of our traditions have come.

Americans of different rank and economic standing address each other informally as equals. A diplomat may discuss foreign relations with a cabdriver. At work nobody is required to humble himself in speech and manners before his superior, as is customary in many other countries. Of course, for a long time all this was true for white society only. "The treatment of the Negro makes a mockery of this value now as it has in the past."[10]

But against this tradition of equal respect for fellow citizens works the trend toward a growing gap between the poor and the middle and upper classes and also the growing power of a military and industrial elite. If America is to continue to grow into a more democratic society these trends have to be checked.

> There are tendencies inherent in human social organization which seek to destroy freedom and to foster inequality. Hence the effort to prevent them from dominating must be a constant one. It must be directed against poverty and related evils at one hand, and against ascription and elitism at the other.[11]

FREEDOM AND ORDER

What would you rather have: freedom or order? Quite a few people will decide against the freedom to act according to their convictions and choose order, especially when times are troubled and tense. Unrest in the streets, widespread poverty, or growing violence place the democratic system under heavy pressure. Cries are heard calling for a big broom to sweep up all dissension. Strong, tough measures are demanded whether or not they may violate the guaranteed freedoms. "In times of [economic] depression, fear and frustration undermine faith in the democratic process, and where the faith in rational methods weakens, *fascism* is the potential gainer [italics are this author's]."[12]

At the end of World War I Italy experienced large-scale unemployment. Bloody fights between political opponents erupted, and government proved to be helpless and inefficient. This atmosphere was ripe for the takeover by the fascist movement under the leadership of Benito Mussolini, who installed himself as dictator. His rule lasted for over twenty years. There were people who admired him because he made the trains run on time. They believed he had done away with poverty because the beggars had been chased off the streets. Little notice was given by these admirers to the fact that the prisons were filled with Mussolini's opponents.

Communism also profits when people lose faith in democracy. In underdeveloped countries plagued by poverty, lack of education, and the greed of a privileged few, the communist system looks very inviting. It holds out hope of more food, greater stability, and less glaring economic inequality. That it allows little freedom of personal movement and expression is of less concern to those who suffer from hunger and disease.

Fascist, as well as communist, regimes have, in several tragic instances, brought about *totalitarianism*. The totalitarian state makes itself the complete master of its citizens. It controls every aspect of their lives, public and private, with an iron hand and enforces its will with barbaric oppression. Totalitarianism is the complete negation of democracy.

Is our government moving toward totalitarianism because it is steadily expanding its power and influence? Some say Yes. They would like to return to former times when rulers were concerned with the defense of the country, order in the streets, and with little else. In general, the principle of *laissez faire* prevailed and the functions of government were few compared to the present. Anybody could act as he pleased. Before the twentieth century the American government stood aside, in most instances, while the merchant, the money lender, the physician, and the speculator did pretty much as they pleased. Little care was given to the old and the sick, the injured and the handicapped. What this amounted to was that the strong victimized the weak and that the rich took advantage of the poor. Only governmental intervention is now beginning to bring about a larger measure of social justice.

Our political structure is under attack by the *Extreme Right*, which says, "The less government we have the better for us." At the same time brickbats of protest are thrown by the *New Left* and by anarchists. The New Left accuses the government of having become a tool of wealthy profiteers, while anarchists want a society without government. This last group holds that any form of government is oppressive and that society would benefit if people were allowed to cooperate voluntarily with one another.

But it appears that a society without any rule and force must remain a dream. There must be laws, and the laws need to "be invoked to induce the recalcitrant, the selfish, or the perverse to recognize the rights of others, the welfare of others, or their own better interests."[13] If we had, for example, no compulsory school-attendance laws, chances are that the number of illiterate Americans would be far greater than it is.

The big problem facing democracy is finding a balance between unrestricted freedom and *coercion*, which squashes all criticism and dissent. At what point does one person's freedom begin to reduce the freedom of others? When does freedom turn into *license*, which is the complete disregard of all commonly accepted rules of proper conduct? Let us take, for example, the freedom of assembly, a topic of frequent heated discussion in the United States. Relatively few Americans will condemn peaceful demonstrations protesting war or the way some universities are run. But should a demonstration be permitted in the middle of a freeway at rush hour? Should noisy protests be permitted outside classrooms when classes are in session? At what point does a peaceful demonstration become violent and infringe on the freedoms of others? There are no easy answers to such questions.

The highest degree of order is attained by allowing the least amount of freedom. Dictators claim that they bring order into chaos. On the other hand, where government exerts little or no control, complete misery and confusion result. When the Congo became independent in the autumn of 1960, the new government was unable to establish any kind of order. Rioting and robbery abounded. Unemployment reigned, and prices soared. Schools were closed, industry stopped, and food became scarce. Soon civil war swept across the unfortunate country.[14]

The ideal solution lies in a workable balance between complete freedom and complete restriction, between license and control, and between chaos and order. The difficulty is that this balance has to be constantly adjusted as conditions change—in public as well as private affairs. The restrictions on a child, for example, must be different from those on an adult. An adolescent of eighteen would justly rebel were he obliged to be home at the same hour as his twelve-year-old brother or sister. The situation changes with the age of the child, and requirements must change accordingly.

Political conditions also change, and so must the requirements of good citizenship and the methods of the officials of government. Most political scientists agree that democracy can only work when there is constant dialogue among all concerned. Freedoms that are not safeguarded and fought for at all times may diminish and eventually disappear.

Main Ideas

1. Democracy is the idea of government in the interest of the people and under the control of the people.
2. Democratic systems allow for a variety of forms and practices.
3. Democratic governments operate under written or unwritten constitutions.
4. The United States of America is a federal republic that is characterized by presidential rule and a system of checks and balances.
5. Equality of all citizens before the law and equal enforcement of the laws are essential requirements of a democratic system.
6. Another important requirement of democracy is freedom to participate in the political process and a willingness to do so.
7. Democracy, whether direct or representative, is rule by the majority but with consideration of the rights and wishes of the minority.
8. In many instances the two-party system seems to further political stability.
9. Democracy functions well where democratic traditions have had time to develop.

10. Democratic government must maintain a careful balance between individual freedom and governmental control.

Important Terms

Absolute rule	Magna Charta
Anarchy	Majority rule
Capitalism	Monarchy
Checks and balances	Multiple-member election district
Coalition	New Left
Coercion	Parliamentary rule
Constitution	Premier
Coup d'état	Presidential rule
Demagogue	Prime minister
Democracy	Proportional representation
Direct democracy	Representative democracy
Executive power	Republic
Extreme Right	Single-member election district
Fascism	Socialism
Federal government	Totalitarianism
Indirect democracy	Town meeting
Judicial power	Two-party system
Laissez faire	Unitary government
Legislative power	Universal suffrage
License	

Conclusion

Democracy is a way of life for people who consider freedom an extremely important value. Democratic forms of government provide the opportunities for equal participation of all citizens in the exercise of political power and for opposition to government actions that the people may not approve.

Notes

1. Plato, *The Republic*, VIII, c. 370 B.C.
2. D. George Konsolas, *On Government: A Comparative Introduction* (Belmont, Cal.: Wadsworth, 1968), p. 49.
3. G. M. Carter and J. H. Herz, *Major Foreign Powers*, 5th ed. (New York: Harcourt, Brace & World, 1967), p. 555.
4. Alexis de Tocqueville, *Democracy in America*, first published 1835 (New York: Harper & Row, 1966). Introduction by Max Lerner.
5. Seymour M. Lipset, *Political Man: The Social Bases of Politics* (Garden City, N.Y.: Doubleday, 1960), p. 56.
6. G. A. Almond and J. S. Coleman, *The Politics of the Developing Areas* (Princeton, N.J.: Princeton University Press, 1960), p. 283.
7. Kenneth E. Miller, *Government and Politics in Denmark* (Boston: Houghton Mifflin, 1968), p. 110.

8. Carter and Herz, *op. cit.*, pp. 51, 53.
9. G. T. Mitan, *Decade of Decision: The Supreme Court and the Constitutional Revolution, 1954–1964* (New York: Scribner, 1967), p. 3.
10. Seymour M. Lipset, *The First New Nation* (New York: Basic Books, 1963), p. 330.
11. *Ibid.*, p. 343.
12. William Ebenstein, *Today's Isms*, 5th ed. (Englewood Cliffs, N.J.: Prentice-Hall, 1967), p. 109.
13. Neal Riemer, *The Revival of Democratic Theory* (New York: Appleton-Century-Crofts, 1962), p. 89.
14. Colin Legum, *Congo Disaster* (Baltimore: Penguin Books, 1961).

Suggestions for Further Reading

Burnham, J. "Can Democracy Work?" *National Review*, 19, May 16, 1967, 510.

"Democracy Has, Hasn't a Future, a Present: Excerpts from a Theater of Ideas Debate," *New York Times Magazine*, May 26, 1968, pp. 30–31.

Koestler, Arthur. *Darkness at Noon.* New York: Modern Library, 1941. A fictional study of totalitarianism.

O'Connor, Edwin. *The Last Hurrah.* Boston: Little, Brown, 1955. Novel about an American would-be political boss.

Orwell, George. *1984.* New York: New American Library, 1951. Novel about a world under totalitarian control.

Spiro, Herbert J. *Government by Constitution: The Political Systems of Democracy.* New York: Random House, 1959. Comparative analysis of how eight different democratic political systems work.

Warren, Robert Penn. *All the King's Men.* New York: Bantam Books, 1950. Novel about an individual's striving for political power and the development of a political machine.

How do you feel toward "Uncle Sam"?
How does he affect your life?
How is this country governed?
What major problems are facing the United States?

17 A LARGER COMMUNITY
the nation

NATIONALISM

Perhaps you watched the moon landing of the spaceship Apollo 11 on television. Millions of people did on that day in July in 1969. They were citizens of many countries, and almost all felt elated about this historic accomplishment. But you probably felt especially proud because the first two men ever to step on the surface of the moon were Americans.

Why might you have felt this way? What difference did it make that Armstrong and Aldrin were your countrymen? Why did you experience a special satisfaction from the fact that the United States had achieved this fantastic triumph? "See what we can do when we put our minds to it!" you might have bragged to your friends. By "we" you meant the people of America with whom you identify yourself. You want to belong to a nation that could do outstanding things, and the moon landing helped to confirm your belief that this is the best country in the world.

Such very common reactions are part of what is called *nationalism*. As for believing that America is "the best country," the average Englishman feels similarly about England and the Frenchman about France.

Nationalism is expressed in many ways: loyalty toward the leaders of your nation, reverence for its past. Most people willingly obey their national government, even to the point of sacrificing their lives as soldiers on the battlefield. No other social institution can command such a degree of loyalty.

We celebrate national holidays, we pledge allegiance to the national flag, and we stand in reverence when the national anthem is played. Plaques or monuments throughout the United States commemorate the dead of the nation's wars. Battlefields are national shrines. By teaching about the beauty of the American countryside and about the valor of American heroes, schools try to instill in our children a feeling of *patriotism* (from *patria*, Latin for "fatherland"), which, for many people, has the same meaning as nationalism.

Nationalism is a force that gives a large number of people, otherwise strangers to each other, a sense of unity. This sense becomes most powerful in wartime, which "merely brings to the surface and makes plain through pathological exaggeration what already exists in peace: an almost universal disposition to place the nation before all other human groupings."[1]

Do you resent criticisms of our government or when someone points out flaws in the American character? Why? Does love of your country prevent you from finding any fault with it? Nationalists have, all too often, the tendency to insist on uncritical acceptance of what the nation is doing at the moment. "My country—right or wrong." This blind ultranationalism is also known as *chauvinism*, named after the soldier Chauvin, who, during the French Revolution, expressed exaggerated fervor in his support of the French army flag.

Chauvinism can take on an "inspirational and sometimes revivalist character."[2] Chauvinistic leaders can sometimes transport people into such a state of fanaticism that even otherwise ordinary citizens will blindly follow their orders and consider it justifiable to suppress other nations that happen to block their ambitions for greatness. The extremes of this appeal to national glory were demonstrated in Mussolini's fascism and Hitler's Nazism.

THE NATION

Nationalism can become a strong, even an overwhelming, force because the *nation* affects our daily life in many ways. Nations come in many sizes, but they usually include a number of villages, towns, and cities. In most instances the members are bound together by a common government, a common territory, a common language, a common history, common cultural features, and a common economic system.

As compared with other nations, the territory covered by the United States is very large. We can travel thousands of miles without crossing any other national borders, without having to show a passport or to have our luggage examined. We consider ourselves part owners of the Lincoln Memorial in Washington, D.C., as well as the Great Lakes and San Francisco Bay.

English is our common and also our official language, but many Mexican-Americans and Puerto Ricans speak and write in Spanish. The English spoken by Americans, as distinguished from that spoken by Australians and the British, is easily recognizable by its accent and by certain expressions peculiar to this country.

In several nations different languages are spoken by different segments of the population. Switzerland has four official languages—French, German, Italian, and Romansh—yet the people who use them work together quite harmoniously. On the other hand, Canada and Belgium, with two official languages each, have experienced some difficulties on this account, and in India, a vast country of numerous tongues and dialects, the conflict over language has caused tragic violence and bloodshed.

Some nations can proudly trace their history back many centuries. Japan, for example, has legends that tell of gods and goddesses who, long ago in a mystery-shrouded past, participated in the founding of that country. In comparison the history of the United States is quite short. Moreover, many of our most patriotic citizens are first-generation immigrants or their descendants.

Occasionally a speaker at a luncheon meeting will refer to the "American way of life," but he might be embarrassed if the audience pressed him to define the phrase. Probably for him the American way of life is what he personally is accustomed to and what he considers right and proper. Perhaps one could name milk shakes, baseball, and blind dates as parts of the American way. Typically American are also drive-in theaters, outdoor barbecues, and baby-sitters. These are not very basic national characteristics, and they change with technical innovations. When dealing with more significant trends in thought and action, we find an immense variety of characteristics, depending on whether we are considering the lives of city or country people, upper, middle, or lower classes, college graduates, or blue-collar workers, blacks or whites. Thus there are many American *ways* of life.

Unlike many Americans, most people of other nations do not seem concerned over the question of what their national goals and purposes are. Perhaps our power and prosperity causes us to wonder if we are making the right use of these gifts. The strong moral and religious interest of early American settlers has kept its hold on their descendants and influences later immigrants, who are now involved in political and economic moves that affect the whole world. It is characteristic that, during the administration of President Eisenhower, a committee of scholars was appointed to define our national goals.

THE NATIONAL ECONOMY

Nations are often described in terms of their economic characteristics. We distinguish between rich and poor, industrial and agricultural, technologically advanced and underdeveloped nations.

You are probably well aware of your personal economic situation. You know what your income is and that of your family. You decide what to do with your income, whether to spend it on a house, a car, or extra clothing. Perhaps your income barely suffices to buy food and other necessities.

But how much money you earn and how you spend it is to a considerable extent related to the economic state of the country. You may find it difficult or easy to find a well-paying job. How you use your money depends not only on your individual wishes but also on the taxes you must pay, on the degree of inflation, and on the availability of goods. For example, can you select a Japanese camera, a German automobile, or a pair of Austrian skis?

These questions depend on the national economy. There are different ways by which nations can reach the goal of economic well-being. A growing number favor some form of *socialism*. Others claim to be dedicated to the idea of *free enterprise*, though completely free, that is, uncontrolled, private enterprise is not found in real economic life.

The wealth of a nation is usually measured by its *Gross National Product*, usually shortened to GNP, which is the market value of all the goods and services produced in one year. In 1967 the GNP of the United States was about $800 billion.[3] Reading some meaning into these gigantic figures is difficult for the average person. Perhaps a comparison will help: estimates indicate that, at best, Russia will have reached a GNP of $500 billion (in terms of United States money) by 1970.[4]

The wealth of a nation as a whole is, of course, no indication that all its citizens share equally in its benefits. America is the wealthiest country on earth, yet extensive poverty still exists in our midst. In fact, it is more visible in our cities and in some blighted rural areas of this country than it is in Scandinavia or the Netherlands. But in comparison to the nations of Eastern Europe, Asia, Africa, and Latin America, we are doing very well, and a greater portion of our population can afford to live comfortably than in these other parts of the world. Economists and historians attribute this high degree of material well-being to the system of "controlled capitalism"[5] that has developed in America over the years. This means that private capital owns factories, mines, means of transportation, and so forth but that it operates under quite extensive governmental controls.

The United States is also the most industrialized of the large nations, and we have already seen in earlier chapters the impact of industry and technology on the individual and society. Though we still have many farms and cattle ranches that produce, in fact, much more than we can use, it is essentially the machine, mechanized transportation, and automation that create the rhythm of our lives.

Some Americans demand more free enterprise in our economy, which means that the production of goods and services would be entirely in the hands of private individuals who would then be free to charge any price they could get. In this system the *market* would determine the price, and government would practice a complete hands-off policy toward business. Actually this extreme form of laissez faire is rarely found in any nation.

The other extreme, often referred to as socialism, is complete governmental control of economic life. In Russia the government owns all factories, warehouses, and stores; it runs the radio stations, publishes the newspapers, and operates airlines, railroads, and buses. This system makes almost every Russian citizen who works a government employee. Each Russian worker earns his money from the government and returns it to the government when he pays for his purchases.

Ours is frequently referred to as a "mixed economy." Clothing stores, bicycle repair shops, and dry-cleaning services are owned by individuals, who, in competition with others, determine what prices to charge. A corporation that runs a chain of supermarkets or a number of steel mills is, like the individual owner, part of the free-enterprise system; so is the dentist who charges a fee for the extraction of a tooth and the gardener whom a suburbanite pays by the hour.

The free-enterprise system has great advantages—high wages and profits to the successful individual and a boost to the national economy. It gives us an incentive to work hard, to take chances, to experiment with new ideas. But now consider the drawbacks: What about those who are less gifted, who suffer from physical, mental, or social handicaps? Should they be left by the wayside? What about needed public services that private enterprise will not or cannot adequately perform, such as garbage removal or the construction of superhighways?

Today the public not only wants but insists that the national government step in to economic affairs. Only the federal government is powerful enough to do something about the problems we face. Here we can only list a few examples of the government's hand in the national economic life.

The record of the government in running important economic enterprises is mixed. Numerous loud complaints have been heard about the way the national postal service operates. More successful seems to be the production, management, and sale of hydroelectric power, which comes from the Tennessee Valley Authority, the Hoover Dam, the Grand Coulee Dam, and the Bonneville Dam. The government influences the free market by paying billions of dollars in salaries to federal employees and more billions to recipients of public assistance of various kinds, who are not employees.

In addition to running its own enterprises the government supervises and regulates certain activities of the private sector of the economy when these activities are considered particularly important to the public welfare. Railroads and airlines, food and drug producers, banks and lending agencies must conform to governmental rules. Here too the results are spotty. Some rules are cumbersome and impractical. Others make sense but are not vigorously enforced. Generally the government attempts to promote economic growth and stability. This is accomplished by allowing or restricting the import of foreign goods that might compete with our own production, by pumping money into enterprises that cannot make it on their own, and by seeing that neither too much nor too little money is floating around. When money is too plentiful, the country may be plunged into inflation; when it is too scarce, the builder or buyer of a home, the small merchant, or manufacturer find it hard to get credit, which makes jobs scarce and business in general sluggish.

A powerful instrument for controlling the flow of money is taxation, especially the federal income tax. It not only attempts to prevent inflation but also pays for the functioning of the governmental machinery. In the past few decades the federal government has nearly always spent more than it received in taxes. Only rarely have we had a *balanced budget,* when expenditures were equal to income. When an individual buys more than he can pay for with his own resources, he has to borrow money. This is also true of the government, and so we are saddled with a *national debt.* The government owes money to all the individuals and businesses that have bought government bonds, such as the United States savings bonds that you can purchase in every bank. In 1900 our national debt was about $1.15 billion. By 1968 it had risen to almost $348 billion mainly because of increased spending for national defense. Economists argue among themselves whether *deficit spending* is good or bad for the country. When you spend more than you take in, you incur a deficit. This goes for governments as well as for individuals. By pumping money into the economy, the government hopes to create more jobs and more profits, and when this happens, increased tax returns will eventually make up for the deficit.

In Chapter 10 we spoke of the continuous flow of money, in the form of currency, checks, or credit, between consumer and producer. We also mentioned that any working person is at the same time a producer as well as a consumer. This process was illustrated by Figure 12 on page 196. Now we must add that the national government plays an often decisive role in regulating this flow. Successful economic policy will keep the current steady, control any runaway trends, and remove obstructions so that there will be full employment for all who want to work and so that the prices of goods and services will remain even.

The government's main tools in this job are *fiscal policy* and *monetary policy.* In its fiscal policy the government uses the power to tax, spend, and borrow. The federal monetary policy is carried out by the Federal Reserve Board, which can increase or decrease the available supply of money.

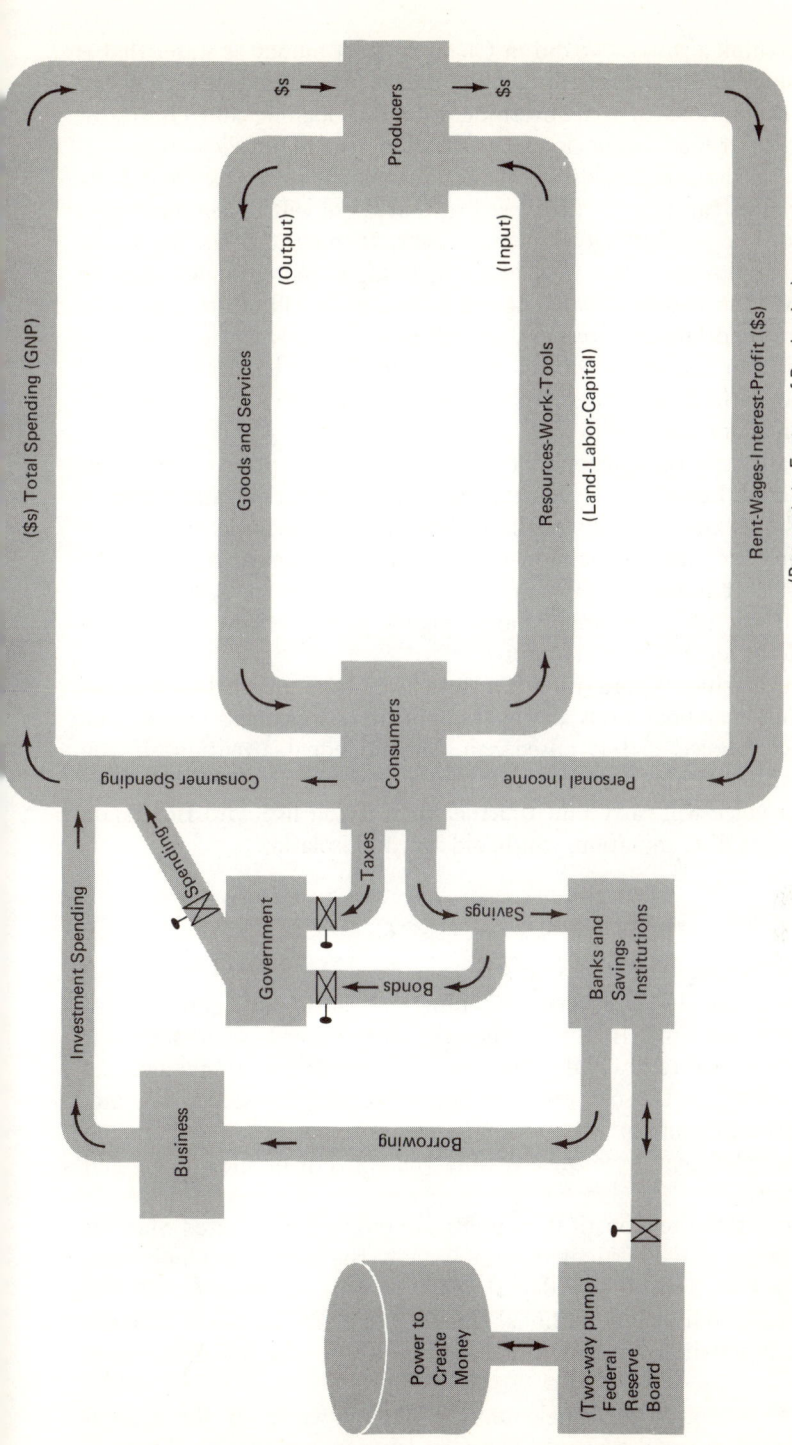

Figure 27 **How the Government Controls the Flow of Money**

* This chart compares the government's influence on the flow of money in the country to an intricate pumping system with many interconnected pipes and with valves that, when open, increase the flow, and when closed, halt or slow it down. The following are important terms:

1. *Two-way pump:* the government can withdraw money from the flow by raising taxes, or it can pump money back through the system by means of public projects (road or dam construction, and so forth), through grants, Social Security payments.
2. *Input:* this is money used to produce goods (buildings, clothes, cars) and services (laundromats, barbershops, hospitals).
3. *Output:* the goods and services produced are sold to the consumer for a price.
4. *Factors of production:* these are all that is needed to produce something: workers, machines, buildings, capital.

If we think again, as we did in Chapter 10, of money as water that is being pumped through a system of pipes and constantly being re-used, we can liken the actions of our government to the opening and closing of valves that either speed up or slow down the flow (see Figure 27).

Suppose that, in periods of inflation, consumer prices rise very high. Then the valves can be partially closed so that there will be less money to compete for the available goods and services. If, on the other hand, the rate of unemployment becomes alarmingly high, more money can be pumped into the system by opening the valves. This will create more jobs and a fuller use of our resources. By operating the various safety valves, the government can indirectly control the economy; yet the decision about what to do with their money still remains in the hands of the private producer and consumer.

Not all steps the government takes find general approval. We hear criticism about bungling, inefficiency, and even corruption, and some of the criticism is undoubtedly justified. But in a democratic society the citizen is free to voice his opinion loudly and also to make it felt in the voting booth. It is the citizenry and its representatives in Congress who decide what role the government should play in the national economy and what should be left to private enterprise.

However, since we are still a few steps away from an ideal democratic situation, not everybody finds an equal opportunity to express his opinion, and not every voice that is raised can demand equal attention. If you possess wealth and high status, if you have important friends in the right places, your voice will carry much farther than if you live with the handicaps of poverty, discrimination, youth, old age, and isolation.

THE NATIONAL GOVERNMENT

Though the American government still operates under a constitution that was drawn up in 1787, government functions have undergone radical changes since that time. In 1787 there were comparatively few issues that the government had to deal with, but gradually the various federal agencies became involved in the control of business, health, transportation, and crime, and in the support of housing, education, recreation, labor, and many other fields that were once mainly the concern of individuals and private groups.

According to the Constitution political power in the United States is divided between the President, Congress, and the Supreme Court (see Figure 28). The three major departments of our government are still charged with handling our national affairs, but their methods and the range of their activities are quite different from those of a few generations ago.

The President is the single most powerful person in the United States and perhaps in the world. The Constitution makes him the chief

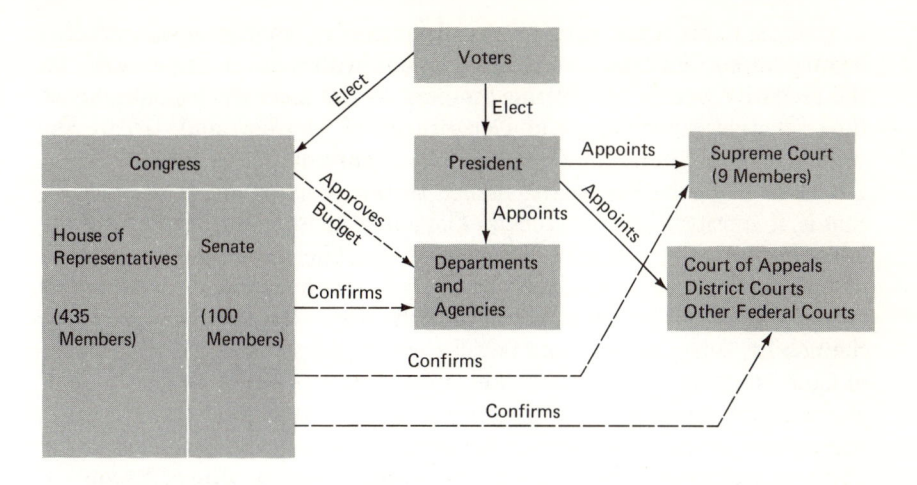

Figure 28
How the Federal Government Operates

executive officer of the government and the commander-in-chief of all armed forces. He is responsible for carrying out the decisions of Congress, but he is also expected to direct Congress in making new decisions. In many instances he need not wait for Congress, but he can issue *executive orders,* which take effect immediately, as when President Eisenhower ordered troops into Little Rock, Arkansas, to protect black children who were entering desegregated schools.

In our relations with other nations the President is our principal representative and spokesman. The Supreme Court has clearly stated that in the field of foreign affairs "with its important, complicated, delicate and manifold problems, the President alone has the power to speak or listen as a representative of the nation."[6] The President is, furthermore, the acknowledged head of his, the victorious, party. By distributing many important government jobs among faithful party members, he keeps the party under his control.

Most important of all, the President acts as the leader of all the American people. They expect him to relieve their hardships, to inform them of important events, and to keep America's position in the world strong and honorable. This is a tremendous job, according to some political scientists, almost too much for one man. "The presidency is the most important of the countervailing forces that have allowed our political system to check its regressive characteristics and to adjust to the pressures of social and economic change."[7]

Obviously the President needs a good deal of assistance, which he receives from a vast bureaucracy stationed in the nation's capital, in other American cities, and in foreign countries. These helpers and advisers—

comprising more than fifty federal departments, commissions, agencies, boards, authorities, and other organizations with various titles—make up the executive branch of government. Among the most recent additions to the executive branch are the Department of Housing and Urban Development (1965) and the Department of Transportation (1966).

Congress, the lawmaking branch of our government, is *bicameral*—that is, it consists of two chambers. The upper house is the Senate, and the lower house is the House of Representatives. This double arrangement is designed to prevent hasty decisions and safeguard all regions and interest groups within the country. In England the upper house once represented the nobility and wielded more power than the lower house, or the House of Commons. As the country became more democratic, the House of Lords gradually lost influence, and many wish to dissolve it altogether. In other democratic countries similar developments have taken place, whereas the prestige and power of the United States Senate have, if anything, grown.

American congressmen are the most influential lawmakers in the world. "Far more than any other legislative body of the major nations, the Congress of the United States makes policy. . . . [and] is everlastingly assertive in revising and rejecting—as well as in accepting—the President's legislative proposals."[8]

When you express disgust with high prices, smog, or mail delays, people will sometimes advise you, "Why don't you write your Congressman?" Contrary to some expressed opinions senators and representatives listen to the voices from back home. Your greatest chance of finding an ear for your complaints and of having something done about them is through this channel.

An important congressional power is that of investigation. The members of each house of Congress form numerous committees, such as the Foreign Relations Committee, the Armed Services Committee, the Commerce Committee, and many others. Senate and House committees hold *hearings* to collect all the facts pertaining to sometimes very complicated pieces of legislation. Sharp political controversies resulted from the hearings of the House Un-American Activities Committee, now called the House Internal Security Committee. Its critics accused it of intimidation, unfounded accusations, and using public hearings for personal publicity.

The Supreme Court enjoys a great deal of independence, as do the other federal courts. Judges are appointed for life, and their positions give them considerable prestige. The Supreme Court is the highest court of appeal in the country, but it makes its greatest impact through the power of *judicial review*. This is the right to declare acts of other governmental branches unconstitutional.

Through its decisions the court has been a major force in shaping American national policy. When it outlawed school segregation in 1954, it opened a new chapter in American race relations (see Chapters 3 and 12).

THE PUBLIC AND POLITICS

In 1890 a political scientist by the name of John Burgess "wrote his two-volume survey of world governments, *Political Science and Comparative Constitutional Law*, without even mentioning parties, pressure groups, or public opinion."[9] Today no scholar would be guilty of such an omission.

The party is the main instrument of political expression, yet much of the time most Americans are only dimly aware that they have any ties with the Republican or Democratic parties. Party life is almost dormant until a few months before a national election, when party buttons, stickers, and posters appear in gigantic quantities. Doorbells are rung, flyers distributed, mass meetings and parades held. People become partisan. Under the onslaught of political propaganda Americans attempt to choose among the candidates of the parties presented on the ballot.

On Capitol Hill in Washington one can observe a number of people who are very anxious to talk to congressmen and to be allowed to testify at committee hearings. These people are *lobbyists*. The National Rifle Association maintains lobbyists in Washington to influence legislators to vote against gun-control laws, and the major oil companies lobby to keep their taxes down. Teachers, physicians, outdoor enthusiasts, veterans, and many others try to inform and influence the lawmakers through either permanent or occasional lobbyists.

Lobbyists represent *pressure groups* (such as the National Rifle Association), which are interested in having certain bills passed or defeated. Students who protest publicly against military power become a pressure group. How successful they are depends on their tactics and how they fare in competition with other pressure groups, for example, the veterans' organizations, which favor a strong army.

Pressure groups also spend time and money in order to influence *public opinion*. Trucking firms buy advertising space in newspapers and magazines in order to persuade the public that longer and heavier trucks should be allowed on the highways. The American Automobile Association, on the other hand, tries to convince the public that such vehicles are too dangerous.

If the public becomes persuaded to take a certain position, it communicates this position to its representatives. Should the legislators refuse to listen to the voters, the voters may choose not to return them to office at the next election. Public opinion is difficult to measure, but unless freedom is completely absent, "government policy, and indeed all important historical events, are shaped by the opinions of the members of the political communities involved."[10]

PROBLEMS OF THE NATION

The nation is constantly demanding more services from its government. As the activities of government increase, so do the arguments about whether it is doing too much, not enough, or acting with sufficient strength and efficiency.

Political controversy involves groups commonly known as "right," "left," and "middle-of-the-road." Generally, the right resists change—that is, it wants to preserve the present social and economic situation (status quo) and denounces its opponents as unpatriotic; the left desires drastic and immediate reforms to provide more freedom and greater well-being to more citizens; the last group takes a moderate stand in political matters. One of the major problems of our time is not the difference in opinions but the ways in which the differences are expressed.

Protest from the Left: American foreign policy, especially our involvement in Vietnam, has caused fierce resentment on the part of many people. After having suffered discrimination silently for a long time, black Americans are now loudly and fervently demanding their rights. The poor want a share of the country's general prosperity. Students are demanding schools and universities that will meet their needs. Each of these groups wants drastic change on some particular issue: racial, economic, military, or educational policies. In other respects they may not see eye to eye at all or may be strongly opposed to far-reaching changes.

Many protesters feel that letters to congressmen are not enough. The message does not seem to get through, and the results are slow in coming or completely lacking. So protesters have been trying more drastic methods to bring themselves to the attention of public officials and the public itself: marches, demonstrations, sit-ins, boycotts. Often these peaceful forms of protest are met with brutal violence on the part of the police.

A small minority of the protesters have also turned to violence. Riots have erupted in the city ghettos, on college campuses, and at draft-board offices. Looting, burning, and destruction often cause harm not only to property but also to the cause of the dissatisfied.

In the face of such excesses, the public has been quick to forget the issues of the protests. Conservative politicians rush to cash in on this "backlash" by loudly declaring themselves for "law and order." In the spring of 1969, for example, Sam Yorty was reelected as mayor of Los Angeles, despite a record of corruption. In his campaign against Tom Bradley, a black, he had stirred up racial antagonism and fears of violence. He even ran a newspaper ad with a picture of Bradley and the caption "Will your family be safe?"

Protest from the Right: Many observers of the political scene are particularly disturbed by the tactics of the radical right. The John Birch Society and the Christian Anti-Communism Crusade engage in "witch hunts" by denouncing as a communist anybody with whom they disagree or whom they dislike. Government officials, Supreme Court justices, and civil rights leaders are their favorite targets. In the *Blue Book of the John Birch Society* the society's leader, Robert Welch, accused President Eisenhower of being an "agent of the Kremlin" and declared that "democracy is a . . . perennial fraud."[11]

Hitler came to power by attacking in a similar way. Freedom can be endangered by both the extreme right and the extreme left. The *extremist* appeal succeeds with the disgruntled and the ignorant and "with people who find the complexities of modern life and the dangers of the nuclear age too fearful and frustrating to live with."[12]

The Welfare State: Much of the political protest from the right is directed against the *welfare state*. Under this heading conservatives group all attempts by the government to guarantee economic security to every citizen. Such attempts are denounced as "creeping socialism"; but, as we have seen, the term "socialism" does not apply here at all. "A socialist society may certainly employ welfare measures, but welfare states are not necessarily socialistic."[13]

Since the Great Depression of the 1930s, the United States has steadily moved toward acceptance of the idea that government should be concerned with public welfare. Many laws and programs resulted, such as Social Security, minimum wage levels, unemployment insurance, graduated income tax, aid to dependent children, medicare, urban renewal, and, more recently, the War on Poverty. Even the laws protecting small businessmen and natural resources are part of the welfare concept.

Most Americans accept the idea that government should be concerned with the welfare of all citizens, but there is wide disagreement on the questions "How much involvement should government have? What kind and what methods should be employed?" Arguments will, in all likelihood, continue indefinitely as new situations arise and new techniques are tested.

Pollution: Not too long ago, Americans would have laughed at the suggestion that government should maintain controls concerning the environment. If anything, air, water, and open space were in plentiful supply and uncontaminated. But urban sprawl, the combustion engine, nuclear reactors, and factories that spew out dangerous chemical waste have changed all this. The air has become foul with smoke and gases, and illnesses of the lungs have increased. Fish die because our lakes and rivers are uninhabitable. Forests and meadows disappear under the bulldozers of housing developers. Our scenic highways and picnic grounds are disfigured by empty bottles, cans, and other refuse. (See Figure 29.) Old trucks and abandoned automobiles are left to disintegrate on city streets, on roadsides, and in junkyards that become neighborhood eyesores. Noise pollution too, caused in part by the roar of jet aircraft over our rooftops and by traffic in our streets, has begun to trouble us.

What should be done about these problems? Leave it to the local

Figure 29
Drawing by Dedini; © 1969 The New Yorker Magazine, Inc.

community to deal with the ugly side of progress? Impossible. Chicago has made strong attempts to stop the pollution of Lake Michigan, but other communities bordering the lake still dump raw sewage into the lake. St. Louis, Missouri, has strict air-pollution controls, but virtually uncontrolled industry from across the state line still contaminates the atmosphere. Smoke, noise, and contamination do not respect political boundaries.

This situation calls for the federal government to act as umpire, conservationist, and protector of the public interest. To determine what is in the public interest in itself becomes a political issue open to unending controversy.

Main Ideas
1. Most members of a nation feel love for and pride in their country; these feelings are part of what is termed "nationalism."

2. In its fanatical form nationalism may lead to an uncritical acceptance of whatever the nation is doing, even when it suppresses other nations.
3. A nation is a large group of people bound together by a common territory, common cultural features, a common economic system, and a common government. Many nations also have a common language and a common history dating back many centuries.
4. The United States has a mixed economic system combining the features of free enterprise with a measure of governmental control.
5. The President is the acknowledged leader and spokesman of the American people; he combines this function with that of being head of his political party.
6. The legislative branch of our government is bicameral; the Senate enjoys a position of high prestige; citizens may influence the legislative process by contacting their congressmen, through the news media, by demonstrations, public opinion polls, and so forth.
7. The Supreme Court is the highest court of appeal and also decides whether laws passed by legislative bodies and executive decisions are in agreement with the Constitution.
8. The average citizen participates in the political decision-making process as a member of a political party or a pressure group and by helping form public opinion.
9. Most issues confronting the nation are the subject of public controversy; the right takes a conservative standpoint and the left desires immediate radical reform.
10. Extremism both on the left and on the right endangers our democratic system and the orderly functioning of society.
11. The government is becoming more and more concerned with safeguarding the economic security of every citizen.
12. The impact of industry and urban expansion on the natural environment makes it necessary for the government to become concerned with pollution and the waste of our natural resources.

Important Terms

Balanced budget
Bicameral legislature
Chauvinism
Committee hearings
Deficit spending
Executive order
Extremism
Fiscal policy
Free enterprise
GNP
Judicial review
Lobbyist
Market
Monetary policy
Nation
National debt
Nationalism
Patriotism
Pollution
Pressure group
Public opinion
Socialism
Welfare state

Conclusion

Nationalism is a powerful force not only in this country but among all nations. It provides unity and strength, but if abused, it may lead to oppressive government and military aggression. A nation that wants to live in peace and harmony must be able to adapt its economic and political life to changing conditions. The problems facing our government are manifold; they overlap and are interdependent. Only a few examples have been mentioned in this chapter. Some problems become meaningless as time marches on, and new ones arise. They seem to multiply faster than solutions can be found.

Notes

1. Frederick L. Schuman, *International Politics*, 7th ed. (New York: McGraw-Hill, 1969), p. 307.
2. Hans Kohn, *The Idea of Nationalism* (New York: Macmillan, 1944), p. 23.
3. John E. Maher, *What Is Economics?* (New York: Wiley, 1969), p. 5.
4. George L. Bach, *Economics*, 5th ed. (Englewood Cliffs, N.J.: Prentice-Hall, 1966), p. 702.
5. Arthur M. Schlesinger, "Our Ten Contributions to Civilization," *Atlantic Monthly* (March 1959), pp. 65–69.
6. "United States v. Curtiss-Wright Export Corporation," in John Vanderzell (ed.), *The Supreme Court and American Government* (New York: Crowell, 1968), p. 129.
7. Harry Lazer, *The American Political System in Transition* (New York: Crowell, 1967), p. 163.
8. Louis W. Koenig, *Congress and the President* (Glenview, Ill.: Scott, Foresman, 1965), p. 22.
9. Austin Ranney, *The Governing of Men*, 5th ed. (New York: Holt, Rinehart and Winston, 1966), p. 393.
10. R. E. Lane and D. O. Sears, *Public Opinion* (Englewood Cliffs, N.J.: Prentice-Hall, 1964), p. 1.
11. R. A. Rosenstone (ed.), *Protest from the Right* (Beverly Hills, Cal.: Glencoe Press, 1968), introduction.
12. Stan Twardy, "Carnival of Hate," in Rosenstone, *ibid.*, p. 59.
13. F. Kinsky and J. Boskin (eds.), *The Welfare State: Who Is My Brother's Keeper?* (Beverly Hills, Cal.: Glencoe Press, 1968), p. 2.

Suggestions for Further Reading

Bone, Hugh A. and Austin Ranney. *Politics and Voters*, 2nd ed. New York: McGraw-Hill, 1967. A short study of parties, voting, and the role of pressure and interest groups.

"Dollars, Trade and Aid," *Great Decisions*. New York: Foreign Policy Association, 1968, pp. 73–82.

Drury, Allen. *Advise and Consent.* Garden City, N.Y.: Doubleday, 1959. Novel on the interplay of political forces in the Senate.

———. *Capable of Honor.* Garden City, N.Y.: Doubleday, 1966. Novel concerning the workings of a national party convention.

Harris, Joseph P. *Congress and the Legislative Process.* New York: McGraw-Hill, 1967. A brief study of how Congress works.

Judge, Joseph. "New Grandeur for Flowering Washington," *National Geographic* (April 1967), pp. 501–539. Pictorial article on the development of the nation's capital.

Ritchie-Calder, Lord. "Polluting the Environment," *The Center Magazine*, 2 (May 1969), 7–12.

Udall, Stewart L. *1976: Agenda for Tomorrow.* New York: Harcourt, Brace & World, 1968. The former Secretary of the Interior talks about population and conservation problems.

White, Theodore H. *The Making of the President 1960.*

———. *The Making of the President 1964.*

———. *The Making of the President 1968.* New York: Atheneum, 1961, 1965, 1969. Chronicles of the last three presidential campaigns.

Wise, Sidney (ed.). *Issues, 68, 69.* New York: Crowell. Annual publication of documents on questions of current controversy.

PART FIVE THE WORLD WE LIVE IN

Vienna Choir Boys give a concert in Miami.
Peace Corps volunteer returns from Ethiopia.
Air Force captain sent to Spain.
Plywood mills around Seattle threatened by Japanese imports.

18 IT'S A SMALL WORLD
interdependency of states

Every day brings reports about contacts with the world beyond our own nation. Americans study overseas in increasing numbers, and students on our college campuses come from every continent. Travel abroad, once the pastime of the very rich, is now available in the form of package deals to vacationing high-school teachers, factory workers, and to the retired.

Earlier in this century the mood of the American people was *isolationist*. "Let's stay out of other nations' quarrels" was our watchword. Today we know that such an attitude is no longer possible. A civil war in Nigeria, trouble in the Middle East, controversies in Southeast Asia affect us deeply, and the decisions we make echo around the globe. The world is becoming smaller and smaller, and the *interdependency* of nations is growing.

HOW SMALL A WORLD?

The ancient Roman and the Chinese civilizations existed at the same time. Both were magnificent, and each ruled vast territories. Yet except for a few wares that passed from merchant to merchant along the caravan routes, no contact existed between the two.

In medieval times many villagers never strayed farther from home than a day's journey on foot. Columbus spent three months crossing the Atlantic Ocean. In their ignorance people imagined that distant lands were inhabited by giants or dwarfs or by monsters with a single eye in the middle of their forehead.

In 1812, two weeks after the Treaty of Ghent had ended the war between the Americans and the British, the armies of both still fought a battle at New Orleans. The news of the peace had not yet reached them. Today air transportation and electronic communication make it possible for all of us to witness important historical events. It is a time of "instant history."

Early in the twentieth century, the first automobile was driven across the country—a journey that took seventy days. Members of the United States Foreign Service enjoy the quip that with modern air travel you can, on the same day, have breakfast in Buenos Aires, lunch in Paris, dinner in New York, and sleep in Los Angeles. It may seem strange, but the traveler often finds himself spending more time crossing man-made boundaries with their customs, passport, and visa controls than covering vast distances. And in our own country the trip by car from Chicago International Airport to downtown Chicago may frequently take longer than the air trip from Chicago International to Kennedy Airport in New York.

In the nineteenth century Europe practically dominated the world. And Europeans noticed little besides what went on in their own continent and their vast colonies. Only occasional glances were cast in the direction of the United States. In 1878 the American explorer Henry M. Stanley wrote a best-selling book about Africa, entitled *Through the Dark Continent*, which introduced readers to this almost unknown continent. In contrast, today, with full coverage of African events on television and in the newspapers the myth of the dark continent is disappearing, just as the myths about cowboys and Indians have given way to more substantial knowledge.

Ambassadors, the chief representatives of a government in a foreign country, once had to make important decisions on the spot. Now all questions may be referred to the home government by telephone if necessary. A "hot line" has been installed between the White House and the Kremlin to be used only by the chiefs of state in case of emergency. By using the phone as a means of communication during the fighting in the Middle East in the summer of 1967, an *escalation* into a major war was prevented.

ECONOMIC INTERDEPENDENCE

Early communities were usually *self-sufficient*—that is, the members produced everything they needed. They gathered or grew their food, fashioned their clothing and built their shelters from materials close at hand. Today only the most isolated and underdeveloped countries preserve some form

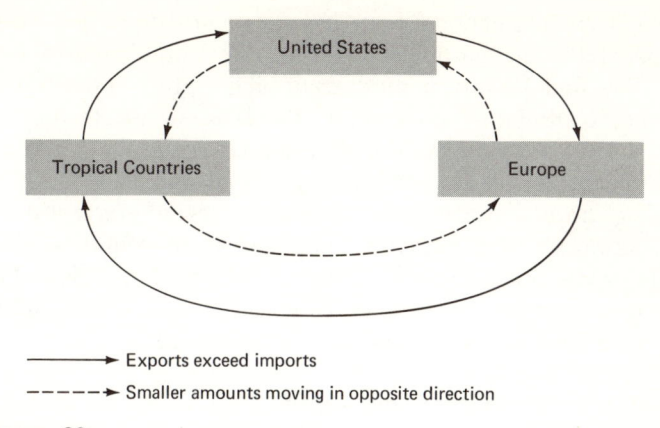

→ Exports exceed imports
--→ Smaller amounts moving in opposite direction

Figure 30
Flow of Multilateral World Trade
Source: George L. Bach, *Economics,* 5th ed. (Englewood Cliffs, N.J.: Prentice-Hall, 1966), p. 622. Reprinted with permission.

of self-sufficiency, while the industrialized nations find themselves increasingly involved in trade, tourist traffic, and in various forms of international organization.

England was the first country to develop modern machine industry. Many Britons ceased to be farmers or sheepherders and became factory workers. Those who remained on the land were unable to feed and clothe the growing masses of city dwellers. Today the country must import most of its food; it pays for food by selling abroad what its factories produce. The same is true of Japan, the major industrial nation of Asia.

By contrast, the people of the United States can easily feed themselves. Our land area is large, and resources are abundant. But America too must trade, and she is doing so in increasing quantities. We export half of our cotton crop, while 90 percent of the tin and nickel used in our industries comes from abroad. Between 1939 and 1964 American exports rose from $4 billion to $37 billion.[1] But imports into the United States have also been increasing. Some government officials and businessmen complain that too much American money leaves the country in payment for foreign automobiles, clothing, electronic gear, and other articles. This money is in addition to the millions of dollars spent abroad by our tourists and our military forces.

A nation's economy is healthy when exports and imports are kept in a rough balance. This does not necessarily mean that the exports of Country A to Country B must equal its imports from the same country. The balance is often achieved not in a two-way exchange but by an arrangement involving three or more parties. For example, Brazilians sell more coffee to us than we sell goods to them. The United States, in turn, does a great deal of export business with Canada and Europe, which then may provide needed industrial products for Brazil. Thus, if everything works smoothly, international trade becomes *multilateral* (see Figure 30).

One of the main troubles besetting the world today is large-scale poverty. We find poverty a most disturbing feature inside the United States, the wealthiest country on earth. Here it affects only a small minority, but in the total world picture we can designate vast stretches as poor or underdeveloped, or, to use the official and more hopeful term, "developing" areas. Poverty causes domestic unrest wherever it occurs, but when it becomes typical for the majorities of many countries, it is also a danger to world peace. Besides, it raises the moral question: Can rich nations enjoy their luxuries in good conscience, while untold millions are constantly on the brink of starvation? (See table below.)

People and Products of the World

	Gross National Product (in millions of dollars)	Population (in millions)
World (noncommunist countries only)	1,875,093	3,420
United States	789,700	200

Conclusion: Approximately 5.7 percent of the world's population produces approximately 40 percent of the noncommunist world's Gross National Product.
Source: *New York Times Encyclopedic Almanac, 1970.*

The *per capita income* (average income per person) in the United States was $3,159 in 1967.[2] By contrast, in the same year, the per capita figure for the East African country Ethiopia was $54 and that of Guatemala, in our own hemisphere, was less than $200. There is one physician for every 137,000 Ethiopians as compared with one doctor for about every 600 Americans; and in this country we complain strongly about a shortage of medical personnel, especially in our rural areas and in the poorer sections of the cities. It is hardly necessary to add that in underdeveloped countries like these few cars are seen on the roads—if there are roads—and few radios, telephones, and electric lights in the homes.

Why are Ethiopia, Guatemala, and many other countries poor? In some instances poor climate and lack of natural resources can be blamed, but more often poverty is man-made. Social conditions are responsible for widespread misery. Small ruling groups cling to their inherited wealth and show little regard for the needs of the masses. The rich often control the machinery of government and suppress any attempt to change the picture.

Wealth in the hands of a few does not in itself help a country, especially when the average citizen lacks education and technical skills. The farmer may work long and hard on his tiny plot yet produce very little. The average yield of cotton in India is 93 pounds per acre; in America the average yield is 419 pounds.[3] The difference can be attributed to ignorance, lack of money for tools and fertilizers, and also to the unwillingness to change cultural patterns abruptly.

In 1962 the unemployment rate in Kinshasa (formerly Leopoldville) in the Congo stood at about 56 percent. Yet at the same time, government

Chart Data

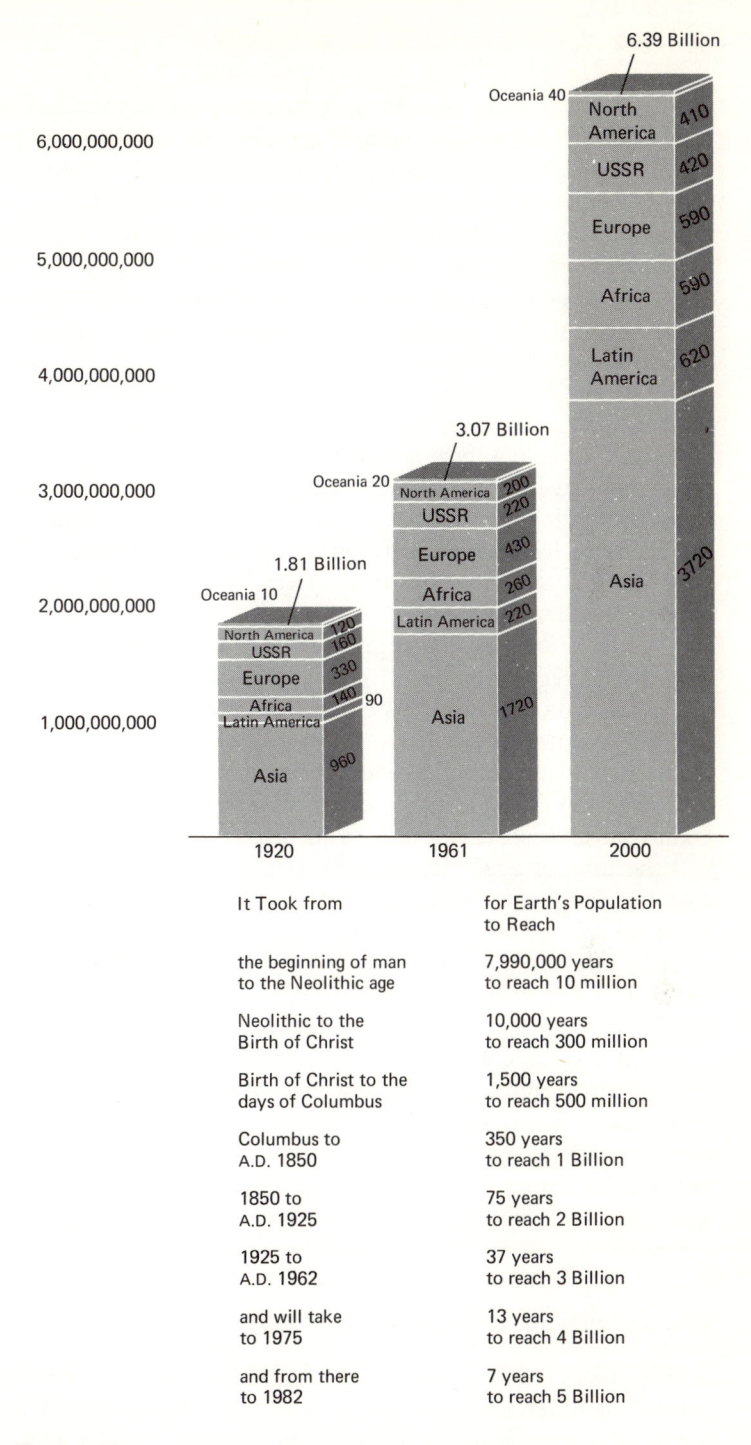

1920: 1.81 Billion
- Oceania 10
- North America 120
- USSR 160
- Europe 330
- Africa 140
- Latin America 90
- Asia 960

1961: 3.07 Billion
- Oceania 20
- North America 200
- USSR 220
- Europe 430
- Africa 260
- Latin America 220
- Asia 1720

2000: 6.39 Billion
- Oceania 40
- North America 410
- USSR 420
- Europe 590
- Africa 590
- Latin America 620
- Asia 3720

It Took from	for Earth's Population to Reach
the beginning of man to the Neolithic age	7,990,000 years to reach 10 million
Neolithic to the Birth of Christ	10,000 years to reach 300 million
Birth of Christ to the days of Columbus	1,500 years to reach 500 million
Columbus to A.D. 1850	350 years to reach 1 Billion
1850 to A.D. 1925	75 years to reach 2 Billion
1925 to A.D. 1962	37 years to reach 3 Billion
and will take to 1975	13 years to reach 4 Billion
and from there to 1982	7 years to reach 5 Billion

Figure 31
World Population and Projection for Year 2000

Source: *Intercom*, 10 (July–August 1968), 28–29. Reprinted with permission of the Foreign Policy Association.

and business in that city were in desperate need of qualified workers. A teacher, nurse, engineer, or simply a high-school graduate with the ability to read, write, and figure could easily find a job. Over half the residents, though, could not qualify. A population with "know-how" can make more things in less time than one that is untrained. Many underdeveloped nations have *single-crop economies,* such as Ghana, another African country, which depends on the export of cocoa. If the world price of cocoa falls, such a nation, which is already at the subsistence level of income, suffers even more.

All this need is compounded by the *population explosion,* which has come about because of the high birth and low death rates. An underdeveloped country's first contacts with wealthy industrialized countries bring about such innovations as inoculation against diseases, better sanitary facilities for children and adults, and more wholesome eating habits. This sounds like a blessing and it is, but the immediate effect is a lower rate of child mortality and a longer life expectancy. The population figures shoot up dramatically. (See Figure 31.)

India, a country that is perennially short of food, covers less territory than the United States, but its population stands now at about 500 million and is still growing rapidly. We find the highest rate of population growth in Latin America with Asia and Africa following in close order. This means that there are more mouths to feed where food is scarcest.

Communism has its greatest appeal among the most frustrated populations. Guerrilla warfare frequently erupts where poverty is highest and the level of education lowest. Here we usually find unstable governments, military men thirsting for adventure, and mobs that are easily led to violence.

In addition economic conditions in one country affect other countries. The Great Depression of 1929 began in the United States but spread from here over the entire world. Since then, as countries have become more interdependent, economic interdependence has become even more widespread. Events in one nation inevitably involve neighboring and distant nations. Positions must be taken in response. Whether we want it or not, we must be our brother's keeper if only to help ourselves. We cannot for long live on an island of peace and prosperity surrounded by a turbulent ocean of revolt and repression. Sooner or later the storms will flood the island.

THE NATION-STATE IN TODAY'S WORLD

Individuals who travel, correspond, or work on projects in cooperation with citizens of other countries are involved in international relations. Merchants, shipping firms, industries, and universities likewise extend their activities across national boundary lines. But the most persistent, best organized, and most crucial international contacts exist between governments.

A nation with a government of its own is a *nation-state*. The nation-state adamantly insists on its *sovereignty*, which means that there is no higher authority above it and that it deals independently with other nation-states. The United States possesses national sovereignty. So do France, Turkey, and China, but Denver or Utah does not, even though a politician may occasionally refer to "the sovereign State of South Carolina" in his speech. An independent foreign policy, an army and navy, a currency and economic policy are marks of national sovereignty.

Yet complete sovereignty exists only in theory, not in fact. It is checked, sometimes quite severely, by boycotts, threats of war, public opinion, and international agreements. If all nation-states were completely sovereign, they would treat each other as equals. "The myth of sovereignty has come to stipulate the absolute and perfect legal equality of all states."[4]

Here we have a paradox. The nation-states demand equal respect for their sovereignty, yet they are obviously not equal. The Maldive Islands, a group of coral atolls in the Indian Ocean having barely 100,000 inhabitants, is not equal to Russia, nor is Ghana equal to the United States, in population, wealth, technological capacity, and—above all—in power.

Each nation-state has a set of goals and values that comprise the *national interest*. Statesmen justify their actions as being in the national interest. During wartime the President of the United States is given almost dictatorial powers; he may even suspend constitutional freedoms "in the national interest." The overriding national interest is survival. Leaders of any country are, first and foremost, charged with the duty to protect their country from external harm. In the name of the national interest armies are maintained, and wars are fought.

The values that a nation holds are reflected in the *objectives* of its government. Hitler's objective was to make Germany the dominant power in Europe and possibly in the world. Some writers claim that Russia has a similar objective. An objective of the United States is to halt the spread of communism, particularly in the Far East. We would expect that, out of sheer self-interest, all nations would pursue the objective of international peace, but their actions don't always reflect this objective.

POWER

Parents have the power to make their children pick up discarded toys or stay home when the children would rather go out with friends. The power of the parents resides to a large extent in their superior physical strength. The teacher has the power to make students do their assignments because he can penalize them with poor grades. Power is, among other things, the ability to *coerce* others into obeying. Within a country the government has the power to coerce the citizens into observing its laws. Through its police forces and, if need be, its army, the government has a monopoly on the means of coercion.

On the international scene power is concentrated in the nation-state.

No superpower yet exists that is capable of coercing nations; so the various nations compete with each other in building up their means of coercion, mainly their military might.

But, in nation-states, power rests not only in the number of soldiers and the size of missiles. It is also "the capacity to influence human behavior. Power in international politics is therefore the capacity of a state to influence the behavior of other states."[5]

In 1968 Czechoslovakia, a communist country, decided to allow its citizens a larger measure of personal freedom. This change in communist policy met with strong opposition from Russia, and in the summer units of the Red Army and several other communist nations invaded Czech territory. Russia, clearly possessing all the military power it needed, stopped many of the reforms. Yet this violation of a weaker neighbor's sovereignty caused such an outcry of enraged public opinion, even in some communist countries, that the Russians had to soft-pedal, for a time, some of their measures and make compromises here and there. They were definitely embarrassed by world reaction to their acts.

In the preceding year a short war erupted in the Middle East. Within six days the Israelis inflicted a humiliating defeat on the armies of several Arab states even though they were numerically weaker. The Israeli power rested not on numbers but on technological skill and a strong feeling of unity. Since then an uneasy stalemate has prevailed.

Power is difficult to measure. Military capability is still the most commonly used measuring stick, but power also depends greatly on such factors as economic resources, technical training, solidarity, and the quality of leadership. Prestige helps to increase a nation's power. When a nation-state presents a favorable image to the outside world, it is better able to influence the behavior of other nation-states. Russia's prestige suffered by its invasion of Czechoslovakia. Czech students, workers, and government leaders wanted to remain communists, but they desired more personal freedom and also more freedom for their country to chart its own course. Russia squashed this desire with its tanks, and its pose as a peacemaker and a protector of the oppressed became slightly tarnished in the process.

Our example as a land of freedom and opportunity and also our generous aid programs have enhanced the prestige of the United States, but when we backed some rather odious dictatorial governments and became involved in a muddled Asian war, we seemed to lose some prestige.

BALANCE OF POWER

The earth is divided among sovereign nation-states, each jealous of its power and prestige. As these states vie with each other, they engage in a struggle for power. More power for one nation means less power for others. This struggle for power, often intensified by strong nationalistic feelings, is being waged with many weapons. The most obvious and also the most tragic one is war. But there are other ways to spar for power, among them acquiring allies who—hopefully—will render help in time of need.

History records numerous wars, but it also notes a number of peaceful years, when no large armies faced each other in battle and no monuments had to be erected for fallen heroes. Such peaceful periods came about not so much because the states sincerely wanted peace but because a *balance of power* prevailed, a situation in which two or more nation-states of about equal strength existed side by side. None was so weak that others could attack it without risk; none was so strong that it could easily get away with trying to push the others around.

The hundred years prior to 1914 were comparatively peaceful. Armed conflict was not completely absent, but wars were rare and limited, mainly because five European powers (England, France, Austria, Russia, and Prussia [later Germany]) formed the balance. Whenever one of the states threatened to become too strong, the others banded together in *alliances* to keep it in its place. This was in particular the policy of England, the world's leading sea power. As long as several European nations kept each other in check, England could concentrate on enlarging her overseas empire.

The outbreak of World War I, which contained all the seeds of World War II, signaled the dismal failure of balance-of-power politics. This kind of international balance failed to prevent the holocaust that occurred in battle abroad and on the homefront and that caused great damage to defeated and victor alike. Since the end of World War II an uneasy balance has prevailed between the two superpowers, the United States and Russia. (See Chapter 19 for a further discussion.) In order to maintain this balance, which has also been called a "balance of terror," each of the two felt it had to outdo or at least match the other in military strength. This has led to the *arms race*, particularly to the stockpiling of nuclear weapons. The aim of each antagonist is not really balance but superiority. When we have atomic weapons that can destroy Russia a hundred times over and they have weapons that can only destroy us fifty times over, we are theoretically "ahead." Scientists and philosophers have pointed out that this striving for "overkill" eventually becomes absurd.

UNITED STATES FOREIGN POLICY

In order to reach its objectives, a nation-state creates a *foreign policy*. How does the United States conduct foreign policy? As it does in all other areas, Congress makes the laws pertaining to our relations with other nations. It has special committees and subcommittees that study all aspects of foreign policy and make recommendations. Declaration of war and ratification (approval) of treaties with foreign powers are important duties of Congress. It also wields the very crucial *power of the purse*; it dispenses the money needed to carry out foreign policies.

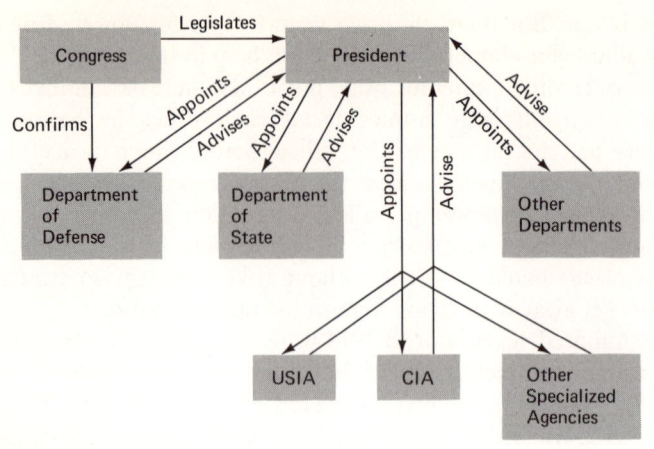

Figure 32
Government Involvement in Foreign Affairs

Foreign policy is not only the business of the diplomats and the generals. Many economic and psychological considerations enter the picture. Since World War II practically all segments of government have had to consider the world beyond our own immediate boundaries. Our military commitment in Vietnam has affected the political and economic position of the United States everywhere and has cast its shadow on conditions inside the country.

The President plays the leading role in shaping and carrying out foreign policy. The country looks to him for leadership, and to the outside world he represents the voice of the United States. At times Congress has complained that a President has invaded its own area of responsibility.

Formal contacts with foreign governments are mainly handled by the Department of State, whose head, the Secretary of State, is the chief adviser to the President in foreign affairs. The President may make all important decisions himself or leave them to his Secretary of State. Franklin Roosevelt kept a tight hand on foreign relations, whereas Dwight Eisenhower allowed his Secretary of State, John Foster Dulles, much leeway.

The Department of Defense is not only responsible for the military security of the United States but administers military aid programs around the world; it is represented by *military attachés* in many of our embassies and occupies a key position in the *National Security Council*. This group of the highest military and governmental chiefs has a strong voice (some say the strongest) in advising the President on the course of foreign policy. Other departments, particularly Agriculture, Labor, Commerce, and the Treasury, are involved in foreign trade, aid to developing countries, and problems of financial stability.

Many specialized agencies have a part in our contacts with other nations. The Central Intelligence Agency (CIA) gathers information needed by our policy-makers. Popular imagination credits it with all kinds of hair-raising spying and counterspy activities; but in reality most of its work is of a routine character. The United States Information Agency (USIA) is our propaganda outlet. It helps to create and maintain a favorable image of America by establishing libraries, arranging exhibits, concerts, and lectures, and by operating the Voice of America, an international broadcasting network.

As the world grows smaller in this age of instant communication and rapid transportation and as the role of government expands, virtually all parts of the governmental machinery will undoubtedly become increasingly involved in foreign affairs (see Figure 32).

INTERNATIONAL RELATIONS

The preceding paragraphs discuss briefly the making of foreign policy in one country. Similar activity is carried on in virtually every other country. Our government makes decisions and takes actions that it believes are in our national interest. Other governments do likewise.

Many Americans are convinced that Russia is a threat to the security of the United States. In the Anti-Ballistics Missile (ABM) argument of 1969 many took the position that these weapons were needed for our defense, while their opponents reasoned that the weapons would only accelerate the arms race between the two major powers. The Russians, in turn, explain that their mighty military machine is absolutely necessary for their national security. They even argue that the invasion of Czechoslovakia in 1968 was a purely defensive measure. In fact, Russians often ask American tourists why we want to threaten Russia. They may or may not know that much is said and written here about the dangers that threaten us from Eastern Europe.

In 1969 Peru seized the Peruvian properties of American oil companies. We regarded this seizure as an act against our national interest and protested strongly. But Latin American and other developing countries resent the heavy investments of American and West European companies because money is taken out of these poverty-stricken countries. Peru was upholding its own national interest, as the Peruvian leaders who happened to be in power at the time saw it.

A diplomat or a general usually tries to carry out the policy of the government that appoints him; he tries to guard his country's national interests. In the national interest diplomats bargain with the representatives of other countries, and generals prepare for wars, and if governments decide to do so, war is waged. As long as the generals stay home and let the diplomats handle contacts with the rest of the world, these gentlemen in business suits engage in the normal business of international relations.

> In a sense, the study of international relations is a study of the interplay of the foreign policies or of the national interests of nations.

But while the architect of foreign policy tends to regard the world from the vantage point of his own nation, the student of international relations must look at the world in the round.[6]

Main Ideas

1. Technological progress, especially in the fields of transportation and communications, is bringing about greatly increased contacts between the nations of the world.
2. Most countries, particularly industrialized ones, are not economically self-sufficient but depend on foreign trade.
3. A healthy national economy shows a rough balance of trade.
4. Underdeveloped countries suffer from large-scale poverty, lack of skills, unpopular governments, and sometimes also from the adverse effects of a single-crop economy.
5. Underdeveloped countries suffer most from the world-wide population explosion.
6. The nation-state insists on its sovereignty and considers all its objectives to be in the national interest.
7. The power of the nation-state is its capacity to influence the behavior of other nation-states.
8. The power of the nation-state is derived from its military strength, its prestige in the civilized world, the quality of its leadership, and from its natural and human resources.
9. A balance of power prevails when two or more nation-states of about equal strength exist side by side.
10. The balance-of-power situation in Europe is credited with helping keep the peace prior to 1914; the two world wars, however, shattered the belief in the effectiveness of the balance-of-power system.
11. The President of the United States plays the most important role in stating and carrying out the foreign policy objectives of the United States.
12. Practically all parts of government are, to some extent, involved in foreign relations.

Important Terms

Alliance
Ambassador
Arms race
Attaché
Balance of power
Coercion
Escalation
Foreign policy
Interdependency
Isolationism

Multilateral world trade
National interest
Nation-state
Per capita income
Population explosion
Power of the purse
Self-sufficiency
Single-crop economy
Sovereignty
Supranational

Conclusion

Writers sometimes use the term "world community." If we can speak of a world community at all, it is not to be thought of as a replica of the local or national communities as we have encountered them in earlier chapters. World problems are different from local ones. These problems are especially distressing since no effective force yet exists on a supranational level to curb the aggressive appetites of sovereign nations or to make these nations introduce reforms although their people may live in poverty and without personal freedom. Some students of international politics look at the world as an international system of anarchy beset by a struggle for power among all the nations in the world. However, checks do exist on the actions of modern nation-states, but as yet they are limited and often ineffective, depending on the power of the nation that must be coerced. (See Chapter 20.) We must come to view the problems of the world realistically instead of through our personal or national biases. We cannot afford to do otherwise.

Notes

1. George L. Bach, *Economics*, 5th ed. (Englewood Cliffs, N.J.: Prentice-Hall, 1966), p. 613.
2. *World Almanac*, 1969, p. 138.
3. Elgin F. Hunt, *Social Science*, 3rd ed. (New York: Macmillan, 1966), p. 778.
4. C. O. Lerch and A. A. Said, *Concepts of International Politics* (Englewood Cliffs, N.J.: Prentice-Hall, 1963), p. 102.
5. W. W. Kulski, *International Politics in a Revolutionary Age*, rev. ed. (New York: Lippincott, 1968), pp. 39–40.
6. John G. Stoessinger, *The Might of Nations*, 3rd ed. (New York: Random House, 1969), p. 30.

Suggestions for Further Reading

A Cartoon History of United States Foreign Policy Since World War I. New York: Random House, 1968.
Church, Frank (Senator). "Making Foreign Policy: Treaties, War and the Constitution," *Current*, No. 91 (January 1968), pp. 6–12.
Commager, Henry Steele. "1918–1968: Is the World Safer for Anything?" *Saturday Review*, 51, November 9, 1968, 21–24.
Lunsford, Terry F. "Making Democracy Work," *Current*, No. 106, pp. 44–53.
National Policy Panel. *World Population*. New York: United Nations Association of the United States, 1969 (pamphlet). A short look at world population growth and some suggested means of attacking the problem.

Nelson, Joan M. *Aid, Influence and Foreign Policy.* New York: Macmillan, 1968 (paperback). The purpose of and the many types of foreign aid.

"Our Overcrowded, Underfed World," *America,* No. 120, May 24, 1969, p. 609.

Ward, Barbara. *The Lopsided World.* New York: Norton, 1968. Series of lectures on how underdeveloped nations can develop.

"The World Population Crisis," *Intercom,* 10 (July–August 1968), 18–56.

*Government overthrown in Indonesia.
Riots in Northern Ireland.
Syrians bomb Israeli outposts.
Incidents along the Indian-Pakistani border.*

19 A TROUBLED WORLD
revolution and war

Such news items appear daily in the newspapers and over television and radio broadcasts. In the various trouble spots of the world armies lunge at each other, mobs burn and loot, and conspirators imprison government leaders or drive them into exile. Unrest is widespread and can easily lead to war. And in this age of the interdependency of nations what begins as a civil war threatens to mushroom into world war.

RISING EXPECTATIONS

One of the chief reasons for unrest in many parts of the world is poverty. "Why is it now a cause?" you ask. "There has always been poverty." Yes, poverty has definitely existed all through history. In fact, it was the lot of most people, and they accepted it without question. But today modern travel and communication touch the lives of the African villager, the Asian coolie, the South American Indian. The poverty-stricken are becoming aware that large numbers of people elsewhere live in comfort and eat three nutritious meals a day, and thus they ask, "Why not us?"

The inhabitants of distressed areas do not want poverty and starvation as their way of life, even if this kind of life was the only one their fathers and grandfathers knew. People everywhere are joining the "revolution of rising expectations." They want a share of the wealth they see so prominently displayed, and they want it immediately. If it is not given to them willingly, they are increasingly determined to take it by force.

The revolt against poverty began in the nineteenth century with various socialistic and communistic movements. In a number of West European countries socialistic ideas led to the creation of the democratic welfare state. Communism took over in Russia in a bloody revolution that was followed by an even bloodier civil war. Since the revolution of 1917 Russian living standards have been rising, though they are still below ours. But for this economic progress the Russian people have had to pay a high price. They are living under a dictatorial regime that allows no political opposition and muzzles free expression.

Communist leaders had hoped that the events in Russia would spark a world-wide revolution, but this has not been the case. Still communist propaganda carries its message, at times very effectively, to many places.

Karl Marx, who created the theory of modern communism, addressed himself mainly to workers in the most industrialized countries. But in the second half of the twentieth century the appeal of communism seems to be strongest in places, such as Vietnam and Guatemala, where there is little industry but where a small wealthy group monopolizes power.

It is more the Chinese than the Russian type of communism that appeals strongly to the disgruntled people of Asia and Africa. China, the most populous country in the world, is still largely a land of peasants. Poor peasants in underdeveloped areas can easily identify with their Chinese counterparts and with their more revolutionary words and gestures.

Poverty on a world-wide scale—with the poor no longer meekly accepting their fate—creates tensions similar to those within our own national community. The world can be divided into "have" and "have-not" nations. The "haves," who enjoy a high living standard, are industrialized, while the "have-nots" still try to eke out a living with primitive plows and underfed livestock. The tension between these two worlds can only be eliminated by eliminating its cause—poverty. "Mankind will find out its unity when the barriers of exploitation and inequality have been thrown down."[1]

AID FOR THE "HAVE-NOTS"

The "haves" can no longer ignore the plight of the "have-nots." Many poverty-stricken countries are beset by guerrilla warfare, which the communists call "wars of national liberation." Poor people are attracted to rebel leaders who ask their support and promise them a better life free from the misery of hunger and disease. In Cuba Batista, a petty dictator, shamelessly exploited the population. Our government did little about it, and so Fidel Castro, a social revolutionary turned communist dictator, is now installed right at our doorstep.

Can prosperous nations help poorer ones and in what ways? Providing aid is not an easy task. The newest nation-states, which are usually also most in need of help, are very sensitive about their sovereignty. They jealously insist on all the outward symbols of national independence even when they can ill afford them. Most states attempt to establish a modernly equipped army immediately. The new leaders in Africa hurried to obtain limousines with motorcycle escorts though their citizens could not afford shoes. They establish national airlines, which are not particularly needed, and must spend money they do not have to hire foreign pilots and technicians.

These are mistakes caused by lack of experience. Advice is needed, but it must be extended tactfully and only when requested. The advanced nations can train administrators and technicians or send in their own experts to bridge the gap until local manpower is able to do the job.

Even more urgent than providing training is giving economic aid. The foreign trade of underdeveloped nations has steadily increased in volume, but at the same time their share of world trade has fallen from approximately 27 percent in 1953 to 19.9 percent in 1965, mainly because agricultural products decreased in value.[2] What is happening is that the gap between the rich and the poor nations is widening with every passing year, and frustration is increasing accordingly.

Some of this imbalance could be redressed fairly quickly. *Tariffs* and import duties of all kinds could be lifted from the products of these nations. Efforts have been made to establish a higher world-market price for such products as coffee and cocoa, which come primarily from "developing" nations, and to maintain a guaranteed price that would assure these nations a set income.

Many of the new nations are too small and too weak to have a healthy economy. They should be encouraged to establish *common markets* with their neighbors. The outstanding success of the European Common Market sets a good example (see Chapter 20).

The United States and other prosperous nations give direct aid in the form of money and goods. Here again good judgment and delicacy are required. The receivers proudly reject any "strings" being attached to such assistance; yet some controls seem needed to counteract corruption. Only too often it has been the wealthy few who have profited from the aid rather than the many poor.

Unfortunately, aid is at times used as a weapon in the Cold War between the communist and noncommunist worlds. Russia built the Aswan Dam for Egypt's late President Nasser with the idea of gaining political influence in the Middle East. On the other hand, the United States has often extended military and economic aid in order to ward off the threat of communist expansion. Effective aid to all "have-not" nations is definitely in the self-interest of the "haves" but not only because of their thirst for more power and influence. Unrest in any part of the world casts its shadow over all nations, even those that are far away from the immediate trouble spot. Our involvement in Southeast Asia is a good example. What we can do to bring comfort and hope to underdeveloped and strife-ridden areas will, in the long run, be of benefit to us.

Help of many kinds is needed, not only to boost backward economies. In addition, political impatience, outdated social imbalances, and the destructively high birth rates must be overcome. Is it possible to overcome these problems? The experts think it is. "The downward spiral of the 'revolution of rising frustrations' can be checked with realism and not by trying to arouse again a 'revolution of rising expectations.' "[3]

COLONIAL IMPERIALISM

When a country extends its territory, by conquest or by threat of war, beyond its original boundaries, we speak of *imperialism*. According to this definition Russia could be considered the major imperialistic power of this century. In the wake of World War II it swallowed up considerable amounts of territory in East Europe and also in the Far East (Estonia, Latvia, Lithuania, parts of Poland and of Japan). Besides, she holds sway over a number of *satellite* countries (East Germany, Czechoslovakia, Bulgaria, etc.), which have the outward trappings of sovereignty but must bow to the dictates of the Kremlin.

More often the term "imperialism" is applied to the possession of overseas colonies. Earlier in this century most of Africa and a large part of Asia were the properties of certain European nations, particularly England and France. Japan possessed some colonies in the South Pacific, and the United States controlled the Philippines.

The colonies were treated as property to be exploited for profit, like real estate. Slowly a spirit of defiance spread among the colonial peoples. It erupted in a vigorous nationalism, which in turn gave rise to powerful independence movements. The most dramatic independence movement occurred in India under the leadership of Mahatma Gandhi. He inspired not only the inhabitants of this British crown colony, but his influence extended far beyond to other young colonials who smarted under foreign domination.

The end of World War II brought a series of struggles for independence. Today the period of colonial imperialism has almost come to an end, and Portugal is practically the only colonial power left. Poor and backward itself, it holds on tenaciously to its African colonies, Angola and Mozambique, though Portuguese troops must fight continuous guerrilla uprisings. (See map of Africa, Fig. 33.)

With the newly won independence of the colonies a number of problems have arisen. Most of the former colonies find themselves in the ranks of the "have-nots." Some are so small that they lack the population

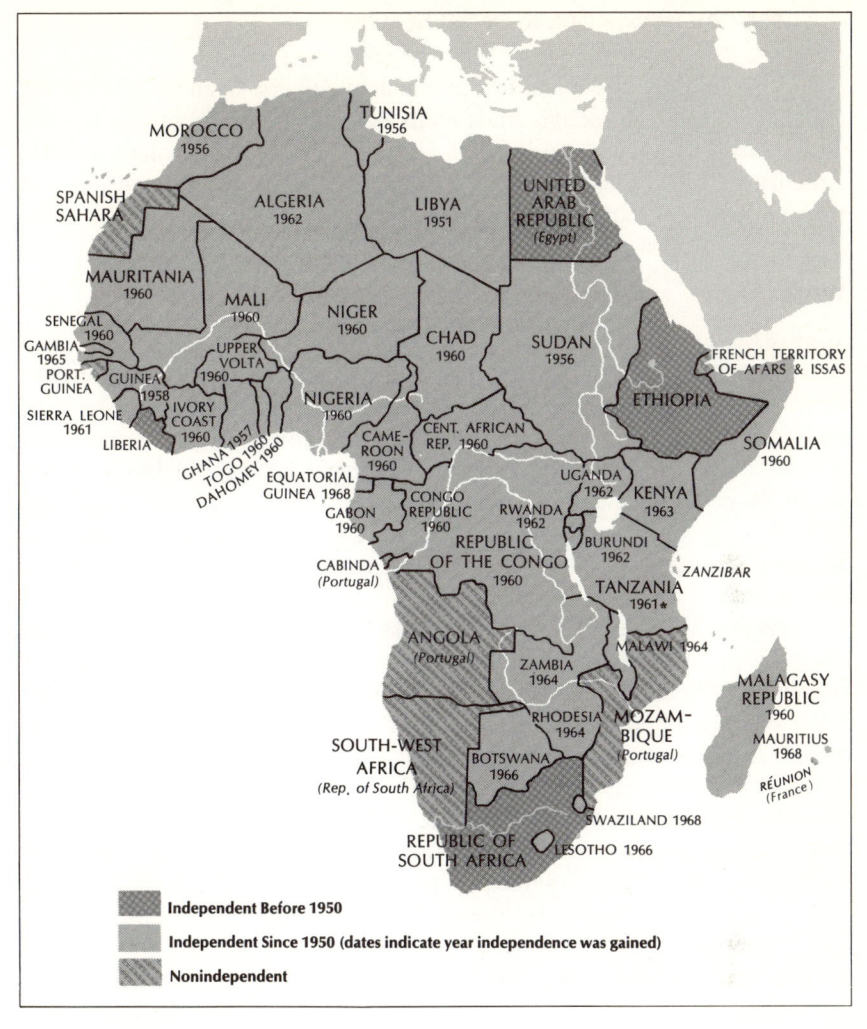

Figure 33
Africa Before and After 1950

* Tanganyika became free in 1961, the island of Zanzibar in 1963; on joining in 1963 they took the name of Tanzania.

and the resources to develop. Gambia on the west coast of Africa has a population of about 350,000, roughly equal to that of Birmingham, Alabama, and depends entirely on the sale of peanuts for its income.

The former colonial subjects retain strong feelings of hostility against their former masters, the Western powers. Though the United States acquired few colonies, it stands guilty of economic imperialism. Some giant American corporations, owning oil wells, iron mines, and fruit plantations in Latin American countries, have at times used their power to dictate the policies of those countries. Thus the United States has become the main target of bitterness against the West. Economic aid is often interpreted as *neocolonialism,* an attempt at economic domination. The presence of

American military bases has led to the familiar cry "Yankee, go home." American officials in foreign lands are booed and stoned. Riots occur, such as the protests against the official visit of Nelson Rockefeller to Latin America in 1969. The shadow of colonialism lingers on and continues to threaten peaceful cooperation among nations.

WAR

War is the gravest danger facing mankind today. There was a time when two armies engaged in battle while the rest of the world went unconcernedly about its business. This is no longer possible. With the advent of atomic weapons man now has it within his power to make the earth uninhabitable for life as we know it. Hydrogen bombs can bring instant death to millions, and the fallout can harm future generations. Military arsenals now contain rocketry of increasing sophistication, nerve gases, and means of bacteriological warfare. All this makes the idea of world war a nightmare.

World War II (1939–1945), the last large-scale war, brought death to over 22 million people, many of whom were the civilian victims of bombing raids. No count is possible of the additional millions who died from starvation and disease caused by the war. But the end of the war in 1945 did not bring world peace. Since that time opposing troops have continued to fight each other in some corner of the globe.

Guerrilla warfare has emerged as the characteristic style of fighting. Small armed bands operate from jungle bases or from mountain hideouts. Often they swoop down suddenly upon their enemies, and after striking they filter back to prepare for the next attack. There are no front lines in the traditional sense. Peasants who work their rice paddies by day may become guerrilla soldiers at night.

The Sudan, Laos, Vietnam, Thailand, Malaysia, and the Portuguese colonies have had their share of guerrilla warfare. Guerrilla tactics were used very successfully by the Chinese communists in wresting control of the country from President Chiang Kai-shek. Mao Tse-tung, the leader and father figure of Red China, elevated guerrilla warfare almost to a political creed.

Though guerrilla bands wage mostly civil wars, other countries are often drawn into the conflict. The United States has supplied military advisers and technicians to a number of governments, along with troops and weaponry. Since the end of World War II we have been involved in two shooting wars, both undeclared. Our fight against North Korea (1950–1953) was officially labeled a "police action." What label should be applied to the struggle in Vietnam is still disputed.

In Korea and in Vietnam the United States has been engaged in *limited wars,* wars in which the intention is not to use the full might of our army, navy, and air force. *Conventional weapons* have been used in all fighting, meaning that all instruments of war have been used with the exception of atomic bombs. Many countries are not yet capable of producing atomic "hardware." But it is characteristic of our time that even the nations that have large stockpiles of these superweapons are afraid to use them for fear that a limited war may escalate into the major calamity that will bring the end of humanity.

WHY WAR?

History books, especially older ones, contain an endless chronicle of wars. Battle after battle was fought between tribes, kingdoms, and empires. Even bishops and popes participated at times in the deadly sport. These questions arise: "Why does war exist? Is it inevitable? Is man by nature a warring animal?" Only in the past few years have scholars begun to seriously tackle the problem. "For the first time in history, we can speak of a Peace Research Movement, characterized by rigorous *empirical* inquiry into the nature and origins of violence in international conflict [italics are this author's]."[4]

In the sixteenth century King Francis I of France was engaged in almost constant warfare with the Holy Roman Emperor Charles V. When Francis was asked what differences of view had led him and Charles to fight each other, he replied: "None whatever. We agree perfectly. We both want control of Italy."

Greed and hunger for power are obvious causes of war. So are aggressive nationalism, intolerant religious attitudes, and the desire to spread certain ideologies, such as communism. Often the combatants claim to fight in the name of religion or ideology when the real reason is the quest for more land.

From among those who have pondered the causes of war three main ideas have emerged:

> 1. Man is by nature capable of doing either good or evil, and it is the evil in him that drives him to wage war. Some thinkers view man as striving for improvement. Once the good in him gains the upper hand, war will be averted. This is an optimistic point of view.[5]
> 2. The cause of war lies in the character and purpose of the state. Spokesmen for democracy feel that monarchic governments tend to bring about armed clashes. But the record shows that democracies have been involved in many wars along with absolute monarchies and dictatorships. "There is no demonstrable historical correlation between devotion to democracy and devotion to peace."[6]
> 3. International anarchy brings about war. In the Wild West, where police power was weak or absent, the law of the six-shooter prevailed. Similarly lack of police power on the international scene permits uncontrolled competition among the nation-states.[7]

The conclusion that can probably be drawn from this list is that no single cause is responsible for most wars but rather a combination of many causes. Psychologists find that continued frustration can lead to aggression, which helps explain violent forms of crime and delinquency. The frustration of a whole nation may express itself in war. Rarely are all people who participate in war frustrated; they will fight, nevertheless, because of patriotism or because they have no other choice.

Nothing gives a group greater cohesion than having to face a common enemy. Science fiction writers have suggested that one situation in which mankind might achieve unity is if we were threatened by an invasion from outer space. This is interesting to contemplate, but it would be unwise to wait for such an event to solve the problem of war on earth.

To study the causes of war and the possible ways of avoiding conflict remains a fruitful undertaking because "there is nothing in human nature that makes war inevitable. This conclusion is strengthened by the undeniable fact that warfare is by no means a universal phenomenon."[8] The Semai in the hill country of Malaysia and the Bushmen of Africa are examples of societies that do not engage in war. In the Eskimo language there is not even a word for war. Perhaps the civilized nations can learn something from their "primitive" brothers.

THE COLD WAR

It was a hot day in August 1945. The news of the Japanese surrender blared from thousands of radios. World War II was over. Fighting in Europe had ended three months earlier. Americans streamed out of factories and offices in jubilation. Peace had finally come—so they thought as they danced and frolicked in the streets. But they were mistaken, for what has followed the most terrible war in history is neither a shooting war nor peace—it is the Cold War. (See map, Figure 34.)

True, the Cold War excludes shooting, and this is the only good thing that can be noted about it. Otherwise, most other elements of war are present: closed borders, suspicion, bitter accusations, loud propaganda, a race for armaments and allies, and a jittery and tense atmosphere filled with the fear that open hostilities could break out any minute.

The Cold War is a new phenomenon in history. The military machines of Nazi Germany and imperial Japan lay shattered in the wreckage of World War II, and the United States and Russia, allies during the fighting, emerged as the two most powerful nation-states in the world. Wartime comradeship quickly gave way to competition. A power struggle developed over the control of the ravaged European continent and other areas. Each superpower frantically collected allies among the less powerful countries and kept its own destructive weapons in preparation. The world could be viewed as *bipolar*, with the United States and her allies (England, France, and West Germany, for example) occupying one pole and Russia and her allies (Poland, East Germany, and China, for example) the other.

For the two-and-a-half decades following World War II the two

Figure 34
The Cold War in Europe

major adversaries in the Cold War kept an uneasy balance of power. Prime Minister Winston Churchill of Great Britain spoke of an *iron curtain* that had been lowered between the communist world and what our statesmen like to call the "free world." Joseph Stalin, a ruthless Russian dictator, left no doubt that his country intended to occupy and control as much territory as possible. The United States made it just as unmistakably clear that it intended to stop Russian ambitions. President Truman declared, "Unless Russia is faced with an iron fist and strong language, another war is in the making. Only one language do they understand—'how many divisions have you?' "[9]

Bipolar World: The Balance of Power in the Cold War

United States	Russia
England	Poland
France	China
West Germany	Hungary
Canada	Bulgaria
Turkey	East Germany
Italy	Other allies
Other allies	

In March 1947 President Truman set forth the principle that the United States would "support free people who are resisting attempted subjugation by armed minorities or by outside pressure." The *Truman Doctrine* was primarily aimed at Greece and Turkey where, at the time, communist guerrillas were fighting the government and receiving Russian aid. Since then the same reason has been given for American intervention in other parts of the world, such as the divided city of Berlin, Korea, the Middle East, and Vietnam. When one superpower lent support to one side in a local conflict, the other superpower would inevitably lend assistance to the opposing side.

Russia gathered about it all communist parties of the world into an organization called COMINFORM (Communist Information Bureau). Later it concluded the *Warsaw Pact*, a military alliance, with its East European satellites. America's response was, and still is, an effort of *containment*. To contain the spread of communist control, the United States has created an opposing cluster of alliances, such as NATO (North Atlantic Treaty Organization), CENTO (Central Treaty Organization), and SEATO (Southeast Asia Treaty Organization).

The Treaties to Contain Soviet Imperialism

NATO
    United States, Canada, West European countries, Greece, Turkey

CENTO
    Turkey, Iran, Pakistan

SEATO
    United States, England, New Zealand, Australia, Thailand, Philippines, Pakistan

END OF THE COLD WAR?

Cold war is certainly preferable to "hot" war, but it means the situation is far from peaceful. Peace exists when nation-states can go about their business behind securely fixed borders without the fear that, at any time, a small fight in a remote place may bring about a general call to arms. Peace means that people can travel across borders without danger or harassment, that they can carry on trade with each other and cooperate in many ways even though the passports they carry identify them as citizens of different countries.

Russia and the United States, the two superpowers, have frequently expressed the wish for a "thaw" in their frozen relations. Communist party chief Khrushchev, who followed Stalin, voiced a desire for *peaceful coexistence* of the two countries and their political philosophies. Hesitant steps were taken to exchange visits of scholars and artists. A few American tourists began to visit Russia. However, suspicion continues to exist, especially on the Russian side, and so Western newspapers and magazines are kept from circulating, and visitors are forbidden to enter certain parts of the country. Each side asserts that its dislikes do not extend to the people of the other country, only to the other country's politics.

The United States and Russia may be the strongest powers ever to rule on earth, but they don't seem to be strong enough to keep their own allies in check. Yugoslavia, for example, a communist country in southeast Europe, bolted the Russian bloc in 1948 and has since kept out of Cold War entanglements. Russia threatened all kinds of reprisals against Yugoslav President Tito, but he continues to remain neutral much to the benefit of his country, which is happy and prosperous.

Small nations have defied Russia's bidding. In order to gain more influence around the shores of the Mediterranean Sea, Russia befriended the weak Arab states and supplied them with arms and other war materials. Against the advice of their benefactor the Arabs went to war against Israel in 1967 and were severely beaten. Afterward the Russians had to replace the enormous quantities of weapons and planes that the Arabs had lost. Bigness has its problems too.

The most painful sore on the Russian body opened not in the Middle East or Europe but on the remote 4,000-mile border with China, the giant of the Far East. Since 1949 China has been under a communist regime and during the 1950s it submitted to the leadership of Russia, as did most other communist countries.

But in the next decade the meek follower turned into a fierce competitor; the disciple defied the master. Heretofore the Russian interpretation of Marxism and communism had been accepted by China practically without question. But as time went on, Chinese spokesmen began to issue their own versions of communist doctrine in defiance of Russian leadership. From lecture halls and editorial offices the rebellion extended to the

border regions. China feels hemmed in. Her population of 760 million[10] casts hungry glances into the nearly empty spaces of Mongolia and Siberia, which the Russian fellow communists control.

China openly disputes the present boundary lines with Russia. Heavily armed troops face each other, and a number of bloody border clashes have already occurred. The conflict seems deep and serious and "will almost certainly be recorded as one of the most significant events of the twentieth century."[11]

Looking across the iron curtain might comfort Russia in her troubles, for Russia's American antagonist also has some problems of her own. CENTO and SEATO have become so beset with difficulties as to be practically useless. In Vietnam, for example, American troops were left to do most of the fighting, while SEATO members acted as little more than interested spectators.

NATO is supposed to keep a heavily armed watch against a possible invasion of Europe by the Red Army. But since the Kremlin and the White House have been talking about peaceful coexistence, the danger has seemed less urgent, and much of the original enthusiasm has evaporated from the NATO camp. President Charles de Gaulle severely cut France's participation in this military alliance. "The more fully Soviet-American relations assume the form of a *détente* [relaxation of tension], the more logical appears de Gaulle's argument that Europe cannot count on America for the defense of its vital interests [italics are this author's]."[12]

Our European allies want to act independently, and so do the new states that were formerly parts of European colonial empires. The latter follow the lead of India, which holds the position of belonging to neither camp in the Cold War but of willingly accepting aid from both. This policy of *nonalignment* is expressed in the words of Prime Minister Modeiba Keita of Mali: "We examine international problems in the light of our national interests and of the interests of Africa—and we decide our policy in the light of these principles alone."[13]

The Cold War has not disappeared, but its nature is changing. The nuclear powers, mainly the United States and Russia, have so far deliberately avoided direct confrontations. They clearly fear the escalation of local conflicts into all-out war. Besides, many other world problems require their attention. Instead of a bipolar world, a multiple balance of power seems to be taking shape. What we once spoke of as a balance of power mainly in terms of Europe now extends over the whole world.

FOREIGN POLICY AND MORALITY

We have discussed war and the dealings among nations without raising the question of right and wrong. Does morality have place in foreign relations? Many people are anxiously searching for an answer.

In our personal affairs we consider the question of morality. We respect our neighbor's property. Many occupations have codes of ethics. The merchant is under obligation to deal honestly with his customer, the doctor with his patient. Help is frequently rendered to those who are weak or in danger. We point with pride at the teachings of the various religions, which contain such commands as "Thou shalt love thy neighbor as thyself."

Does morality end at the national border? The record of international events seems to support such a contention. Governments act in the national interest, and the primary goal of the national interest is the pursuit of power. But millions of people are not satisfied with such a conclusion. They feel that if moral principles are at all valid they ought to be valid in the most important acts of organized mankind.

There is some evidence that national politics need not always be motivated solely by selfish goals. A number of countries—Sweden, for example—seem perfectly content with their second- or third-rate status among nations and don't strive for power, at least not military power.

America has given enormous quantities of material and technical aid to other countries. It can be argued that giving aid is in the national interest, since it wins us friends and helps combat communism; but this is not a sufficient explanation. Americans, as well as the people of other nations, carry a certain missionary zeal within their value system. They feel better helping others.

Moral concern shows itself in the criticism that we level at the actions of our government. Was it *right* to drop atomic bombs on the Japanese cities of Hiroshima and Nagasaki in the summer of 1945? These bombings served the national interest because they helped us win the war, yet many consciences have been troubled by the decision.

America's involvement in Vietnam has also come under severe scrutiny on moral grounds. In this case both advocates and critics of the war claim to have morality on their side. The advocates of the war argue that we ought to help the South Vietnamese maintain their independence against threats from their communist neighbors, while the critics point out the damage that we are inflicting on a nation that has done us no harm and is no threat to us.

Apparently it is extremely difficult to bring morality and national interest into agreement. "The realistic moralist must return to . . . problems of power, of the gulf between individual and collective morality, and of the relation of national interest to higher aims and purposes."[14] The conflict between morality and day-to-day politics will agitate us for some time to come.

Main Ideas
1. Poverty at a time of rising expectations is one of the main causes of unrest in the world.
2. It is in the self-interest of the "have" nations to help the "have-

nots" by removing trade barriers, stabilizing prices, and by tactfully providing material and technical aid and advice.
3. The struggle of Asian and African populations against colonial imperialism has brought about much strife in the current century.
4. Most former colonies are now independent states, but many suffer from lack of stability and retain hostile feelings toward Western nations.
5. Warfare with modern superweapons could make the whole earth uninhabitable for mankind.
6. Since the end of World War II numerous limited wars have been fought with conventional weapons.
7. The causes of war are now the object of systematic study.
8. Evidence indicates that there is nothing in human nature that makes war inevitable.
9. World War II was followed by the Cold War between two groups of nations, one led by Russia and the other by the United States.
10. The Cold War created a bipolar world for about two-and-a-half decades.
11. During that time the United States followed a policy of containment of communist expansion.
12. More recently, both the United States and Russia have made attempts at peaceful cooperation with each other.
13. The conflict between Russia and China has disrupted the pattern of the Cold War.
14. A number of newly independent countries and several European nations, particularly France, are trying to follow a policy of nonalignment.
15. The difficulty of aligning national interest with moral principles poses grave problems for the consciences of nations and individuals.

Important Terms

Bipolar world	Iron curtain
Cold War	Limited war
Colony	Neocolonialism
Common markets	Nonalignment
Containment	Peaceful coexistence
Conventional weapons	Satellite
Détente	Tariff
Guerrilla warfare	Truman Doctrine
Imperialism	Warsaw Pact

Conclusion

It is clearly beyond the power of even the mightiest nation to maintain peace in every corner of this earth and to eradicate poverty and inner tension inside every country. The only hope of achieving these revolution and war 373

ends is for nations to group together, share their resources, manpower, and prestige. In the next chapter we will discuss such groupings and also the possibilities of all nations joining hands in peaceful cooperation.

Notes

1. Barbara Ward, *The Lopsided World* (New York: Norton, 1968), p. 95.
2. *Ibid.*, Appendix C, p. 116.
3. Lucian W. Pye, *Aspects of Political Development* (Boston: Little, Brown, 1966), p. 199.
4. D. G. Pruitt and R. C. Snyder (eds.), *Theory and Research on the Causes of War* (Englewood Cliffs, N.J.: Prentice-Hall, 1969), p. ix.
5. Reinhold Niebuhr, *The Children of Light and the Children of Darkness* (New York: Scribner, 1944).
6. Frederick L. Schuman, *International Politics: Anarchy and Order in the World Society*, 7th ed. (New York: McGraw-Hill, 1969), p. 283.
7. Kenneth N. Walts, *Man, the State and War* (New York: Columbia University Press, 1959).
8. Otto Klineberg, *The Human Dimension in International Relations* (New York: Holt, Rinehart and Winston, 1964), p. 16.
9. Harry S Truman, *Memoirs* (New York: Doubleday, 1955), I, 551.
10. *World Almanac*, 1969, p. 502.
11. Robert A. Scalapino, "Sino-Soviet Split in Perspective," *Annals*, 351 (January 1964), 11.
12. David S. McLellan, *The Cold War in Transition* (New York: Macmillan, 1966), p. 130.
13. F. M. McEwan and R. B. Sutcliffe (eds.), *Modern Africa* (New York: Crowell, 1965), pp. 240–241.
14. Kenneth W. Thompson, *Christian Ethics and the Dilemma of Foreign Policy* (Durham, N.C.: Duke University Press, 1959), p. 143.

Suggestions for Further Reading

Burdick, E. and H. Wheeler. *Fail-Safe*. New York: Dell, 1962 (paperback). Novel about the imaginary accidental discharge of nuclear weapons.

Davis, Kingsley. "Population Control: Can Family Planning Do It?" *Current*, No. 91 (January 1968), pp. 50–64.

Findlay, Paul. "United States Foreign Policy: Are Frequent Wars Necessary?" *Vital Speeches*, 35, June 15, 1969, 520–523.

Fisher, Roger. "International Conflict for Beginners," *Atlantic*, 223 (June 1969), 47–52.

Gallico, Paul. *Trial by Terror*. New York: Knopf, 1951. Novel about the Cold War in Europe.

Horowitz, Irving L. *The War Game*. New York: Ballantine, 1963 (paperback). An attack on civilian militarists and on war as a game of politics.

Ward, Barbara. *The Rich Nations and the Poor Nations.* New York: Norton, 1962 (paperback). The growing gap between the rich and the poor; the politics and economics of development.

Wightman, David R. "Food, Aid, and Economic Development," *International Conciliation,* No. 567 (March 1968).

*They shall beat their swords into ploughshares,
And their spears into pruninghooks;
Nation shall not lift up sword against nation,
Neither shall they learn war anymore.*

—MICAH 4:3

20 WILL THE WORLD DESTROY ITSELF?
the quest for peace

In these immortal words the ancient biblical prophet expressed his dream of a future world at peace. Many men have tried to make this dream a reality, but thus far the goal has eluded them. The earth is still an arena in which approximately 150 sovereign nation-states are locked in a fierce struggle for power. Unlike sports, no stringent rules govern the competition, and no umpire could enforce them if they existed. "The management of power is the real issue."[1] Many attempts have been made to control the forces that bring about war. Most have failed, but whatever progress has been achieved gives us hope that Micah's magnificent vision may yet come true.

DIPLOMACY

When neighbors disagree on the boundary line between their property, they don't usually attempt to resolve the issue with knives or clubs. They may talk the problem out, and if this does not bring results, they may ask a judge to settle their dispute for them.

This procedure is such an obvious way for civilized people to settle things that we wonder why nations don't always follow it. The fact is that only too often it isn't the procedure used. However, attempts are always being made to have representatives of nations get together and discuss their common problems. As long as words are used in disagreements, chances are that guns will remain silent, and although talks may become tedious and drawn out, certainly they are preferable to fighting.

Nation-states talk to each other in the framework of *diplomacy*. If the United States wishes to communicate with a foreign country, our *ambassador*, stationed in that country, acts as our spokesman. On particularly important matters the foreign ministers or even the chiefs of state themselves meet face to face. If successful, such negotiations will result in treaties or alliances, or at least in agreement on some point of international concern.

The very fact that statesmen are willing to sit down at the conference table shows that they have at least some interest in a peaceful agreement. They would rather compromise than immediately call out the armies. But the difficulty is that no country can be forced to negotiate with another.

In the past the United States has peacefully settled border disputes with England and Mexico. In each case the parties involved were anxious to avoid war. If any one of the parties had been determined to fight, talks probably would have had a scant chance of success.

Alliances between states have a long history. However, they were not always arranged to serve the cause of peace. When the ancient Greek city-states were threatened by the superior Persian armies, they banded together to form the Delian League for their common defense. But soon Athens, the strongest of the city-states, began to oppress its allies and eventually turned the league into an empire, which it exploited shamelessly and cruelly.

Traditionally, diplomatic negotiations were carried on in secret. Only after the pacts were signed and sealed did the people learn what fate had been decided for them. In this way cities and provinces were traded back and forth without the consent of the people living in them. To prevent such deals, President Woodrow Wilson pleaded during World War I for "open covenants openly arrived at."

To some extent Wilson's demand was heeded. Certain diplomatic gatherings now take place in front of large audiences, with microphones humming and flashbulbs exploding. But we find that under such circumstances the representatives of nations don't really attempt to communicate with each other; instead, some tend to perform for the public and become propagandists. Completely open negotiations are no negotiations at all. When labor unions bargain with management or when congressmen try to iron out their differences, they prefer the quiet atmosphere of a closed room. This gives them more flexibility to arrive at a compromise and makes it less imperative to save face. Modern diplomacy must find a middle ground between irresponsible secrecy and ineffective performance in the public limelight.

COLLECTIVE SECURITY

When Hitler, the dictator of Germany, began to show a voracious appetite for territories belonging to other nations, diplomats held many meetings to try to fashion a system of *collective security*. According to this idea if all participating governments agreed to stand together and act collectively against anybody who broke the peace, then nobody would dare, in the first place, to face the combined might of all the peace-loving nations. This is a noble idea, but it did not work. Hitler guessed correctly that some countries would be unwilling to live up to their obligations, and so he continued to swallow up more territories till the world was plunged into all-out war. If collective security is to work, it would have to be backed up by some form of permanent international organization.

A serious flaw in the concept of collective security is the difficulty of defining *aggression*. When two boys get into a fight, usually each boy will claim that the other started it. "I punched him because he shoved me first." There have been few wars in history in which one side did not blame the other for starting the conflict.

INTERNATIONAL ORGANIZATION

Once, organized life existed only within the tribe or village. Beyond these confines was no man's land, where no rule prevailed except that of the fist. Slowly political organization was extended until it encompassed the whole nation. From then on, it was no longer man against man in the struggle for power but nation against nation. The individual had been brought under control but not the nation.

Ideas for drawing all or most nations into some form of supernational organization have been expressed for a long time. One obvious way of doing this would be for one nation to conquer all the others, a prospect that is neither very likely nor desirable. World-wide conquest has never been achieved, but some powers have come close to it. Ancient Rome held sway for several centuries over most of the then known Western world. It referred to its rule as the *Pax Romana*, the Roman peace, which was not peace at all in the modern sense but submission to a strong master. Over 1,000 years later Genghis Khan and his Tartar hordes founded a vast empire reaching from the Danube in Central Europe to the Pacific coast of Asia. Again, the *Pax Tartarica* forced upon a number of nations some sort of supernational organization.

But obviously, when we speak of international organization today, we have in mind the voluntary joining of hands to achieve a common purpose. When you mail a letter in Baltimore, you can be reasonably sure that, after some time, it will be delivered to your friend in Montevideo or in Teheran. This service is possible because in 1878 an international organization, called the Universal Postal Union, was formed. Most governments cooperate in this venture because it is to their advantage.

The advent of modern technology brought about the need for other international organizations to regulate telegraph and telephone service, aviation, weather reporting, and so on. Today we have also world-wide federations of students, scientists, labor unions, and many other special interest groups. The Catholic church maintains a very tight international organization, and other religions also have bonds that extend from nation to nation.

International cooperation among individuals and groups with common interests helps dispel hostility and prejudice. An atmosphere is created that, in the long range, will help preserve peace. But private or semiprivate organizations don't have the power to keep the guns muzzled and missiles grounded. This can only be achieved by cooperation among national governments. What is crucially needed is the *international organization* of the nation-states themselves.

The most successful organization of states so far does not extend over the whole world but only over a small part of it, Western Europe. It is the European Economic Community (EEC), usually called the *Common Market*. Six countries (France, West Germany, Italy, Belgium, the Netherlands, and Luxembourg) decided to drop all barriers of trade and travel between them. (See map, Figure 35.) For economic purposes they have almost become one country. Workers from any one of the six can find jobs in the other five countries. Talent and natural resources, such as coal and iron, are pooled to make the Common Market area a gigantic industrial complex and one of the most prosperous areas in the world.

What is particularly amazing about the success of the Common Market is that its two most important members, France and West Germany, were archenemies only a few years ago. The children of each were taught to hate people of the other nation, and when they grew to adulthood, blood was spilled in a number of destructive Franco-German wars. The example of the Common Market should give us hope that old enmities can be forgotten and that old nationalistic competition can make way for friendly cooperation.

The success of the Common Market has been so dramatic that other nations are anxious to participate and to share in the bounty. Great Britain applied several times, but it has not been granted membership yet. Charles de Gaulle harbored an old grudge against the British, and as long as he was the President of France, the application from London was vetoed. Now Britain's prospects for admission seem more favorable.

In the meantime, Great Britain has found friends in the European Free Trade Association (EFTA), which has a total of seven members. (See map, Figure 35.) They too cooperate in their economic relations and

Figure 35
The EEC and the EFTA

grant each other different kinds of relief from restrictions, but they have not pooled their resources to the degree the Common Market has.

UNITED NATIONS

As wars became more destructive and engulfed larger areas, the call was heard for an organization of all nation-states with enough power to police the whole world. Appalled by the unprecedented misery of World War I, President Woodrow Wilson became the prophetic spokesman for all men in his demand for an organization "which shall make it certain that the combined power of free nations will check every invasion of right."[2]

President Wilson's earnest plea led to the founding of the *League of Nations*. In a gleaming white palace on the bank of beautiful Lake Leman in Geneva representatives of many countries met to discuss the ways to prevent war and eradicate its causes. Their theme was that "violence against any member constitutes violence against all members."[3]

It was a noble theme, and millions of people everywhere looked toward the League with profound hope. Yet the League failed. It was powerless to prevent the onslaught of World War II. When the war broke out, the League was its first casualty.

Why did the League fail? Many member nations were not yet ready to subordinate their private quests for power to the overriding goal of world peace. They gave lip service to the creed of the League but continued to play the old game of power politics. Perhaps the hardest blow to the League was the failure of the United States to join it. Despite Wilson's impassioned pleading the spirit of American isolationism prevailed at the time. Even so "the League might have succeeded in its task had its members been willing to put collective security into practice, but of course they were not."[4]

The League of Nations did have some small successes to its credit; it prevented several conflicts between minor powers. But its major achievement was that the world saw in the League an experiment needing repetition. If mankind was to continue its existence, another try had to be made, and the second experiment could profit from the mistakes of the first.

Thus, while World War II was still being waged, the *United Nations* was born. The United States was one of the prime movers in its founding and joined it immediately. By 1969 membership had grown to 125 nation-states. The sprawling organization (see Figure 36) has its headquarters in New York City, but various branches and associated agencies are located in Geneva, Paris, Rome, Vienna, and other places.

The *Security Council* is the organ of the United Nations that is most frequently in the news. It can be called together at short notice and should always be ready to act when the peace is threatened anywhere in the world. Fifteen states are represented on the council, five of them permanently (United States, Russia, England, France, and [Nationalist] China). The

the quest for peace **381**

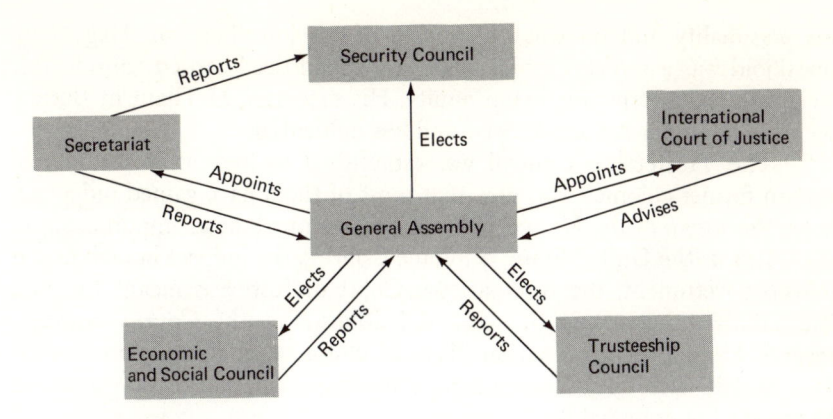

Figure 36
The United Nations Organization

other ten seats *rotate* among the delegates of various member nations, which are elected by the total membership of the General Assembly. Decisions are made "by an affirmative vote of seven [now nine] members including the affirmative votes of the permanent members."[5] This provision marks the often discussed *veto power* of the five permanent-member nations. Nothing can be done unless the *Big Five* agree.

The most spectacular gatherings of the United Nations are the yearly sessions of the *General Assembly* in which all member nations are represented. We can picture this assembly as an infant world parliament. Speakers from every corner of the earth give their views in English, French, Russian, or Chinese. Delegates listen, with the help of earphones, to immediate translations of the speeches, which "discuss any questions or any matters within the scope of the present Charter" and make recommendations in the framework of "the general principles of cooperation in the maintenance of international peace and security."[6]

The General Assembly was not originally intended to act as a kind of world-wide fire department that would quickly extinguish any threatening conflagration. This was to be the task of the smaller Security Council. But since the Security Council is often stymied by the veto of one of the Big Five, the General Assembly has taken over some of its functions. For example, when North Korea invaded South Korea in 1950, the General Assembly decided by majority vote that the invaders should be repelled. American and other troops therefore fought in Korea under a mandate of the United Nations.

The Secretariat, manned by employees from many member nations, sees to the functioning of the whole United Nations machinery and carries out the directives of the various organs. At its head is the Secretary General, whose official role is that of the number-one international statesman. Actually the importance of the Secretary General depends oftentimes on his personality and on what he makes of his job. The late Dag Hammarskjöld was a forceful leader whose word and deed carried considerable weight in the international community. His successor, U Thant of Burma, seems to be somewhat less decisive and less influential.

The Trusteeship Council was established to look after the fate of certain former colonies. But now that most of them have gained independence, this organ of the United Nations has lost much of its importance.

Just as the United States Supreme Court is the judicial branch of our federal government, the International Court of Justice is meant to fulfill the judicial functions of the United Nations. But the Court's power is severely limited, since no nation-state can be forced to abide by its verdict. It is as if it were up to every offender to decide whether or not he wants to pay the fine imposed by the judge.

The Economic and Social Council (ECOSOC) does not receive much publicity, yet, in its quiet way, it easily represents the most successful aspect of United Nations activity. Its interests range from the curbing of narcotics traffic to the status of women and from providing rototillers for Pakistani peasants to staffing Indonesian schools with teachers. The Economic and Social Council coordinates the activities of a number of specialized agencies (see table that follows), all of which aim at raising living standards, improving health, knowledge and freedom, and creating better understanding between the peoples of the world.

Some Specialized Agencies of the United Nations

International Labor Organization (ILO)
Food and Agricultural Organization (FAO)
World Health Organization (WHO)
United Nations Educational Scientific and Cultural Organization (UNESCO)
International Development Association (IDA)
International Monetary Fund (IMF)

THE UNITED NATIONS—SUCCESS OR FAILURE?

What has the United Nations accomplished in its first quarter century of existence? "Hardly anything" say many newspaper columnists and people who write letters to the editor, among others. The critics point out that the United Nations could not prevent the Cold War, nor can it prevent the smaller shooting wars that seem to occur with frightening regularity. The United Nations looked on helplessly as Russian tanks crushed a popular movement in Hungary in 1956. When Czechoslovakia was forced into submission by Russia in 1968, the United Nations again demonstrated its impotence. While the struggle in Vietnam and the tension in the Middle East continue unchecked, speakers at the Security Council and the General Assembly endlessly repeat propaganda phrases and do not give the impression that they are interested in finding solutions.

The United Nations has a much larger membership than did the

League of Nations, which preceded it, but critics have noted the absence of several important nations, particularly China, with its over 700 million inhabitants. The fact that in the General Assembly every nation has one vote, the tiniest and weakest having the same vote as the United States or Russia, is also regarded as a serious flaw by many detractors.

The United Nations is further plagued by financial problems. All member nations are obliged to contribute to the immense cost of patroling trouble spots in various parts of the world and of supporting the other activities this superorganization is supposed to be involved in. In reality, nations pay their dues and assessments only voluntarily, and there is no way to force them as our Internal Revenue Service forces us to pay our taxes. It is mainly through the cash contributions of the United States that the United Nations machinery can continue working.

But the difficulty lies as much with the critics of the United Nations as with the United Nations itself. Many had grand illusions about what the United Nations could accomplish, and when miracles did not happen, they could not hide their disappointment. The United Nations is a device for creating world order, but it cannot do any more than the member nations, especially the powerful ones, want it to do.

Some nation-states, though participating in an international forum, still pursue their national interests and use the United Nations for this purpose. Russia, for example, wanted to befriend the Arab nations for its own advantages. Therefore it helped condemn Israel as an aggressor following the Six Day War in 1967. Moscow did not sit as an impartial judge at this international forum, but cynically tried to gain political advantages from that tragic event. "The major theme that emerges . . . is the controlling role that the superpowers' national interest has played in the evolution of the UN."[7]

If we take into account all the obstacles and the half-hearted support of the major powers, it is remarkable that the United Nations has had as much success as it has. There has, after all, been no major war since 1945, and a number of minor ones have been averted through United Nations machinery. Valuable time was bought when mediation silenced Indian and Pakistani guns and when Greece and Turkey were persuaded to suspend their fight over the island of Cyprus.

The meetings of the United Nations provide a safety valve for national frustrations. Diplomats state their countries' official positions before a world-wide audience, but in the privacy of cloakrooms and lunchrooms they can and do make more informal personal contacts.

As long as the United Nations exists, there is the chance that it will eventually develop more muscle, that it will show greater strength in policing the world and silencing guns. Many improvements will have to be made to this end. One of the most important of these improvements would be enlarging the membership list to include all the independent countries on the map.

The history of international organization demonstrates that troublemaking states tend to be a much greater nuisance when they are not inside the organization. When they are outside they feel freer to be defiant . . . as were Italy, Germany and Japan, and Communist China after it.[8]

In the balance the United Nations has undoubtedly been a strong factor for peace. Measured against an ideal world order, it has fallen short, but measured against the political realities, it deserves more praise than criticism.

DISARMAMENT

Individuals may fight each other with fists, but nations use weapons. So far the United Nations has been powerless to make governments relinquish the tools of war. On the contrary, they are engaged in a stupendous *arms race*, which swallows unbelievable amounts of money and resources. The best brains are put to work to fashion ever more destructive devices, and as soon as one major power discovers a new means of killing people, another tries to outdo it by stockpiling an even deadlier weapon.

From time to time statesmen have recognized the folly and waste of this race and have met in *disarmament conferences*. After World War I, Europeans pinned their hopes on the much publicized Locarno Conference in 1925. A few years later, in 1930, the United States, England, and Japan agreed in the London Naval Treaty to limit the size of their war fleets. The carnage of World War II proved how futile those promises were.

After the shooting and the bombing had stopped in 1945 and the world totaled its losses in human lives and in cities and villages laid waste, governments again began the game of "if you reduce your arsenal of weapons, we will cut down on ours." Long drawn-out meetings were held, mostly in Geneva, Switzerland, all with disappointing results. The endless negotiations around the green conference tables have "had no effect whatever on the realities of the armament problem. Indeed, the only tangible effect [has been] to soften the will and the capacity of the democracies to survive as they came to view weapons as villains rather than as only sometimes the tools of villains."[9]

Eventually the ever-present nightmare of an all-out nuclear holocaust that might destroy our whole world moved the negotiators to some small tokens of action. In 1963, twenty-five nations, represented in Geneva, signed the Partial Nuclear Test Ban Treaty, which prohibits nuclear explosions for testing purposes in the atmosphere, in outer space, and under water.

But nuclear bombs have remained stored in secret hiding places and new ones have been constantly added. The threat of total destruction, by intent or by mistake, has continued to hover over mankind. Once more the diplomats sat down together to talk things over. Still no nation was ready to abandon its nuclear arsenal. Instead they established the Nuclear Non-

Proliferation Treaty, in which the nuclear powers pledged not to pass their bombs and missiles on to other countries that did not yet possess them. The United States, England, and Russia signed the document, but France and China, which also possess nuclear arms, did not. So the agreement lost much of its value.

Another attempt to prevent global suicide began in the spring of 1970 when the two "superpowers," Russia and the United States, opened the Strategic Arms Limitation Talks (SALT) in Vienna. The tone of the talks seems friendly so far, but the talks are apt to stretch out for many months or even years. In the meantime, Washington and Moscow—and Peking too—keep on adding to their stock of atomic missiles and submarines.

A major stumbling block on the rocky road to disarmament is the question of inspection. Unfortunately, nations do not easily trust one another, just as some individuals will not trust the word or even the written pledge of their neighbors. Governments hesitate to dismantle their stockpiles of weapons unless they have firsthand proof that the other parties to the agreement are doing the same. But how does one nation check up on another's military machinery? The obvious answer would be to go and take a good look, but this raises objections concerning national pride and national sovereignty and involves the fear of spying. Russia has been particularly wary of letting any foreign observers come close to any place that has even the remotest connection with its military activities.

Some political scientists feel that disarmament efforts in general make little sense. They argue that arms don't cause war, but nations, who gather weapons when they expect conflict for a variety of reasons, do. "War machines are reduced only when peace seems probable . . . and armaments spring from war and from the anticipation of war."[10]

On the other hand, nations cannot use weapons that they don't have. We can speculate that Hitler probably would have dropped atomic bombs on the Allies had he possessed them, and we did drop two on Japan. People who have guns strapped to their sides are tempted to use them, especially when they fear defeat. Research into the causes of war seems to indicate that the more heavily nations are armed the greater is the possibility of military conflict.

INTERNATIONAL LAW

You don't usually take pot shots at the neighbor across the street, even if you have cause to hate or fear him. Laws punishing the offender serve to prevent people from engaging in such activity. If you intend to break the law, police, courts, and penal institutions stand ready to enforce it. If whole nations were also bound by law and if there existed a world police force strong enough to enforce that law, the danger of war would probably disappear or at least be greatly reduced.

International law does, in fact, exist, but it is vague and difficult to enforce. Often it is based on long-standing customs rather than on a written code, and sovereign states always insist on interpreting it as they see fit—which means to their own advantage. In addition, there must be courts to interpret the laws. And we have already seen that the International Court of Justice cannot do much more than act as a mediator between two parties who have agreed ahead of time to abide by its findings.

International law has worked quite well when it was in the interest of all nations to observe it. Ambassadors, consuls, and their staffs enjoy *diplomatic immunity*; that is, they are free from arrest in foreign countries even when those countries are rather hostile.

How much of the ocean does a country own? This is an old legal question. In times of peace the high seas were generally considered free to all shipping. But countries with coastlines claimed that their sovereignty extended three miles outward. This used to be the maximum distance a cannon shot could carry. Modern guns can go much farther, and so countries have pushed the limit to twelve, twenty, and in some cases, 200 miles, causing all sorts of minor quarrels about fishing boat violations of these artificial limits.

Various international conferences, such as the ones held in Geneva, Switzerland, have tried to devise rules of civilized warfare. The use of poison gas was outlawed before World War I, and so were attacks on hospitals and medical personnel. Prisoners of war and civilians were to be treated humanely; white flags were to be recognized as signs of surrender or of a request for a truce. Sometimes these rules were observed, but on many occasions they were not. War is by nature inhuman and cannot always be played according to rules, like a football game.

International law tends to be highly conservative. The "have-not" nations are the ones that often most flagrantly violate established rules. They claim, with some justice, that international law is unfair, that it was introduced by the "haves" and serves to maintain the status quo. As in our own country, law on the international scene must move closer toward justice. "All proposals to give law a greater role in international relations, to say nothing of the 'peace-through-law' and the 'no-peace-without-law' movements, would involve profound changes in present attitudes and concepts."[11]

WORLD GOVERNMENT

To enforce the law is one of the prime duties of the national government. It has long been suggested that only a world government, a kind of "United States of the World," could effectively enforce international law. Such a government would need to have sufficient power to police the now sovereign nation-states, a power that the present United Nations definitely does not have.

Famous personalities, such as Albert Einstein and Justice William O.

Douglas, have spoken in behalf of world government. The World Federalists and similar movements work for its realization. But they run into loud and highly emotional opposition. Communists have attacked such moves as a "Wall Street plot," while the American Legion and the Daughters of the American Revolution see them as part of a communist subversive plot.

World government is a lofty ideal, and it will be advocated with ever greater urgency as time goes on. But its chances for realization in the immediate future are not too certain. Nationalism remains an extremely strong motivating force, and nation-states have given no indication of a willingness to surrender any part of their sovereignty.

Main Ideas
1. Nation-states communicate with one another through the instrument of diplomacy.
2. In order to be successful, diplomacy has to be secret, at least to some extent.
3. Collective security is the concept that peace-loving nations should stand together to repel any aggressor.
4. Many types of international organization exist and function well when their success is in the interest of the participating nations.
5. The European Common Market is a particularly successful example of international cooperation.
6. The League of Nations failed as a peace-keeping international organization because the member-nations used it to further their quest for power and because the United States never joined it.
7. The United Nations provides elaborate machinery for the preservation of peace; success so far has been limited.
8. Various United Nations agencies are engaged, with considerable success, in improving the economic, social, and cultural climate of the world.
9. The effectiveness of the United Nations depends largely on the role that the major powers allow it to play.
10. The arms race raises the possibility of war, yet attempts at peaceful disarmament have so far had scant results.
11. International law is based mostly on established customs and is subject to interpretation by the individual sovereign states.
12. According to a number of proposals only a world government will be able to ensure peace.

Important Terms
Aggression
Ambassador
Arms race
Big Five
Collective security
Common Market
Diplomacy
Diplomatic immunity

Important Terms (*Cont.*)

Disarmament
General Assembly
International law
International organization
League of Nations
Nuclear Non-Proliferation Treaty
Pax Romana
Pax Tartarica
Rotating membership
Security Council
United Nations
Veto power

Conclusion

I do not wish to seem overdramatic, but I can only conclude . . . that members of the United Nations have perhaps ten years left in which to subordinate their ancient quarrels and launch a global partnership to curb the arms race, to improve the human environment, to defuse the population explosion, and to supply the required momentum to world development efforts.[12]

This warning was given to the world by Secretary General of the United Nations U Thant on May 9, 1969. It is grim, but it leaves an avenue of hope that selfish national interests will cease to dominate mankind and that the various urgent challenges confronting us will be met by the combined efforts of all nations.

Notes

1. Inis L. Claude, *Power and International Relations* (New York: Random House, 1962), p. 7.
2. R. S. Baker and W. E. Dodd (eds.), *The Public Papers of Woodrow Wilson: War and Peace* (New York: Harper, 1927), p. 234.
3. W. N. Hogan and A. Vandenbosch, *Toward World Order* (New York: McGraw-Hill, 1963), p. 40.
4. A. F. K. Organski, *World Politics*, 2nd ed. (New York: Knopf, 1968), p. 454.
5. *United Nations Charter*, Article 27.
6. *Ibid.*, Articles 10 and 11.
7. John G. Stoessinger, *The United Nations and the Superpowers* (New York: Random House, 1965), p. 168.
8. Frederick H. Hartman, *The Relations of Nations*, 3rd ed. (New York: Macmillan, 1967), p. 208.
9. Lincoln P. Bloomfield, *The United Nations and U.S. Foreign Policy*, rev. ed. (Boston: Little, Brown, 1967), p. 93.
10. Frederick L. Schuman, *International Politics: Anarchy and Order in the World Society*, 7th ed. (New York: McGraw-Hill, 1969), p. 251.
11. Hogan and Vandenbosch, *op. cit.*, p. 152.
12. "UN Notebook," *Vista* 5 (July–August 1969), p. 5.

Suggestions for Further Reading

Buckmaster, Henrietta. *The Lion in the Stone.* New York: Harcourt, Brace & World, 1968. Novel about a fictional crisis in Asia and how it is handled by the Secretary General.

Cousins, Norman. "Towards a New Language: World Law," *Saturday Review,* 52, May 24, 1969, 24 ff.

Coyle, David C. *The United Nations and How It Works.* Rev. ed. New York: Mentor, 1965 (paperback).

"Disarmament: A Guide to Understanding the Problem," *Intercom,* 10 (January–February 1968). Feature article.

National Policy Panel. *Controlling Conflicts in the 1970s.* New York: United Nations Association of the USA, 1969 (paperback). Problems of regional and United Nations peace keeping.

National Policy Panel. *Stopping the Spread of Nuclear Weapons.* New York: United Nations Association of the USA, 1967 (paperback).

Scheinman, Lawrence. "Nuclear Safeguards, the Peaceful Atom, and the IAEA," *International Conciliation,* No. 572 (March 1969).

UN Monthly Chronicle. New York: UN Office of Public Information. Monthly report on United Nations activities around the world.

Vista. Bimonthly magazine published by United Nations Association of the USA.

PART SIX SUMMING UP

Can we see any order in the chaos of facts? What does it add up to?

21 ONCE MORE: I AND WE
some basic concepts

The preceding pages have covered much ground, from the rural hamlet to the United Nations. We have looked into mental hospitals and jails and also into factories, banks, and universities. We have seen man declaring his love to woman and abusing his fellow-man because of the color of the other's skin. The members of society have been shown at work and play. Now it is time to sum up and organize the many details around a few basic concepts.

PERSONALITY

We started out with the most important of all topics—you. You have a distinct personality, which is the product of three factors: (1) your physical make-up and mental capacities, (2) your unique experiences and contacts, and (3) the culture of which you are a part. You did little or nothing to determine your basic physical and mental condition. You are tall or short, your skin is black or white, regardless of your preference; your hearing is excellent or poor, your memory photographic or just average; these conditions were not left to your choice.

Nor could you control all the experiences that helped shape your personality. Perhaps you were orphaned in early

393

childhood, or your parents migrated to America from southern Europe. An accident might have impaired your eyesight, or a distant aunt might have left you a considerable fortune.

It is the third element, the culture of which you are a part, that is the main subject of this text. Actually culture also makes itself felt in the first two factors we have listed. You were born black or white, but how this affects your life depends on the culture around you.

Color is not what is important. Rather it is what color means in particular social contexts. Men, like animals, get hungry, but only men wait until dinner time to eat because their culture demands it. You feel like sneezing—a very natural reaction—but culture makes you suppress the urge or, at least, say, "Excuse me." Pain is natural, but whether or not you show it by crying or grimacing is again dictated by your culture.

Culture also casts you into various *roles* that you must play either for a limited time or for life, the roles of student, relative, friend, consumer, voter, church member, and so forth.

CULTURE

What do we really mean by the term "culture," a term that seems to be a steady companion on our journey through the social sciences? Briefly, *culture* is the sum of all the ways of a group. Or to put it in a more scholarly definition, "a culture is a historically created system of explicit and implicit designs for living which tends to be shared by all or specially designated members of a group at a specified point of time."[1]

Usually the term "culture" refers to the ways of *societies*, which are, in general, large groups of people, such as the North American, Chinese, or South African societies. But isolated primitive groups may also have distinctive cultures of their own though their memberships are small. When a society has reached the point of creating a system of writing and can therefore keep records, we speak of a *civilization*. A civilization then is the culture of a literate society, whether that society chisels its records into stone pillars or keeps them on microfilm.

Culture is *learned*. By growing up in a family, going to school, and generally coming into contact with other people, you gradually become *socialized*, or *enculturated*. An American who, for some reason, is brought to Japan at an early age and grows up as a member of a Japanese family, will exhibit the usual characteristics of the Japanese, not the American, culture.

You cannot invent your own private culture; it must be *shared* with others. If nobody else is around, there is no culture. In a number of cases unfortunate children were deprived of all human companionship for years. Out of shame mothers have hidden their illegitimate offspring in attics or locked rooms. When these children were eventually found, they resembled infants or wild animals more than youngsters of five, six, or older. Unable to walk upright, to talk, or to control their bowel movements, they were human beings without human culture.[2]

Though man is a comparatively weak and clumsy animal, culture enables him to more than compensate for his deficient eyesight, hearing, smelling, and running ability. Using his superior reasoning ability, man invents weapons against stronger animals, medicines for wounds and disease, and religion to soothe his fear of death. He does not flee from the harshness of nature but fights it on his own terms. He installs air conditioning in Arizona, central heating in Minnesota, and he builds earthquake-proof buildings in Tokyo.

Human culture displays unending variety. There are innumerable ways of doing almost anything you can think of, whether it is cooking, courtship, punishing offenders, or dealing with political opponents. Yet all human beings, from naked hunters in the jungle to corporation presidents and prime ministers, have certain basic needs in common. Culture provides ways to fill these needs; therefore we find the same basic elements in all or most cultures.

BASIC ELEMENTS OF CULTURE

Economic System: Man must eat and find shelter from storm and frost. Each culture devises means of providing these material necessities. We have encountered some nomadic cultures, others with agricultural systems, and still others with industrial economic systems. In one culture free trade with distant regions is encouraged, while in another members are secluded for fear that contacts with foreigners will make them dissatisfied.

Family System: No society can survive unless it provides for the bearing and raising of offspring. Our American culture insists on monogamy, favors a democratic family spirit, frowns on sexual relations outside marriage but seems to be moving toward greater sexual freedom.

System of Status: Man wants to know where he stands in relation to his fellow members in the group. According to the ways of society his place is determined by race, caste, and class. It may also depend on education and wealth. In older cultures old age, physical strength, unusual courage, or the supposed ability to control supernatural forces were rewarded with high status.

Government: To safeguard life and property against dangers from without and within, some authority is needed. It may be exercised harshly or mildly, by a god-king or a ward boss. Governmental structures range all the way from simple one-man rule to complicated networks of local, national, and, to some extent, international bureaucracies.

Education: The socialization of the child has been the job of parents, tutors, priests, schools, or a combination of all these. Some provision is always made for passing on culture from generation to generation, either informally or through special institutions such as schools, colleges, universities, and so forth.

Beliefs: "There is no god but Allah." "Idleness is sinful." "Man's first loyalty is to his tribe." "Be practical." "Enjoy yourself—it's later than you think." These are ideas that different cultures consider proper and important. They can be imposed as the only permissible notions. If this is the case, anybody who attacks them incurs ridicule, censure, or even severe punishment.

Language: No culture can be formed without communication between its members. Drumbeats and smoke signals are means of communication, but they cannot compare with the richness and variety of human language. If you have traveled in a foreign country without understanding its language, you know the feeling of utter frustration that accompanies being cut off from contact with people who walk past you on the street or sit elbow-to-elbow with you in a restaurant.

Aesthetic and Recreational Needs: In the Altamira Caves of northern Spain magnificent mural paintings—the work of unknown Stone Age artists—were discovered. They had magical and religious significance, but they are also the product of man's need to create and enjoy beauty. Preliterate people fashioned musical instruments from reeds and bones and danced to simple tunes. Today's housewife selects pleasingly patterned wallpaper for her living room. Sculptors fashion monuments for the parks and plazas of our cities. These are not objects man needs for survival; he could exist without them, but his life would be drab and dreary.

Once the necessary tasks are done, men of all cultures want to relax. They may bring out a deck of cards, drink together in a beer garden, smoke waterpipes in a café by the bazaar, or gamble with sticks around the campfire. Whatever energy is left from the working hours is spent on an unending variety of leisure-time interests.

TRAITS AND COMPLEXES

A wedding ring may seem to have little relation to a man's necktie, and yet they are both material objects of our own culture, which consists of many material and nonmaterial items called *culture traits*. Fingerprinting, the job of a referee, and the belief in the desirability of being young are also culture traits.

A number of traits are grouped around *culture complexes*. The wedding ring, together with the bridal shower, the honeymoon, and the taking of the husband's name by the bride, all belong to the culture complex called wedding. The behavior of the business or professional man, police work, and boxing matches are other culture complexes.

FOLKWAYS AND MORES

Now let us observe man in action. Latin Americans interrupt work at noon and rest till 4 P.M. Italians like to walk around the central plaza in the early evening. Chinese eat with chopsticks. Frenchmen kiss their male friends on both cheeks when they meet. These are *folkways*, that is, the accepted forms of behavior in a particular culture.

People who don't observe the folkways of their society are considered odd, though as a rule nobody will interfere with their unusual behavior. If a Mexican decides to work through the early afternoon or if a Chinese tries to handle a fork and knife, he will probably encounter nothing worse than curious stares or giggles behind his back.

But other folkways are considered so important that deviations from them will often cause serious trouble. These are the *mores*. Walking around in the nude may be very pleasant in warm weather, but in a place where the mores require clothing punishment will be swift and, perhaps, painful. Breaches of the sex mores can have particularly severe consequences. The mores regulate the behavior of children toward their parents and vice versa, of high-class to lower-class people, of rulers to subjects.

When regularly enforced by society or written down in special documents, the mores become *laws*, and special *institutions*, such as government, courts, and police, are charged with guarding these laws.

Mores and laws can come into conflict with other values of a society. British records reveal several cases of shipwrecked sailors who, before they could be rescued, had killed and eaten some of their companions. The sailors had violated the mores against cannibalism and the law against murder, but they had upheld the value of self-preservation.[3]

ARTIFACTS

Every society fashions certain objects—called *artifacts*—that are characteristic of its culture. The Egyptians had their pyramids, medieval knights their armor, and the Vikings their sturdy ships. Australians throw boomerangs, and Eskimos build kayaks. Suppose that a thousand years from now archaeologists excavate the remains of our present society. What artifacts do you think they will consider particularly characteristic: the automobile, the bathtub, the Coca-Cola bottle, the pill, or the guided missile?

CULTURAL CHANGE

As each individual grows older, his appearance changes, and so do his habits, tastes, and thoughts. The same is true of cultures. They are in the process of constant change. American life today is different from what it was 20, 100, or 200 years ago.

Change was slow in the early stages of the development of mankind.

It accelerated with the invention of writing 6,000 years ago, broke into a run with the coming of modern science in the sixteenth century, and is now racing at great speed, urged on by electronics, automation, and urbanization.

Some historians believe that these changes follow a certain well-defined pattern. Oswald Spengler thought that civilization, like human beings, goes through periods of youth, maturity, old age and ends in death. In 1918, in his book *The Decline of the West* he announced, somewhat prematurely, the impending death of his own, the Western, civilization.[4]

Jacob Bronowski, a philosopher of science, points at social changes caused by scientific discoveries and inventions. The automobile drastically transformed human sex habits. "It is evident now that the car provided young people with more privacy than the home, and that as a result it became usual to begin sexual experience in the back seat of a motor car." Bronowski further speculates on the impact of future discoveries that now seem feasible, for example, the raising of edible plants in salty water or the large-scale desalinization of sea water.[5]

Not all elements of a culture change at the same pace. Some surge forward rapidly; others lag behind. We have seen how *cultural lag* poses many problems. The international peace-keeping machinery lags behind the perfecting of destructive superweapons. The processes of government cannot keep pace with the rapid spread of the metropolitan community. Many citizens criticize the laws concerning abortion, divorce, and homosexuality as being outdated. Our prison systems fall behind the findings of modern criminology. The French armies were beaten by the Nazi war machine because French generals refused to update their obsolete methods of warfare.

Generally man's social achievements have lagged miserably behind his technological innovations. Though we can hear astronauts talk to us from the moon, we fail to communicate with people a few city blocks away who are of a different race or class. We can transplant kidneys and hearts but know of no sure way to cure alcoholism or to mend troubled marriages.

War sometimes brings about rapid changes, even changes for the better, though it is not easy to acknowledge that anything good can come from war. New medical techniques, such as the transfusion of blood plasma, were developed in World War II. The "GI Bill," an outcome of World War II, speeded up class mobility by enabling thousands of working-class veterans to train for professional careers.

CULTURAL DIFFUSION

Thus far in this chapter we have spoken of various cultures as if each were completely separate from the other. In reality no culture is surrounded by an impenetrable wall. Even the iron curtain between the communist and noncommunist worlds has many holes.

Cultural diffusion.
George W. Gardner

Cultures borrow constantly from each other. There is much interchange, much *diffusion*. As an example, we might look at the elements of our own culture that originate elsewhere. We drink coffee from Brazil, eat Italian-style spaghetti and pizza, celebrate the festival of Saint Patrick, an Irish saint, and play chess, which probably came from India. In our language we use "kindergarten," "sauerkraut," and other German words. American churches and synagogues practice religions that originated in the Near East. We are enlightened by the sayings of Confucius, an ancient Chinese teacher, and we imitate Japanese landscaping in our backyards.

At the same time that North Africans abandon their camels and drive American-built jeeps across the Sahara Desert, Afghanis watch Hollywood-made cowboy movies. Frenchmen have incorporated such terms as "sandwich" and "weekend" into their language, and "jeans" have become the uniform practically everywhere and "rock" the anthem of the young generation.

Cultural diffusion is by no means a recent event. Before man had learned to write, traders in frail boats exchanged goods between Mesopotamia and the Indus valley. Some scholars detected such strong similarities between South American and Polynesian cultures that they concluded that the seafarers of both must have visited back and forth thousands of years ago. Others speculate that similar contacts account for the resemblance of the Mayan pyramids in Mexico to those of the ancient Egyptians.

GROUPS

Man lives in groups, and in most cultures there is room for many kinds of groups. The functioning of these groups and the individual's relationship to them is the main concern of the social scientist.

Each of us belongs to a variety of groups. Student bodies and baseball teams receive us into their membership for only a limited time, whereas we belong to a race or caste for as long as we live. Communities and nations are more permanent than are friendship circles or car pools.

In earlier chapters we frequently pointed out man's need for primary-group relationships. In the primary group we experience a sense of belonging; we are recognized as individuals. The larger secondary group offers no such recognition, but it often allows the forming of small subgroups in which face-to-face relations exist. The United States Army is a secondary group, but within it a squad of soldiers or a clique of buddies affords opportunities for intimate bonds. In our urban mass society keeping old and establishing new primary contacts looms as an important task.

How often have you made these statements? "My country is best." "Our team can lick anybody's." "I live in the best neighborhood in town." "Let's keep those inferior people out of our club." Such statements are expressions of *ethnocentrism*, which means, approximately, "My group is in the center." We have encountered ethnocentrism in the spirit of nationalism, in the attitudes of racial superiority and class exclusiveness. It manifests itself in the team spirit of a football squad, in the loyalty toward school or place of employment. The snobbishness of a high-society clique and the intolerance of a religious community are also forms of ethnocentrism.

Willingly or unwillingly, John is a member of a certain group. What is his position inside it? How does he relate to it? Generally he has three options: *accommodation, competition,* and *conflict.*

If he has joined the group voluntarily, he is probably willing to accommodate himself to its goals and practices. Upon entering a fraternity, he pledges to follow its rules and uphold its principles. He joins in its parties and pranks. If he becomes a member of a juvenile gang, he adopts the mores of the gang, which may conflict considerably with the mores of adult society. He now holds stealing from a fruit stand or candy store permissible, but he abhors informing on a gang member as the supreme sin.

Some groups encourage competition among their members. In a classroom you are constantly competing for grades with other students. Workers in a plant vie for promotions, lawyers for clients, merchants for customers. Whole groups may compete with other groups. Political life in a democracy is based on the competition between parties, and sports on the competition between both individuals and teams.

Conflict, too, will occur between the individual and the group and between one group and another. The rebel turns against his school, his community, his nation. A number of rebels may band together and stage an uprising, which with enough mass support can swell into a revolution. If successful, the rebels will replace the old system with a new one. The American scene is troubled by conflicts between black and white, old and young, moderates and radicals though it retains enough *stability* to make a major revolution unlikely.

War is conflict in the raw. Though our efforts to prevent war lag woefully behind the inventions that make war ever more destructive, optimists hopefully predict that, because of its very destructiveness, war will eventually become obsolete.

SOCIAL PROBLEMS

Though everybody belongs to a culture, not everybody is happy with all its aspects. When a large number of people are dissatisfied, when they experience anxiety and clamor for a change, we are confronted with a *social problem*. The confusion of metropolitan government, poverty, large-scale unemployment, violence in the streets, and war anywhere in the world are in this category, but an earthquake is not, nor is a tornado. The latter are natural events that man has so far been unable to control. However, the effects of such catastrophes on a community may easily become very urgent social problems.

Generally, "a social problem is a problem in human relationships which seriously threatens society itself or impedes the important aspirations of many people."[6] The issue involved in a social problem must be important to the welfare or the safety of the whole group, and the difficulty must be solvable through group action. Human death, though it is a tragic problem, cannot at present be prevented by any amount of group action. Thus it does not fall within the definition of a social problem.

MANY CULTURES

We could devote much time and use innumerable words to describe the differences between the various cultures. But in order to distinguish, let us say, the North American from the East European or the Indian from the North African culture, it is not necessary to enumerate all the mores, folkways, artifacts, and so forth. Scholars have tried to pinpoint certain main themes, or *focuses*, that characterize each culture in a few short words.

Historians point to the organizational genius of ancient Rome, the otherworldliness of the Middle Ages, and the emphasis on man and beauty during the Renaissance as the main themes of those bygone periods of Western civilization. How justified these generalizations are is uncertain, since historical research has largely been limited to famous and powerful individuals and has not given much attention to the average man, who is precisely the concern of the modern social scientist.

What are the focuses of our North American culture? And how do we find them? An interesting way is suggested by Peter L. Berger. He advises us to look for "statements that represent a consensus so strong that the answer to any question concerning them will habitually be prefaced by the words, 'of course.'"[7] If we use this device, we are likely to hear such assertions as, "Of course, monogamy is the natural form of marriage," "Of course, the democratic process works nearly perfectly in the United States," or "Of course, private property should be respected by the government."

Other frequently named themes of our North American culture include an emphasis on youth, personal success, particularly in a material sense, speed, and "businesslike" procedures. "Time is money" is among the typical slogans of the successful American. In contrast, time is valued much less in Latin America, where lengthy conversation before coming to the point is a sign of good manners and where being late for an appointment is expected and approved of.

We have spoken of the universal needs of all human beings and have stated that all cultures provide ways to satisfy these needs. "Why then," one is prompted to ask, "isn't there just one culture? Why are there so many cultures and such differences between them, since they serve, after all, the same purpose?"

This is a good question and not an easy one to answer. What would anthropologists, archaeologists, and historians do if there were only one culture? There would not be much for them to write and teach about. Of course, the reason for the great variety of cultures is not to give these worthy scholars something to explore. We must look further.

A very obvious and significant factor that shapes human culture is the physical environment, the *habitat*. Climate, altitude, availability of water, the presence or absence of mountains, rivers, lakes, or seashore all have their impact on the way man acts. But except for the *geographic determinists* we don't necessarily feel that we are completely the product of geography and that there is nothing we can do about it.

The Eskimos in the northernmost parts of our continent and the tribes of Arctic Siberia live under approximately the same natural conditions. But their cultures are far from being carbon copies of each other. The Eskimos build igloos from snow blocks, train dogs to pull their sleds, and hunt walrus in waterproof kayaks in which they can turn over completely and still survive. The inhabitants of Arctic Siberia, on the other hand, have a very different type of culture.

> The igloo is unknown, and shelters are made from skins that are attached to a framework of wood, even though wood is as scarce here as elsewhere above the Arctic Circle. The Siberians are herders rather than hunters, their economic mainstay being the reindeer rather than the walrus.[8]

Man is a creative being. In adapting himself to the conditions of nature, he can make choices. He invents, and he improves on earlier inventions. So, instead of monotony, we find color and variety as we make the rounds of human culture.

Perhaps it will not always be so. Distances between different cultures shrink as contacts become more frequent, and men seem to grow more alike in many ways. We not only know practically in an instant what goes on anywhere in the world, but we can also view actual events on our television screens. In the conference halls and offices of the United Nations representatives of most countries in the world meet and work together intimately. Western techniques, dress, food, and entertainment are being introduced to non-Western continents, while Asia and Africa send their art forms and spiritual notions in other directions too.

Conceivably mankind might arrive at a single culture in the distant future, but it is not likely that this will occur during your own lifetime. Discovering the many ways in which various societies live will remain a fascinating pursuit for quite a while.

Main Ideas
1. The personality of a human being is determined by his physical and mental make-up, his unique experiences and contacts, and the culture of which he is a part.
2. Culture is the sum of all the behavior of the members within a society.
3. Culture is learned and shared.

4. The basic elements of a culture include an economic system, a family system, systems of status, government, education, beliefs and language, and means to satisfy aesthetic and recreational needs.
5. Each culture features a number of culture complexes around which are grouped various culture traits.
6. Folkways are the accepted forms of behavior in a particular culture.
7. Mores are folkways considered so important to a society that they are enforced informally or through special institutions and with the help of laws.
8. An artifact is a man-made object that is typical of a certain culture.
9. Culture undergoes a continuous process of change.
10. Cultural lag occurs when one phase of a culture lags behind others in the process of change.
11. Through cultural diffusion cultures borrow from each other and influence one another.
12. Primary groups are based on intimate person-to-person relationships; secondary groups are too large for such relationships.
13. Ethnocentrism attributes a particular worth or superiority to one's group.
14. Individuals relate to groups and groups relate to each other by the processes of accommodation, competition, and conflict.
15. Social problems involve difficulties that are threatening the welfare or safety of the group and that are solvable through group action.
16. The central beliefs or attitudes of a culture form its focus.
17. Mankind shows great cultural diversity, but lately, in some ways, various cultures have shown a tendency to become more alike.

Important Terms

Accommodation	Ethnocentrism
Artifact	Folkways
Civilization	Geographic determinism
Competition	Habitat
Cultural diffusion	Institution
Cultural focus	Mores
Cultural lag	Personality
Culture	Role
Culture complex	Socialization
Culture trait	Stability
Enculturation	

Conclusion

It is easy to recognize the shortcomings of our society. When we wrestle with the grave problems of the time, we may become disheartened. We may feel that mankind is in such trouble that there is no hope. To combat this bleak attitude, the study of cultures provides us with not only a welcome diversion but also a source of comfort. We see convincing proof that, at least up till now, society has always been able to adapt itself to changing conditions, though often slowly and with painful setbacks. It becomes obvious that reforms and corrections are possible provided they don't upset too radically and too quickly the current mores and beliefs.

Notes
1. C. Kluckhohn and W. H. Kelly, "The Concept of Culture," in Ralph Linton (ed.), *The Science of Man in the World Crisis* (New York: Columbia University Press, 1945), pp. 78–107.
2. Kingsley Davis, "Final Note on a Case of Extreme Isolation," *American Journal of Sociology*, vol. LIII (March 1947), 432–437.
3. L. Broom and P. Selznick, *Sociology*, 4th ed. (New York: Harper & Row, 1968), pp. 63–64.
4. Oswald Spengler, *The Decline of the West* (New York: Knopf, 1926).
5. Jacob Bronowski, "What We Can't Know," *Saturday Review*, July 5, 1969, pp. 44–45.
6. E. Raab and G. J. Selznick, *Major Social Problems*, 2nd ed. (New York: Harper & Row, 1964), p. 3.
7. Peter L. Berger, "Sociology as a Form of Consciousness," in Peter I. Rose (ed.), *The Study of Society: An Integrated Anthology* (New York: Random House, 1967), p. 31.
8. Melville J. Herskovits, *Man and His Work* (New York: Knopf, 1948), pp. 157–158.

Suggestions for Further Reading
Berelson, B. and G. A. Steiner. *Human Behavior*. New York: Harcourt, Brace & World, 1964 (paperback). This short book is an inventory of the state of knowledge in the behavioral sciences.

Bradbury, Ray. *Fahrenheit 451*. New York: Ballantine, 1953. Novel depicting a future static and anti-intellectual society but leaving some hope for change if members will show initiative.

Dictionary of the Social Sciences. New York: Free Press, 1964. This collection of short articles was compiled under auspices of the United Nations Educational, Scientific, and Cultural Organization.

Heyerdahl, Thor. *Kon-Tiki: Across the Pacific by Raft*. Chicago: Rand McNally, 1950.

Huxley, Aldous. *Brave New World*. New York: Modern Library, 1932 (paperback). Well-known novel set in a future society shaped by profound technological and social changes.

International Encyclopedia of the Social Sciences. 17 vols. New York: Macmillan, 1968.

Szilard, Leo. *Grand Central Terminal*. New York: Collier, 1952. Novel in which archaeologists from space try to reconstruct our civilization from the ruins of a railroad station.

Within the broad color spectrum of a culture, there is room for distinct patches, subtle shades, and contrasting hues.

22 GROUPS WITHIN GROUPS
subcultures and contracultures

Switzerland is a breathtakingly beautiful country of high mountains and narrow valleys, formerly accessible only by steep and winding trails, which for many months were blocked by deep snow. Having only limited contacts with neighboring valleys, the people developed their own unique ways. Visitors to the country today find that the dialect spoken in one valley varies slightly from that of the next. The women of different valleys wear different costumes, the children sing different songs and learn to yodel different tunes. Even the method of stacking hay in the field varies from place to place.

Yet the Swiss, regardless of the different valleys they may inhabit, are much more alike than different from one another. They belong to the same culture, but the individual valleys and mountain regions have, in the course of time, developed their own *subcultures*, which can be defined as "the *normative* systems of groups which are smaller than societies"[1] (italics added).

Often the differences from subculture to subculture are so subtle that they can only be noticed by an observer who has been familiar with the area for many years. But we can also find strong contrasts where the accident of history has left *enclaves* of one ethnic type surrounded by a majority of another. Until World War II whole villages deep inside Russia spoke only German. In Spain the Basques still stick firmly to their language and peculiar music and dances. The Gypsies, who have roamed the highways of Europe for many centuries, fiercely resist any attempts to *enculturate* them to the ways of a particular nation.

REGIONAL AMERICAN SUBCULTURES

The American culture is strongly *heterogeneous* and has an abundant variety of subcultures. One reason for the variety is the extensive size of the country. Traveling across the country from the Atlantic to the Pacific Ocean, we encounter many climates and many different land formations. History has dealt in various ways with the North, the South, the East and the West, and with the smaller regions within these broad sections. The people of the various sections and regions represent many diverse backgrounds, and they can be distinguished by their likes and dislikes, by their favorite foods and their favorite ideas.

In the South, for example, certain chivalrous gestures, such as a man taking off his hat when a woman enters an elevator, are long-established customs. Also longstanding but very destructive is the blight on Southern social life caused by deep-seated racial fears and strong antagonisms against outsiders. These remain from the old plantation economy and the institution of slavery.

The climate has had its impact on Southern ways. Before the days of air conditioning Southerners moved slowly in the long months of extremely hot weather. Tempers were short, and the danger of violence was ever present. Other characteristics of this region are the well-known "Southern drawl" and a strong loyalty toward certain traditions, including conservatism in politics and a preference for fundamentalist and highly emotional religion. Now, with increasing horizontal mobility and instant communication, the old stereotype of the Southerner is slowly fading into history.

The South extends over such a wide area that a number of smaller subcultures can be distinguished between the Mason-Dixon line and the Gulf of Mexico, each displaying different traditions and folkways. The bayou country of Louisiana, the mountains of Tennessee, the gracious old ports of Savannah and Charleston—all have their own unmistakable identities. Stuart Chase shows that we live inside a number of *cultural rings*, one enclosed in the other. Figure 37 depicts a slightly different arrangement of these rings.

Suppose you live in the Louisiana bayou country. How would you fit into these concentric circles and rings? You are still part of *human society*, which produced a system of written communication some 6,000 years ago, developed urban living and a highly diversified economy. This is the outermost ring. Next, with all other members of *Western civilization* you share

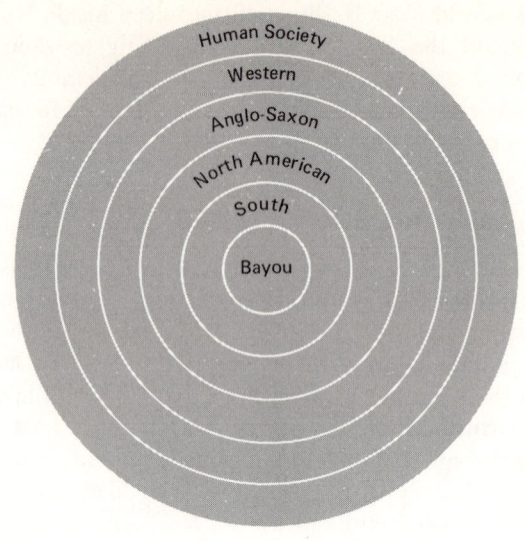

Figure 37
Cultural Rings

Source: Based on data from Stuart Chase, *The Proper Study of Mankind*, rev. ed. (New York: Harper & Row, Colophon Edition, 1963), pp. 76–78. By permission of Harper & Row, Publishers, Inc.

certain ideas of right and wrong, a monotheistic religion, a liking for technology and its products, and probably the conviction that you should be free to choose your partner in marriage, preferably through romantic love.

Moving toward the center of the circle, you find yourself inside the ring of *Anglo-Saxon* culture together with Englishmen, Australians, and New Zealanders. Its strongest bond is the English language, which enables English-speaking people to communicate easily. They read the same books, attend performances of the same plays, and laugh at the same jokes. A common historical past has given them certain forms of legal justice and a preference for political democracy but has also fostered discrimination against darker races. Members of the Anglo-Saxon culture hesitate to show their emotions too openly. Women may be excused for shedding a tear at weddings or funerals, but men try not to cry when they mourn, nor do they jump for joy unless they are spectators at a football game.

The *North American* way of life is a subculture of the Anglo-Saxon culture and contains such elements as a strong reliance on the automobile, a love of baseball, and a taste for short-order snacks. We treat our neighbors and even strangers with an informality that would shock residents of the Old World, and we grant our young people a very generous amount of freedom. Culturally Mexico does not belong to the North American ring, despite its geographic location, but it is rapidly changing.

The customs and traditions of the original Indian population element have remained strong throughout Mexico. Beneath the outer appearance of Spanish culture, which the European conquerors brought with them, their way of life has been maintained. But in recent decades intensive trade with the United States and visits from many tourists, students, and older people in search of inexpensive retirement places have helped to bring the Mexican way of life closer to that of its neighbors to the north.

Nearer to the center of the circle is located the regional subculture, New England, the Middle West, the South. The smallest circle is your own locality. As a native of the bayou country, you probably speak a curious French dialect besides the English language. You are well acquainted with various seafoods, and you are versed in the skills of boating. You have childhood memories of legends about pirates and seafaring conquerors, which you heard from parents and teachers.

ETHNIC SUBCULTURES

Geographical location alone cannot account for all the subcultures and combinations of subcultures that we encounter in this country. America is a nation of immigrants who came to these shores at various periods, bringing with them their cultural heritage, which they tried to perpetuate in a strange setting.

The oldest Americans are the Indians, though they too migrated ages ago from Asia, probably on a land bridge between the two continents that later broke up to form the Aleutian Islands chain. Since these early migrations thousands of Indians have lost their identity among the general population of our cities and villages. Others maintain tribal enclaves on the various reservations, constantly faced with intrusion from the outside world. As the white man imposes his schools and health services, his machinery and marketing methods on the Indian, old Indian cultural patterns become confused.

In the novel *Laughing Boy*, by Oliver La Farge, the life of a young Navaho in the 1920s is depicted. The young man can make jewelry and handle horses and sheep, skills that are part of his cultural heritage. Gambling is "in his blood," but the loss of money means very little to him. He is much more concerned about keeping the respect of his *peers*. He never questions the traditional religious belief in the spirits that control nature and man's fate. His idea of a good time is sitting around a blazing fire with his friends, eating chunks of mutton, rolling cigarettes, singing, joking, and laughing. On other occasions, however, the rigid mask of his impassive face completely conceals his true feelings. He cannot marry a girl from his own tribe, and he expects his wife to weave blankets on her loom as his mother and grandmother had done. But his world begins to come apart. His girl sells herself to white ranchers. The salesman proffers forbidden whiskey, and the policeman enforces incomprehensible laws.

Navahos and members of the hundreds of other Indian tribes have found it almost impossible to maintain their culture in a society in which the majority of the people trace their heritage from Europe. By giving up some old ways and adapting others to changed conditions, Indians now form various subcultures mainly in the southwestern and mountain states.

American culture as we know it today was cast into its particular mold not by the Indians but by immigrants who came from northwestern Europe from the seventeenth century on. They brought with them the English language, Protestantism, and various concepts of morality, community life, work, and play. The white Anglo-Saxon Protestant population element (WASP) set the tone or style of American life.

New and more massive waves of immigration followed. Early in the seventeenth century blacks came in the fetid holds of slave ships. Two centuries later Irishmen fled from famine, and Asians came to labor on the transcontinental railroads. After the Civil War the floodgates opened for the masses of persecuted East European Jews and poor Italian, Polish, Yugoslav, and Greek peasants.

The immigrants landed in a country that possessed an established culture to which they were strangers. Excluded by the dominant group and

The oldest Americans are the Indians.
George W. Gardner

subcultures and contracultures 411

huddling together for warmth and security, they formed a variety of subcultures. It was possible to walk through the Italian or Greek sections of our cities and almost forget that one was on American soil. Posters in a foreign language announced unusual festivals. Family life was strictly patriarchal, and parents forbade their children to marry outside their own subculture (see Chapter 14).

The Lower East Side of New York City was the haven for East European Jews. Bewhiskered men in long black frock coats read newspapers printed in the Yiddish language, while their wives and daughters labored for endless hours in the "sweat shops" of the garment industry. On Jewish holidays whole city blocks of tightly shuttered shops could be seen.

America's most famous Chinese community survives in San Francisco; Chinatown is a throbbing and exciting city within the Golden Gate City, with its own fraternal organizations and its own social rank order. The grocery stores display exotic vegetables, and the theaters offer Chinese motion pictures. Tourists come to walk through the narrow streets, stare at strange sights, and buy trinkets, which, incidentally, are now mostly made in Japan.

Puget Island is a dreamy patch of emerald green located in the

Columbia River about fifty miles from where the river empties into the Pacific Ocean. In the late nineteenth century Norwegian settlers discovered the empty island, with its low pastureland crisscrossed by countless sloughs that reminded them of the fjords in their ancestral homeland. A little village sprang up. The houses fronted on the sloughs, and travel was almost completely by boat. Life resembled that in a typical Norwegian fishing community. The native language prevailed in the wooden church and in the shingled schoolhouse. Smorgasbord was served on festive occasions in the community hall, and after the hefty meal the floorboards vibrated to the rhythms of Norse country dances. Once a week the mailman brought a Norwegian language newspaper in his boat.

The village on Puget Island is still there, but the Norwegian flavor has almost completely disappeared. Today the little schoolhouse is empty, and a big yellow bus delivers the children to a consolidated school by way of a highway bridge. The children prefer hot dogs to smorgasbord and the latest dance to the old country dances. They even dislike hearing their parents speak the native language and feel somewhat ashamed when the older generation cannot pronounce English words correctly.

The colorful ethnic subcultures created by the first generation of immigrants have not disappeared, but they have undergone profound changes. The children and grandchildren of the new arrivals have been educated in American public schools, have entered American occupational life, and have participated in the affairs of the American community. But after hours, so to speak, and in their more intimate contacts, they still preserve the old-country heritage.

> Within the ethnic group there develops a network of organizations and informal social relationships which permits and encourages the members of the ethnic group to remain within the confines of the group for all their primary relationships and some of their secondary relationships throughout all stages of the life cycle.[2]

Thus "hyphenated Americans," such as Norwegian-Americans, Polish-Americans, and Greek-Americans, still tend to maintain their own church clubs, service organizations, lodges, hospitals, and rest homes. To this extent *pluralism* continues to be a characteristic feature of the American culture.

RELIGIOUS SUBCULTURES

Organized religion imposes on its followers a whole set of habits and precepts for living (see Chapter 8). In Europe some countries are almost completely Catholic, while others are solidly Protestant. They show marked differences in their style of life. Though religion may not be the only reason why Sweden, for example, presents a cultural character that is quite unlike that of Spain, it is undoubtedly an important factor.

Originally American Catholics, Lutherans, Jews, Mormons, and others formed distinct subcultures. Since practically all Irish and Italian immigrants were Catholic and most Scandinavian immigrants Lutheran, religion and national origin often reinforced one another. Today these religious subcultures, like ethnic ones, remain in existence largely on the level of primary relationships.

But besides religious subcultures we find a number of small sects that reject important features of the general American culture. In a sense they form completely distinct cultural enclaves. But since they still retain American citizenship, participate in the American economic life, and share many moral and even certain basic religious concepts with the American majority, we are justified in referring to them as American subcultures.

Probably the quaintest example of such a sectarian subculture is furnished by the Amish.[3] They reside mostly in Pennsylvania, but some of their settlements are also found in the Middle West and in the Northwest. Their faith, which is rooted in the *Anabaptist* movement of sixteenth-century Germany, was bitterly attacked by both the Catholic church and the newly formed Protestant religion. Cruel persecution drove the early Amish to the shores of America.

The unique feature of Amish life is the stubborn resistance to change. Any innovation is held to be sinful and must be strictly avoided. Farming is the only acceptable occupation, and the Amish pursue it diligently and with utmost simplicity.

The Amish live in houses without electricity, telephones, curtains, or soft upholstered furniture. They are not allowed to ride in automobiles. The men, who dress in dark suits, without belts or buttons, and broad-brimmed hats, let their whiskers grow long. Women, with their hair uncut and always covered by a kerchief, wear ankle-length dresses. Make-up and jewelry are forbidden.

But even Amish boys hanker for competitive play, and so deprived of "hot rods," they like to race their horses. A date means taking a girl out for a buggy ride with all the hazards this may cause in modern highway traffic. Courting and marriage always remain within the bounds of the Amish community.

Church buildings are not permitted. For Sunday services the sixty to eighty villagers, old and young, meet alternatingly in their own farm houses, which are built with removable partitions just for this purpose. Prayers and hymns are in an old-fashioned German dialect, and no musical instrument is permitted. After the service all sit down to a hearty meal, which the women have cooperatively prepared.

These Sunday get-togethers also function as the town meetings, at which decisions are made that control all individual and group action. Transgressors are called before this forum and given stern warnings for such offenses as using lipstick or seeing a motion picture on a sneak visit to the nearest city. If the culprit persists in his wrongdoing, the community punishes him. The severest penalty is the *meidung* (German for "shunning"), which makes the condemned person an outcast in his own village.

Nobody, not even his closest relatives, is allowed to have any dealings with him or even speak to him until he has cleared the blemish from his record.

The community cares for its sick, the elderly, and its widows and orphans. There is no need for fire insurance, for when a barn burns down, all neighbors appear with their axes and saws, and in a day or two the structure is rebuilt. Crime and delinquency are nonexistent, and so is worry about an uncertain future.

The Hutterite Brethren, another sect, share with the Amish many beliefs and customs and a similar historical fate.[4] One distinctive feature is that they practice religiously motivated communism. Farmland and buildings in the small village are not privately owned but belong to the whole community. Food is prepared communally. All eat at the village mess hall, men at one table and women at another.

Everybody works with his hands, even the manager of the collective farm and the preacher, who are voted into office by the membership. A Hutterite enjoys little privacy. All work is done in groups. Certain members are appointed to care for the children, while mother and father go about their tasks in field, craftshop, and communal kitchen.

These sects offer an example of how distant a subculture can become from the cultural mainstream of the society that surrounds it. Though sharing many values with the general American culture, these sects cling to their own traditional value system. To preserve that value system, they try to limit contact with the outside world to the absolute minimum.

But modern urbanism and technology also threaten these values to an increasing degree. It is becoming more difficult to keep the younger generation from straying into the cultural territory beyond the village. Society is knocking at the doors of the Amish and Hutterite communities with such "worldly" demands as Social Security payments, compulsory attendance at public schools, and the military draft. When the believers feel that such demands go contrary to their faith, they resist stubbornly.

CONTRACULTURES

The subcultures described so far are rooted in the past. Groups inherit certain customs, which they try to continue while making the necessary adjustments to the general culture around them. Some change faster in this process of adjustment; others, especially those with strong primary ties, preserve the traditional life to a much greater degree.

Now we turn our attention to subcultures that arise as protests against the accepted mores. To them we apply the term *contraculture*. "In a contra-culture . . . the conflict element is central; many of the values, indeed, are specifically contradictions of the values of the dominant cultures."[5]

Where do we find a contraculture? We don't have to search for long or in remote places. A contraculture can be found in practically every town and city. All we have to do is observe some of the members of the younger generation, the adolescents.

The dancers swing through the hall. Jungle beats roll off the drums, and amplifiers vibrate with the throbs of trumpets and electric guitars. Hoarse cries issue from the throat of the vocalist. Alternatingly, the hall is plunged into darkness and illuminated by rotating lights that reveal weird wall decorations in extremely bright colors. Long-haired boys in bell-bottom trousers dance with girls in beads and miniskirts. Their bodies sway in complete abandonment, never touching each other. Eyes are half closed, faces stained with perspiration. A few such evenings, having begun as youthful entertainment, have ended in outbursts of senseless destruction.

Older people shake their heads in bewilderment and comment on the loud music and frenzied dances, which to some seem to resemble the fertility rites of primitive tribes. The adult generation is shocked, and this is exactly the effect that the long-haired boys and the short-skirted girls have intended. Much of the adolescent contraculture is acted-out protest that is aimed at a shock effect. Having learned standard usage of the English language in school, young people create their own idiom in which such terms as "cat," "square," "groovy," "chick," "play it cool," "pad," and many others have their own special meaning.

Objects that figure prominently in young society are nonfunctional jewelry, guitars, and motorcycles. The popularity of "drag races" and hopped-up engines indicates the fascination that power-driven machinery has for the adolescent male. There is an intense desire to conform to the norms of the *peer group*. Friendship and loyalty are of overriding importance, especially in the face of adult criticism or hostility. In contrast to the morality and ethics of the Protestant culture to which adult society adheres or at least gives lip service, the adolescent contraculture openly, even proudly, embraces as its chief purpose, "to have a good time."

The battle lines between the old and the young are not clearly drawn, and they are certainly not permanent. Some adolescent fashions become generally accepted. Many young people, especially those who enter the working world early, show little resentment against their elders and soon fall in step with the older generation's ways. Others who express contempt for the adult generation in general may nevertheless worship certain adult heroes, whether these idols are pop singers or sports stars.

Youth cultures that are critical of adult society are not new. The Romantic poets and artists of the nineteenth century and the German youth movement of the early twentieth century tried to create new forms and express new ideals. Though much that the young generation attempts and proclaims is later discarded as immature and ill-conceived, there is usually a residue of innovations that enters the dominant culture and contributes to cultural change.

At times, young people become so disgusted with the ways of their elders that they decide to "drop out" of adult society and create a culture of their own that is meant to avoid the injustices, hypocrisy, and coldness of the dominant culture. They form small *utopian* communities in which they try to create the same *in-group* feeling and sharing of material goods that we found among the Hutterites, but without the religious base. A number of such communities were begun with a high degree of idealism but did not prove to be very durable.

The hippies have similar intentions, and their peculiar movement seems to have reached its peak in the summer of 1967.[6] Young men and women, many with years of college training, decided that the older generation had made a mess of American society. They were disgusted with the feverish—and to them senseless—rush for power and material goods around them. They wanted to demonstrate their deep opposition to war and violence.

The hippies literally "dropped out" of the adult culture. Customary clothing was discarded in favor of long robes, ponchos, and tunics adorned with flowers and beads. Large buttons proclaimed "Love." Barefoot hippies gathered in public parks for their "happenings," strumming guitars, smoking marijuana, and listening to the recital of mystic poetry.

Many hippies gave up studies and jobs to live in self-imposed poverty. Symbolically they burned paper money in public. Every hippie was willing to share his shabby "pad" and his frugal meals with others. Though the movement began in the big cities, its followers gradually moved out into rural areas, where they attempted to form agricultural communities based on common ownership and freedom of personal expression.

The hippies demonstrated their desire for peace and human relationships based on love. Yet they came into conflict with society and ran afoul of the law through the use of marijuana and psychedelic drugs, such as LSD, which became one of their trademarks. This brought about police action and strongly expressed hostility on the part of "straight" society.

Only a small fraction of American youth became full-time hippies. Many more were impressed enough to adopt some of the hippie characteristics, such as nonconformist dress or hair style or participation in dance and music festivals that were celebrated with unusual abandon. In the late summer and early autumn of 1969 a number of youth festivals, held in different parts of the country, were attended by an incredibly large number of young people who came by car, on foot, by motorcycle, and by every other conceivable means of transportation. One of these "happenings," the Woodstock Festival at Bethel, New York, attracted approximately 400,000 participants, about ten times as many as the organizers had anticipated. All plans for housing, feeding, and caring for the sanitary needs of the guests broke down. Yet the huge crowd remained friendly and helpful. None of the fears of large-scale rioting and destruction materialized. The young people "did their thing," namely listening to earsplitting rock music, strumming their guitars, camping, smoking "pot," and occasionally shedding their clothes as a kind of testimony to their freedom from adult ideas of propriety.

Hippies live differently from the way we usually think narcotics addicts do, though some hippies may eventually join the addict society. Under the outspoken condemnation of most other segments of society the users of habit-forming drugs form still another type of contraculture. They don't advocate that everybody adopt their ways, nor do they attack the dominant culture; but they insist on carrying on their customs and upholding their values within their own group. Similarly, homosexuals and various types of deviants also develop a set of mores and folkways all their own.[7]

A gang of delinquent boys, which can be observed in the slums of many of our cities, combines youth with *deviant* practices. It develops its special code of behavior. Since the boys have usually given up hope of achieving success by upholding dominant values, "such values are repressed, their importance denied, [and] counter-values affirmed."[8] (See also Chapter 4 on Crime and Chapter 12 on Education.) Contracultures seem to spring up in societies that exhibit much tension and in which sizable portions feel neglected and frustrated.

Main Ideas

1. Subcultures are the normative systems of groups that are smaller than societies.
2. Subcultures and cultural enclaves are found in heterogeneous societies.
3. American culture can be viewed as one particular ring in an arrangement of several cultural rings.
4. Because America has been populated by successive waves of immigration, its culture is a composite of a number of ethnic subcultures.
5. The descendants of immigrants perpetuate a system of subcultural pluralism mainly in their primary-group relationships.
6. This pluralism also exhibits itself in the subcultures formed by the major religions.
7. Sectarian subcultures, such as those of the Amish and the Hutterites, show considerable divergence from the dominant culture.
8. Many values of contracultures are definite contradictions of the dominant values.
9. The adolescent subculture shows characteristic elements of a contraculture.
10. The hippies formed a contraculture in protest against what they considered the hypocrisy, violence, and the competitive materialism of the dominant culture.

11. Contracultures are formed by groups of narcotics addicts, homosexuals, juvenile delinquents, and other deviant groups.

Important Terms
Anabaptist
Contraculture
Cultural ring
Deviance
Enclave
Enculturation
Heterogeneous culture
In-group
Normative systems
Peer group
Pluralism
Subculture
Utopian communities

Conclusion
Subcultures exist in a culture, such as ours, to which many different population elements have contributed and which is in the process of rapid transition. Despite growing general mobility the members of subcultures find themselves in social isolation and therefore carry on their accustomed behavior for a long time. Frustration and confusion of values lead to the formation of contracultures. Some subcultures seem to persist; others become substantially modified, or they make room for new subcultures. Thus a heterogeneous culture offers a picture of great variety and continuous change.

Notes
1. J. Milton Yinger, "Contraculture and Subculture," in Peter I. Rose (ed.), *The Study of Society* (New York: Random House, 1967), p. 827.
2. Milton M. Gordon, "Assimilation in America: Theory and Reality," in Rose, *ibid.*, p. 449.
3. John A. Hostetler, *Amish Life* (Scottsdale, Pa.: Herald Press, 1959).
4. John A. Hostetler, *Hutterite Life* (Scottsdale, Pa.: Herald Press, 1965).
5. Yinger, *op. cit.*, p. 831.
6. M. Harris, "Flowering of the Hippies," *Atlantic* (September 1967), pp. 63 ff.
7. Albert K. Cohen, *Deviance and Control* (Englewood Cliffs, N.J.: Prentice-Hall, 1966), pp. 109 ff.
8. Yinger, *op. cit.*, p. 834.

Suggestions for Further Reading

Adamic, Louis. *A Nation of Nations*. New York: Harper, 1945. Survey of immigrant groups in the United States, their subcultures and adjustment problems.

Asch, Shalom. *East River*. New York: Putnam, 1946. Novel on Jewish subculture in New York City.

Glazer, N. and D. P. Moynihan. *Beyond the Melting Pot*. Cambridge, Mass.: Harvard University Press, 1963. Even though ethnic groups in America change, they still retain their cultural identity.

Hagan, William T. *American Indians*. Chicago: University of Chicago Press, 1961. Indian-white relations and the attempts to form an Indian subculture within the North American culture.

Handlin, Oscar. *The Uprooted*. New York: Grosset and Dunlap, 1951. Movingly told story of the hardships and the adjustment problems of immigrants in American cities.

Hedgepeth, W. "Inside the Hippie Revolution," *Look*, August 22, 1967, pp. 58 ff.

La Farge, Oliver. *As Long as the Grass Shall Grow*. New York: Alliance, 1940. Compassionate picture of American Indians and their attempts to incorporate modern techniques into their ethnic culture.

Schermerhorn, R. A. *These Our People: Minorities in American Culture*. Boston: Heath, 1949.

Schreiber, William. *Our Amish Neighbors*. Chicago: University of Chicago Press, 1962. Description of all phases of Amish life.

Smith, Betty. *A Tree Grows in Brooklyn*. New York: Harper & Row, 1947. Novel about the Irish subculture in the American city.

*What are the social sciences?
And what is science in general?
What does a social science do?
And what use can be made of its findings?*

23 WHAT, WHY, AND FOR WHAT PURPOSE?
the social sciences

This book has tried to introduce you to matters dealt with by the social sciences. It has offered you a glimpse into the variety of human society. By cutting across the individual disciplines of the social sciences, we are able to behold the broad panorama of mankind with all its troubles and in all its glory.

We have ranged over topics as widely different as the Supreme Court, gangland, television commercials, lonely hearts clubs, Chinatown, labor unions, kleptomania, and many more. At first glance they don't seem to have much connection, yet these and hundreds of other topics are part of social behavior. And they all fall within the scope of one or another of the social sciences.

WAYS OF KNOWING

Look again at the two words "social science." We understand by now to a large extent what the word "social" entails. But what about "science"? Science is a way to gain knowledge. But it is far from being the only way, and it is a comparatively new method next to the others that we will now mention briefly.

In everyday life people quite commonly gain knowledge by listening to somebody who, they believe, knows more than they do—a teacher, priest, family doctor, fortuneteller. They depend on an *authority*. We all do to some extent. In order to continue living, we must take the word of experts, since we cannot possibly be experts in everything ourselves.

A man becomes an authority by virtue of his training or skill or because he holds a certain position in the community. Many, probably most, people also believe in a supernatural authority, which in our culture is called God. When God speaks through Scripture or through a man, a prophet, who claims to be his mouthpiece, most of the faithful feel that the absolute truth has been revealed, a truth that must not be questioned.

There are other avenues to knowledge. Looking through various college catalogues, you frequently find that the course offerings appear under three main headings: Natural Sciences, Social Sciences, and Humanities. Previous chapters have indicated that the humanities include such fields as philosophy, literature, and the history and interpretation of art and music. Like the social sciences, the humanities deal with man's thoughts and creations. Deep insights are gained from beholding such creations and from pondering such thoughts. They enrich the mind and lift it to the heights of idealism, but they are not sciences.

Many people claim to gain knowledge without the help of books or college courses. Some still believe that finding a four-leaved clover brings luck. Why do they believe this? They have heard it from their parents, who in turn heard it from their grandparents. The belief is part of their *folklore*. Certainly some people will experience luck after finding this rare plant, while others will not. The lucky ones then are likely to be convinced that this piece of folklore is correct.

For thousands of years men believed that the sun moved around the earth. Why? Well, all anybody had to do was look up to the sky and observe the fiery disk travel its daily course! It was *common-sense* knowledge.

Yet common sense is not foolproof, and to point out errors in it can be dangerous. In the seventeenth century Galileo, an early astronomer and physicist, proved that the earth was not the center of the universe but that it circled continuously around the sun. This not only hurt the pride of his fellow-men but also went against the authority of the church. Galileo's attack on common sense landed him in a dungeon.

Even in our own century, it can be dangerous for science to step into the path of religious authority. As recently as 1925, a high-school teacher by the name of John T. Scopes was convicted by a Tennessee court for having taught the scientific theory of *evolution*, which proposes that all life developed from simpler to more complex forms. According to this theory man's ancestors are a long-extinct species of large apelike creatures. The Book of Genesis in the Bible describes how the first man was created by God out of dust and the first woman out of a rib of the first man. Thus those religious spokesmen who interpret the Bible literally object to the theory of evolution.

WHAT IS SCIENCE?

Science does not blindly accept any authority. It is not folklore or common sense or inspiration through poetry and art. What is it then?

Briefly, science is "finding a pattern in a set of *phenomena*."[1] The scientist collects facts, which are as accurate as he can find, arranges them in order, interprets and explains them, and then tries to arrive at some generalizations, which are called *theories* or *laws*. He assumes that there is order in the material universe and also in the relations of human beings and that the same causes will always have the same effect under the same circumstances.

On July 21, 1969, men walked for the first time on the surface of the moon. This feat was possible because the scientists and technicians who had prepared the trip could safely assume that the law of gravity and other natural laws hold true anywhere and at all times. Such assumptions enable us to make predictions. From what we see, hear, or smell now we can draw conclusions about events that will happen in the future. For example, scientists have been very accurate in predicting eclipses of the sun and, so far, somewhat less accurate in predicting tomorrow's weather.

The scientist, whether he investigates natural or social behavior, proceeds according to rules that we call the *scientific method*. The scientific method is not a hard-and-fast list of instructions like those printed on the pages of a cookbook, but rather a set of general principles that the scientist adapts to the task at hand. Basically the practitioners of the scientific method follow these steps:

1. Find a problem. This depends on the interest of the researcher and also on what his particular scientific discipline has found before. For example, what makes a person become a criminal? (See Chapter 4.)

2. Collect data. Cesare Lombroso (1835–1909), for example, a criminologist, did not gather facts by referring to old books, nor did he listen to his friends and neighbors. He went to the prisons and carefully examined many inmates.

3. Form a *hypothesis*, that is, an educated guess that contains the answer to the problem. Lombroso's hypothesis was that there are born criminals and that one can recognize them by certain physical characteristics, particularly the shape of the skull.

4. Rigorously test the hypothesis in order to prove or disprove it. Criminologists have since done a great deal of research on the cause of criminality. They found Lombroso's hypothesis to be wrong and therefore discarded it.

5. Form a theory or law, provided the hypothesis holds up under thorough objective testing. Using this method, students of the natural

sciences have developed many laws and theories, such as the law of gravity and the theory of evolution. Social scientists are trying to do the same. Some criminologists developed the theory that crime is related to poverty and other features of lower-class society. But this theory too had to be modified when more knowledge was gained about "white-collar" crime, which is practiced by people of greater means.

SCIENTIFIC ATTITUDES

In collecting his facts and arriving at his theories, the scientist adopts a set of attitudes that are quite different from those of the nonscientist and that may even conflict with the attitudes the same scientist displays after working hours:

1. Science is *skeptical*. It does not subscribe to emotional statements like, "Our Federal Government is controlled by communists" or "All long-haired youths are addicts." It withholds judgment until all the evidence has been gathered. The scientist answers rash assertions with, "Show me. Convince me with facts."

2. Science is self-corrective. The criminologists, we have just seen, made errors, which they admitted. The scientist does not claim that his findings are true for all future times. Instead he stands ready to correct them when new evidence turns up.

3. Science is public, not secret. Reports are made available to competent persons so they can check on the investigations and repeat them. Also, before beginning any new research project, scientists are advised to check carefully the literature in their field. This preliminary research can prevent the unnecessary heartbreak of finding out, after a project has been completed, that somebody else has already done the same or a very similar piece of work. Unfortunately, some types of research, mostly connected with the development of military weapons, are now carried on in great secrecy. In this way scientific know-how and ingenuity are used for destruction rather than for the benefit of mankind. Secrecy also prevents the scientists of various countries from communicating with each other. The progress of the human mind should not be limited by national boundaries. Many great scientific achievements were accomplished by one scholar building on the findings of others who lived and worked in different places.

4. Science is precise and objective. The predictions of ancient priests and *oracles* were often vague, but the scientist must make sure that there will be no misunderstandings. He must record what he sees and "let the chips fall where they may." Science does not suppress findings that are unpleasant or unpopular.

5. Science must aim at *generalization*. The hobbyist may collect rocks or busy himself in his home laboratory, but he usually does it just for the pleasure of looking at interesting specimens or chemical reactions; the

scientist engaged in the same activity, on the other hand, uses these observations as a means of arriving at general conclusions.

HOW SCIENTIFIC IS SOCIAL SCIENCE?

When someone hears the word "science," he will probably automatically connect it with the biological or physical sciences, such as zoology or chemistry. There are doubts whether the study of human behavior can be undertaken with the same methods used to study magnetism or the mating habits of earthworms.

Without question the relations between human beings are extremely complex and difficult to observe. For one thing, the social scientist is part of what he is investigating—he belongs to a class, a nation, a family; he earns money and consumes goods like everybody else. Therefore, he finds it much harder to suppress his personal *bias* than the investigator of, say, mosses or gases.

This brings up another difficulty: few laymen would consider arguing with atomic physicists or biochemists about their respective fields, but most people consider themselves experts on matters of social concern. Millions of blue- and white-collar workers, businessmen and housewives, who exchange their views over coffee or after church, seemingly know exactly what should be done about juvenile delinquents, unwed mothers, or Red China. Their judgment is based more on emotion and hearsay than on real knowledge. We hear such statements as, "I know all about unemployment; I have been unemployed myself." But then the social scientist will show that the problem of unemployment is very complex and that it has many causes. The layman may be quick to propose an easy solution, while the scholar finds it much more difficult. To the layman the scientist sometimes seems to have the curious habit of obscuring matters that many claim are obvious.

In probing into issues of deep personal concern, the social scientist touches, at times, upon raw nerves. Sometimes what has previously been accepted as a correct assumption becomes doubtful or relative. Long-cherished ideas about the role of the parent and the teacher, about sexual behavior, poverty, crime, and foreign relations are being challenged. Social science is "always potentially dangerous to the minds of policemen and other guardians of public order, since it will always *relativize* the claim to absolute rightness upon which such minds like to rest [italics are this author's]."[2]

Despite all these difficulties social science is making rapid progress from being a general philosophy and a collection of curiosities toward being true science. Because of the nature of its subject matter, social scientists hesitate before making flat assertions. Often such assertions are qualified by words like "usually," "mostly," or, "as far as our evidence shows." As one of its practitioners, Karl Deutsch, says, social science is a "probabilistic field."

Qualifications in this field are not necessarily an expression of failure or weakness, but rather . . . an expression of strength and *sophistication*. Truth is not served if the complicated is made simple or the difficult unduly easy—and human life in all its richness is extremely complicated in itself and extremely difficult to study scientifically[3] (italics added).

Social science is still very much in its beginning stages, for its history goes back not much more than one hundred years. Social scientists have devised their own methods of collecting data and testing hypotheses. They adopt whatever is applicable from the older natural sciences.

HOW SOCIAL SCIENTISTS COLLECT DATA

Experiment: The word "science" usually immediately suggests experimentation carried on in laboratories. Experimentation in the social sciences does not mean putting individuals or groups into test tubes or dissecting them physically. Still some limited forms of experimentation are possible. Experiments in the social sciences are restricted mostly to small groups, such as a working team in industry (see Chapter 13) or a class of school children.

For example, a class is taught arithmetic by a new method, while a similar class is taught by the old method. If the two groups are equal in mathematical skill at the outset, one can later compare the results and decide which method produced the better math students.

Sample survey: Perhaps you were once polled as to what brand of refrigerator you own or what television programs you prefer to watch. Investigators also ring doorbells to get your opinion on political questions. Students are asked to complete questionnaires on their dating habits. If the sample covers both sexes, various age and racial groups, different levels of education and so on—in other words, if it is *representative*—important conclusions about attitudes or about the impact of communication and propaganda can be drawn.

Case study: A patient in a mental institution, a primitive tribe in the Amazon jungle, or a small community in our Middle West is being carefully observed over a long period of time. Such investigations may be undertaken by a single researcher or by a whole team of researchers. At the end of the study the findings are analyzed, and possible generalizations are suggested.

Tests: The test is familiar to all students. It is a device used to measure the knowledge gained in a certain class. Besides schools, employment agencies, and personnel officers in business and industry, the military and other branches of government employ many different kinds of tests to measure intelligence, attitudes, abilities, and interests.

Statistics: Many important facts that help the social scientist prove or disprove a hypothesis are expressed in figures. Such statistics provide different kinds of information—for example, whether populations of countries or cities are growing or decreasing, the number of families living on certain incomes, how many juveniles have been arrested for a particular violation, how many blacks hold skilled or professional jobs, and so forth. But statistics are valuable only when carefully interpreted; otherwise they can be very misleading.

Historical analysis: Mores, folkways, political systems, religious practices, and many other social situations can only be properly understood if their origin and development is studied.

Cross-cultural method: By comparing the behavior of different societies in different parts of the world, we learn how similar needs are met in many and often contrasting ways.

Records: In many instances the social scientist has to rely on the written word. He may, for example, study the nature of communism from Marxist writings or glean insights into past and present civilizations from legends, novels, and public documents. Propaganda material, court records, letters, and diaries yield clues from which the social scientist may make generalizations and predictions.

THE VARIOUS SOCIAL SCIENCES

Because the whole field is so new and its subject matter so diversified, we cannot even agree on what is or is not a social science. But we can begin with one group of disciplines that qualifies without rousing too much opposition. These are the *behavioral sciences,* namely sociology, anthropology, and psychology. Many people use the terms "behavioral science" and "social science" interchangeably, as if these three disciplines were the only true social sciences.

Sociology: "Positions, relationships, and groups represent the basic categories of sociology."[4] Sociology deals with man's relations to groups, with the structure of groups, and with the relations of groups to each other. The subject matter seems very general, and the same statement can be made about most of the other social sciences as well. Actually sociology overlaps with many other fields, and such overlapping, as we will see, is true of all the social sciences. Since sociology developed later than some of the other academic disciplines, it undertook the investigation of topics that they had neglected, such as crowd behavior or mobility.

Anthropology: Anthropology (from Greek, meaning the "study of man") covers more territory than any other subject. It embraces "the full geographical and chronological sweep of human societies."[5] Traditionally it has concentrated on the racial history of mankind and on the study of *preliterate* cultures. But lately anthropology has been extended to the study of advanced societies as well. In fact, the concept of culture (see Chapter 21) was first introduced by anthropologists. More than most other social scientists, they spend months or even years in fieldwork, which might take them to Central America, distant Pacific islands, or to any other point on the globe.

Psychology: "Psychology is the scientific field that attempts to understand, describe, predict, and influence behavior."[6] The stress is on *human* behavior, though psychologists also work with rats, pigeons, and monkeys. They feel that findings on animal behavior can sometimes be applied to the human species.

The psychologist deals with such topics as learning, perception, conditioning, and motivation. All these pertain to the individual, but since we are in perpetual contact with other people, the individual cannot be studied in isolation.

The relation of the individual to his society is the special interest of the field of *social psychology*, which, according to one view, "is a set of topics that have exceeded the grasp of non-social psychology but which are being effectively investigated by a psychology that draws upon the social sciences."[7] Briefly then, social psychology is psychology with a strong emphasis on the interplay of the individual and society. A few examples of research topics will illustrate its scope: the socialization of the child, leadership, role and role conflict, and behavior under situational stress.

Aside from the behavioral sciences two fields that are quite generally accepted as social sciences are economics and political science.

Economics: Economics studies man's ways of making a living. It investigates the production of goods and the performance of services necessary to man's survival and his pursuit of prestige; it observes the distribution and consumption of such goods and services. The interests of the economist range from the individual and the family to the activities of local and national governments and even to the international scene.

Political science: Political science is the study of governmental institutions and man's political behavior. It investigates how political power arises and how political decisions are made. In older times political scientists could more accurately be referred to as political philosophers because they spent much time speculating on what would be the best form of government. Recently the field has moved closer to the behavioral sciences, as it is concerned with public opinion, pressure groups, voting habits, and other forms of politico-social behavior.

To complete our survey, we still must mention several fields that are partly considered to be social sciences.

History: History attempts to reconstruct and interpret the past of man, especially of literate man. As the historian tries to unravel human relations in various periods, he shares the interests of the social scientist. But he also pays much attention to the magnetism of great personalities and to the spiritual and aesthetic expressions of bygone ages. This emphasis puts the historian more in the realm of the humanities.

Geography: Geography is a description of the planet on which we live. As far as it deals with climate, the outlines of mountains and valleys, and with vegetation and the habitats of animals, it resembles the natural sciences. But as it also studies the distribution of population, economic conditions, and routes of communication, it crosses the boundary into the social sciences.

Psychiatry: Psychiatry is a branch of medicine that deals with diseases of the mind. As we have seen (Chapter 2), mental disturbance often results from a break in the communication line with society. The psychiatrist tries to mend or restring the line, as the electrician does in the case of a power break, so that the patient can function once more as an accepted and participating member of the group.

It is quite evident that the various social sciences are not separated from each other by impenetrable walls. Often two or more branches may deal with the same problem but from slightly different angles. Frequently sizable research projects are undertaken by teams of specialists drawn from different fields. Suppose, for example, a community wants to do something to amend its racial problems. An effective course can best be charted when economists, sociologists, psychologists, and political scientists pool their techniques. The same procedure has been applied in finding ways to help underdeveloped countries stabilize themselves.

Not only do the tasks of the various social sciences overlap, but social and natural sciences intrude on one another's fields of investigation. Human knowledge cannot be neatly divided into different piles and stored in different bins or drawers. For example, we have recently become greatly concerned about the dangers of pollution, which, according to many scholars, threaten the very existence of man and his society. To study pollution and the ways to overcome it calls for the combined efforts of natural and social scientists. Psychiatry links medicine with psychology and anthropology. Psychology, for its part, covers some of the same area as *physiology*, the science of the functions of living organisms, as it examines the physical roots of man's thinking and feeling. By enlisting the help of statistics and computer programming, all social sciences, but especially economics, rely heavily on mathematical knowledge. The findings of physics are drawn upon when criminologists employ fingerprinting or when historians and archaeologists use the *carbon-dating* method to ascertain the age of an artifact.

We notice two trends seemingly leading in opposite directions. On the one hand, the sciences are drawing together, sharing research goals and borrowing each other's methods. But in a startling contradiction, we observe, at the same time, constantly increasing *specialization*. Accumulated knowledge is so vast that it is becoming impossible for one scholar to master entirely even one field. In the social sciences, as in all sciences, this is the age of the specialist who comes to know more and more about less and less.

Some Specialized Fields in the Social Sciences

Sociology
- Industrial Sociology
- Rural Sociology
- Urban Sociology
- Criminology
- Human Ecology
- Demography (study of the distribution and migrations of populations)
- Sociometry (measurement of attraction and repulsion of members in small groups)

Anthropology
- Physical Anthropology (physical development of men and races; overlaps into biology)
- Cultural Anthropology
- Archaeology (study of cultures from their artifacts)
- Linguistics (study of languages)
- Semantics (study of the meaning of signs, symbols, and words; a subfield of linguistics)

Psychology
- Social Psychology
- Clinical Psychology (treatment of patients with psychological problems)
- Developmental Psychology (man's behavior through his growth from infancy to adulthood)
- Learning Theory
- Psychometrics (testing and the measurement of the test results)
- Information Theory (coding, transmitting, and receiving of messages)

Economics
- Agricultural Economy
- Labor Economy
- Business Economy
- Consumer Economy
- Money and Banking
- Price Theory
- International Economy

Political Science
- American Government
- International Relations
- Public Administration
- Parties and Pressure Groups
- Public Opinion

WHAT DO WE DO WITH SOCIAL SCIENCE?

Students frequently ask a teacher, "I like sociology (or political science or history), but what can I do with it?" What they really mean is: How can I make a living after having majored in this field in school?

There are many ways, but first let's make a few clarifications. Why does anybody study anything? Is it only to obtain grades and credits as an entrance ticket to an occupation?

When Sir Edmund Hillary, the first conqueror of Mount Everest, was asked why people want to climb such a dangerous mountain, he gave the famous answer "Because it is there." People want to find facts about themselves and about the world around them because they are there. They want to search for order and predictability in what they observe. Man is a curious animal, and since you belong to the species of man, a course in anthropology or international relations will help satisfy your natural curiosity.

Even those who become experts in any of these fields are motivated by curiosity, by a desire to find out more than is already known and to better arrange what they have found in a body of solid theory. This is *pure science,* as contrasted with *applied science.* Pure science explains and searches for patterns; it does not ask, "What can we do with it?" When Michael Faraday discovered the law of magnetic induction more than a hundred years ago, he had no idea that this piece of knowledge would be applied in making generators for automobiles.

Pure science is an end in itself, but it is also the basis for applied science. When an engineer designs a bridge that will hold heavy loads, he applies what physicists have found out about stress and the qualities of metals. Producers of paints and drugs apply the findings of chemistry. In the case of the medical scientist who studies the nature of diseases and also cures them, pure and applied science are thoroughly intertwined.

What really is a scientist? Some people consider only the scholar engaged in pure science as deserving of this title. They would refuse it to an economist whom government might call upon to devise a better system of taxation or to a psychologist who helps select employees for management training. The argument as to who deserves the designation of scientist is a rather futile one. Certainly a good engineer is well grounded in a number of sciences. Diplomats, ministers, journalists are not social scientists in the strict sense, but those who do the most constructive job will have absorbed much knowledge from the social sciences in a formal or an informal way.

What use, then, do you make of social science? You study it to better understand yourself and your human environment; you teach it to others; you apply it in order to bring about improvements in social relations. What constitutes improvement depends on your ideas and on the ideas of the people for whom you work. In earlier chapters we have already encountered many ways of application, and more are coming into being every day.

Social Scientists Employed by Colleges and Universities

Approximately 86% of holders of doctor's degrees in sociology
Approximately 76% of holders of doctor's degrees in political science
Approximately 69% of holders of doctor's degrees in economics

Source: Based on data from Talcott Parsons, "Sociology as a Profession," in Peter I. Rose (ed.), *The Study of Society* (New York: Random House, 1967), p. 62.

Most social scientists find employment as teachers or researchers at colleges, universities, business schools, medical schools, law schools, schools of public health, and in the seminaries that train ministers, priests, and rabbis. In fact, the whole field of education, with its special interests in curriculum, learning techniques, school administration, and school finances, is really one large complex of applied social science.

Jurisprudence, which is the study and designing of laws and court procedures, also combines many social sciences. Jurisprudence concerns itself with the training of attorneys and judges and with the role of law enforcement in the community. Thus the field is in close contact with political science and also with criminology while retaining its traditional connections with logic and moral philosophy.

The application of various social sciences is strongly evident in public health and even more so in *social work.* The layman tends to confuse social work with sociology, though the latter is a science and the former an applied activity.

Career Opportunities in Which Training in the Social Sciences Is Useful

Social Work
    Case worker in child welfare, family welfare, and mental health agencies
    Psychiatric social worker
    Probation and parole officer
    Social worker in correctional institutions
    Recreation and playground director
    Community center director
    Executive in the Boy Scouts, Girl Scouts, YMCA

Government Employment
    City, county manager
    Community planner
    Foreign service
    Intelligence services
    Various positions in the departments of Agriculture, Labor, Commerce, Housing and Urban Development, the Bureau of Indian Affairs, and so forth

Employment in Business, Labor Unions, Churches
    Personnel officer
    Statistician
    Market and cost analyst
    Opinion research
    Consultant on human relations, planning, organization, investment, sales promotion, and so forth

SOCIAL SCIENCE: GOOD OR BAD?

For some people the term "sociologist" is a bad word, since it connotes to them a meddlesome do-gooder who constantly attempts to upset established ways. This is, of course, a case of misunderstanding and confusion.

Neither sociology nor any other social science sets out to change conditions for better or worse, as this is not the purpose of any science.

Here we come to the distinction between facts and *values*. The scientist wants to discover facts and develop concepts. He does not want to attach values to the facts. This is the business of the reformer, the politician, the religious leader, and the philosopher. Philosophers, in particular, have always pursued the question of values. *Ethics* and *aesthetics* are special branches of philosophy dealing with values in moral behavior and in the consideration of beauty.

Values are *subjective*; they depend on the tastes and the convictions of the individual and the group. In the search for values you don't ask how things are but how they *ought to be*. On the other hand, the zoologist investigating the flight pattern of migratory birds does not decide whether what they do is good or bad. Neither does the social scientist condemn or praise suburbs, automation, or polygamy. His job is to see why they exist, how they work, and what their consequences are.

It is easier to be objective about migratory birds than about migrant workers. Erupting volcanoes are less upsetting to the distant observer than riots erupting in the slums to the urban dweller. The social scientist is, after all, a person who has his own value system. He does not always find it easy to separate the philosophy behind his work from the opinions he expresses after work. Whether you have a degree in one of the social sciences or not, you cannot easily evade the value judgment that alcoholism and poverty are undesirable and that ways should be found to eliminate them. Layman and expert share such convictions.

Though the scientist is not a rebel or even a reformer when he is doing his job, he is frequently called upon to help those who want change, and most times he is glad to oblige. He can chart a course for the reformer that is more likely to lead to success, since he is trained to appraise social situations accurately. Thus mistakes based only on good intentions and emotional judgments can be more easily avoided.

Social scientists did not bring about World War II or the Korean War, but they proved to be very useful in evaluating enemy propaganda, advising intelligence and counterintelligence workers, charting the course of wartime economy, and obtaining the cooperation of local residents in occupied territories.

We can only hope that the valuable knowledge of the social sciences will always be employed in the service of the ethical values that our particular civilization upholds. Fears have been expressed that this will not always be the case. Once learned men thoroughly understand the mechanism of human behavior, some of them might be tempted to control and manage mankind for the sake of power. Several novelists have created nightmarish pictures of such controlled societies.[8] To some extent the management of human thought and action is already being tried in certain techniques of sales promotion and political campaigning.

To dream the dream of a better world and to keep the dream constantly before our eyes is the task of the *social philosopher* rather than the social scientist. In this age of the megalopolis and of ever increasing technology the philosopher warns us not to let the machine become our master, or we will become a society in which "men live for the artifacts they have created instead of bending these to the human spirit."[9] Most social scientists, though, cannot help but be deeply concerned about the sickness of society and the privations that individuals must suffer, often unnecessarily. It is in the nature of the work that sociologists, psychologists, economists, and other social scientists perform that they gain a deeper insight—more than most other people—into what is wrong with man. Conscience and compassion may call them from their quiet libraries and sheltered studies into the arena of civic and political reform.

What makes it particularly difficult for the social scientist to avoid making value judgments is the fact that he deals with other people's values all the time. They are part of his raw material. Though this imposes a difficulty, it also provides a great benefit. The student of the social sciences realizes that there are many different cultures with many different value systems. It may come as a surprise to him, at first, that monogamy is not universally accepted as the "right" form of marriage or representative democracy as the only "right" form of government, though our own culture values these forms highly. But he finally understands that "good" and "bad," "right" and "wrong" are relative terms.

The serious practitioner of the social sciences inevitably becomes less ethnocentric than he was before. This is a "fringe benefit" of his efforts but one that should not be underestimated. It may yet turn out to be the most significant benefit not only for him but for mankind.

Main Ideas
1. Human knowledge is gained by relying on authority, by *contemplative* insight, by relying on folklore and on common sense, and by the process of science.
2. Science collects facts, arranges them in order, interprets and explains them, and tries to arrive at theories or laws.
3. The usual steps in the scientific method are: find a problem, collect data, form a hypothesis, test the hypothesis, and form a theory, provided the hypothesis holds up under thorough testing.
4. Science is skeptical, self-corrective, public, precise, objective, and oriented toward making generalizations.
5. It is particularly difficult for the social scientist to remain unbiased and regard values as relative.
6. Social sciences gather data by means of experiments, sample surveys, case studies, tests, statistics, historical analyses, cross-cultural methods, and written records.
7. Sociology, anthropology, and psychology are grouped together as behavioral sciences.
8. Other social sciences are economics and political science.

9. History, human geography, and psychiatry belong, to some extent, to the social sciences.
10. The fields of inquiry and the methods of the social sciences overlap; in many instances, interests and techniques are also shared with the natural sciences and the humanities.
11. Each of the social sciences contains a growing number of specialized subfields.
12. Social science findings are applied in numerous fields, among them education, jurisprudence, public health, and social work.
13. There are numerous careers in which training in the social sciences is required or, at least, useful.
14. Every social science should, like any other science, avoid value judgments; this is difficult because of the personal involvement of the researcher with his material.

Important Terms

Aesthetics
Applied science
Authority
Behavioral science
Bias
Carbon dating
Common sense
Ethics
Evolution
Folklore
Generalization
Hypothesis
Jurisprudence
Oracle

Phenomena
Physiology
Preliterate cultures
Pure science
Relativize
Representative sample
Scientific method
Skepticism
Social philosopher
Social psychology
Social work
Specialization
Theory
Value

Conclusion

Though he is called upon to be objective and avoid favoring any value system, the social scientist operates under a value system of his own in which objectivity plays an important role. This value system requires that he exercise integrity and refrain from slanting, exaggerating, or withholding his findings. His professional ethics will compel him at times to investigate situations that are unpleasant or even repulsive with the same care that he lavishes on those he finds agreeable. Hopefully, he will never promise more than he can deliver but will humbly admit the youth and limitations of his field.

Notes
1. Stuart Chase, *The Proper Study of Mankind*, rev. ed. (New York: Harper Colophon, 1956), p. 8.
2. Peter L. Berger, "Sociology as a Form of Consciousness," in Peter I. Rose (ed.), *The Study of Society* (New York: Random House, 1967), p. 31.
3. B. Berelson and G. A. Steiner, *Human Behavior*, shorter ed. (New York: Harcourt, Brace & World, 1964), p. 197.
4. Theodore Abel, "What Is Sociology?" in A. W. Thompson (ed.), *Gateway to the Social Sciences*, rev. ed. (New York: Holt, Rinehart and Winston, 1961), p. 98.
5. *International Encyclopedia of the Social Sciences* (New York: Macmillan, 1968), Vol. I.
6. Richard A. Kalish, *The Psychology of Human Behavior* (Belmont, Cal.: Wadsworth, 1966), p. 4.
7. Roger Brown, *Social Psychology* (New York: Free Press, 1965), foreword.
8. See, for example, Aldous Huxley, *Brave New World* (New York: Modern Library, 1932) and George Orwell, *1984* (New York: Harcourt, 1949).
9. Henry Winthrop, *Ventures in Social Interpretation* (New York: Appleton-Century-Crofts, 1968), p. 510.

Suggestions for Further Reading
Berelson, Bernard (ed.). *The Behavioral Sciences Today*. New York: Basic Books, 1963. Series of talks by experts in various social science disciplines in the forum series of the Voice of America.
Bronowski, J. *Science and Human Values*. New York: Messner, 1956. Brief and simple discussion of the relationship of science to truth, human dignity, and the creative mind.
Conant, James B. *Modern Science and Modern Man*. New York: Columbia University Press, 1952. Short discussion of science in the twentieth century and of its relationship to human conduct and spiritual values.
Hersey, John. *The Child Buyer*. New York: Knopf, 1960. Psychological novel about a firm that buys exceptional children and conditions them to become dehumanized thinking machines.
Oliver, Chad. *Shadows in the Sun*. Greenwich, Conn.: Fawcett, 1954. Novel by and about an anthropologist.
Social Science Perspectives. Columbus, Ohio: Merrill. Series of six paperbacks, each introducing one of the social science disciplines: Henry S. Commager, *The Study of History*; J. O. M. Broek, *Compass of Geography*; Frank Sorauf, *Perspectives on Politial Science*; Pertti J. Pelto, *The Nature of Anthropology*; R. S. Martin and R. G. Miller, *Prologue to Economic Understanding*; Caroline B. Rose, *The Study of Sociology*.
Stokley, James. *Modern Advances in Science: A Layman's Guide*. New York: Ronald Press, 1964. The author combines professorships in astronomy and journalism.

INDEX

Absolute rule, 310
Abstinence, 109
Accommodation, 401
Acting crowd, 34
Adult education, 237
Advertising industry, 201–202
Aesthetic goals, 190
Aesthetic needs, 396
Aesthetics, 432
Affluence, 204
Afterlife, belief in, 144
Aggression, 377
Agnosticism, 142
Air pollution, 279, 299, 337, 338
Alcoholics Anonymous, 67
Alcoholism, 66–67, 398, 432
Alliances, 353, 376
Ambassadors, 346, 376
American Federation of Labor—Congress of Industrial Organizations (AFL-CIO), 182, 316
American Indians, 85, 205, 409, 410
Amish (religious sect), 413–414
Anabaptist movement, 413
Anarchy, 312
Anglo-Saxon culture, 408
Animism, 140
Anthropology, 426, 429
Anthropomorphic gods, 141

Anti-Semitism, 82–83, 150
Anxiety neuroses, 22
Appalachia, 205
Applied science, 430
Arctic Siberian culture, 403
Arms race, 353, 384
Artifacts, 397
Aryan race myth, 81
Assessment, 296
Assets, 196–197
Atheism, 142
Attack response, 25
Audiences, 45–46; Beatle fans, 45; concert hall, 45–46; stadium, 46
Augustine, St., 219
Australian ballot, 304
Authority, 421
Automation, 179–181, 243
Automobile industry, 199
Aztec Indians, 279

Backlash, 336
Balance of power, 352–353; Cold War, 368
Balanced budget, 330
Barter economy, 166
Behavioral sciences, 426–427
Beliefs, basic elements of, 396
Bias, 424

437

438 Index

Bible, 82, 104, 375–388; education, 236; evolutionary theory and, 421; literal interpretation of, 421–422; myths, 141; translations, 155; on white supremacy, 79; on work, 164
Bicameral legislature, 334
Big business, 199
Bigot, 81
Bipolar world, 366, 368
Birth control, 55, 133
Black power, 89–90, 108
Black studies programs, 250
Blacks, *see* Negroes
Boroughs, 297
Bourgeoisie, 220
Buddha, 144, 148
Buddhism, 145–146, 152
Budgeting, 199–201
Building codes, 295
Bureaucracy, 176
Burglary, 57, 58
Business, 170–172
Bussing issue (school), 247

Capitalism, 169, 314
Case poverty, 205
Case study, 425
Caste system, 217–218
Casual crowd, 32–33
Central Intelligence Agency (CIA), 354–355
Central Treaty Organization (CENTO), 368, 370
Centralization, school, 238
Charisma, 43, 266
Charter, 296
Chauvinism, 326
Checks and balances, 313, 318
China (ancient), 345
Church of Jesus Christ of Latter-day Saints, 62, 125, 147, 152
Churchill, Sir Winston, 309, 368
Cities, 278–287; characteristics of, 279; ecology of, 282–284; government, 297–299; heterogeneity and mobility, 281–282; megalopolis, 288–289; origin of, 280–281; planning, 289–290; slums, 284–287; suburbia, 287–288; taxes, 302–303
City-states, 280, 376
Civil Rights Act of 1964, 88, 314
Civil rights movement, 87–88
Civilization, defined, 394
Class: lower, 226–228; lower lower, 224–226; lower middle, 224–226; lower upper, 224–226; middle, 226–228; upper, 226–228; upper lower, 224–226; upper middle, 224–226; upper upper, 224–226
Class system, 219–229; Marx on, 220–221, 222, 223, 227; religion and, 226–227; in Soviet Union, 221–222; theories of, 219–222; in United States, 222, 228
Classless society, 220
Cliques, 217
Coalition government, 317
Coeducation, 105
Coercion, 351–352; unrestricted freedom and, 321
Cohesion, 264
Cold War, 361, 366–370; balance of power, 368; changing nature of, 369–370
Collective behavior, 32–50; audiences, 45–46; casual crowds, 32–33; expressive crowds, 44–45; leadership, 43–44; lynching, 35–37; mobs, 34–35; panic, 33–34; propaganda, 48–49; publics, 46–48; riots, 37–41; rumor, 41; social movements, 41–43
Collective security, 377
Colonial imperialism, 362–364
Commission form of government, 298
Common Market, 380. *See* European Economic Community (EEC)
Common markets, 361
Common sense, 421
Communism, 142, 319, 321, 350, 360, 387; religious, 414; as secular religion, 156–157
Communist Information Bureau (COMINFORM), 368
Community, 273–340; democracy, 309–323; from hamlet to megalopolis, 273–292; government, 294–307; national, 325–340; as place to live, 273–274
Competition, 401
Compromise, response to stress, 25
Compulsive neuroses, 22
Compulsory education, 235–236
Concentric Zones, theory of, 283
Conditioning, 11
Conflict, 23, 401
Conflict behavior, 56–57
Conformity, 11, 53
Congress of Racial Equality (CORE), 88
Constitutions, democracy and, 312
Consumer: advertising industry and, 201–202; budgeting, 199–201; freedom of choice, 198–199; habits of, 196–198; income and consumption, 189–210; living standard, 202–204; protection of, 202
Containment, policy of, 368
Contraceptives, 133, 227
Contraculture, 414–417
Conventional weapons, 364–365
Conversion, 144
Corporation, 170–172
Cosa Nostra, 60

Council-manager form of government, 299
County unit of government, 297
Coups d'état, 317
Courtship: in America, 105–109; breaking off of, 108; choosing a mate, 103–105; love and, 97–114; premarital sex, 109–111; prospects of marital success, 112–113
Credit rating, 201
Crime, 52–72; alcoholism and, 66–67; annual cost of (in dollars), 57; conflict behavior and, 56–57; deviation, 55–56; folkways, mores, laws and, 55; homosexuality and, 70–71; increase in, 62; juvenile delinquency, 64–66; major kinds of, 58; narcotics and, 67–70; organized, 59–60; prevention of, 64; retreatist behavior and, 66
Criminal behavior, 57–59; narcotics and, 68
Criminals, 60–63; contraculture, 417; punishing, 62–63
Criminologists, 57
Crisis therapy, 29
Cross-cultural behavior comparisons, 426
Cultural change, 55, 397–398
Cultural diffusion, 398–400
Cultural focus, 402
Cultural lag, 55, 398
Cultural ring, 407–408
Culture, 7, 393–418; artifacts, 397; contracultures, 414–417; elements of, 395–396; folkways and mores, 397; groups, 400–401; many kinds of, 402–403; meaning of, 394–395; personality, 393–394; social problems, 401–402; subcultures, 406–414; traits and complexes, 396; values, 10
Currency, 190
Curriculum, 240–241

Dating, 106; computer, 106, 107; social background and, 108
Declaration of Human Rights (United Nations), 181–182
De facto segregation, 86, 89
Defensive behavior, 25–26
Deficit spending, 330
De jure segregation, 86
Demagogue, 43, 315
Democracy, 309–323; ancient Greece, 310; direct, 306, 316; freedom and, 318–322; Great Britain, 314–315; indirect, 317; limitations and obligations of, 319; majority rule and minorities, 316–317; meaning of, 310–312; participation in, 315–316; representative, 316–317; rule of law, 314–315; tradition of, 318; types of, 312–314; voting, 315–316, 319–320
Denomination, 149
Depression (personality problem), 22
Depression of the 1930s, 337, 350
Dervishes (religious sect), 44
Desertion, family, 117, 134
Détente, 370
Determinism, 12
Deviation, 55–56, 417; forms of, 56
Dictatorship, 310, 320, 322
Diplomacy, 375–377
Diplomatic immunity, 386
Direct democracy, 306, 316
Disarmament, 384–385
Discrimination, 80, 204; Black resistance to, 87–89; caste system, 218; religious, 150
Dividends, 171
Divorce, 132
Dominant group, 81
Double standard of morality, 130; premarital sex and, 109
Drive, personality, 5
Dropouts: school, 248–249; society, 416
Dukhobors (religious sect), 149

Ecology, 282–284
Economic imperialism, 363
Economic interdependence, 346–350
Economic system, basic elements of, 395
Economics, 427, 429
Ecumenical movement, 150,152
Education, 232–253; adult, 237; American school system, 236–251; basic elements of, 395–396; control of school system, 237–240; curriculum, 240–241; dropouts, 248–249; federal aid to, 239–240; formal, 235–236, 241–243; in France, 238; generation gap, 249–251; goals of formal education, 241–243; income and, 193–194; informal, 233–234; meaning of, 232–233; minority groups and, 246–248; role of government in, 239–240; role of teacher, 244–246
Ego, the, 6
Egypt (ancient), 18, 58, 148, 397, 400
Electra complex, 5, 102
Electronic propaganda, 48
Electrotherapy, 19
Embezzlement, 58
Employment, 163–186; automation, 179–181; Bible on, 164; businesses, 170–172; as a curse, 164–165; farming, 172–173; finding, 177–178; and getting along, 255–268; group cohesiveness, 263–265; human relations, 258; kinds of jobs, 174–177; labor force, 173–174; and leisure, 184–185; leadership, 265–267; morale, 259–263; money and machine,

Employment (*continued*)
169; organizations, 182–183; Protestant concept of, 180; reason for, 163–164; rewards of, 166–168; satisfaction of needs, 255–258; social science and, 430–431; successful secretary, 261–263; as a virtue, 165–166; without pay, 168; unemployment, 181–182
Enclaves, 406–407
Enculturation, 394, 407
Endogamy, 103, 218
Energizers, 20–21
Engagement (wedding), 106; breakup of, 108
English language, 327, 408; and adolescent contraculture, 415
Enlightenment, 310–311
Equality before the law, 314
Erotic passion, 99
Escalation, 346
Eskimos, 397, 403; language, 366
Esprit de corps, 264
Establishment, 223
Estates, 218
Ethical concepts, 53
Ethics, 147, 432
Ethnic groups, 83
Ethnic subcultures, 409–412
Ethnocentrism, 400
European Economic Community (EEC), 361, 378
European Free Trade Association (EFTA), 378–380
Euphoria, 68
Evolution, theory of, 421
Executive orders, 333
Executive power, 313
Experimentation, 425
Expressive crowds, 44–45
Extended family, 126–127
Extreme Right, 321
Extremism, 42, 337
Extrovert, 4

Factory system, 169
Fads, 48
Faith healing, 18
Family, 117–136; 395; communication, 119–120; divorce, 132; extended, 126–127; functions of, 128–130; genealogy, 216; monogamy, 124, 125; names, 127–128; nuclear, 126–127; poverty line (1966), 206; roles, 130; signs of trouble, 117–118; as social institution, 123–124; survival, 118–119; system, 120–123
Farming, 172–173; poverty, 205
Fascism, 326
Feast days, religious, 145–146

Federal Bureau of Investigation (F.B.I.), 60, 176, 214
Federal Reserve Board, 330
Federal Reserve System, 190
Federal system, 312
Feedback, 121
Feminist movement, 127–128
Fetishism (Totemism), 140, 141
Fiscal policy, 330
Fixation, 102
Fluid ascription, 219
Folklore, 421
Folkways, 53–55; basic concepts of, 397; Southern, 407
Food and Agricultural Organization (FAO), 382
Forced labor camps, 165
Foreign policy (U.S.), 353–355; morality and, 370–371
Forgery, 58
Formal education, 235–236; goals of, 241–243
Frame of reference, 9–10; learning, 10–11
Free-enterprise system, 198–199
Free will, 12
Freedom: democracy and, 318–322; meaning of, 318; and order, 320–322
French Revolution, 35, 311, 326
Freud, Sigmund, 4–7, 12, 29
Frustration, 23
Fuehrer concept, 43–44
Fundamentalist religions, 143

Gambling, 58–59
Gandhi, Mahatma, 43, 88, 362
Genealogy, 216
Generalization, scientific, 423–424
Generation gap, 118, 249–251
Genetics, 12
Geographic determinism, 403
Geography, 427–428
Gerrymandering, 302
Getting along, 255–268; group and, 263–265; human relations, 258; leadership, 265–267; morale, 259–263; satisfaction of needs, 255–258
Ghettos, 285–286; in the Middle Ages, 83
Gods, 140–142
Good-luck charms, 146
Goods, consumer, 195
Government: aid to education, 239–240; basic elements of, 395; community, 294–307; democracy, 309–323; local, 294–303; national, 325–340; voting, 303–306; world, 386–387
Greece (ancient), 235, 276, 280; city-states, 376; democracy, 310; homosexuality, 55; myths, 141; religion, 141, 144, 147; slavery, 164–165

Gross National Product, 170, 348
Group cohesiveness, 263–265
Group dynamics, 263
Group therapy, 29
Groups: basic concepts of, 400–401; contracultures, 414–417; subcultures, 406–414
Growth-motivated persons, 27
Guerrilla warfare, 350, 360, 362, 364
Gypsies, 57, 274, 407

Habitat, 403
Hamlet (community), 274
Hair styles, 90, 415, 416
Happenings, 149, 416
Hassidim, 144
Headaches, 22
Heart transplants, 398
Hebrew language, 83, 145
Hebrews (ancient), 142, 147–148, 205
Henotheism, 141, 142
Heredity, 11–12
Hero worship, 45
Heroin, 68
Heterogeneity, city, 281–282
Heterogeneous culture, 407
Hierarchy, 215–216
Hinduism, 34, 35, 142; caste system, 217–218; holy men, 66; temple carvings, 100
Hippies, 69, 156; "doing their thing" movement, 416–417
Historical analysis, 426
History, 427
Hitler, Adolf, 43–44, 81, 82, 165, 315, 326, 337, 351, 385
Holiness sects, 226
Homosexuality, 55, 70–71, 100, 102, 417
Horizontal movement, 281
House of Representatives, 334
Human mind, problems of, 16–30; defensive behavior, 25–26; getting help, 27–29; mental health, 26–27; mental illness, 16–26; new era change, 20–21; older social attitudes, 17–19; pressure, 23–24; and response to stress, 24–25; stress, frustration, conflict, 22–23
Humanities, 235
Hutterites (religious sect), 148–149, 168, 414, 416
Hypnotism, 18
Hypothesis, 422

Id, the, 6
Identity, 167
Ideological movements, 42
Ideology, 157
Image, political, 48
Immigration, 410–411
Imperialism, 362–364
Incest, 58, 103

Income and consumption, 189–210; advertising, 201–202; budgeting, 199–201; choice, 198–199; consumer, 195–196; consumer habits, 196–198; fight against poverty, 205–208; inflation, 191–193; living standard, 202–204; money, 189–191; poverty, 204–205
Income tax: federal, 330; state and city, 303
Independence movements, 362
Indirect democracy, 317
Indoctrination, 242
Industrialization, 169
Inflation, 191–193
Informal education, 233–234
In-group, 416
Initiative, 306
Institutionalized events, 46
Institutions: cultural, 397; family, 119, 123–124
Integrated personality, 14
Integration, 87
Intelligence, 12
Interaction, 32, 120–121
Interdependency of states, 345–357; balance of power, 352–353; economic, 346–350; international relations, 355; power, 351–352; today's world and, 350–351; U.S. foreign policy, 353–355
Interfaith marriages, 108
Internal Revenue Service, 383
International Court of Justice, 382, 386
International Development Association (IDA), 382
International Labor Organization (ILO), 382
International law, 385–386
International Monetary Fund (IMF), 382
International organization, 377–380
International relations, 355
Interracial marriages, 108
Interstimulation, 44
Introvert, 4
Investments, 191
Isolationism, 345

Jews, 66, 81, 82–83, 152; American goals, 155; interfaith marriages, 108; rumors about, 41; Sabbath service, 145; as scapegoats, 82
Job Corps, 248–249
Job satisfaction, 167–168
John Birch Society, 337
Johnson, Lyndon B., 37–38, 208
Judicial power, 313
Judicial review, 335
Jurisprudence, 431
Juvenile delinquency, 64–66

442 Index

Kerner Commission, 37–38
Khrushchev, Nikita, 369
Kidney transplants, 398
King, Martin Luther, Jr., 56, 87–88
Kinsey, Alfred, 109–110
Kleptomania, 22
Korean War, 364, 381, 432
Ku Klux Klan, 74–75
Kurnai tribe (Australia), 103
Kwoma tribe (New Guinea), 100

Labor force, 173–174
Labor unions, 181–182
Laissez-faire, 265, 321
Language, basic elements of, 396
Larceny, 58
Laws, 53–55, 397; enforcement of, 314; Jim Crow, 86; scientific, 422
Leadership, 43–44, 265–267
League of Nations, 380, 383
Learning experience, 10–11
Leary, Timothy, 69–70
Legislative power, 313
Leisure, 184–185
Lesbianism, 70
Liberals, religious, 147
Libido, 5, 6
License, freedom and, 321
Limited wars, 364
Living gods, 148
Living standard, 202–204
Lobbyists, 335
Local control of schools, 238
Local government, 294–303; activities of, 295–296; city, 297–299; financing, 302–303; problems of, 299–302; types of, 296–297; voting, 303–306
Long ballot, 306
Louisiana bayou country, 407, 409
Love, 97–114; choosing a mate, 103–105; courtship, 105–109; experiencing, 98–99; falling in, 99; meaning of, 97–98; premarital sex, 109–111; prospects of success in marriage, 112–113; romantic, 97–98; and sex, 99–103; sex roles, 111–112
Lynching, 35–37
Lysergic acid diethylamide (LSD), 69–70, 416

Machine politics, 302
Mafioso, 59–60
Magic, religion and, 146–147
Majority rule, minorities and, 315, 316–317
Management, business, 172
Manic-depressive psychoses, 22
March on Washington of 1963, 88
Marijuana, 69, 70, 416, 417
Market (free enterprise), 198

Marriage: choosing a mate, 103–105; forms of, 125; interfaith, 108; interracial, 108; Middle Ages, 104; for money, 105; parental matched, 104; partners, 108–109; prospects of success, 112–113
Marx, Karl, 142, 157, 360; on class system, 220–221, 222, 223, 227
Mass communications, impact of, 46–48; informal education and, 234
Masturbation, 102
Materialistic values, 204
Mates, selection of, 103–105
Matriarchal system, 130
Matrilineal descent, 128
Maya Indians, 279, 400
Mayor-council form of government, 297–298
Mead, Margaret, 40–41
Median family income, 194
Medicare, 134, 208, 337
Medium of exchange, 189–191
Megalopolis, 288–289
Mennonites, 148–149
Mental age, 20
Mental health, 26–27
Mental illness, 16–26; attitudes toward, 17–21; misconceptions about, 19–20; and personality problems, 21–22; types of disturbances, 22
Mental retardation, 20
Metropolitan area, 288
Mexican-Americans, 89, 218, 286
Middle Ages, 165, 402; caste system, 218; cities, 279; status groups, 217; universities, 241
Minority groups, 81; majority rule and, 316–317; school and, 246–248
Miracles, belief in, 143
Mobility, 223, 281–282
Mobs, 34–35; lynching, 35–37
Mohammed (prophet), 143
Monarchy, 312
Monetary policy, 330
Money: government control of, 330–333; meaning of, 189–191. See also Income and consumption
Monogamy, 124, 125
Monotheism, 141, 142
Morale, employee, 259–263
Morality: double standard, 109, 130; foreign policy and, 370–371
Mores, 53–55; basic concepts of, 397
Morphine, 67
Moslems, 35, 125, 142, 144, 145, 147, 152, 235
Motion picture industry, 234
Motivation, 12–14
Muhammad Elijah, 90
Multilateral world trade, 347–348

index **443**

Multiple-member election districts, 317
Multiple Nuclei, theory of, 284
Municipal corporation, 296
Murngin society (Australia), 100
Mussolini, Benito, 44, 320, 326
Mysticism, 144, 228
Myths, 141

Narcotics, 67–70
Nation, 325–340; common binding forces, 326–327; economy, 326–331; interdependency of, 345–357; national government, 331–335; nationalism, 325–326; problems of, 336–338; public and politics, 335–336
Nation-state, 350–353; balance of power, 352–353
National Advisory Commission on Civil Disorder, 37–38
National Association for the Advancement of Colored People (NAACP), 87
National debt, 330
National interest, 351
National Security Council, 354
Nationalism, 157, 325–326, 362, 387
Nationality, 81
Natural resources, protection of, 337
Navaho Indians, 409, 410
Nazi party, 26, 326, 366, 398; Aryan race myth, 81; extermination of Jews, 81, 82; *fuehrer* concept, 43–44; propaganda, 81; unemployment and, 181
Negroes, 13, 84, 87, 89–90, 218, 286; first mayor in South, 89; lynching of, 35–37; population (1968), 85; poverty, 205; pride in African heritage, 90; riots, 37–38
Neocolonialism, 363–364
Nervousness, 22
Neuroses, 22
New Left, 321
Nixon, Richard M., 208
Nomads, 273
Nonalignment, policy of, 370
Nonpartisan ballot, 302
Normative systems, 406
Norms of society, 10
North Atlantic Treaty Organization (NATO), 368, 370
Nuclear family, 124, 126–127
Nuclear Non-Proliferation Treaty, 384–385

Objectives, government, 351
Obscenity, 100
Oedipus complex, 5, 102
Old age, 134; poverty, 205
Open-country neighborhood, 277
Opium, 67
Optimum size, work group, 266

Ordinances, 295, 299
Organic mental disturbance, 21
Organization man, 175–176
Organized crime, 59–60, 204, 282
Orthodox Jews, 144, 152
Orthodox religions, 143

Pacific Northwest Indians, 215
Panic, 33–34
Parish (county), 297
Parliamentary rule, 312–313
Parochial school, 237–238
Partnership, 170
Partial Nuclear Test Ban Treaty, 384
Patriarchal system, 129
Patrilineal descent, 127
Patriotism, 326
Patronymic, 124, 127
Pax Romana, 377
Pax Tartarica, 377
Peace, quest for, 375–388; collective security, 377; diplomacy, 375–377; disarmament, 384–385; international law, 385–386; international organization, 377–380; United Nations and, 380–384; world government, 386–387
Peace Corps, 168
Peace research movement, 365
Peaceful co-existence, 369
Peer group, 409, 415
Pentecostal sects, 226
Per capita income, 348
Permissive attitude, 99
Persecution, feelings of, 22
Personal adjustment, problems of, 27–29
Personality, 3–15; basic concepts of, 393–394; frame of reference, 9–10; Freud on, 4–7; heredity, 11–12; learning, 10–11; mental illness and, 21–22; motivation, 12–14; self-concept, 8; traits and roles, 7–8; types of, 4
Phallic stage, 102
Phenomena, 422
Phobias, 22
Physiology, 428
Plains Indians, 55, 233
Pledge of Allegiance, 149, 315, 326
Pluralism, 153, 412
Political science, 309, 427, 429
Pollution, 337–338
Polyandry, 125
Polygamy, 125
Polygyny, 125
Polytheism, 141, 142
Population explosion, 350
Pornography, 60, 133
Potency, 111
Potentials for development, 12
Poverty, 204–208; fight against, 205–208; geography of, 205; population (U.S.),

Poverty (*continued*) 206; underdeveloped nations, 348; world revolt against, 359–360
Power, nation-state, 351–352
Power of the purse, 353
Power of suggestion, 18
Prayers, public school, 153
Prejudice, 62, 80–81; policemen, 38
Preliterate cultures, 426
Premarital sex, 109–111; abstinence, 109; double standard, 109; liberal and conservative positions on, 110
Premier, parliamentary role of, 313
President, role of, 331–334
Presidential rule, 312–313
Pressure, 23–24
Pressure groups, 335
Primary group, 124
Prime minister, 313
Primitive religion, 139
Prison: reforms, 63; riots, 38; work punishment, 165
Private schools, 237–238
Productivity, employment, 173
Progressive tax, 303
Projection, 26
Proletariat, 220
Propaganda, 48–49; Nazi, 81
Proportional representation, 317
Prostitution, 58, 59, 60, 100, 299; narcotics and, 68; religious, 59
Protest: from the Left, 336; from the Right, 337
Protestantism: American goals, 155; capitalism and, 165; concept of work, 180; interfaith marriages, 108; percent of (U.S.), 152; rules of conduct, 147
Psychedelic drugs, 69–70, 416
Psychiatry, 428
Psychoanalysis, 29; development of, 5–7
Psychology, 427, 429
Psychoses, 22
Psychosomatic illnesses, 22
Psychotherapy, 21
Public opinion, 335
Public opinion analysts, 48
Public utility district, 296
Publics, 46–48
Pueblo Indians, 163
Puerto Ricans, 13, 85, 89, 218, 286
Puget Island, 411–412
Pure science, 430
Puritanism, 100

Quakers, 42, 148

Race, 74–92; anti-Semitism, 82–83, 150; and blood type, 79; classification of, 77; consciousness, 75; discrimination, 80, 204; dominant and minority groups, 81; hatred and frustration, 74–75; issue (1970s), 85–92; meaning of, 76–77; migration and, 78; mixture, 77–79; personality and, 12; prejudice, 62, 80–81; purity, 78; as social problem, 79–80; superiority, 83–85
Racism, 81
Radical movements, 43
Rank, 211–229; achieved status, 216; ascribed status, 216; caste system, 217–218; class system, 219–229; hierarchy, 215–216; status, 211–215; stratification, 216–217
Reapportionment, 302
Recreational needs, basic elements of, 396
Referendum, 306
Regressive tax, 303
Rehabilitation, 63
Reincarnation, 217–218
Religion, 138–158; American, 152–155; class system and, 226–227; communism, 414; drawing together of, 150–152; existence and death, 143–144; expressionism in, 44–45; fervor and panic, 34; freedom of, 314; gods, 140–142; important moments in, 144–146; of many kinds, 150; meaning of, 139–140; membership, 153; mob atrocities, 35; need for comfort, 138–139; organization, 148–150; primitive, 139; prostitution, 59; ritual and ceremony, 146–147; rules of conduct, 147–148; science and, 143; secular, 156–157; as social control, 53–54; social movements, 42; and status quo, 153; subcultures, 412–414
Representative democracy, 316–317
Representative (of sample survey), 425
Repression, defensive behavior, 26
Repression, libidinal, 6
Republican government, 312
Restrictive attitude, 99
Retreatist behavior, 66
Revivalism, 44–45, 144
Riots, 37–41; Blacks and, 37–38; prison, 38; student, 38–40
Role conflict, 8
Role playing, 267
Roles, cultural, 394
Roman Catholic Church: American goals, 155; hierarchy, 215; interfaith marriages, 108; marriage between first cousins, 103; parochial school system, 237–238; percent of in U.S., 152; rules of conduct, 147; as state religion, 148
Romantic love, 97–98
Rome (ancient), 45, 104, 148; laws, 54; religion, 141; slavery, 164–165
Rumors, 41
Rural community, 274–278; types of, 277–278

Sabbath, 145
Saints, 144
Satellite city, 287
Satellite countries, 362
Scapegoats, 43, 82
Schizophrenia, 22
School boards, 236–239, 297
School system, *see* Education
Science: applied, 430; meaning of, 422–423; religion and, 143; and social science, 424–425
Scientific attitudes, 423–424
Scientific method, 422–423
Secondary groups, 124
Secondary sex characteristics, 102
Sector theory, 283
Sects, 148
Secularism, 155
Segregation, 78, 85–86, 87, 218, 246–247, 385; *de facto*, 86, 89; *de jure*, 86
Self-actualization, 167
Self-concept, 8
Self-employment, 170
Self-mutilation (religious), 44–45
Self-sufficiency, 346
Semiprofessional occupations, 175
Serfdom, 165, 172
Service occupations, 176
Services, consumer, 195
Sex: American attitude toward, 100–101; class system and, 226–227; crimes, 62; in development of child, 102; drive, 5–6; education, 133–134, 242; and love, 99–103; premarital, 109–111; Puritan influence and, 100; roles, 111–112; while dating, 106
Shakers (religious sect), 44
Shareholders, 171
Shintoism, 152
Short ballot, 306
Single-crop economy, 350
Single-member election districts, 317
Skepticism, 423
Slavery, 164–165, 172
Slums, 284–287
Snobbery, 225
Social climbers, 225
Social control, 53–54
Social movements, 41–43
Social philosopher, 433
Social problems, defined, 401–402
Social psychology, 427
Social sciences, 420–434; career opportunities, 431; employment, 430–431; kinds of, 426–429; science and, 424–425; specialized fields in, 429; use of, 429–431; value judgments and, 431–433; ways of knowing, 420–422
Social Security, 134, 207–208, 337
Social work, 431

Socialism, 314, 360; welfare measures and, 337
Socialization, 119, 394
Sociology, 426, 429
Socrates, 57, 147, 235
Southeast Asian Treaty Organization (SEATO), 368, 370
Southern Christian Leadership Conference (SCLC), 87–88
Sovereignty, 351
Specialization, 428
Spock, Dr. Benjamin, 118
Stalin, Joseph, 165, 368, 369
State government, financing, 302–303
State religions, 148
Statistics, 425–426
Status, 211–215; achieved, 216; ascribed, 216; basic elements of, 395; work and, 167
Status symbols, 214, 228
Stereotype, prejudice and, 80
Stimuli, responses to, 9
Stock-purchasing plans, 263
Strategic Arms Limitation Talks (SALT), 385
Stratification, 216–217
Stress, 22–23; coping with, 24; response to, 24–25
Student Nonviolent Coordinating Committee (SNCC), 88
Student unrest, 41–42; riots, 38–40; sit-ins, 38
Subcommunity, 277
Subconscious mind, 6–7
Subcultures, 406–414; regional American, 407–409; ethnic, 409–412; religious, 412–414
Subjective values, 432
Sublimation, 6
Subsidies, farm, 173
Substrata, 217
Suburbia, 287–288
Superego, 6
Surface traits, 7–8
Survey, 425
Systems, 120–121

Taboos, 147
Tariffs, 361
Taxes, types of, 302–303
Teacher, role of, 244–246
Team spirit, 263
Teamsters' Union, 124, 182
Ten Commandments, 54, 147
Tests, 425
Thant, U, 382
Theism, 141
Theology, 142
Theories, scientific, 422

446 Index

Television, 185, 227, 234; commercials, 202
Torah, 145
Totalitarianism, 321
Town meeting, 316
Towns, 277
Traffic engineers, 296
Tranquilizers, 20–21
Transcendental meditation, 156
Transvestite, 55
Truman Doctrine, 368
Two-party system, 317

Underdeveloped nations: aid for, 360–362; fight against poverty, 359–360; foreign trade of, 361; single-crop economies, 350
Unemployment, 181–182; compensation, 182; in the Congo, 348–350; insurance, 337; poverty and, 205
Unincorporated community, 277
Unions, 181–182
Unitary government, 312
United Nations, 380–384, 386; criticism of, 382–383; ESOSOC, 382; financial problems, 383; General Assembly, 381; Korean War and, 381; membership (1969), 380; rotating membership, 381; Security Council, 380–381; specialized agencies, 382; Trusteeship Council, 382; UNESCO, 382; veto power, 381
U.S. Congress: committee hearings, 334; foreign policy and, 353, 354; legislative role of, 334
U.S. Constitution, 62, 86, 153, 311, 331; Bill of Rights, 314, 319
U.S. Senate, 334
U.S. Supreme Court, 153, 331, 333; role of, 334–335
Universal suffrage, 319
Universities: campus unrest, 250; factory-like system, 40; Middle Ages, 241; population, 250; programs, 250; riots, 38–40
Urban areas, 33
Urban renewal, 290, 337
Urbanization, 279
Utopian society, 168, 416

Values, 432; culture, 10; materialistic, 204
Vertical movement, 281
Vietnam war, 46, 90, 336, 364, 370
Village, 277
Virginity, 106, 109
Vocational education, 241
Voluntary organizations, 281
Volunteers in Service to America (VISTA), 168, 281
Voodoo, 146
Voting: in a democracy, 315–316, 319–320; election of 1968, 294; participation in, 315–316; rights, 304; in U.S.S.R., 304; women, 314, 319

War, 364–366; causes of, 365–366; limited, 364
War on Poverty, 337
Water pollution, 337, 338
Weathermen (radical group), 315
Wedding: ceremonial symbols, 106; engagement, 106, 108
Welfare, 182
Welfare state, 337
Welfare system, 206–207
Wilson, Woodrow, 376, 380
Witchcraft, 17, 58
Withdrawal, 25
Woodstock Festival, 416–417
Women's suffrage, 314, 319
Work, *see* Employment
Work culture, 164
World: interdependency of states, 345–357; population (projected), 349; quest for peace, 375–388; revolution and war, 359–373
World government, 386–387
World Health Organization (WHO), 382
World War I, 44, 353, 376, 380
World War II, 353, 364, 371, 380, 432

Yiddish language, 83, 411
Yinger, J. Milton, 140, 147, 148, 157
Yogi, Maharishi, 156
Youth cultures, 414–417

Zen monks, 144
Zoning rules, 290
Zuñi Indians, 214

Paula Ann
Shargel